ONEIDA LIVES

The Iroquoians and Their World

EDITORS

José António Brandão
Mary Druke Becker
William Starna

Oneida Lives

Long-Lost Voices of the Wisconsin Oneidas

EDITED BY
Herbert S. Lewis

WITH THE ASSISTANCE OF
L. Gordon McLester III

WITH A FOREWORD BY
Gerald L. Hill

UNIVERSITY OF NEBRASKA PRESS
LINCOLN & LONDON

Publication of this book
was assisted by a grant from
The Brittingham Fund at the
University of Wisconsin–Madison.

Printed by Edwards Brothers, Inc.
Library of Congress
Cataloging-in-Publication Data
Oneida lives: long-lost voices of the Wis-
consin Oneidas / edited by Herbert S.
Lewis with the assistance of L. Gordon
McLester III; with a foreword by Gerald L.
Hill.
p.   cm.—(The Iroquoians and their world)
Includes bibliographical references and
index.
ISBN-13: 978-0-8032-2943-3 (cloth: alk.
paper)
ISBN-13: 978-0-8032-8043-4 (pbk.: alk.
paper)
ISBN-10: 0-8032-2943-7 (cloth: alk. paper)
ISBN-10: 0-8032-8043-2 (pbk.: alk. paper)
1. Oneida Indians—History—Sources.   2.
Oneida Indians—Interviews.   3. Oneida
Indians—Social life and customs.   I.
Lewis, Herbert S.   II. McLester, L. Gor-
don.   III. Series.
E99.045 053   2005
977.5004'975543—dc22
2005009909

CONTENTS

ILLUSTRATIONS

In the fall of 1998 the Oneida Tribe was contacted by the provost at the University of Wisconsin–Madison asking the protocol for the university to return to the tribe copies of a cache of handwritten notebooks from the Oneida Ethnological Study of the Works Progress Administration (WPA). Professor Herb Lewis, looking for information about an undergraduate student from the 1930s (Floyd G. Lounsbury), found his way into the vast basement storeroom of the anthropology department. It was there that he found a large carton with the word "Oneida" written on its side. While looking through the contents, he was stunned to find 167 spiral steno pads filled with pencil-written texts of different lengths and subjects about the Oneida people.

When Professor Lewis discovered these long-forgotten manuscripts, he recognized their historical value in general as well as their importance to the Oneida people in particular. As chief counsel, I played a small part in the return of a full set of copies to the Oneida Tribe. When notified about them I immediately asked to examine the originals. Within a week I went to Madison at least as excited as Howard Carter finding the tomb of Tutankhamen in 1926 or Napoleon's army discovering the Rosetta Stone in 1799. While those were ancient artifacts, these were relatively recent recorded oral histories of the Oneida people in Wisconsin. The detailed information that had been lost to us for several generations is incalculably more directly connected to us because the informants, transcribers, and translators were of our own living families, both direct and extended. This is our community speaking to us from recent generations.

As a longtime student of world, United States, indigenous, Iroquois, and Oneida history as well as of the Oneida language, I recognized that this find was full of significant implications in law, history, and Oneida culture for our people. During 1939 and 1940, the WPA project, led by the noted linguist Morris Swadesh and his assistant Floyd Lounsbury, then still an undergraduate, collected hundreds of interviews, stories, and anecdotes with the help of native speakers of the Oneida language. Some were extended narrations by individuals directly, while others were simple word lists, recipes, jokes (some quite ribald), and short observations of a sentence or two. Others were the result of Oneidas interviewing other Oneidas, many of whom did not speak English.

Originally these linguists had planned an extensive training period for Oneida speakers in the use of a new orthography, but within two months the Oneidas were eager to get started, thoroughly enjoying shocking their trainers with their quick grasp of the system. The Oneidas had been literate for generations using an older Mohawk orthography, which is the basis for the written versions of many of the Oneida hymns still sung in the Holy Apostles Episcopal Church and the Oneida Methodist Church.

When the continuation project began late in 1940, under the direction of another graduate student, Harry Basehart, the focus changed from language to history, ethnography, and autobiography. As the text of this book shows, the range of topics renders this collection a historical treasure trove. To the Oneida people, this is the equivalent of the Rosetta Stone for its insight into the Oneida community just prior to World War II.

America, with the rest of the world, was emerging from an economic depression, and the insights provided in this collection show how one Native community, Oneida, was affected. Many of our ancestors had served in World War I, the Civil War, back to the Revolution, and even the French and Indian Wars in the 1760s. So the history of the Oneida people is intertwined with the European colonies that would become the United States and Canada.

The Oneidas were aware in 1939, 1940, and 1941 that they would be called upon again with the war that was brewing in Europe even while this collection was being gathered. That mood of scarcity, struggle, and the attitudes and worldviews of 1940 America are reflected here. Perhaps even more important to us is the vibrancy of Oneida life and customs also reflected in these stories of our most recent ancestors.

Approximately a quarter to a third of the entire collection is in the Oneida language. That portion of these newly discovered materials is now being indexed and translated by the Oneida Cultural Heritage Department. This is being accomplished with great urgency, for obvious reasons, given the continuing decline of the use of the Oneida language and the corresponding shift to English in Oneida as well as other Native communities. In the sixty years since this collection was gathered, the number of speakers of the Oneida language has fallen to fewer than several dozen. This is a sad but universal phenomenon that some linguists predict will result in the extinction of all but a few Native languages within the next fifty years. We do not agree with that prognosis, yet we understand that this is a pivotal time in our history to take the gift of this book as a wake-up call.

The stories in the present volume have been selected from those originally written in English. It is expected that the collection from which these stories were taken will yield many more books and studies by Oneidas as well as other Native and non-Native scholars.

The earlier collection, already in the Oneida archives, from which the present collection was inadvertently separated, included hundreds of other stories. Some of those stories were copied, studied, translated, and transcribed by the Oneida Language Program in the 1970s and published internally as *Stories from the Olden Days, Bear Stories, Animal Stories, Medicine Stories,* and assorted other books and pamphlets. Many have been committed to audiotape and CD. Like long-separated families, these two Oneida collections together combine a rich source of information about the Oneida people in Wisconsin: what they thought about, their observations of life around them, their opinions about government policies, and the strength and power of our Oneida heritage.

Often it is assumed that a Native people's culture and historical information is passed on only through formal and ancient religious ceremonies. This text refutes such a simplistic myth. Traditional ceremonies serve to connect the knowledge of the past with the need of the present. These ceremonies are still practiced and highly respected by the Oneida people today. Such rites are imbued with religious teachings that inform us about relationships and responsibilities. In contrast, the present volume is a secular expression of the Oneida people, our recent ancestors, in their own voice, some still among us, telling of mundane yet vitally important minutiae of daily life in a vibrant community. This book resonates with the intelligent vitality that characterizes the Oneida people, Onʌyotaʼaka. May our generation and those of the Oneidas who will follow amplify the work begun in this humble yet important book.

Finally, let us be grateful to Professor Herb Lewis for his generous, honorable scholarship in putting this together.

Ta ne thoniyole wakaliwatkweni,
Gerald L. Hill

Kaihuhatati ni yukyats
*Okwali wakitalot^*

ACKNOWLEDGMENTS

This book contains the work of the writers on the Oneida Ethnological Study, a project sponsored by the Works Progress Administration (WPA). It is composed of their words, their lives, their troubles, their wit and eloquence—and that of the people they interviewed and who were so frank and willing to talk about themselves and their world. It was my great fortune to find these and to be able to identify them, with the help of others. We owe a great deal to Gita Gebauer, Joseph Mingele, Jim Stoltman, Harold C. Conklin, and Cliff Abbott, each of whom played a role (both wittingly and unwittingly) in the discovery and identification of the papers. Cliff shared in the early work of processing these marvelous writings, and he continues to teach me much about Oneida.

Casey Nagy, then special assistant to the provost of the University of Wisconsin–Madison, and John Wiley, then provost and now chancellor, could not have been more supportive. They helped to arrange for the processing of the collection and for the transfer of the original documents to the Wisconsin State Historical Society and a complete set of photocopies to the Oneida Nation. They also aided in financing subsequent work on the project and this publication. Gerald L. Hill, counsel for the Oneida Nation at that time, also played a major role in the process. I am especially grateful to him for writing the foreword to this book and for his unflagging support for the project.

Kathryn Klein of the Maxwell Museum of the University of New Mexico graciously facilitated my search through Harry Basehart's papers. Carrie Thompson of the University of New Mexico has my special thanks for her devotion to finding and copying material from that collection. Helmut Knies, archivist at the Wisconsin State Historical Society; Susan Otto, Ann McMullen, and Dawn Scher Thomae of the Milwaukee Public Museum; and Debra Anderson of the Area Research Center at the University of Wisconsin–Green Bay—all of these helped in various ways.

I owe most, perhaps, to Elizabeth Hassemer for her devoted, intelligent, and accurate transcription of the more than eighteen thousand handwritten pages that she converted to forty-five hundred typed pages ready for editing and processing. Thanks are due also to Nathan Martin and Shawn Murray, who photocopied most of the text, and to Sandra Kennedy of the Social Science Copy Center, who has always been a great help. Steven Dast of the Memorial Library made possible the photocopying of the project's maps, and Steve Sundell of Mills Music Library tracked down and recorded Oneida hymns from their collection.

Special thanks are due to Larry Hauptman, SUNY–New Paltz, extraordinary historian of the modern Iroquois, for his wise advice and enthusiastic support. Jack Campisi has willingly shared some of his deep knowledge of the Oneida and the Iroquois, and Barb Landis has conveyed her great enthusiasm for the Indian students and community of the Carlisle Indian Industrial School. Mary Druke Becker read the first draft of manuscript scrupulously and made numerous editorial and substantive suggestions of great value, for which I am very grateful. Thanks are due as well to Judy Cornelius, the late Lloyd Schuyler, Danette Woodmansee, Leabeth Miller, Michael C. Coleman, Stephanie Kellerman, Bernie Kemp, Bruce Basehart, Betty McLester, Susan Daniels and Omie Baldwin. I must thank Dr. Carol Cornelius, Loretta Metoxen, Thelma McLester, and Vera Wilson of the Oneida Cultural Heritage Center, and Roberta Hill.

It is a pleasure to acknowledge the support of the staff of the University of Nebraska Press, and above all the work of Jonathan Lawrence, extraordinary copyeditor; Linnea Fredrickson, who has guided this work from manuscript to book; and Gary Dunham, who was there when I first presented the Oneida material publicly and has supported its publication ever since.

I am pleased to acknowledge the financial support of the Brittingham Foundation for work on and transcription of the notebooks, research travel, and publication.

We must also remember Morris Swadesh, who conceived of the original project, secured the funding for it, and set it in motion. In addition to the extraordinary dedication and contributions of Floyd Lounsbury, it was Harry Basehart who intelligently oversaw the Oneida Ethnological Study. Just a small portion of the work from that project appears in this volume. Robert Ritzenthaler also contributed through his research in the summer of 1939 and especially through the photographs he took of so many of the workers and other members of the Oneida community at that time. Professor Scudder Mekeel was the caretaker of the papers until his sudden and untimely death in 1948.

As always, Marcia, my wife, was there, delighted and enthusiastic when I would telephone her from the office to read remarkable passages as I came across them. Her gentle reminders and prodding have helped to move this work along in a timely fashion.

Finally, I want to express my profound appreciation to Gordon Mc-Lester for his enthusiastic moral and practical support. His untiring devotion to the history of his people is an inspiration.

yaw^ʔkó

During these lean years of the Great Depression, the whole nation was hard pressed to furnish employment to its millions of unemployed inhabitants. The result was the national, state, local government officials and every other capable organization was thinking up work or occupations of many types and descriptions. It will take no great stretch of imagination to be convinced that the Indian early became part of this great army of unoccupation.

It was thus then that the University of Wisconsin sponsored what is called a social research project. By a streak of fate (some Oneidas say it was through the intervention of their native God, Dehaluhyawá•gu), the once eminent but now humble Oneida Indians, a former member of the great Iroquois Confederacy, were given consideration. The project affecting us, the Oneidas, had for its object the recording, for the first time, of the language . . . of the Oneidas, in a methodical or scientific manner.

The results from this undertaking were so satisfactory and interesting that a correlated research project, the historical study, was immediately sponsored and approved. This embraces the writing of biography, autobiography, and consulting newspaper and other records.

Andrew Beechtree (1941)

Andrew Beechtree was one of more than a dozen men and women of the Oneida Tribe of Indians of Wisconsin who were employed for a period of thirty-six months on two unique projects funded by the U.S. government through the Works Progress Administration (WPA).[1] For the first project, the Oneida workers recorded their language through the collection of texts in the form of folktales, anecdotes, jokes, recipes, plant and place names, stories of personal experience, and some observations about historical and contemporary events. The results of this work are well known and have been used by the Oneida themselves and by scholars since that project ended in 1940. The second project, the Oneida Ethnological Study, produced a much larger body of material, more than eighteen thousand pages of handwritten text with information on

Oneida life and experience. Unfortunately, it was set aside and forgotten for most of six decades, until its rediscovery a few years ago. This volume contains sixty-five autobiographical narratives by fifty-three different men and women, selected from more than five hundred individual accounts. The following section gives a brief historical account of the Wisconsin Oneida and of the project that produced these remarkable documents.

Historical Background

The Oneidas were one of the five original nations of the Hodenosaunee, the People of the Longhouse, the League of the Iroquois, who inhabited and controlled the great region that is today upper New York State. [2] Although they were strikingly few in number by the standards of world history—probably fewer than fifteen thousand souls—their strategic location and remarkable social and political organization and skill literally placed Iroquoia squarely on the map of colonial North America. [3]

The Five Nations formed a confederacy to maintain peace among themselves and to protect themselves from others. [4] When the French, Dutch, and English came into these lands beginning in the seventeenth century in search of furs, souls, and land, they had to contend with the political and military power of these Indian nations. The presence of the foreigners and their insatiable demand for furs led to greatly enhanced trade and war throughout a vast region. Hunting, trapping, trading, and making war, men of the Iroquoian groups ranged far beyond their own homelands. According to Campisi, the Oneidas alone took furs, booty, and prisoners from the St. Lawrence River Valley to the Carolinas (1974:60), and together with other Iroquois "their influence extended west to Green Bay and Illinois, while to the south they held control through Pennsylvania" (1978:482). [5] "As both France and England knew, their contest for control of the North American continent ultimately would be decided by the choice the Iroquois made between them" (Tooker 1978:418). And Iroquois warriors did, indeed, play significant roles in major and minor conflicts, above all the war between the French and English for control of Canada (the French and Indian War) and the American Revolution. The Iroquois left their mark not only on the history of the United States but also on its culture and consciousness. [6]

Despite being weakened by losses through disease and war, and not infrequently divided by competing interests and alliances in an extremely complex political arena, the Iroquois confederacy maintained its importance until the 1770s and the American War of Independence. That war found different Iroquois groups deeply split and obliged to choose between the opposing forces. The Oneidas and Tuscaroras generally fought with the American settlers while the others took the side of the British Crown and the Loyalists. Being on the winning side in the war did not give the Oneidas any lasting advantages, however, though they did receive some monetary rewards from the new government. Like the other peoples of the league, they suffered the destruction of their villages and many deaths due to violence, disease, and other consequences of the war. The population of all the Iroquois nations was reduced to perhaps five thousand by that time.

After the war the Iroquois were no longer united; their military strength counted for little, and they were unable to play one European power off against the other. They had become only a hindrance to the ambitions of the rapidly growing population of Euro-Americans. They were in the way as the region between the Hudson River and Lake Erie became an area of booming economic growth. The Erie Canal, completed in 1825, was the gateway to the West, and the whole region was a primary area for economic expansion for the new nation. Farmers moved in, towns and cities were established, trade flourished, and the region became an important center for grain production.

The population of Oneida and Madison counties, the center of Oneida settlement, grew from under 2,000 in 1790 to more than 83,000 in 1820 and 110,000 in 1830 (Hauptman and McLester 2002:24). In contrast, the Oneida population at that time numbered about 600 in 1800 and 1,031 in 1819 (Hauptman and McLester 2002:23), but they were the formal owners of most of the land. The drive to obtain the tribe's lands became paramount for individual settlers and speculators, organized land companies, and the state of New York, and these interests prevailed. According to Vecsey, "in 1783 the Iroquois held half of what is now New York State; by 1842 their property was negligible" (1988:10).

The pressures on the New York Indian groups became intense. Some Oneida sold their land in order to get money to stay alive. Others had the land taken from them through fraudulent treaties and a variety of deceitful practices. "By bribes, threats of dire punishment for refusing to obey the supposed wish of the United States government for such a move, and deliberate misrepresentation of the facts to federal authorities," writes Anthony Wallace, "Seneca and other Iroquois chiefs were brought unwillingly to sign treaties by which some of the reservations were sold to the Ogden Land Company and the State of New York" (Wallace 1970:323–324; cf. Hauptman 1986:18–19 and Hauptman 1999).[7]

The Move to Wisconsin

After the Revolution, the Oneidas were exhausted from almost two hundred years of warfare. They were dislocated, disheartened, disorganized, and at odds with most of their former allies, who had been on the British side during the war. "Alcoholism, murder, suicide, and factionalism all attest to the patterns of disintegration in the post-war period" (Campisi 1974:74–75). Traditional chiefs (sachems), whose offices derived from the matrilineal lineage and clan system, were at odds with the so-called pinetree chiefs, who had achieved their leadership primarily from their personal achievements as warriors, orators, and men of wisdom and generosity.

Factions developed along religious lines, which, according to Campisi, "had at their core a controversy over the degree of acceptance or rejection of white society" (1974:104). The Presbyterian followers of an influential New England missionary, Rev. Samuel Kirkland (known as the First Christian Party), were at odds with the "Pagan Party" of the tradition-minded sachems and others who answered the call of a Mohawk prophet who preached a return to old rituals (Campisi 1974:104).[8]

The religious divisions would become less marked by 1816–17, however, as the result of the missionary activities of a new figure, Eleazer Williams. The descendant of distinguished Mohawk and white forebears, Williams was raised at the St. Regis (Akwesasne) reservation, became an Episcopalian lay preacher, and was designated missionary to the Oneidas in 1816. He soon succeeded in convincing the remaining Presbyterians of the First Christian Party to switch their loyalties to the Episcopal church. Next he converted the members of the Pagan Party, who then took the name Second Christian Party. (Another group was induced to join the Methodist church soon after, and they called themselves the Orchard Party.)[9]

By 1820 the Oneidas held only a tiny fraction of the land in their heartland and were besieged by the state government, the Ogden Land Company, and other speculators who desired their removal to the West.[10] Powerful governmental and private interests wanted to push all the Indians out of New York State and into the far frontier, at least as far as what was then Michigan Territory, west of Lake Michigan, if not all the way to Kansas.[11] At the same time, Eleazer Williams dreamed of creating an Indian empire in the West with himself as its leader. And capable Oneida leaders, such as Chiefs Daniel Bread and Elijah Skenandore, could see no way out for their people other than such a move (Bloomfield 1907:167ff.; Hauptman and McLester 2002:27–28).

The Oneidas were offered land on the frontier in the area west of Green Bay, in what would become the state of Wisconsin in less than thirty years, and about half the members of the tribe decided to accept the offer. Eleazer Williams and Chief Elijah Skenandore (d. 1897) took a group of settlers from the First Christian Party and moved west in 1823, and members of the Second Christian Party and the Orchard Party joined them within a decade. Eventually they were settled on a reservation just outside the small settlement of Green Bay on a block of land that runs from northeast to southwest following a watercourse known as Duck Creek. (The reservation is divided between what became Brown and Outagamie counties.) In 1838, through the Treaty of Buffalo Creek, the reservation was fixed in size at just over 65,400 acres—100 acres for each of the 654 Oneida settlers living there at that time (Campisi 1978:485).[12]

Wisconsin Oneidas in the Nineteenth Century

By the time they moved to Wisconsin, the Oneidas had undergone many economic, cultural, and sociopolitical changes since first encountering the Europeans two centuries earlier. Before the coming of the fur trade the Oneidas were largely self-sufficient—growing, hunting, collecting, and making what they needed. The women were in charge of horticulture, planting gardens and tending maize, beans, squash, and tobacco and collecting berries and other wild plants. Both men and women fished and foraged, while the men cleared land for the gardens, built and maintained structures, and manufactured tools, weapons, containers, utensils, lacrosse sticks, snowshoes, and other items. And the men hunted wild game, traded, and warred with others, often traveling considerable distances and staying away from home for long periods, leaving the women behind to take over many responsibilities (Campisi 1974:36–38).

With the coming of the Europeans and the fur trade, the men spent much more time trapping, trading, fighting, and attending council meetings and intergroup negotiations. While the women continued the horticultural activities, people became more and more dependent on trade for their tools, guns, powder, shot, traps, metal vessels, clothes, blankets, and the new foods they had come to value, including flour, tea, and sugar. By the beginning of the nineteenth century the fur trade had long been finished, there was little left to hunt for food, and there were no more wars to be fought.

The early sociopolitical organization of the Oneidas had been based on longhouses and single-family dwellings set in compact villages and on strong matrilineages and clans that featured a formal system of sachems, nominated by the leading women of the descent groups. At a higher level, these villages and the larger tribes to which they belonged were linked in the great Iroquois Confederacy. By the time the Oneidas moved to Wisconsin, however, virtually none of this remained.

The Oneidas settled on the land in Wisconsin in log-and-frame structures that housed individual family units, strung along roads and footpaths or clustered in hamlets and a few small villages. The nuclear family had become the primary social unit, and bilateral kindreds replaced the matrilineal kinship groups that had been so important. People now looked to kin on either the mother's or the father's side without preference.[13] Although the nearly functionless clans still claimed the right to appoint chiefs, these were not the sachems of old, nominated by leading mothers of the clan and installed in an elaborate ritual system. Important leaders were also drawn from the three religious parties, and new pinetree chiefs arose as well (Basehart 1952; Campisi 1974, 1999).

The Wisconsin Oneidas had become Christians, and their leading chiefs—notably Daniel Bread, Elijah Skenandore, Jacob Cornelius, and Cornelius Hill (later)—were all practicing Episcopalians or Methodists and were expected to support the churches and set examples of Christian behavior for their followers. White Episcopal and Methodist missionaries were influential throughout the nineteenth century as well, although leadership of the church councils and associations was always in Oneida hands. Almost all of the ceremonial rituals and practices of precontact days were abandoned, except for a residue of the False Face curing society, and a few Iroquois practices carried over into funeral customs and New Year's and Easter celebrations (Campisi 1978:486).[14] Christian cosmology, belief, and worship prevailed, despite the fact that few people could speak English; church services were translated by interpreters. A strict brand of Christian morality was upheld as the ideal with regard to marriage, the family, and sexual relations, and the churches were important instruments of social control.

The missions maintained the few scattered day schools that educated some of the children of the reservation until the establishment of government boarding schools, and the churches were also the center of much of Oneida social life. Lay church leaders, both men and women, organized mutual aid associations, church socials, bees, and hymn-singing groups. Early visitors to the reservation noticed the social and cultural importance of choral groups that sang classic Christian hymns in the Oneida or Mohawk language—groups that remain important to the Oneidas to this day.[15]

The most successful Oneidas in Wisconsin took to clearing the land and farming, with men doing most of the cultivating, using the plow and draft animals. Women also worked in the agricultural sphere in various ways, and they continued to participate in the cultivation of corn (Campisi 1999:71). Within a short time some families were successfully farming on land they had cleared and tilled, growing wheat, oats, maize, potatoes, beans, and many other crops. Some owned livestock, especially cattle, pigs, chickens, and horses.

Farming was supplemented with fishing, hunting, gathering berries, collecting and working with materials from the forest, and producing barrel hoops, shingles, ash splints for baskets, and other items. Women also made baskets, made dolls, mats, and mattresses out of corn husks, and, much later, made lace. Men also engaged in wage labor, especially in the lumber industry that grew rapidly from the 1840s. They cut timber on their own lands, hauled logs to sawmills on and off the reservation, and worked as lumberjacks in camps further north.

Visitors were impressed with Oneida farms and their "good management" (Hauptman and McLester 1999:16). As one Oneida elder, Rachel

Swamp, told a WPA interviewer, "They were ambitious people, they did all kinds of work to make a living, such as cutting wood and selling it, they sold logs, they hunted and sold the hides and some even found work in Green Bay" (Hauptman and McLester 1999:122). As Campisi notes, the families that had the highest status in civic and religious life were those that "placed strong emphasis on education, hard work, sobriety, and family responsibility" (1999:78). The WPA narratives demonstrate that these were still the ideals by which people were judged in 1941–42, even if, as in any society, not everyone could live up to them all.

Alcoholism was a serious problem, even though the chiefs made a concerted effort to keep taverns and other sources of alcohol off the reservation. And not all were equally lucky or worked equally effectively and hard, so a stratification system developed in which the "better families" were distinguished from those not so well off or well respected.

Apparently the new start in Wisconsin did not begin badly. There was enough good land, plenty of timber, lots of fish and game, and a profusion of wild berries and other products. The Oneidas were developing a local infrastructure with a gristmill, two sawmills, and a blacksmith's shop. The Oneida leaders were capable men, and from 1853 they had a supportive ally in an Episcopal missionary, Rev. Edward A. Goodnough. But once again events and the ambitions of the growing white population conspired to make life much more difficult.

The Loss of Reservation Timber and Land

The moving frontier followed right behind the Oneidas. The Michigan Territory they had moved to in 1823 became part of the state of Wisconsin in 1848. The population of Wisconsin grew from less than 12,000 in 1836 to 31,000 in 1840, 305,000 in 1850, and 1,055,000 in 1870 (Hauptman and McLester 2002). The city of Green Bay grew rapidly as well, and it became an important port for the rapidly expanding lumber industry of northern and central Wisconsin. Wood was needed for the population boom and the development of the new state: for fuel, houses, and barns; for the new towns and cities; and for the new plank roads and railroads (for ties and fuel). "By the 1850s Green Bay had become the shingle capital of the United States" (Campisi 1974:143–145; Hauptman and McLester 2002:130).[16]

Entrepreneurs eagerly sought Oneida timber, and sawmills were soon operating on and around the reservation. Some Oneida men preferred the relatively easy money from work in the timber industry to the labor involved in developing and maintaining farms. Between 1830 and 1870 much of the Oneida land had been stripped of most of its timber resources; erosion and decreasing soil quality followed as well. The loss of the land itself, however, would be a bigger blow.[17]

Land speculators, politicians, and farmers followed on the heels of the Oneidas. Once again leading political figures called for the removal of the Indians to regions still further west, but this time the Oneidas successfully resisted (Hauptman and McLester 2002:104ff.). What could not be resisted, however, was allotment, the division of Oneida Reservation land into separate parcels to be doled out to individuals.

At the time the reservation was established it had a protected status, as did other Indian lands. It "was subject to federal statutory restraints on alienation; those statutes not only precluded outright sale of Indian land but also made Indian lands immune from state law and procedures that might result in alienation such as taxation, lien, and foreclosure" (Locklear 1988a:83). The land belonged to the whole tribe, not to individuals. Chiefs could allocate and control land, or individuals might occupy and use available land, but no one could sell the land or otherwise transfer it to others.

Obviously, this arrangement did not suit the designs of those who wanted to gain control of Indian land for their own purposes, but others began to question the wisdom of this policy as well. Not only whites but also some Indians believed that there could be no economic or cultural progress unless individual families held their own land, took pride in it and responsibility for it, and developed it the same way that many white farmers did. They argued that farmers needed security of tenure in order to be willing to put in the labor and capital to develop their land. Individual landholding would have a salutary civilizing and assimilating effect on the Indians, they argued, forcing them to become yeoman farmers and abandon communal and "tribal" ways. So both the friends and the enemies of the Indian peoples, and some influential Indians themselves, called for a change in the laws.

Among the Oneidas, Chiefs Daniel Bread and Jacob Cornelius came to believe that allotment was necessary. They complained of the growth of lawlessness and irresponsibility among their people. It was difficult to control individuals who had an independent source of income, who cut down trees with no thought for the future, and who had no stake in the land and wouldn't improve or care for it (see Hauptman and McLester 2002:132ff.). Others, of course, bitterly opposed allotment.

In 1887, Congress reversed its long-standing reservation policy and set in motion the processes that would deprive the Oneidas—along with most other Indians groups in the United States—of most of the land the government had previously granted them. Congress passed the General Allotment Act (also called the Dawes Act), which was effective in bringing about the transfer of Indian lands to whites while hardly ever achieving the desired economic independence for Indians.

Under the provisions of the General Allotment Act, reservation land was to be divided among tribal members in amounts to be determined by the government. Beginning in 1891, 1,530 allotments were made to the Wisconsin Oneidas, with each individual over the age of eighteen given forty acres and those younger given twenty-six acres. In theory these allotments were to be held under what was called a "trust patent," which would protect them from alienation for twenty-five years. In practice, however, there were many ways to separate Oneidas and other Indians from their new landholdings (Locklear 1988a).

The application of the act and subsequent legal decisions permitted Indians to sell their land and then subjected the land and its owners to taxation and complex legal restrictions (see Campisi 1974:148–151; Locklear 1988a; Metoxen n.d.). The laws and rulings left landholding Indians prey to sharp dealers and crooks.[18] Eager white speculators and farmers soon had most of this land "as trust periods expired, incompetent allottees died, and competent allottees failed to pay property taxes" (Locklear 1988a:85).

White farmers had been moving into land adjacent to the reservation and could not wait to get their plows into Oneida lands. In 1906, when the Oneidas were given fee-simple patents (which gave them the power to mortgage and sell their land), and in 1908, when town and county taxation was instituted (Campisi 1978:487), they were besieged by merchants eager to sell them the latest farm implements and machines, cattle, horses, wagons, and carriages. The Oneidas needed to invest in these items in order to make their farms succeed in the developing economy, and just like their white neighbors they wanted improved housing, furnishings, clothing, and carriages. Few older Oneidas could speak English well, and fewer still could read, but they were encouraged to put up their land as collateral for loans to buy these items. Many Oneidas signed papers that put up their farms as security and soon found themselves foreclosed for failure to repay their debts. Others failed to pay their taxes and their land was seized. By the 1920s the Oneidas owned only 3,590 acres out of the original 65,400.[19]

With the loss of the land the Oneidas also lost local political influence. Whites settled on reservation land and by the 1920s outnumbered the Oneidas.[20] Local government was reorganized and parts of the reservation were assigned to different townships; by 1910 the Oneida Township Council replaced the former Oneida Tribal Council. At first the Oneidas controlled the new council, but the number of whites increased and by the mid-1920s they were outvoted (see Basehart 1952:219; Campisi 1974:149–151; also see accounts in this volume by Ida Blackhawk in chapter 1 and by Stadler King in chapter 3). Tribal government was restored in 1934 as the result of New Deal reforms.

By World War I, Oneida men and some women turned increasingly to wage labor, primarily as unskilled and semi-skilled workers on farms and in industry. Many of those who tell their stories in these texts speak about their work with satisfaction. They were proud of being good and able workers, worthy of promotion and respect from foremen and bosses, and they made salaries that they deemed reasonable for those days. But the Great Depression changed all that, and after 1929 most Oneidas lost their jobs. Many had been living in Green Bay, Milwaukee, Chicago, and Detroit, but they were forced to return to the reservation to look for housing, perhaps live with kin, and try to live more cheaply. They had not begun to recover at the time these texts were written. The loss of their land and the impact of the depression had left the Oneidas of the 1930s in the poverty that is so evident in these accounts.

The New Deal at Oneida

The Indian policies of the New Deal, implemented by the Franklin D. Roosevelt administration, brought a number of badly needed services and improvements to Oneida after 1932.[21] The Wheeler-Howard Act of 1934 (the "Indian New Deal") contained provisions that encouraged the reorganization of reservation self-government. Despite active opposition by some at Oneida, the faction that supported the New Deal succeeded in winning a referendum in 1934 that called for a new tribal government under the Indian Reorganization Act (IRA). "In 1936, the Oneidas, through the efforts of the Indian Service, drew up a constitution and bylaws under which these Indians would operate as a political entity, the 'Oneida Tribe of Indians of Wisconsin' " (Hauptman 1981:84–85). This organization gave the Oneidas stable elected leadership with functioning committees. The executive body of the tribe, then and now, is the elected Oneida Business Committee.

Other provisions of the Indian New Deal made it possible for the Oneidas to buy back small amounts of land to be allocated for home and garden sites. There was also a building loan fund that contributed to the repair of many buildings and to the construction of twelve new houses by 1939. "Labor was furnished by W.P.A., and about a dozen homes have been built with the loans being paid on a long-term basis" (Ritzenthaler 1950:15). There was also a revolving fund for the purchase of stock and farm implements, to be repaid at 3 percent interest. As a result, "by 1939 approximately 1,300 of the 1,500 Oneidas [on the reservation] were receiving government aid, either in surplus commodities, W.P.A. [work], outdoor relief, old-age pensions, dependent-children pensions, or C.C.C. aid" (Ritzenthaler 1950:15). [22]

Boarding Schools

A major force for change and acculturation was the institution of the Indian boarding school. From the late 1880s until the 1930s most of the education Oneida children received was in special residential facilities, both on and off the reservation. Oneida children usually started their schooling at the Oneida Indian Boarding School (on the reservation) after it opened in 1893, and some went to the Indian schools at Tomah and Wittenberg in Wisconsin. Those who went furthest in their education, however, attended the famous non-reservation schools. The most prominent of these were the Carlisle Indian Industrial School (Carlisle, Pennsylvania), Hampton Institute (Hampton, Virginia), Haskell Institute (Lawrence, Kansas), Chilocco Indian Agricultural School (Chilocco, Oklahoma; before 1907, Indian Territory), and Flandreau Indian Boarding School (Flandreau, South Dakota). [23]

The young pupils received intensive exposure to the culture of mainstream white America in these institutions. Those who stayed long enough learned English, and some forgot or abandoned the Oneida language—which was exactly the intention of those who ran the schools (see Basehart 1952:220–221; Coleman 1993; and chapter 7 in this volume).

The non-reservation Indian boarding schools have acquired an almost entirely negative reputation, above all because their declared purpose was to make the young people in their care forget their Indian culture and language and assimilate to Euro-American ways. The aim was to remove the children from the influences of their parents, kin, and home communities and to place them in institutions controlled by white administrators and teachers where they would be taught only in English and learn only the things that their teachers thought would make them "proper Americans." There have been many criticisms of the health and physical conditions, the quality of the food and adequacy of the diet, and the treatment of children by teachers and staff. The first narrative in this volume on this topic, by John A. Skenandore, captures most of these harmful aspects in a few vivid pages. The other accounts of individual recollections and reactions, however, present a more favorable and complex picture. While several boys tell of running away from the Oneida and Tomah boarding schools, experiences at the major non-reservation institutions seem to have left at least these former students with more positive feelings. [24]

Schools like Carlisle, Haskell, and Hampton played a significant role in creating an educated elite at Oneida who played a role in local and national Indian affairs. In addition to the greatly admired athletes who came from these schools (a recurrent theme in the WPA papers), there were lawyers, a physician, nurses, teachers, musicians, political leaders, and women and men who had learned various industrial skills and arts. And by bringing young Indians from many different tribes together, a sense of pan-Indian consciousness was formed more effectively than it otherwise would have been (Lurie 2002:36).

Acculturation and Identity

By the time of the Oneida Ethnological Study, Oneidas had been living near or with Europeans and Euro-Americans for almost 350 years and had adopted many of the ways of the outsiders. Contact intensified in the twentieth century as whites bought Oneida land and moved onto the reservation, where they soon outnumbered the Oneidas. In increasing numbers, Oneidas went to work for wages on white farms and businesses and went to live in nearby cities, and many young Oneidas spent at least a few years at the non-reservation boarding schools and were instructed in the ways of the whites.

A reader who seeks classic Iroquois culture and traditions in these WPA texts will be disappointed. By the early 1800s, matrilineal kinship was abandoned and the kin terminological system—beloved by generations of anthropologists studying comparative kinship—had changed to one appropriate to the bilateral kindreds now favored by the Oneidas. The central institution of chiefship was first simplified and then discarded by late in that century. Their economic life and material culture, except for its relative poverty, was basically indistinguishable from that of the surrounding non-Indians.

Almost nothing was left of the elaborate and well-documented ceremonials of the Iroquois (there is reference to just one individual who is a follower of the Longhouse religion). The Oneidas had become fervent Christians, and traces of earlier beliefs, although detectable in the accounts of some of the older people, are not as prominent as those beliefs they shared with their white Christian neighbors. Although they retained skills in basketry, woodwork, and other handicrafts, women also made lace, and their favorite art form was the singing of hymns based on European-derived texts, melodies, and harmonies. The writers do not mention drums or powwows, but they do speak of pianos, organs, cornets, and brass bands. A few of the older men speak of playing or watching lacrosse, but football and baseball were much more popular.[25]

Despite all of the obvious acculturation, the individuals who speak in these texts never—not for a moment—forget that they are Oneidas, Iroquois, and Indians. The evidence of these continuing identities is in every narrative. These writings bear out Jack Campisi's contention that "to a casual observer many Oneidas are indistinguishable in White society. But even assuming an apparent behavioral assimilation it soon becomes clear that Oneidas are institutionally distinct, that their primary group relations are almost exclusively Oneida and are ordered on distinctly different premises" (1974:495). Nancy O. Lurie makes the following claim:

...ida language for the next eighteen months, through July 1940. They ...ssed this material either directly from their own knowledge or ...ugh interviews with others. They would then translate the texts, ...e typists employed by the project transcribed and typed all the ma-...l in triplicate. The workers were paid at the standard WPA "white ...r" rate (which varied, but was fifty-seven dollars per month in 1941; ...nty-five dollars for the timekeeper, who recorded their hours on ...ob), and they worked in conditions that were clearly preferable to ...king on the roads around Green Bay in January—or August. Stadler ...g, one of the workers, wrote of his experience:

...uring these times we were able to write our language and we can read it. ...e have made words for [an] Indian dictionary. We have written stories ...hich we solicited from many of the Oneidas. Some of these stories are ...d stories from way back. Some are true stories that really did happen, ...d some of the stories are about the customs and belief of the Indians. ...e have translated all the Indian stories and the words for the dictionary ...to English. We have written biographies of some of the older people. We ...ave written in Indian and translated some old Indian medicines which ...ey used long ago. All this work has been done by Oneidas under the ...pervision of some university students. [29]

...he Oneida writers produced a major body of material for the study ...Oneida and other Iroquoian languages, and Lounsbury helped to ...pare the material for use in teaching, for scholarly analysis, and for ...own master's and doctoral theses. As Campisi and Hauptman say, ...s research and teaching [drawing on this Oneida material] virtually ...nded the contemporary interest in Iroquoian linguistics" (1981:448). ...ce then, generations of Oneidas have learned from, studied, and ...lished these writings. [30] As John Skenandore told Laurence Haupt-...n, "We all realized that we were attempting to preserve and pass on ...language for the future" (Hauptman 1981:176). Aside from its use ...language learning and linguistic analysis, these pieces are contribu-...ns to Oneida history, folklore, and ethnography.

...s Andrew Beechtree reported, after the language and folklore pro-...t was completed, the Department of Sociology and Anthropology at ...University of Wisconsin applied for and received funding for a new ...ject: the Oneida Ethnological Study (WPA Project no. 9476). The ...licit aim of this research was to study the modern community, with

In their difficult dealings with Whites, Indian communities have something more than misery seeking company holding them together. Indian people are aware of being different from Whites, and in the matters that count to themselves the differences are not equated with inferiority but with meaningful social identity. Their humor is different; their decision-making processes are different; their religious attitudes are different, even if based on Christianity and church membership; their canons of politeness are different; their attitudes toward land and material wealth are different; and their expectations of one another are different. (Lurie 1962:829, quoted in Campisi 1974:11)

The Oneida WPA writings illustrate this. The men and women who speak through these narratives opened up and told the world about their lives and their feelings. Together they give us a portrait of a group of individuals with a variety of different personalities and different experiences who have retained a distinctive and well-recognized identity and social and cultural patterns of their own. They offer an excellent example of a people who had undergone massive change and acculturation over several hundred years, who share the majority of their culture with their non-Indian neighbors, but who nevertheless remain distinctively themselves. Indeed, this seems equally true of the Oneidas today, more than sixty years later.

Oneida since 1942

Despite the litany of losses and the constant press of poverty that is so prominent in the narratives in *Oneida Lives*, this small population contributed a remarkable cohort of capable people who accomplished things both on and off the reservation. [26] Robert L. Bennett (1912–2002) became the second Native American to become U.S. commissioner of Indian Affairs (he was the first Oneida but the second Iroquois), and other Oneidas, such as Norbert Hill Sr. (and Jr.), were also active in government, labor, and Indian affairs beyond the reservation as well as at home. And when a few opportunities opened up for Indians, as they did during the New Deal, the Oneida leadership took advantage of them.

The condition of the Oneida Nation is very different today from what it was in the 1930s. Although there was still a great deal of poverty, unemployment, ill-health, and substandard housing at Oneida in the mid-1960s (Campisi 1974:166ff.), conditions began to improve about that

time because the tribal government took advantage of the increased federal assistance to Indian communities that was available in the Kennedy
and Johnson administrations (Richards 1974:90ff.). Beginning in 1973
they could make use of funds from federal revenue sharing (Campisi
1974:249). When they received money from success in a land claims
case, and when it became possible for Wisconsin Indians to call upon
their special treaty status to operate smoke shops and bingo parlors,
they finally had revenues to use for community development. Making
use of some of the small parcels of land that they still had, they began to
buy back available reservation land with their new funds. They created
an industrial park on their land at the edge of Green Bay, and they built
a hotel and convention center next to the Green Bay airport. They built
a magnificent new elementary school, a public library, and the Oneida
Nation Museum, and they acquired a large building—a former Catholic
seminary—for their tribal offices and a high school.

Since the early 1990s, with the advent of full-scale gaming, the
Oneida Nation has been able to capitalize on its successful casino and
expanded bingo operations. These allow the nation to give annual per
capita payments to tribal members and to offer all manner of health,
housing, education, and social services. The Oneida Nation is one of
the largest employers in that part of Wisconsin, and its numerous enterprises enable it to offer a great variety of occupational opportunities
to Oneidas who want to work in the area. The population of the Oneida
Nation today is estimated at fifteen thousand, of which approximately
six thousand live on or near the reservation. Many people have decided
to return to the reservation to take advantage of the opportunities for
work and to be with their kin and fellow Oneidas. [27]

The WPA Project and the Book

This book contains more than sixty first-person accounts of the lives
and experiences of fifty-three Oneida Indians who ranged in age from
twenty-nine to ninety at the time they contributed their stories to the
Oneida Ethnological Study. The material for this collective self-portrait
resulted from a unique research endeavor. Between February 1939 and
March 1942, a score of Oneida Indian men and women worked on two
related projects that produced a massive body of material about their

language, folklore, history, ethnography, sc
lives.

The original project was conceived in 1938 ฺ
linguistic anthropologist, was teaching at the ໄ
Madison. Swadesh wanted to do research oɩ
which belongs to the Iroquoian family. Wheɩ
Oneida leaders, they were immediately recepti
that their language was in danger of dying out a
and only a few young people cared to speak
research would contribute to its maintenance. I
the Oneidas manifested a desire to preserve thei
their history, an interest that has blossomed in ɩ
nomic conditions have improved (e.g., Hauptm

In 1938 the main source of paid employme
work provided by the New Deal programs—th
Conservation Corps (CCC). For the most part th
on a dam, and quarrying, while a few worked
Morris Swadesh conceived a plan to support a
WPA funds while they worked full-time to reɩ
guage. He applied for and received a grant from
ers Project, administered through the Universi
called the Oneida Language and Folklore Projɛ
project see Campisi and Hauptman 1981; Haup
bury 1988).

Bilingual and literate Oneidas were invited tɩ
project, and about twenty were selected for preli
testing. Eventually, two women and nine men
project for eighteen months, beginning in Fɛ
could not continue beyond the planning stage,
contract at the university was not renewed, and
tunity to work in Mexico (Campisi and Haupt
1971:241). Fortunately, a remarkable stand-in ⱱ
the project. Floyd Lounsbury, an advanced und
mathematics who had taken courses in anthropo
and several prominent linguists, was able to ƥ
remarkable skill and enthusiasm. [28]

After two weeks of intensive training and te
January 1939, those who were selected proceedɛ

special emphasis on acculturation: the nature and processes of change in Oneida society and culture. [31] This project ran from October 1940 through March 1942 and employed eight men and two women, most of whom had also worked on the original project.

The men and women who did most of the work on the project are, in alphabetical order, Oscar H. Archiquette, Andrew Beechtree, Ida Blackhawk, Hyson Doxtator, Guy Elm, Stadler King, William Metoxen, David Skenandore, John Skenandore, Sherman Skenandore, and Alma Thomas. [32] The supervisors were Ronald Elperin, a sociology graduate student from the University of Wisconsin (October 1940–February 1941), and then Harry W. Basehart, a graduate student in anthropology at the University of Chicago (March 1941–March 1942). [33]

As with the first project, these bilingual men and women went among their fellow Oneidas with pencils and stenographers' pads (six by eight, eighty pages each) and recorded by hand what their kin, neighbors, and friends told them. Most also wrote down their own observations, recollections, and opinions. [34] Together they filled up about 180 notebooks with their own accounts or verbatim records of interviews with others. They recorded life histories, interesting experiences, beliefs, funny stories, lists of useful plants and recipes, observations, and analyses of Oneida life. In addition, they produced maps of the reservation and carried out two or three small social and economic surveys. Several other workers were hired to abstract articles about the Oneidas that had appeared in the Green Bay, Appleton, and De Pere newspapers from the 1890s until 1941. For this research, too, typists were hired to transcribe the handwritten accounts in triplicate.

It is significant that the Oneida workers and their informants largely determined what material was collected. "Unlike other WPA projects of the time, [these narratives] are unique because they were collected, translated, and transcribed by the Oneidas themselves" (Hauptman and McLester 1999:xviii). Elperin and Basehart prepared two surveys (one on work histories and the other on diet and food expenditures), Basehart arranged an ethnobotanical study, and both suggested some topics to write about (e.g., social stratification, child development). Basehart apparently recommended taking down more and longer autobiographical accounts. But the interviewers seem to have had no restrictions on what they could ask or record, and what they collected depended on the interests and knowledge of the respondents and the writers themselves. Many of the selections take unusual turns; often the interview has a formal title, but what actually appears in the text may be quite different as the narrators move from one topic to another. Above all, and uniquely, these are the stories, thoughts, feelings, and attitudes of the Oneida people themselves, unmediated by interviewers from outside the culture.

There are three major differences between the two projects. First, all the material for the first project was collected in the Oneida language and then translated word for word, for linguistic purposes, and subsequently translated freely into English. Most of the material for the ethnological study, however, was either collected in English or taken down in the Oneida language and then translated freely into English. Second, the emphasis of the second project was on social, cultural, and autobiographical matters, not language and folklore. Third, while most of the pieces in the first project are short—usually one or two paragraphs in length, at most a few pages—the selections in the ethnological project are much longer, usually running for many pages. This permits sustained autobiographical or topical narratives that were impossible in the first project. Both in its nature and its vast scope, this collection is without parallel in American Indian literature.

The Fate of the Oneida Ethnological Study

Although the material produced for the Oneida Language and Folklore Project has been well known and widely used all these years, the results of the Oneida Ethnological Study were almost completely forgotten until they were rediscovered in 1998. As best as we can reconstruct it at this time, the following is what happened.

The project had been conceived on a large scale, to include mapping, the collection of genealogies and life histories, social and economic surveys, and participant observation by Basehart. When the war came, however, Basehart was drafted into the army, and the WPA funding ran out in any case. After the war, Basehart drew on his fieldwork experiences and some of the material in the notebooks for his dissertation, "Historical Changes in the Kinship System of the Oneida Indians," completed at Harvard in 1952. A few years later he took a position at the University of New Mexico, where he turned his attention to the Apache peoples and to research in Africa. He never returned to the Oneida material.

The original notebooks and maps were left at the Department of Anthropology in Madison. The anthropologist who acted as caretaker of the project materials, H. Scudder Mekeel, died unexpectedly of a heart attack in 1948. He was the only cultural anthropologist on the faculty at that time, and apparently no one else was aware of the significance of the material. As a result, a large carton containing 167 notebooks, a number of maps, the labor survey, and abstracts of newspaper articles was put in the department storeroom, along with Mekeel's library and other items from his office. The collection lay in various storerooms from then until 1998, when I was led to the treasure by a series of unlikely but fortunate coincidences and was able to identify it with the help of Harold Conklin and Clifford Abbott.[35]

The original notebooks and other materials from the project are now in the archives of the Wisconsin Historical Society and are housed at the society's Area Research Center on the campus of the University of Wisconsin–Green Bay. The collection can be seen and used there by the public and professional researchers. A full set of photocopies of the originals was presented to the Oneida Nation in May 1999 and are in the care of the Oneida Cultural Heritage Department, where a team of researchers has been working with them. Members of the Oneida Language Program are studying those newly found texts that are in the Oneida language.

The long-forgotten accounts collected in this book represent only about 15 percent of the total collection, which, when transcribed, totals almost forty-five hundred manuscript pages. The full collection includes more than five hundred separate entries, some of them quite lengthy. For this volume we have selected a group of autobiographical accounts from among the many that were available. They will introduce these distinctive voices and give a taste of the Oneidas and their lives from the late 1880s until 1942.[36]

A Note on the Selections

With the exception of the speech and letters relating to the "Boland affair" in the appendix, all the pieces are personal and autobiographical. I chose these narratives because they seemed to me the most interesting

and the most substantial and because they offered a wide range of topics
and a well-rounded view of Oneida life by men and women of different
ages. They document both the sorrows and the joys, the good times and
the bad. We could not include many other excellent accounts and still
keep the book to a reasonable size.

In addition to more memoirs, the other 85 percent of the collection
contains many accounts of Oneida history (mostly what was then recent
history) and what might be called ethno-sociology. These are recollections, observations, and the expression of attitudes on many topics,
including economic life (jobs and earning a living, cooperation, getting
credit at local stores); birth, baby care, naming, child rearing, and discipline; changes in family, marriage, and social behavior; social stratification, prominent people, rich and poor; the contemporary political situation, leadership, Oneida political organizations and attitudes; church
organization, mutual aid societies, and other voluntary associations; religious beliefs and practices, funerals and wakes, witchcraft, False Face;
allotment and the loss of land; hunting, sports, gambling, recreation,
taverns and dance halls, friendships; and much more.[37]

Principles Followed in Editing

The narratives in this volume presented a number of distinct editorial problems. To begin with, there are fifty-three different voices here,
each with its distinctive style, and written down by ten different people.
Most of these were rapidly transcribed recordings of extemporaneous
speech, which must have contained false starts, incomplete sentences,
and numerous lapses. Some of the narrators were monolingual Oneida
speakers, and many interviews were given in the Oneida language and
then translated by the bilingual workers. The knowledge and education of even those who spoke in English varied considerably, and the
translator-writers themselves varied in their level of formal education
and their control over written English. Each writer had his or her own
way to punctuate, spell, and divide sentences and paragraphs. In the
light of all this it is remarkable how little editorial intervention has been
necessary, but some is called for.

There is a great range of expression found in these many selections,
and it is neither possible nor desirable to print everything exactly as it
was put on paper or to edit out the variation and the individuality. It

is impossible to be completely consistent in editing punctuation and grammar. We have had to be flexible in order to do justice to the flavor of the narratives; we have had to make compromises between conforming to American English publication standards and retaining the rhythm and style of the individual speakers and those who recorded their words.[38]

As in any body of writing, there are inadvertent errors of spelling and grammar in the original documents—deviations from the norms set by such guides as the *Chicago Manual of Style*. One of the functions of editors (and word-processing programs) is to catch and correct such errors. The Oneida workers did not have the benefit of these tools, but we do. We are extending the same courtesy to these writers that we would to all authors.

We have followed these general principles in editing:

1. Where an editor would normally change the spelling in a manuscript to save it from unintended spelling errors, we have done so. It wouldn't serve a useful purpose to leave "forty" as "fourty," "fifty" as "fiffty," or the town of Wittenberg as "Wittenburg." It was not uncommon for the writers to separate compound words that would usually be joined into one, as in "how ever," "any thing," "some thing," and "may be." We have reconnected them. There are a few cases of creative idiosyncratic use of the language that we have retained. These include "whipple snapper," "warppling," "spunning," and "*painecious* anemia."

2. Only rarely was it necessary to make changes in syntax. Sometimes the writers were working in haste and slipped up unintentionally; there is no point in publishing something that will present an unintended and unnecessary puzzle. Sometimes we have added the article "a" or another word in order to correct an obvious omission; such minor changes are not indicated. In only a few cases have substantive words been changed or added, and these are marked with a note or question in brackets following the word: [thus].

   It seemed advisable to punctuate some long sentences with commas, semicolons, or dashes, or even divide them into two, and to separate long blocks of text into paragraphs. Some authors wrote for many pages without making new paragraphs. Any loss of narrative authenticity is balanced by the easier reading that results.

3. Most of the narratives are presented in their entirety, but several have been excerpted from longer pieces. In a very few instances, paragraphs have been deleted because they represented unnecessary digressions or were more appropriate to another volume, one presenting Oneida history, sociology, and ethnography. These excisions are noted in the text.

4. Whenever possible we have presented a very brief sketch of the narrator of each piece. Unfortunately, we were not able to do so for everyone.

5. Each narrative in this volume has been given a brief title, some of which accompanied the originals. Not all the pieces had titles, and some titles were not very informative (e.g., "Religion" or "Family"), so we retitled those. Because the author might address a number of different topics in any account, however, the titles are often poor guides to the contents. Accounts of family life, economic conditions, or boarding schools, for example, may be found in any selection, regardless of the title. Nevertheless, the titles indicate a central concern of the selection.

6. Regarding anonymity and confidentiality, many of the individuals who told their stories were very frank about their lives, their problems, their relationships, and other people. It does not seem that they thought their stories would or should be kept secret. Indeed, several people (e.g., Ruth Baird, Guy Elm, and Tom Elm) speak of the "book" that will result. In the early days of the project the identities of those who wrote their autobiographies were disguised by replacing their names with code letters or numbers, but later this practice was dropped.[39]

Some narrators did have their identities concealed, however. The thirty-three-year-old woman who is identified as "Confidential" explicitly requested that the interviewer not use her name. For some reason, three other individuals were presented as Mrs. M. E. S., G. O., and Anonymous, although in the latter two cases the accounts contain obvious identifying information.

In addition, we have concealed the identity of one man (Anonymous no. 2) because he relates things that might cause discomfort to his descendants. His story seemed too well told and too good as a picture

ACKNOWLEDGMENTS   xli

of the human condition to leave out. His name was not hidden, and he might have been happy to have his name known, but we have chosen to omit it.

Unfortunately, the first names of Mrs. R. Hill and Mrs. James Skenandore were not given.

ONEIDA LIVES

1.

A Brief Economic and Social History

This chapter consists of just one account: a detailed memoir in which Ida Blackhawk describes the changes in economic and social life that she experienced over the course of her lifetime. It is a story of steady decline from the days of her childhood, when the Oneidas as a tribe owned a considerable amount of land and there were still timber resources, wild berries galore, and no lack of fish in the creeks. Over the next forty years she witnessed the near-total loss of land by the Oneidas, the depletion of the stands of timber, the growth of wage labor, and then the Great Depression that wiped out so many of those jobs.

Ida Elm Blackhawk, who was born in 1884 and died in 1971, was a prominent member of the WPA team. She wrote her own accounts of Oneida life and interviewed many others, especially women. She was educated at Hampton Institute, where she met her husband. They moved to his home state of Nebraska, where she worked as a teacher for several years. They had two children who died young, and when her husband also died she returned to Oneida. She was a sister of Guy Elm, another prolific participant in the project. She gave this account, dated January 13, 1942, its title.

Hard Times at Oneida

There is a vast difference in the Oneida community in the periods between 1888–1896 and 1927–1942. When I was about six years old I remember we lived on my father's allotment. He settled there after he married my mother. He put a claim on this land, and when the government issued trust patent to the Oneidas in 1888 my father got a ninety-acre allotment east of his father's and mother's allotment, where he had staked his claim. When I was six years old he had cleared about fifteen to twenty acres, and had built a log house and also a log barn for his horses and cows. I remember we had two cows then. We practically lived in the woods. There were other people; about 75 percent of the Oneidas were in the same circumstances. There were some Oneidas who lived along the ridge road who had their ninety acres mostly cleared and were farming extensively, but very few had stock. [1] Some of them had many horses, but they were the pony breed. These horses grazed all over. The Oneidas had rail fences surrounding their cultivated fields, but horses, cattle, pigs, and sheep were turned loose. No one pastured their stock.

The farmers along the ridge road were getting along fine and had plenty of everything. They raised big crops of corn, beans, and potatoes and raised lots of grain. My grandfather Elm had a ninety-acre farm by the church, but some of his land was not cleared then. He had a big herd of dairy cows, and he was one of first farmers to have a dairy farm. He milked as many as twelve to fifteen cows. He sold butter all year round. My father used to do his planting, and then he worked for the big farmers and he worked for my grandfather at times. When they used to cut grain by hand and shock by hand the farmers used to have to hire lot of men and my father was a good worker, and my mother stayed home and managed the work at home. My two oldest brothers were away to school at that time, so my brother, who was two years older than I, did the work with my help. In the summer time he had to look for the cows, and he and I milked the cows after he brought them home. Then we helped mother weed the garden, and my brother cut brush every spare time he had.

My father made enough money to buy groceries and clothing for us. There were only four of us at home at that time. My father had a small hay field and a small oat field, and sometimes he planted wheat too. He always planted potatoes, navy and kidney beans, onions, Indian and yellow corn, squashes, and pumpkins. Everything he planted used to yield abundantly, because he had a good rich new land. When he started to clear land he had a yoke of oxen, but when I could remember he had a pony team, and they did all the work on the farm consisting of twenty acres. My mother raised chickens, and in spite of the fact that hawks and other wild animals killed the chickens, she always managed to have about a hundred chickens in the fall. We also used to have several pigs—one sow that had a litter of pigs every summer.

My father was a good manager. Although we did not have any more resources than other similar families, my father looked ahead. He always found something to do. He cut brush every spare time. In the winter he would go and cut hoop poles in his woods, besides cut wood for our own use.[2] I remember he would make some trips to De Pere with a load of bolts,[3] or wood or rail ties during the winter, and at that time we had no orchard so when my dad went to town we children knew he would bring us some apples. He used to buy one or two bushels at a time, and that was the only fresh fruit we got in the wintertime. We always had plenty to eat. Fresh pork in the wintertime and salt pork in the summer from corn-fed hogs raised by my father. Our main diet was homemade butter, milk, potatoes, beans, carrots, beets, squash, onions, cabbage, turnips, and cornmeal, oatmeal, and bread.

My father used to have his wheat ground and he always had about four 100-pound bags of flour in the wintertime. My mother always put up wild blackberries and raspberries and dried some apples. The berries were boiled in open kettle, and put in crocks covered with clean white muslin, and tied securely. When my mother was ready to use them she just added sugar. All the groceries my father bought in the wintertime are beef, sugar, coffee, tea, oatmeal and cornmeal, apples, and crackers and cheese and candy. My father used to buy us only peppermint candy and stick candy, but he always brought us candy whenever he went to town. It seems as though we never got enough of sweet things because we got that only occasionally, and my mother divided the candy so that we all got an equal share. My mother did not know how to make a cake, but she could make good pies, cookies, and gingerbread. She used to put too much flour in her cakes; otherwise it was alright. It was not light. We got plenty of fruit in the summertime, because right near our home on my father's land was where blackberries grew plentifully. Oneidas from the neighboring homesteads came there to pick berries. But my father would get up at daybreak and go with a big basket, and by the time my mother had breakfast ready my father would be back with about six or eight quarts of blackberries. My brothers and sisters all remember how we used to enjoy our breakfast with fresh blackberries or raspberries.

My parents taught us to work, but not real hard labor. My mother used to leave me to take care of my little sisters and brothers, even the baby, while she went to pick berries or work in the garden. She used to even keep me home from school at planting time to take care of the children while she worked outside. I often tell my brother and sisters that I was the one that raised them. I went to the mission school [in Oneida] until I was about twelve years old. Then I went to Philadelphia to [an Episcopal] school.

One winter when I was about five years old my father decided to go to the northern woods near Wittenberg, Wisconsin. There were about 25 percent of Oneida men went to the woods that winter. There were four of us children; then two of my brothers were away to school. My father chopped lot of wood, mostly hardwood. We had a woodshed that my mother used for a summer kitchen. My father filled that up with wood, and left some outside in case we got short. Soon after Christmas he left for the woods. He had butchered two hogs and we were well stocked with both fresh and salt pork. We always have homemade sour kraut, and cucumber pickles. He had bought about fifty pounds of sugar, and we had our own flour, besides we had Indian corn, and my mother could make corn bread. We had a neighbor whose husband went too. She only had one child, but she soon got out of fuel, and she came over and stayed with us. My father was gone two months, and it seemed a long time to me. We got along alright. We did not run out of groceries, but we had a very heavy snowfall, and severe weather. And our wood got low, so my mother got my uncle to chop wood for us. Coal was unheard of those days.

While my father was gone one of the cows fell in the well. She broke through the ice and could not get out. My mother tied a logging chain around the cow's horns and hitched the horses to the chain and they pulled her out. I remember my mother got so excited because my brother was not much help to her. When my father came back my baby sister was about two years old, and I was about six. My little baby sister was afraid of him. I was a little shy of him myself. That was the only time that he was away from home during my childhood. I don't think he ever went to the woods again after that. He made some money that time. He made about $150, but he had to buy some things from the store at Wittenberg. He brought boots for himself, and that used to cost about fifteen or sixteen dollars. I always remember what a nice pair of shoes I got that time. I guess he bought shoes for all of us.

Other winters he hauled wood, logs, etc. to De Pere and he used to make a little money at that too. It seems to me that my father was working all the time. He used to haul hardwood timber to Joe Smith's sawmill, and had it sawed into lumber. About this time he put an addition to the log house and we used it for the kitchen and we ate in the kitchen. He had to enlarge the house, as the family was increasing all the time, and we were all growing. A log house is very warm, because our house was never very cold, and yet at one time we only had a cook-stove, but we had plenty of hardwood and small stumps and they are as good as coal.

As I said I guess we did not get enough vegetables in the wintertime, or a variety of foods, but we used to eat carrots, turnips, and cabbage raw. Once in a while my mother would make soup. We got plenty of potatoes. We always had eggs. My mother used to get eggs all winter from her hens composed of mix breeds—mostly leghorns. Every now and then we had chicken cooking in different ways.

I presume the Oneidas who lived by the ridge road were in better circumstances and did not work as hard in the wintertime. Some of the Oneidas—if any of them had a hard time in winter at that time it was because the father neglected to support his family. The man either drank intoxicants to excess, or he was too lazy to work, because there was all kinds of ways for an Oneida to make money in those days. There were about 50 percent of the Oneida men who made progress the same as my father. About the time I went away to school my two older brothers came home from school to spend their summer vacation at home. My father put them to work. He rented a piece of land, about forty acres, and he planted grain, barley, or oats. My brothers helped him all summer, and in the fall my oldest brother went back to [boarding school at] Hampton Institute in Hampton, Virginia, and the other brother went to Flandreau Indian Boarding School in Flandreau, South Dakota.

I was away four years, and when I returned home the old homestead was quite different. My father had cleared quite a bit of land, and he had more cows. They had a separator, and father sold cream to Fairmont's Creamery in Green Bay and my mother made butter for home use. My two youngest brothers, Louis and Guy, were the only ones at home. My sisters were all going to school at the Oneida Boarding School. [4] My oldest brother was already graduated at Hampton Normal School and was teaching at Flandreau. My two other older brothers came home that summer. We all stayed home that winter. Whenever my three sisters came home from the boarding school every month there would be ten of us at home. We only had three bedrooms, and we realized that we were getting crowded, so my brothers and parents and I decided that we needed a new house, or another addition to the house.

My brother and I had lot of red oak trees on our twenty-five-acre allotments, so I let them cut all the red oak trees on my land that were large enough to be sawed at the mill. Our land was west of the Oneida town, and my father and brothers started to haul timber to the sawmill. They also sold some wood and pine bolts, which brought good money at that time. We used to get up about four o'clock in the morning, and while they got the teams ready and milked the cows I helped my mother get the breakfast, and sometimes we made lunch for them. During January, February, and March they worked in the woods. The only time they stayed home was when there was a blizzard. They worked out in all kinds of weather, cold, snowing, or blowing.

At the end of March they had taken a lot of timber to the sawmill and had brought big logs to the place. They also had cleared about a hundred dollars for the wood and bolts they sold. When the snow started to melt and the roads got bad for sleighs then they went to the woods and cut hoop poles and made hoops next day. They worked on that for about a month then took a load to town and sold them. That brought in some more cash. When it was time to work in the fields we had quite a lot of money on hand. And they used it to buy groceries and clothing or whatever we needed. They did not put the money in the bank. My mother was the treasurer. I made lace in my spare time, but I was kept busy helping my mother do the housework, and we had pretty large washings.

At that time my father had two teams, and they were all draft horses medium weight. He raised his own horses. One of my brothers had a pony team, and we used them for riding, or driving on the road. That summer my two brothers cleared a lot of the land. My father had lot of pine timber, and they sold that too, and some they saved. They cut brush every spare time they had. That summer we were all at home but my oldest brother. That was the time Larson Canning Company had all the big Oneida farmers plant peas. Some white farmers planted peas too. Larson hired Oneidas to pull the vines and take off the pods. I don't remember what he paid, but we all picked together and punched on one ticket. My father got the biggest checks. My two oldest brothers did not pick peas, and my father went occasionally. We were so busy that the summer went quite fast. The mosquitoes were not so numerous, and we did not have to make a smudge every evening near our house. [5]

In the fall two of my sisters went back to the boarding school. One was far enough advanced in her studies to go to Haskell Institute, Kansas, and one returned to Flandreau, South Dakota, to continue her studies. Quite late in the fall one of my brothers also went to Haskell Institute to join the school band. They were getting the band ready to go to St. Louis World's Fair. I almost went to Haskell Institute with my brother but I had already signed up to go to Hampton, Virginia, and I was just waiting for my transportation. That winter the old folks were left alone again with just my two young brothers six and eight years old, but they were both good milkers already. About this time the Oneida Creamery was in operation and August Ferm was the cheese maker. My father sent his milk over there. Other Oneida farmers had started to take interest in dairy farming.

I went to Hampton, Virginia, in January 1904 and was gone four years. While I was away my father started to build a new nine-room house up on the hill and also put up a larger barn, but it was not modern.

He had stalls for about twelve cows and a few heifers or calves and room for two teams of horses. The cows had wooden stationary stanchions made by my father.

At this period the Oneidas were permitted to sell inherited land. Parents were also permitted to sell their children's land if deceased. Those who sold land either improved their homes, or bought cattle and horses and implements, or else lived on easy street until the money was all exhausted. In the fall of 1907 the Kansas claim, which was often discussed by the old Oneidas, was partly liquidated and each individual received about a hundred dollars.[6] The parents received the children's share if under age. My father got my share. My three oldest brothers got their payment. The following year the Oneidas got the balance, about seventy-five dollars a head. I received my money this time, but I sent some of it home for my father to use in building the house.

My father was quite a prosperous farmer at this time, and most of the Oneidas were in good circumstances. My father bought new farm implements, also put up a good barbwire fence around his ninety-acre farm. My mother bought new furniture for the home. Oneidas who had not been able to own horses bought horses and buggies so they could ride around. At this time the majority of the Oneidas were in the height of prosperity. Everybody was in good circumstances. They had plenty to eat. There is a joke about one family who had always been more or less in want. The mother bought all kinds of good things to eat, and after she had spread it on the table one little fellow looked on the table and asked if she had corn soup and corn bread. He was so used to having those foods in his diet that he missed them.

There were quite a few marriages at that time. Most of the young fellows could afford to get married. At that time a fellow had to have about a hundred dollars cash in order to pay the wedding expenses. It used to be the custom for the man to buy his fiancée's wedding outfit and also give the wedding feast, and usually most all the Oneidas on the reservation were invited. His relatives usually helped him to some extent. The bride's relatives are the guests of honor on this occasion, and friends and distant relatives are usually invited. We have had two weddings lately where it was vice versa. Oneidas are adopting white people's way.

After being away four years I returned home from Hampton, and I found the Oneida community somewhat different. There was a distinct sign of progress. While out East and in New England I had seen some automobiles, and I had a trip in one of them. In Oneida there were no automobiles, but the Oneidas were well fitted out with nice carriages or buggies pulled by nice-looking teams. The roads were in better condition, and they had better homes. There were many new houses, and some had put improvements to their homes, and some had new barns and more livestock to most farms. I think at this period most of the Oneidas who were farming were at the height of their advancement. About 75 percent were farming, the rest were laborers, but had their gardens, and lived on their allotments.

The reservation had been divided into townships, and white people were buying Indian land. About a year or two before, Oneidas were given their fee-simple patents, and they had started to pay taxes, both land and personal property. [7] The Oneidas started to borrow money, and mortgaged their property. Some of them would use the money in building a better house, or they bought horses and cattle. Most of the heavy timber had been cut, but there were still patches of good timberland; the Oneidas were not selling so much wood and bolts or ties. Wooden hoops were off the market, but there was road work. The two town chairmen were both Oneidas, and the other officials were all Oneidas. Josiah Powless (Dr. Powless) was chairman for the Town of Hobart.[8] Chauncey Baird was the treasurer, Eli Skenandore was town clerk, Moses Elm was the assessor, and Anderson Skenandore and Solomon Webster were supervisors. The town officials for the Town of Oneida were Nelson Metoxen, chairman, Josiah Charles, treasurer, Lehigh Wheelock, clerk, and Richard Powless, assessor. The supervisors I cannot recall. Anyway, the town officials were all Oneidas in the start, but as the white settlers increased the Oneidas started to lose votes. It took about twenty years before there was no Oneida town official in Hobart. I think Bill Metoxen is still treasurer in the Town of Oneida. I think what accounts for that is there are still quite a few Oneidas in Outagamie County.

The way the Oneidas lost their land was through failure to pay the interest on their mortgages and not paying their mortgages when due and neglecting to pay their taxes. They did not know how to take the taxes. There was some opposition regarding taxation by some of the Oneidas and they did not take it seriously. Anyway there was an Oneida man who spread propaganda that the Oneidas did not have to pay taxes and the laws of Wisconsin could not enforce them. Some people listened to him and did not make any effort to pay real estate or personal property tax from one year to another and the result of that was they were evicted from their home. I know two such cases, where they were forced to get out of their homes. I think there were some that were cheated by not being able to read, and they thought they were mortgaging only a small portion of their land, but they would find out too late that they had mortgaged the whole place. The people started to lose their homes one way or another, and white people bought them from the real estate men. White farmers started to settle on the reservation land, and they bought Oneida land as cheap as they could.

My father kept up his taxes and he was taxed heavily. They put a district school near his home, and he had to pay extra taxes for that, and all his children were too big to go to school there. One of my brothers had an accidental death in Green Bay when he was about twenty-four years old, in 1906, and he had a twenty-five-acre allotment, so my father sold that and used some of it to pay his funeral expenses. While I was home I sold my allotment too, because my sisters and brothers had all sold their land, and it was sort of swampy, and I decided I did not want to live there. When the white businessmen of Green Bay took over all the swampland they had a ditch put through, and drained the land, then the land was sold to farmers, and is now under cultivation. Everybody was selling land about this time; some people used their money, others wasted their money.

After I sold my land, I accepted a government position at Springfield, South Dakota, as an elementary teacher. I was gone two years then I returned. My father was farming extensively, and he had about twelve milk cows, and two work teams and one extra horse. He was the road supervisor at that time, and part of the time he had a hired man. He let his team work on the road and he paid his taxes that way. My father bought ten acres of land, so he was now farming a hundred acres. Part of that was still bush land, and he used that for pasture. About seventy acres was under cultivation.

All the Oneidas who were farming were in good circumstances. They were paying their taxes, and were progressive farmers. Some of these farmers (about 10 percent) had money, but did not bank their money. Land was cheap, and quite a few farmers invested their money in realty. Some of the Oneidas had moved away from Oneida, and some were working in the neighboring towns. Some had gone as far away as Racine, Manitowoc, Fond du Lac, Sheboygan, and Madison. The families who had sold their land or had mortgaged it and were not able to redeem it had moved away to some town, and found work in some factory; others had gone north to work in the woods. Some of these people may have been hard up at the time they went away from Oneida, but I never heard of anyone speak of any Oneida as being destitute. Some of the Oneidas lived in small log houses and did not have much furniture, but they dressed well and had plenty to eat.

I was married September 5, 1912, to a Nebraska Indian, whom I had known while at the Hampton Normal School. He was a postgraduate and was working at the mission at Winnebago, Nebraska. He was the interpreter for the missionary. We stayed at the mission about a year, then we went on a rented farm. I lived out west about twelve years. I made several visits home during that time. My parents were getting along fine on the farm.

During the last world war the Oneidas had to do just the same as the white people. They had to buy oatmeal flour, potato flour, and cornmeal every time they bought wheat flour. My mother had to mix her flour to make bread. The other Oneidas did the same. My sister who was a nurse had joined the army as a Red Cross nurse. She was sent overseas for two years, and she used to send some money home.[9] My parents bought about three hundred dollars' worth of Liberty Bonds. My brother Guy N. Elm was drafted, but he did not go any further than the training camp. The Elm family is not a large family because some stayed in Oneida, New York, and some migrated to Canada. Only two brothers came to Wisconsin to settle here, but there were quite a few Elms represented in the last world war. There were seven including my sister. Today she has the same privileges as the soldiers. She is entitled to free hospitalization, and pension when she reaches the age.

There were quite a number of Oneidas who went overseas and saw real action. Dr. Josiah Powless went with the U.S. Medical Corps and was fatally wounded just at the close of the war. His body was cremated and sent back to Oneida. His widow got ten thousand dollars in government insurance. Mrs. Powless bought a home near the Guardian Angel School. She has two daughters, and they all live together. Her daughters both have government school education. They always have a new car every year. Now the ten thousand dollars is gone, but she gets soldiers' widow's pension. After the war the soldiers came home and were all given a warm reception by all Oneidas.

There was a slight difference in the Oneida community after the last world war. There were just patches of woodland here and there, and so woodcutting was practically discontinued excepting for home use. Oneida men went to northern part of the state to work in the woods, but they got such low wages that some of them could not even make enough to pay their board. The men came home one by one. That winter work was kind of scarce for the laboring men. I remember all my brothers were home that winter and my father's two nephews were there, and my mother had two of her nephews come to stay with the old folks. My father could afford to keep all these men, because he had everything there to feed them with. He butchered two hogs and one cow that winter so they had plenty of meat. He put these men to cutting wood for him, and he sold some, and the rest he kept for home use. He had them put up some ice that winter. He had five men working for him that winter. All of them were relatives.

Other Oneida farmers had their men relatives home. These men had no work, but they were being cared for by their relatives. The Oneida farmers were really in a position to help their people. No one was really hard up, but money was not floating around on the reservation. There might have been a very small percent who were real pressed, but everyone was living on whatever resources they had. In the spring work picked up and some Oneida men worked for the Oneida farmers, some for white farmers. Some of them secured road work, others found work in Green Bay paper mill, and some went to Appleton, Neenah, Menasha, Little Chute, and Kaukauna. The young girls who had left school worked in the neighboring towns as housemaids or as factory workers. [10]

During the last world war several of the large and small government schools were abolished. Carlisle Indian School was closed at that time, and Indians could no longer attend Hampton Normal School unless they paid their own transportation and board. [11] The government discontinued paying their expenses. The Oneida government school was not closed until about the year 1922. That was quite a blow to the Oneidas. It had helped them so much. The children got their board and clothing, and that kept the Oneidas' expenses down in the winter months. The children used to stay there all winter, and went home once a month Friday after school until Sunday evening. Most of the employees were Oneidas. The nurse and two teachers, disciplinarian, assistant matrons, assistant seamstress, laundress, baker, dining room matron, and farmer were all Oneidas. Some of these Oneidas got transferred; others lost their jobs. That made it hard for the man with a big family, but it was not noticeable the first year that the school let out.

Only the boys and girls who were quite far advanced in school could sign up for non-reservation schools such as Tomah, in Wisconsin, or Flandreau, in South Dakota, and other large government schools. Very few Oneidas could afford to send their children to high school in Green Bay or De Pere. The Oneidas at this time had started to buy automobiles, and some children, a small percent of them, were able to go back and forth to town to school. Many of them quit school as soon as they were sixteen. About 60 percent of them continued to go to the big schools like Haskell Institute and Flandreau. Children who had no father or no mother, and orphans were permitted to go to government school away from Oneida even if they are not far advanced in school.

The Oneida Episcopal Mission Day School was well patronized again. The Methodist day school had turned to a government day school about 30 years before this time, and it became a district school in the year 1910 or 1911 after the white people settled on the reservation. Both white and Oneida children attended the school. There were other district schools opened up, and Oneidas belonging to a certain district attended these. At first white and Indian children were hostile to each other. It was usually the white children who showed superiority that got in trouble with Indian children. The teachers usually discouraged race prejudice, so that the white and Indian children got along fairly well. It was that way when the Oneidas started to go to the high school in De Pere in 1938 or '39. The white children tried to act superior. There were some friendly white children, but there were a few that made remarks, one girl in particular, that the Oneidas resented, so one Oneida girl took it upon herself to fix the white girl, and she did. After that the Oneidas had no more trouble. If there was a feeling against the Oneidas the white children did not show it after that, and no one picked on them. At the present time the white and Oneida young people are on friendly terms, and don't seem to have any trouble, even at the taverns.

We always got along alright with the white settlers. My father was well known in Green Bay, and De Pere, and most all the white farmers knew him, and were on friendly terms with him. When we used to have thick wooded land some of the businessmen of Green Bay used to come out on Sundays and holidays, and they used to leave their horse and buggy at my father's place while they went hunting in the woods. There used to be peddlers come out on the reservation and they used to always ask to stay overnight at my father's, and he would let them stay there. One winter the schoolteacher of the High View School roomed there. She was supposed to board herself, but she liked my mother's cooking so well that she started to eat with them. She was boarding there when my father's house burned down to the ground in March 1926, but the fire was just before school closed about 4 p.m. It was so windy that they could not hardly save anything in the house. My father had just butchered and had two barrels of salt pork and smoked hams. All potatoes and canned stuff burned. He figured he lost about six hundred dollars that time. The house was partly covered with fire insurance, so he was able to build again.

That was the time my father went behind. He had to go in debt for spring planting. We were all grown up then, and each one of us helped him with cash. The people, white and Indians, helped him to some extent with donations of old furniture and provisions.

At this period the Oneidas were finding the winter a little hard on account of the scarcity of hardwood or wood of any kind. They had to substitute coal, and if a person had no income it was hard to buy coal and groceries. All the families who had become landless, either by putting a mortgage on their land and not able to redeem it, or by selling their farm, or losing it by failure to keep up the taxes, had moved away from Oneida. Some went to Bowler, Wisconsin, some further north, and some went to the nearby cities in Wisconsin. Quite a few went to Milwaukee about this time and did not have any difficulty in getting a job of some kind. Three of my brothers-in-law moved to Milwaukee, and two of my brothers with their families. They all found good steady jobs. My two brothers-in-law and one of my brothers worked for the city as laborers and my brothers-in-law are still working for the city, but my brother was laid off during the winter months in 1937 and he came back to Oneida and never went back again. There were some Oneidas that went back and forth. They would stay in Oneida a while then return to Milwaukee.

The Oneida girls and women found work too in the cities. The girls worked in the different factories, and the women also worked in laundries, hotels, and as attendants in the different hospitals. One tuberculosis sanitarium had as many as twelve Oneida girls working there at one time. Some of them quit because they got married, and some took other jobs. One of them stayed so long that she became a practical nurse, and is still working there in the TB ward at Muirdale, Wisconsin.

When the depression started, the Oneidas were usually laid off first because so many white people think that all Indian people have some other income, besides their earnings, or that they get a yearly payment from the government. So the Oneidas started getting laid off, and one by one returned to Oneida, because they could not keep up with their rent and grocery bill. So if they had a relative living in Oneida, they came back expecting to get help from them. That worked alright for a year or two, but as the years passed and no relief in sight the residents of Oneida were beginning to feel the depression.

The farmers were not getting very much for their milk or butter, cattle, or anything they had to sell. Their taxes were high and had been high ever since 1920, so they were hard pressed too, and could not very well help their relatives, or give them free room and board as they had been doing. The Oneidas who had bought automobiles or some expensive farm implement and had put a mortgage on their land just could not redeem it, so about 40 percent of the Oneida homeowners lost their land and homes. The families crowded in small houses together, two or three families together. Some fixed up deserted log houses and lived there. My father and mother were quite aged at this period, but they had a large house, and had collected some old beds, and had been able to buy some new beds, so that even at this time about the year 1930 they were able to keep some of their grandsons and nephews while out of work.

My father had no trouble getting helpers in the wintertime, but they would all go again when spring came, because they would rather work for some rich white farmer, who had a modern farm, than to work for my father who did not have a hay loader or manure spreader. My youngest brother, who was about thirty years old but was still single, died in the winter of 1929, and my oldest brother who was a widower died the following summer. So my father had to pay two funeral bills, as both had no property or money. My father was getting so he could not do the heavy work of the farm. My youngest brother had been working for my father, and had bought a car before his death. It was rather a blow to him to lose two grown-up sons within four months, but he kept on farming as it seemed the only thing for him to do. He could not sell out as everything was slump. He kept about ten milk cows and one team of horses. He was able to pay his taxes and live on the proceeds from the sale of milk. He still could milk the cows and hoe the garden, and pick beans and cucumbers. During this time my mother was sickly, and they had to have someone do the work, and I came home from Nebraska to help them out because I had no children and my husband was in a government hospital. They were not able to pay me for my work, but I stayed. My mother died in January 1931. My father needed someone to keep house for him and he asked me to stay and I did.

The following winter was about the hardest winter in Oneida. The majority of the people were hard up for fuel especially; some were destitute. The people had no funds to buy wood or coal. Oneida men went and cut wood anywhere they found timber that was not fenced. My father still had some timberland, so we were fortunate in having wood of our own, but we had to buy coal and used coal and wood together. We had hardly any money to use for clothing. We all wore our old clothing. That winter the town gave out Red Cross and army clothing such as two-piece underwear for men, socks, gloves, and shirts and army overcoats and caps. The people who were destitute got groceries such as salt pork and flour, but all the able-bodied men had to cut brush for some of the town officials first before they were allowed to get the groceries. Some of these men were poorly clad, and yet they had to walk three or four miles to their work. The women got some dress goods, outing goods [a type of cloth] for nightgowns. When the town officials gave the Red Cross and army clothing away, there were as many white farmers there as Oneidas and the clothing went like "hot cakes." That was about the hardest time the Oneidas ever had.

The Episcopal mission gave out some canned stuff to the large families belonging to the church. All this time the unemployed of Milwaukee and other cities were being given aid, and the Oneidas who stayed in the cities were included. The Oneidas who were here were trying every possible way to get help too, but the two town officials shifted the responsibility to the state, and the state placed it on the government. For a while the Oneidas felt like they were treated worse than the aliens. Finally in November 1933 a relief office was set up at the Morgan store, and Miss

Nelson, a social worker, was in charge. [12] The Oneidas were told that they had to come and make an appointment, and then return on the day, and at a certain time of the day, for an interview. Sometimes there were so many people there that she would not have time to interview all who came and they would have to make another trip before they would get their order. Later she had an investigator and two clerks to help her; then the people did not have to make so many trips.

For some reason she gave some people everything they called for, and others in the same circumstances could not get what they asked for. That winter she gave out some coal, but not very much to a family, but she gave out some clothing to children, and goods to make dresses with. The Oneidas made a complaint about her management. It seems that she did not give the orders according to their budget. She and the investigator had trouble, and the following winter Mr. Smith was placed here. The investigator was surprised how many poor unemployed people she found on the reservation, and what poor housing condition they lived in. I have heard of one particular place where the people were living in a house with a dirt floor.

In 1934 the government gave out some materials to repair houses on the reservation. There were some men put on a government project to do the carpenter work, and the Oneidas had their houses repaired. Anyone with income did not get their houses repaired, but about 50 percent of them received materials such as roofing paper and wallboard, and flooring, and windowpanes. After Mr. Smith came he sent the old people to the pension office for application for pension, and unwedded girls with children were also sent there. The Oneidas got aid, and I only know of one family case that were found destitute in the wintertime, but that was because the man was a habitual drunkard.

In 1935 the Relief [Office] paid the rent for those that could not pay their rent, and gave orders to farmers to give fresh milk to families with children, and the farmers were paid by the Welfare Office. That same year they got free medical care, and a relief nurse was put on to go and visit the sick and give them first aid, and show the mothers how to nurse their children. The nurse had such a large field to cover, and some of them thought that she was supposed to stay there and nurse them. Her orders were to visit the home of the sick person and take their temperature, and see if they really needed a doctor, or just some medicine for cold, cough, or if they just needed a physic [purgative or laxative]. If she thought they did not need a doctor she would leave some medicine with them and tell them how often to give it and how much a dose. With obstetric cases she helped the doctor, and she called and took care of the mother and baby every day for ten days. She was on a WPA project and was supposed to work only six hours a day. The Oneidas complained because she did not stay all day and take care of some chronic cases. It was just a temporary project, for the winter months, so the next winter it was abolished. Then the government nurse was sent out here to visit those that was sick and made arrangements for them to be sent to Tomah hospital and be cared for there.

A special doctor was appointed for the Oneidas at government expense. The government field nurse does not do any nursing. She just visits the families that have children and sees that they get the right care. If they have poor eyes, she makes arrangement for the child to be taken to some eye specialist and have the child's eyes examined and fitted with glasses, at half expense by the parents and half by the government. The nurse also checks each child that goes to school how they are fixed with clothing, and the parents are given an order to buy clothes for their children. So now no matter how poor they are the children have good warm clothes for school. About the year 1938 the government provided transportation for the Oneida children that went to the high school. Now there are two government buses that carry the Oneidas to school. White children are permitted to ride in the Oneida bus, but they have to pay. There is a government dentist that comes every year to the relief office and extracts teeth, but the government does not pay for false teeth. Very few Oneidas can afford to pay for plates of false teeth, and that is why so many Oneidas have had their bad teeth extracted and have no replacement. For emergency operations Oneidas are taken to the Green Bay hospitals, and the expenses are paid by the towns of Hobart and Oneida if the patient has no means. After Mr. Smith took charge of the relief office for two winters, WPA men cut wood for the relief clients, but no coal is ever given out—only to extreme cases. The Oneidas have had to get their own fuel. Most all the Oneidas use either wood or coal or kerosene, but very few use wood alone. Hardly anyone has woodland except those who occupy New Deal land.

Today some of the Oneidas who were the most destitute when relief came are better off than those who had a little income, because for awhile if a person had two cows they would not be considered to get relief, even if the two cows were both dry. I think the majority of the Oneidas are living in better circumstances than they ever did. A very small percentage of them still complain of their living condition, but I think that is mostly their fault. They either waste their money or are too lazy to work in the summer months.

The assignment of government land to a few of the Oneidas has been a help to those who want to farm. They don't have to pay taxes, so they really have an advantage over the Oneidas who are still holding their land. They get all sorts of help, and get the preference in regards to putting improvement on their land—but which really belongs to the government. A New Deal farmer can borrow money from the revolving fund with 3 percent interest without security, but if a person with taxable land wants to borrow money they have to give first mortgage for security.

2.

Recollections and Opinions of Elders

Almost all of the men and women who related the accounts in this section were at least seventy years old at the time. Some could not speak English, so the interviews were translated from Oneida. They were a generation or two older than most of the WPA workers and had grown up when the Oneida still had chiefs, before Indian boarding schools were common and before the Dawes Act of 1887. Their stories are varied, dealing with such topics as childhood; the loss of their land after allotment; changes in social life, cultural practices, and morals; childbirth and midwifery; attitudes toward whites; and the story of a marriage told separately by husband and wife.

Tom Elm, one of the oldest of the narrators, was interviewed a number of times by several different project workers.[1] He had a long and excellent memory. Here is his account of what he recalls of Oneida in his youth, of how things had changed, and of his youthful aspirations. The narrative has been reorganized a bit, and some material has been cut in order to avoid redundancy. The interviewer, Stadler King, introduces the narrative.

Some Recollections

Tom started the story but first asked what has become of that other man who they called Ad^ná•tsle [Floyd Lounsbury]. He said we used to have fun over him because he was able to understand and talk so much in Oneida. It seemed funny to hear a white man talk in Oneida. He came to see us a few times, and I was always interested in helping what I can in what they wanted. Some of the Oneidas seem to think that this would never be of any use to anyone, so they were not interested. They say the government is throwing away that much money, but I do not think the government would do that; the government is too wise to do that. It knows that it will make use of this sometime, and it knows that there has nothing ever been written down as records about the Oneida right from the beginning when the Oneidas first came here from New York. It also knows that now is the only time left that it could ever get information about Oneidas, because we old fellows are passing away and it will not be long when those of my age will all have passed away and the younger ones that will take our place do not know anything of those olden days. If they waited twenty years or so they would not have been able to find anyone that knows and would be interested in telling of the life of Indians. Those who have gone to school have their minds on something different, so they are not interested and would not know.

I was a child when I started to remember things. We lived just about where Doctor Hill lives now. There is where we had our house. I do not remember my grandparents, but my father and mother I remember them real well. My mother lived longer than my father. My mother used to tell of the time when the Oneidas came here and that the government had promised to send food by boat from Buffalo, New York, to Green

Bay. The boat came every month, but sometimes the boat would be late on account of the wind. If they had good wind in their favor they would get here on time, but sometimes if the wind would be against them they could not make it and they may be late a few days. The Oneidas used to go in a big bunch to meet the boat. They would go on foot and came back the next day with loads of food on their backs. My mother said that there were so many wolves and bears that one person would not dare to go alone, but they did not come near when there were so many Oneidas walking together. There were no real roads but it was just a trail, but through the heavy woods, and they could see these wolves sneaking along at a distance.

The Oneidas in those days were planters of corn because that was nearly all they lived on outside of what they got from the government. At the time when I remember there were some farms then. All along the ridge road there were clearings where they raised grain like oats and wheat. Wheat always done well in those days because there was better ground and there was not so much wind. There was a man whose name was Thomas House who had great farms where the Larson Company has their farms now. He raised so much wheat and oats every year. Nearly all others had small fields where they raised corn, potatoes, and beans.

My mother told of a story that many families had pigs and chickens, so one day a woman who had chickens heard so much noise so she went out to see what was the matter. She went around the house and there was a great big wolf after them and when the wolf saw her it made for her. She ran back, and as luck had it there was a ladder against the house so she climbed this and got on the roof of the house, then she cried for help.

Some sawmills came into operation about thirty years after the Oneida had been here. The first was started in the south end near what is now known as Mason Wheelock place. A man by the name of Rockefeller started a sawmill and bought logs from the Oneidas or made lumber for them with which they started making frame houses. There were two other sawmills in the northeastern part, but they were both outside of the reservation and they also bought logs. Then there was a sawmill where the golf grounds are now. A man named Foster started this mill. He made other houses and buildings like a store and resident house near the mill. The understanding they had was that when he goes away he would leave everything and take only what cash he made so when he moved away he left all the buildings and the mill just as they were. The chiefs sold some of these houses and the lumber that was used on the sawmill. The chiefs kept this money to themselves and never paid it to the tribe.

It was about this time that we moved over in that part of the reservation, but I was still a small boy. Up to this time we lived where Doctor Hill lives now, and my days were spent playing with my neighbor's boys. [2] Our neighbor's name was Solomon King, who had boys that were the same size as I was. They would be at our place or I would be at their place playing some games or we would be going around with our bows and arrows. We would hunt squirrels and go swimming in the little stream that goes through not far from where we lived. My mother did not like it when we went swimming. She would tell us not to do this because she was afraid I might drown. Sometimes we would sneak away and go swimming, and if she finds out she would give me a whipping with a switch. She told us that when we try to fool her or disobey her and if we did drown we would not go to heaven because we were lying to her. She was rather strict about us children trying to fool her, and after she had told us not to do things and we went and did it she would give us a whipping. Also if we brought anything that she thought we might have stolen, she would make us prove that we did not steal it. My mother was always telling us that we must never steal or tell lies to her or to anyone else.

During these times all the Oneidas live chiefly on corn; that is the bread we had was corn bread and nearly all the time we would have corn soup. [3] All the Oneidas pound corn for bread and it was easy for them to start in the morning and boil the corn in ashes and wash it clean and dry it a while, then pound the corn in a bowl made in a log which would be cut to about three feet long. This stood on the ground with the bowl up. They would pound this corn with pestle. It was easy for them to have made a few loaves of corn bread by dinnertime, and some of them made bread like this every day.

They always had a big kettle hanging over the fireplace. When they are ready with the corn bread this big kettle of hot water would hold about eight or ten loaves of corn bread, and it takes one hour to boil this done. They could also bake bread in the coals of the fire. They put this loaf of dough in the ashes and then put red coals over it, and in a little while they take this out and take a dish towel to clean off the ashes. They also fry meat in a spider over these coals.[4]

In the wintertime when the nights are so long, my sisters and myself would go sliding with our neighbor children. We did this almost every night, but there were nights that we did not go; then I would stay and listen to some old man tell stories. Sometimes the old men would come to our place, and if we don't go sliding I would stay in and listen to some of them. Sometimes they told scary stories. I remember one old man telling a funny story. He said that a man went hunting in the woods. It must have been in the fall of the year because there were so much leaves on the ground in the woods. As he was going along, he thought he heard something so he stopped to listen. Soon he heard the leaves rattling in a spot not far from where he was standing, so he moved closer to that spot. Then he saw that two snakes were fighting in the leaves. He saw that each snake had bitten the other snake at the tail and both were drawing or eating the other, and soon there was only a small, hooplike circle and after a while he could not see anything so both snakes had swallowed the other.

When we moved to the place near the sawmill, I was about thirteen years old and this was about the time that I started to work out for different men. I was able to hold my end of a long crosscut saw, so men were willing to hire me to saw with them and sometimes I would work on a farm for different men. They would pay me twenty-five cents a day, and in this way I was able to help my mother. I would also work on the farms for white men, and these all paid me twenty-five cents a day. My father hardly ever stayed home because he was a laborer, so he would be gone most of the time. He would come home only once in a while. So I learned how to work by working with others.

I had two brothers who were older than I was. One of them was twelve years older than I was, so he was away a lot working at other places, and the oldest of my brothers had enlisted in the army, and that is where he died so I never knew him. I had four sisters who were older, and they were working around and two of them were married. None of my brothers or sisters got to be old as I did, but they all died young; some had grown up and married and then died, but I haven't died yet. I am the only one in my family that got to be old. At my age now, I think that I am old because I do get tired from the little work I do each day.

It was the wish of my mother, and she often told us, that we would be more happy all through life if we did what was right in all things and to go to church on Sundays to hear the teachings of the minister. As I did not go to school in my young days, the only thing I could do is to listen to what my or our minister tells us what he reads in the gospel. The church has been the first thing in all my life that I looked to as a guidance. I remember when they started to build the big stone church it took about three years to complete this and that was a long steady job for the Oneidas but they had enough stone. When the church was done the old church was taken down. This was in the year 1886. [5]

The government is rather funny in some ways. It seems that it should have done something about burials of Oneida. It has never bothered itself when people die and could not afford a coffin. Some people would have a hard time getting a coffin. It used to be cheap, but people did not have money to buy it. A person could get a good coffin for fifteen dollars, but in those days they did not have the coffins covered with cloth like they do now. They were all plain boards. Sometimes they could not afford to get a coffin; then they would have one made out of lumber. The government should have bought these coffins for the Indians. Since the towns were organized they have been paying for the coffins for the Oneidas.

The furniture that were used by the Oneidas as far back as I could remember were sometimes made at home, like chairs would be made with splints woven for the seats and then the beds would have rope woven for springs. Some are made of boards in the bottom, but this makes a hard bed. They use candles for lights because there were no lamps. Sometimes they made their own candles out of pig rind. This rind would be heated up and allowed to curl. This was placed in a saucer and lighted same as a candle would be. It would be easy to make a table and things like benches. One thing we never had is a bureau. Some people had them, but those are people who are supposed to be better off.

The women long ago used to dress different altogether than what they do now. They would have a heavy dress of some dark goods, and the waist would be red or some bright color. Then they would have sort of leggings of some real expensive dark goods which was rather loose on their legs, and these leggings would be trimmed with shiny buckles or buttons, and they wore moccasins made from real buckskins. They hardly ever wore a hat, but they always had just a band of black or red cloth around their head. If they went anywhere they would wear a heavy shawl.

The men were dressed rather thin even in the wintertime as I remember when I was a small boy. There was no heavy underwear like we have now. They wore just fleece-lined goods [material] and one pair of trousers. The overalls those days were yellow instead of blue. I remember when I was a small boy I was cutting wood on one side of the house to keep out of the wind. It was very cold. A man came to our house, so he went in and after a little while my feet were cold so I went in and sat by the fire. I took off my shoes and stockings and warmed up my feet. This man asked me if my feet always got cold, and I said yes they do if I stay out long enough. He said his feet never got cold, and he took one of his boots off. He had a piece of cotton cloth around his foot and the boots over that. There were some heavy goods like wool for pants, but they cost more. For shirts they wore a fleece-lined cloth and this yellow overalls over that.

The old men those days did not do much work, but they visited each other very much, especially at nights. One evening some men came to our place and some of them started to tell stories. One man would finish telling his story and another would start up, so one of them told this story. He said that he remembers long before that time when men did not wear pants. He said that a man would only have a long shirt and then he would have some sort of band fashioned behind and come under and fashioned to the front part of his shirt or what is called now a G-string. This is all the men wore. They would have a pair of moccasins on but no pants. He told of a man who went out visiting when he was like that, so he went into someone's house and he was asked to sit down. The chair that he sat down on was one of these old homemade chairs with splints seat. The splints on this chair was old and broke in, in the center. The man began talking with the people and he laughed a great deal. The G-string that he wore must have worked to one side from him moving so much. The people at this house had a cat that must have been a good mouser. All at once this cat crawled sneakingly toward the man. As the man laughed, something must have shook under his chair in the broke-in seat. The cat made a jump and caught that thing, but it was the man's. . . . So that would not be a good way to dress.

The winters those days were just as cold or colder than winters nowadays, so those Indians were really more tough than they are nowadays. The winters were longer too them days when I was a small boy. I remember that it used to start snowing in October and the snow would stay until way later in March. It used to be that when the Christmas holidays are over we used to consider that the winter was half gone, because it used to set in so early in the fall.

I have noticed a change in people since the time I first remember. As I have said that men in the old days did not work so much, they did more visiting around and telling stories and maybe joking on one another. That's all they had to talk about was something in fun. They never talked of anything about the good for people or what they are doing or how to make money or what they have planted or anything that might be of value to them. But today people do talk of money and what they are doing and how much money they made, what they have planted, or how their crops are, and all that kind of talk. This kind of talk may be of more value than just joking. That is the change that has taken place since I remember from a boy up. When I started to work around, here and there among white people, I have noticed that they hardly ever talk of anything else—only about business and something that may help one or the other. They exchange ideas and advise each other of what they should do or not do. It would seem that the Oneidas are taking up the ways of the white men in this respect.

This has started lately, I would say since the depression set in, in 1930. Before that year, many men did not bother about a job or about working, but when that depression started men went around trying to get a job and he was lucky to find work for a week. Even the farmers quit hiring men because they were hard up too and were not able to pay if they hired anyone, and it was no wonder because their main source of income was very low—like milk was way down to about sixty cents a hundred pounds. There was no sale for pigs, and grain was way down. When those milk strikes came many farmers gave their milk away. It was at this time the change in Oneidas took place because they could not get any work and a man was lucky to find anything, so then they began to ask each other if they have any work or what they are doing, and when work started up on projects each man was interested about knowing what his neighbor was doing, and all that joking and storytelling were cut out among other people. They do that today but they do it while they are working, but they do not visit so much now.

Long ago or when I was still a small boy I remember that even big men would play what they called in Indian *dehudlaháhdayuhe* [snow snake].[6] Because they did not work they passed away the time by playing some kind of a game, and this was what could be called a game. They made arrows like pieces of sticks about a half-inch thick and five or six feet long out of hardwood such as ironwood. In those days there was a lot of good straight timber of ironwood. This would be split into long, narrow pieces and made smooth with a knife. They made these so smooth and shiny, and at one end it was made almost like a runner would be, that is, it was turned up or bent up a little. When there was a hard crust on top of the snow, as there is sometimes toward spring when the snow would melt a little during the day and freeze again at nights, this is where the men play with these long arrow-like sticks. They would have a piece of something heavy like lead at the head end of this stick. They would throw this arrows over the top of this hard snow, and this arrow would run or slide on the top of the snow for a long way. This was the game to see who threw the farthest. Some of the men would be able to throw this and make it run on the crust for a quarter of a mile. If a couple men would go out to play like this, it would not take long before a bunch of others would be there with them. Each man would throw his arrows, and then they would walk over to see whose arrows went the farthest. They would have to be able to tell which is their arrows. Well, when they all get their arrows picked up and saw or agreed whose arrows went the farthest, they would go back and try again. It was nothing for them to do this all afternoon. They seemed to enjoy this game, and they would make a date when they would meet again. Of course, it was not only the throwing of these across but it was also the fun they had of teasing each other. They would be laughing and having a good time. This kept up for a few years, but when I was grown up they did not do this no more. Another game they played after this was marbles.

During the time that I was single and my mother was still living and when I was old enough to be called a young man, I often went around with young men and young ladies. This was when I was about nineteen or twenty years old. We used to get a bunch together and go to dances. If we hear of a dance even at the south end of the reservation we would tell our friends and a bunch of us would walk to that dance and back after the dance. It was nothing for us to walk six or seven miles to a dance. Most of them did not have a horse or buggy, and we could not all ride in one buggy, so we walked together. Sometimes we were all night about this, but we were all young and did not mind losing sleep. But I had one partner who was with me more than anyone else. He was Peter Danforth, about two years younger than I was. We were good friends and we took in all the doings. Most of the time he and I were on foot so that we were not bothered with a horse. Once in a while we would drive my horse, but we had the trouble of caring for it all the time.

About this time the men began to work out same as I did, but they usually work in bunches. Like a bunch would get together and go up north in the big logging camps. There they worked all winter by the month or by the day, and some of them who were real hard workers would work by the piece. These fellows made more, but they had to pay for their board. These men who work by the month got their board, so they were not paid so much. Sometimes if bad weather comes for a few days these fellows that are working by the month would make more money because they got paid even if they could not get out to work. Sometimes these fellows or lumberjacks as they were called would have earned about two to three hundred from early fall until late the spring after. The wages by the month was around forty to sixty dollars a month because the Oneidas were good men at sawing with a crosscut saw. Some men used to make ties for the railroads. Of course, one man would hire them to make these ties and he paid the men for making them, and afterwards he would sell the ties to some railroad company. At first all the ties were hewed with a broad ax and men made them by the piece. They would be paid around ten to fifteen cents apiece for making ties.

I had three uncles and an aunt on my mother's side; that is, she had three brothers and one sister. My uncles and aunt were all married and had families, so they did not live with us when I came to, or when I remembered things. My uncles were all equally good to me, and I looked up to them all with equal favor. [7] When any of the uncles saw me they would say se•gù wùt, and I was taught by my mother to say se•gù gnulhù. When my aunt sees me she would say se•gù gyu and I would say se•gù nû. She was real good to me, and I was always happy when I saw her or any of my uncles. My father hardly ever was home so that it was my mother who took care of me, and I was constantly with her at home and when she went I always went with her. I was very much attached to all my uncles and aunt because they came often to see us.

My mother and I always went to church on Sundays, and she used to tell me to always attend church when I am older, so I have obeyed her and I still attend the church each Sunday. I did not go to school much because I was always helping my mother. There was no Sunday school at that time, and the only lessons I did get about the church and Christianity was what I heard the minister say, and at that time we always had an interpreter who spoke in Oneida because there were many Oneidas who could not understand English. It was a good thing that we had an interpreter. The services were almost the same as now, only that they didn't sing in English until sometime later, but when I was a small boy they sang all the hymns in Oneida. The change took place when Father Burleson was here. They sang in English from that time on. It has changed from low church to high church and that's when they started to sing all through the service. Even the creed and Lord's Prayer is sung now.

They had what is called the vestry who looked after the church, and they used to look after the congregation too. The church was much more strict those days. Sometimes if a man or person would go to a dance he or she would be barred from taking their communion for three months, and if someone got drunk he or she would be barred from taking her communion for one year. And if anyone does worse things than that—like if they commit adultery—they would be barred for a longer time. This was where the vestrymen looked after their congregation. If they hear or see anyone being or had been drunk or did any other act violating sacred rules, they would see that they are barred from Holy Communion. It was not so much because they are strict that people were kept from doing these things, but it was right in them to look out for those things, because chances are the vestrymen may never hear of it but it was truly in their belief that it was wrong to do these things.

I did hear when I was a boy that long go about the time when my grandparents were in New York that they did believe in other ways of worship. They say that they used to dance to worship. A big bunch of people would get together and keep going round and round and singing some sacred song; that was the way they worshipped. They believed in one God and they never had any services to worship or pray for any other being, like the saints, but they did hear of, and believed that Virgin Mary was the mother of Christ Jesus as they were taught by the minister. But they did not have any services for her.

When the Oneidas came to Wisconsin they brought along Christianity, which was adopted and started in New York. This was the Episcopal church under the leadership of Aleyaza [Eleazer] Williams [see the introduction]. This man Williams was a good man. He was interested in Oneidas who moved from New York. He wanted to be with them and started to teach the Oneidas Christianity. He wrote books about the Oneidas and also hymnbooks in Mohawk as near the right spelling as he could. The Mohawks and Oneidas and all the others of the five tribes used the same spelling, but the dialect was somewhat different.[8] The books that Williams wrote about the Oneidas afterwards became very important in the early history of Oneidas in Wisconsin.

When I was a boy I remember that our church did not confirm small children because they thought that a small child would not know what it was all about and why they should be confirmed, so I was not confirmed until I was a big boy. They usually confirmed children when they are about twelve years old, but I was older than that. There were some grown-up people who were confirmed with each class every summer, same as they are nowadays. The older Oneidas must have had more faith and a firmer belief in what was taught them by the minister. The ministers always preached on the way Christ went into the wilderness and fasted forty days and forty nights. The minister told them that that is what we should do, we should fast and pray all through the days that is called Lent. Most of the people did fast and quit eating so much or quit something that they really did like to eat, or sometimes men would not drink beer or they wouldn't chew tobacco all through Lent. But there was one old man who must have had a stronger belief in fasting. He would eat just a little and he would not go anywhere, so by the end of Lent or after Easter he would be so much lighter, that is he would have lost quite a few pounds.

It was way before the Oneidas moved from New York that they used to dance to worship, but that was done away with when the ministers taught these Oneidas the real way to worship. But there is a small bunch of Oneidas in New York now who do that on some occasions.[9] The Oneidas did not do that after they were in Wisconsin, because they really did go to church then, but the Menominees did that up to lately, and some of them who are called pagans do that to this day.

I imagine that all children are the same when they are young—about some sort of longing or daydreaming of something that would still be something they could not do. When I was thirteen years old we lived near a railroad tracks. I like to watch a train go by, and the man who made it go would be looking out of the window on the engine. I often thought that when I was big I would be an engineer—that is what I was longing for or daydreaming about—but after I was a little bigger I found out that I could not do that because I did not have any education. I found out that an engineer has to have quite a lot of education in order to understand all the orders they are given and they must go to school to learn all the signals that a railroad man must know, so I could not be an engineer. That has been my setback all through.

There were two things that I longed for when I was a child, and this other was to be a musician, but I took right hold of this real well and I managed to learn this without much trouble. Of course, this does not require much education if only one could get on to the notes. I learned to play the cornet. It was not much of a trick to get wise to this instrument, and the notes I learned by myself so that I could play any music if I hear it played. I could play the cornet, which is supposed to be leading the rest, but I have played in the band a long time and I always made good, so this was one wish I longed for which was granted me.

I stuck to this and I was glad of it afterwards because I had a chance to travel and see the country away from Oneida. We began to travel under the leadership of a man whose name was James Wheelock. He was a great musician, and he was able to get jobs for the band all over. We were gone one summer for three months, starting from about July and continuing until late that fall. We played at picnics, lodge meetings, and other gatherings such as county fairs. We were looked to as a great band because we were all Indians, so when bills or notices were seen that the Oneida Indian National Band was playing there would be big crowds there to see and hear Indians play. While we were on this tour we always stopped in the biggest and best hotels so that no one will say we were a cheap band. We stopped in high-class places because we were a high-class band and we got high wages. Other years we went out for a week or two weeks and we went often. I would never have seen or visited some of these big cities and I would not have traveled if I was not in this band.

It was too late for me to go to school, which would have been the only way I could ever have traveled if I did not belong to this band. We went and traveled in thirteen different states so I could say that I have seen many big beautiful cities.

In playing with other little boys when I was still small I noticed that some of the boys had thoughts of being a policeman because it was their greatest fun to play police. If he came across another boy he would pretend that he caught him in some act and would take him by the arm and say "you come along with me," and he made believe that he put him in jail. This was the game that was played most by boys, so that must have been what they had in their minds all the time.

As I did not go to school I did not know much about talking English, but I could understand some. When I started to work around among white people I did pick up a little more English, but not enough for a good conversation.

SOLOMON WHEELOCK

Solomon Wheelock, ninety years old at the time of this interview, spoke of his own age, of pensions, of the deterioration of the environment, and of how the Oneidas lost their land. He was interviewed by John Skenandore on July 15, 1941.

How the Oneidas Lost Their Land

I cannot answer much of your questions, but I can tell you just what I think of the old-age pension I am getting every month. First I tell you it is not enough. I am only getting twenty-three dollars a month, and one month is a mighty long time, more so when you can't do anything else but sit around. But why should I complain when I am getting it for nothing—like years ago a man can get to be a hundred years old and still he didn't get any kind of pension. Nowadays at the age of sixty-five they don't want you to do anything, and that was just my prime, and if it wasn't for my one weak leg I could do lots of work yet. Even the doctors told me it was good for me to do some work if I wanted to, so that is just what I am doing every day. I get out in the garden and hoe for a little while until I get tired on my legs; then I'd come back to the house and rest. I don't have any pains, but my legs give out on me.

The only thing that bothers me is that I know a man much younger than I am who has been crippled as a kid and he is getting a bigger pension check than I do, unless that [is because] he has a bigger family than me as I am just living here with my daughter and have no dependents anymore. She has only one acre of land on this place which used to belong to my wife at one time. I had parted with my wife long before she died, and after she died my daughter claimed the property so that is how she is hanging onto it yet. It's a nice little place and we raise lot of vegetables on it, as we use every foot of it each summer.

I often wonder why we are treated as we are today. When we had our own rights, they never had to give us relief or pension and we lived good. Now that they got everything away from us, I wonder why they are going through the trouble of feeding us where they didn't have to if they left us alone in the first place. Now they even shut off the fish we used to get every spring in our creek. Ever since they put up that dam down below we never saw any fish up on this end of our settlement. But they got that all away from us, and if we did went out hunting, on which we used to make our living, we would have to have a license or we get arrested if we didn't have it. License—when there is nothing left to hunt. Why didn't they do that right from the beginning so there won't have been so much wasted? But the way it was the white men came in our settlement just to see how much game they can kill and shot at everything they saw and left it lay only to rot. And lots of them shot and killed one another because they shot at every moving thing.

And farmers from all over the country came with big wagons in the spring of the year to fish in our creek. At that time the fish came so heavy that you can drive into the creek and load up your wagon with fish just as fast as you please, catching them by hand. Lots of those fishes were taken out and only spread out into their fields for fertilizer. And now you would have to look very close before you can see one. And there was lots of the fish left on the banks of the creek each year because the white men doesn't know when he has gotten enough or what his team of horses can pull. Wherever the horses got stuck pulling the load, they unload part of it on the banks only to rot. The Oneidas never did anything like this. They get only what they need and left the rest alone for seed.

Now how is it that they can shut the fish off from coming into our streams for spunning [spawning] like they used to? Can we do something so that they open the dam even on just that period of time say in the month of April? Don't you think that filling out a petition with everybody's names on it would help? I think it would, and we should try it.

I consider myself very fortunate to be as I am at the age of ninety. My one leg is about the only thing that is holding me down, or I would be very handy as yet. I never had any trouble with my eyes, but lately it has been watery and the doctor told me that I would have to put up with it because if he succeeded in stopping it that I would go blind altogether. Otherwise I have no pains no place to complain about, only that one of my legs has given out. I have a very good medicine to show you whenever you wish to have it, and it is in salve form and it is very good for itchy sores. I make it out of plants—as you see on the wall, drying ready for use.

At the time we were made citizens of our country we were called together at one big meeting and we were asked to line up in a row, and all that was in favor of becoming citizens should step up ahead and form a new line. [10] The majority stepped out and just a few stayed in their places. And all of us that stepped out got our deeds for our properties. Lots of people sold their land in just a short time, and as we were not used to paying taxes on anything we had, we just neglected it and left our taxes unpaid, and the money men got a chance to buy up our taxes, and quite a number of them lost their lands in just a few years. You see we were just not used to paying on anything that we thought was ours, and after three or four years our taxes were so high that we were not able to redeem it. And businessmen in towns offered to give us anything we need in machinery even if we didn't have any money as long as we had deeds for our lands.

The people will say the Oneidas drank up their property, and this may be true of some, but the majority have lost it because they were not used to paying anything on what was their own and didn't know anything about the white men's laws. I for instance got into a farm machinery shop one day looking for a wagon, and first thing the manager asked me if I had a deed for my land. And as I told him I had it then he started to coax me to take a grain binder also, without paying any money down. Of course, I needed the machinery bad enough so he didn't have to do much coaxing, and I took home a wagon, binder, mower, horse rake, plow, drag, and few other small tools to work with. And all I had to do was sign my name on a piece of paper.

It didn't seem very long when I was called to sign another piece of paper, and that must have been a mortgage. And my only way of saving myself from becoming homeless was to sell some of my property to redeem the rest of my place. So this was what had happened to most of the Oneidas out here in Wisconsin, and even the men that never got a deed for their land lost out, just how I do not know. But I know for sure that two Doxtators, a man and son, were both smoked out of their home. They wasn't going to move out but they were smoked or gassed out of their homes, and that man is living today and he still says that he never got to see the deed of his place and had never signed off. Just how this could be done I do not know. And today we are only living on small pieces of land and making the best of it, and it certainly cost us old bucks a lot to learn our lessons, and if we knew what we know today, there would be lots of big farmers here amongst the Oneidas.

HYSON DOXTATOR

Hyson Doxtator, one of the WPA workers, was younger than Tom Elm and most of the other elders represented in this section, but he recounted a historic day, November 19, 1913, when some Wisconsin Oneida leaders signed the "Declaration of Allegiance" to the United States.

The Rodman Wanamaker expedition (1909–1914), organized by the son of the department store owner, was an extensive effort to get the "chiefs" of all the 189 recognized Indian tribes in the United States to sign a document called the "Declaration of Allegiance." Expedition members traveled the whole country between 1909 and 1914 and collected nine hundred signatures (or marks), by which all the tribes were presumed to have voluntarily acknowledged the sovereignty of the United States. (Indians in the United States did not become citizens until an act of Congress on June 15, 1924.) In this selection, written on December 3, 1941, Hyson Doxtator records the circumstances under which the Oneidas of Wisconsin signed the declaration.

A Surprise Ceremony

In about 1912 or 1913, a special railroad coach was switched onto the side track, bearing a few officials. They notified the superintendent of the school that there was to be a special tribal meeting that afternoon in the assembly hall. Without notice that they were coming, they went to the superintendent of the boarding school. There were no telephones, so the only way they could notify the people was to go to them with horse and buggy. They gathered a few for the council, only a few. The chairman of the meeting was one of the officials; he made a brief speech which was interpreted to those that could not understand. The subject for the meeting was "Our White Father": "As in one family we unite; White and Red races of people do join together as one family, as a hen gathereth her chicks under her wings."

A phonograph was set on the table; a few records were played on the phonograph. First was that of a speech made by Secretary Lane's daughter. She was at the age of twelve at the time. All were so surprised at what the little girl had to say.[11] There were other records transcribed at this tribal meeting, with only a few present. The chairman of this council asked if anyone had anything to say about the council. As usual, no one said anything. They heard a few records on the phonograph.

After this meeting, which did not last long, about an hour and half, a U.S. flag was given the tribe in token that we are as one under "Our White Father." A group of old men went to hoist the flag on the flagpole that stood on the school grounds.

Twelve old men were chosen to hoist the flag to signify the proceeding of the council. When the flag was at half mast, the guyline broke and the flag fell to the ground. I heard one old gentlemen remark that those old men threw another stone into the lake. He meant that they threw our Indian rights and our treaties into the lake.

As I have stated before, the rope broke while the flag was halfway up the flagpole, which was about forty feet in height. A white man, painter by trade, that married one of our Indian girls volunteered to climb for the rope. (This middle-age painter was Henry Bins, who lived in Oneida with his wife.) A long ladder was brought and placed against the flagpole. Up he went as far as the ladder extended. He had no climbers like those used by the telephone workers. Well anyway he managed to reach the end of the rope, which was only a few feet from the top of the pole.

He pulled the rope down. When he came down they all cheered for him. Now the flag went up for the second time, which went way up to the top of the pole. The officials then shook hands with the twelve old men that helped to raise the flag. The special railroad coach pulled out the same evening to go to other Indian reservation in all parts of the western and southwestern states.

At this flag raising which took place on our reservation, all those who took part in raising of the flag—all the old gentlemen—had to sign their names. Those that could not sign their names were fingerprinted; most all of the twelve men were not able to sign their names for lack of education.

This was the same year, in 1912, when the last investigation of our former reservation took place. This is how Indians have lost a great deal of their rights by fraud. Now with this tribal council, as they call it, only a few people that lived around close to the boarding school were present. It not only happens to the Oneida, but to all other Indians throughout the West and Southwest. Our Indian agents are supposed to attend to the affairs of the Indians, but instead of that our Indian agent now at Tomah, Wisconsin, which is 160 miles away from the Oneida Reservation, is making no investigation as to how the Indians are getting along. Instead of that he is only out here for a joy ride. If there is any complaint made by letter, the letter is laid down on the desk. That is as far as it gets.

Mason Wheelock, Solomon's brother, speaks of some of the changes he has seen in his eighty-six years. He does not believe they were for the better. He was interviewed by Stadler King on June 12, 1941.

Changes in Customs and Ways of Living

I have lived a long time; in fact I think I have lived long enough. I am now nearly eighty-seven years old. There are few men who get that old. There is one man who is older than I am, and that's that Simon Metoxen; he is now ninety-three years old. Long ago it was nothing for Oneidas to get to be a hundred years old. Many of them passed that age. I am now all crippled up. My legs would not carry me anymore. Even last summer I was still able to get outside and sit in the shade when it was too hot. My doctor Randolph from Seymour told me that I had high pressure of the blood. I seem to have a cold, but the doctor says that's not a cold—that's from your heart swelling up.

As far back as I can remember, and that's when I was a boy about six years old, living was altogether different than what it is now. I would say that the people were rather poor because everything was hard to get and nobody had money. I remember that all the Oneidas made baskets. You could hear someone pound the ash timber for splints all over in the woods. They made these baskets and sold it or traded them off for something to eat. I remember going myself into the woods and I looked for a good straight ash tree, so when I found one I cut it down and got started to pound the splints loose. After some time I had got enough for me to carry home. I put this on my back the way older people did. My mother then made baskets.[12]

The only thing that kept the Oneidas in those days was that there were so many wild game like deer, bear, raccoon, porcupine, and rabbits. I saw some of those big bows and arrows they used for hunting. It was about six feet long and it was made so that it had plenty of spring, which made it stronger in shooting. They used to put a piece of pointed steel at the end of arrows so that when they shoot an animal the steel part would go into the flesh deep enough so the animal would die in a little while. One time I happened to visit a man and his wife. They had some of these wild animal meats, all these different kinds of meat were put together and dried, and then it was packed in balls like hamburger balls. This was good to eat, and besides this they had corn bread, and the water in which this corn bread was boiled was used for tea. This was good too, and a person could either put salt or sugar in this and it's good either way.

The Oneidas at that time lived on this wild meat and corn bread and corn soup and sometimes fish, and also there were many kinds of fruit that grew well in the woods. I went fishing many times while I was a young man. I always had to walk down because we did not have a team or a horse. I could bring home about forty fish, but I had them cleaned; that is, I had the insides out, so they were not so heavy. I also remember that the men made hoops out of logs. They would cut down a tree which had straight grain and split this in narrow strips; then they shaved this down to about one and a half inch wide and almost half inch thick. They made these about six feet long. They shaved this down with a drawing knife. Afterwards they made hoops out of smaller poles which they split in two and shaved this smooth. These were made in four- and six-feet lengths which were sold for two dollars a thousand.

I remember when I was about sixteen years old the Oneidas used to play what is called lacrosse game.[13] I knew your father real well; he was the best player at lacrosse. He was so fast and quick that when he got the ball it was hard to stop him from making a goal. One time arrangements had been made to have a game between men of one side of Duck Creek against men of the other side. Your father and I were on the west side, so with others we played against men of the east side. There was a great crowd of people there to see us play. Your father told me just how him and I could work together so we did. He got the ball and ran for the goal, but he was interfered with and he threw the ball to me with his racket. I happened to catch this, so I made for the goal. As I was not a fast runner they would have taken the ball from me, but I threw it back to your father. He caught it, and we had been working towards our goal all the time so when he got it, it was easy for him to get the ball through the goal posts. We beat the east siders by a big score.

In those days there was nothing but woods with places where it was thick and places where only big trees were standing. Some of the Oneidas used to plant corn between trees and they used to come so good on account of it being such good ground. Some were able to clear off a piece of land and got it broke up so they could plant corn and other garden crops. Some of the real good workers cleared land all the time so that in a few years they had quite a piece under cultivation. This clearing was going on especially along the ridge where many people settled and a road was being made. This was easy to make this road because there were no streams going across, and it was sandy all the way on this ridge so it was never muddy.

Times changed in the year 1892 when the government allowed people to sell land that did belong to people who have died, and there were many of these so a big portion of the Oneida lands were sold right from the start. There was hardly a family that did not have a relative who had died, so almost all families received money in this way. That was the beginning of the change. After a few years Oneidas were allowed to mortgage their own land and to sell it, so they began to sell parts of their land. Lot of this selling or trading off land was cheating because some white man might have a horse or team and would hold them so high and the Indians did not know the value of stock and besides this they were always offered a little cash with the trade. Lot of this land was sold cheap, like five or ten dollars an acre. I remember old Abram Smith sold forty acres of land, which he had back in the woods, for twenty-five dollars. This was not even a dollar an acre.

All the cheating was done by this trading land for some stock or machinery, and some of the more educated men—like Dennison Wheelock, who was my cousin—I know that he cheated many of the older people. And that Chester Cornelius was another man who cheated many people. So we could see that our own people would turn right and beat us out of what we have if they had a chance.[14]

There were other men who went around inducing people to sell their land through them. I sold my forty acres and later I sold another forty, but I still had a small piece of land which I have been able to hang onto. But now I am laid up so I could not use it—only what rent I get from it.

I have seen many changes in everything since I have lived so long. A person nowadays would never think that this country was once a reservation for Oneidas. And notice the roads now, all good hard roads, and notice the big, well-kept farms and only once in a while you come across an Indian home; the rest is all white people's homes. Even our church has changed so much that one could not imagine that it was the same church, and this is the same with other churches. My church is the

Methodist church, and the change in this church is unimaginable. The head people at this church now are people who are drunkards and who are adulterers. A person may be drunk today, and tomorrow he is at the church in the choir.

When I was a young man I stayed with our minister, whose name was Dr. Ford. He was altogether a different minister. He would not allow this drunkard to be at the head of the church or any adulterers and there were none in those days. If a person was divorced and living with another person he would not allow them to be leaders of the church, and that is the people we have now. That is not a true Christian, and the church itself is not a true church when it allows this to go on. Those are the changes I have seen.

Ida Blackhawk also interviewed Mason Wheelock, on February 9, 1942, two months after the Japanese attacked Pearl Harbor and the United States entered World War II. She added descriptions of Mr. Wheelock's demeanor in parentheses.

(Laughing) I used to go to school too. I was sixteen years old when I finished the eighth grade from the mission day school. Part of the time I stayed with the Methodist minister, so I learned how to speak English fluently. I never could understand how any Indian would forget his own language. When I learned how to speak a few words of English I was always comparing the two languages. That is why I wonder how anyone can forget a language they are once familiar with. (Smiles) I also attended the Lawrence College at Appleton for two months. I guess that don't count, because I don't remember what I learned during that two long months. I got homesick and came home. (Jokingly) I guess I just wanted to get married.

I got married soon after that and had nine children. There are only three living now. Their names and ages are Foster, age fifty-eight, Mary, age fifty-two, and Josephine, age thirty-five. The names of the dead are Elijah, Kayser, Joshua, Julius, Bailey, and Wilson. My children were all good children. I did not hesitate to use the whip if they needed correction. They had to be good. They were not perfect by any means. They got into mischief at times, but I made them respect my words. If I forbid them to do anything and they disobeyed me, I did not spare the rod. (Grins) Of course, when the oldest ones were big enough they all attended schools away from home. Some went to the Oneida Boarding School and later, Hampton, Carlisle, Tomah, and Flandreau.

My wife and I worked together in disciplining the children. You know that children are sometimes spoiled by the parents—either the father or the mother. If children hear you siding in with them, they realize that and take advantage. They don't mind even the one that takes up for them. I think we old people trained our children to mind better than these younger generation. Of course, maybe we stunted their initiative and made them depend on us more after they were old enough to look after themselves. I would say that the young people get away from home and are more independent.

After I was married my father helped me build a log house, and my wife and I settled on a seventy-acre farm. It was not all under cultivation, but by the time I sold the farm it was all cleared. While I was strong and healthy I farmed. I raised some hogs and cattle. I had lots of grain to sell every fall. It was easy to make a living. We did not have to pay taxes, and wood was plentiful, so we did not have to buy coal. We lived comfortably, but I was not rich but had plenty to eat, and always had money in my pocket. The old people always had enough so they lived easily during old age, and most of them were independent. My wife and I were both Methodist, and we were married in the Methodist church. This house we are living in used to be the mission house.

I have seen a lot of changes during my life. There were four wars that the United States got into since I can remember. Civil War, Spanish-American, World War I in 1914–1918, and the present world war. I think United States will win this war with Japan. Our president seems to rely on God, and God always takes up for the one that is right. So I will be very much surprised if the Japanese licks the U.S.

(Jokingly) I wish I was draft age—I would show those Japs some of the Indian prowess. I often listen to the radio and I can hear it pretty good, so I am posted on the war news. I know that the Japanese are good fighters, quick and alert, and the British are slow, easy-going people, and they may get the worse from the Japs, but I will be disappointed with the United States if they let the Japs conquer our country. I think the Japanese are all trained to be good fighters on sea and they know just where to sneak their soldiers to those islands. Some of those Japs lived in a boat all their lives and their chief food is rice, and they raised that in their own country so they won't get short of food.

The Indians used to have plain meals when I was a youngster, and look what a good tall man I got to be. (Laughs) Now it seems as though we have to eat the same kind of foods that the white people eat. They claim that we have to have certain amount of vitamins in our food to be really healthy. I often wonder why so many white people are sickly, when they know just what to eat that contains vitamins. They are so afraid of disease, yet their hospitals are full of sick people. They have asylums for the insane too. What makes them go insane? There are very few insane Indians. I don't know of any hospital for insane Indians. Maybe they don't use their brains enough to go insane. (Laughs)

We have to hand it to the white people; they are smarter than we are. Now they came here and took the land from us, maybe paid a small sum or practically got it free, but now they are taking care of us. If a fellow has no job they give him relief or put him to work on the WPA. Then some of us old people get pensions for being old, blind, or widows with children.

Before the white people came into our reservation we had to take care of our old people, the blind, and the children whose fathers have died or did not have a legal father. It was easy to make money then, if a person just worked, but now we would not be able to do that if we were thrown on our own resources. The state is pretty nice to us; if we want medicine or treatment we can get it. My eyes were bothering me. Sometimes I can't see at all. The doctor told me to go and see an eye specialist, so I went and he said I had cataracts, and he could not perform the operation because I had a weak heart. He said I would die on the operating table. I said, "Alright let it go; you need not fix my eyes if I die during the operation. Why should I want my eyes fixed if I am going to die during the operation. It would not do me any good. I don't need to have good eyes after I am dead." (Laughs hard)

Interviewers often asked women about childbirth, birth control, experience as midwives, the care of infants and children, and their knowledge of Indian medicine. Mrs. Marion Cornelius, then eighty-four years old, had some experience with these fields, and she also knew something about the role of mothers in the Iroquois political system, as she told Ida Blackhawk on July 31, 1941.

Mothers, Children, and Medicine

When my mother was about sixty years old she went and nursed obstetric cases among her relatives. She helped some midwife, and when she saw how it was done she went and took cases by herself, and she was always lucky and never lost a case. When I was over fifty she showed me how to take care of my daughters-in-law, and as soon as some heard of me they always come after me. Just the other day a neighbor woman sent for me, and I did not know that it was a confinement case until I got over there. They had telephoned for the doctor, but the doctor has not come yet, so I had to get to work and help the woman. Everything was alright. We had no difficulty, and the doctor came after everything was over with. He asked me where I learned to do maternity nursing. I told him I had only practical experience, but he said I was just as good as a doctor.

I always hate to do this kind of nursing because if anything goes wrong and then I would get the blame for it, especially now I am getting too old. I never bought a license to do midwifery, and I would rather they wouldn't ask me every time. I took care of one woman five times now. She has no trouble at all, and I always stay with her ten days.

I never heard of any medicine that would prevent women from getting pregnant. I had nine children, and I never thought of taking anything to prevent myself from getting any more children. I always thought that married women were supposed to have children. So long as my children were all healthy I was perfectly satisfied, and I really enjoyed taking care of my children. Of course, my husband did not use liquor, and he was a good worker, and he tried his best to see that the children did not get hungry. The Oneida Boarding School was a great help to us, and our children were just at school age when the school opened up. We sent four of the oldest children there, and when they finished there we sent them away to a higher government school.

My two daughters both married some other tribe of Indians, and both live away from here. One of them is a widow now and is drawing government retirement compensation. She comes home to visit me, but she does not like to live here. She has lived away from here so many years that she feels like a stranger here. The other daughter has never come home since she got married. We hear from her once in a while, but never mentions of coming home even for a visit. I am lucky that they are not near me, or I would be kept busy taking care of my grandchildren. My children are all married, and two of my boys were divorced and married again. I am not staying with any of my children. I stay with anyone who wants to board me. I am getting eighteen dollars a month pension and so I can afford to pay wherever I go. I sometimes stay with my sons now and then, but I prefer to stay with people who are not related to me. I am still quite spry for my age. I am still healthy, but I am not as strong as I used to be. I get tired easily and I prefer a quiet life, and although I like little babies, I don't like to be taking care of them all the time.

I think the old people are better off today than before they gave them old-age pensions. Of course, very few old people were sent to the poorhouse, but many of them were not taken care of by their children. Some of the old people had to work quite hard and steady. I enjoy working, if it is not too heavy. I can't pick beans or cherries anymore, but I can cook, and for some reason my sons like my cooking. If I make biscuits they always eat so much more. My pies taste much better than their wives' pies.

One time one of my sons got sick and he kept losing weight and he went to the doctor and the doctor treated him, but he kept on losing weight, and finally the doctor gave him up. He said that my son was in the last stages of tuberculosis and there was no chance for recovery. He just had to let the disease take its course. When I heard that I went over there and I asked my boy if he would let me treat him with Indian medicine, and he agreed to take my treatment. He was nothing but skin and bones and bedridden. I made my medicine, and when I had it ready I started to treat him. I gave him the medicine myself, and I cooked his meals, and I gave him hot milk, and I also gave him raw eggs beaten up and I flavored it with nutmeg or lemon extract. I let him rest and I gave him sponge baths. I put all of my time on him. As soon as he drank up the medicine, I made some more. The medicine I used is called elecampane (*gah-deh-la-gu•lùt*ᴱ), and I used the roots only. It is so strong that it takes only a small piece of root to a gallon of water. I stayed there one month, and then I noticed he started to show improvement.[15]

I told his wife to continue giving his medicine at regular times, and I left there to rest up myself. I stayed at one of my other son's place for awhile, and now and then I went back to see how he was getting along. I noticed that his wife neglected him because she had so much to do. They had a few cows and she had to milk the cows. Their children were small then and could not do the work, but they helped. I went back again and kept on giving him his medicine as regular as I could. If he slept through the night I omitted his medicine. I never awakened him to make him take his medicine. At the end of six months he could sit up and he was able to eat all kinds of vegetables, but I made mostly soup for him. He began to have good appetite and to feel gay. I stayed there most of the time, and at the end of a year he was up and around. That was about ten years ago. He is able to work, but of course he has never done real heavy work since, but he is up and able to help with the work.

I had another son that started to fail in health. His trouble was in his stomach, and he started to go to the doctor and finally quit working and stayed home. I never like to interfere when they are using doctor's medicine because I know that the doctors study a long time before they start to practice doctoring, so I realize that they know a great deal about their line of work. But somehow my son did not get any better. Every time he had a bad spell then they would send for the doctor. He was up and around, but he could not do any heavy work. They lived on a farm too, so his wife had to do all the work. They never asked for Indian medicine, so I never tried to administer any Indian medicine to him. One day he seemed to be feeling good and he went to his brother's place and had a haircut. He took sick there, but he went home and died soon after he got home. I often wished I had tried my Indian remedy on him—perhaps it would have helped him. I know of another remedy that is good for tuberculosis and that is princess pine (*gu-dlah-de•zuhs*) and mullun (*zikzik/odahs*ᴬ), sheep tail.

The women that were called "mothers" in olden times when the chiefs were in power were the mothers of the chiefs, or aunt, or some close relatives. They were chosen to be mothers by the chiefs, and they had to be descended from hereditary chiefs—usually the oldest daughter if she has not done anything dishonorable. If she has, then her sisters or some other relative was chosen. The mothers were sort of guardians to the reigning chiefs. They guided them and advised them. If a chief's behavior was not satisfactory to the people, someone had to report to his guardian, and the mother will investigate his case. If she finds that he is guilty of what he has been accused of then it is her place to tell the chiefs. The mothers cooked for the chiefs when they held their council. They sat and listened to the discussions but they were supposed to be silent. If a question of war with other tribes or white settlers came up, then the women could favor for or against it, and whichever side the mothers favored, the chiefs always agreed with them. I never heard of a mother not doing her duty, or what they did if the mothers failed to live as the ideal woman.

SOPHIE HILL

Mrs. Sophie Hill, then eighty-one, contributed these thoughts about family, children, education, and the changing times. She was interviewed by Ida Blackhawk on August 26, 1941.

Child-Rearing and Sex Education

The Oneida people are very fond of their children. A person with a large family is considered very fortunate. If a family becomes motherless, the father can do what he wants with his children. If the father has a way to support his children he usually kept them. Sometimes he lets someone take care of the baby, or he may ask someone to adopt it. They usually ask someone to adopt the child who has no children. They never made out any papers, but they did have a witness. If a man pays someone to take care of his child he could get his child back anytime, but if he gives it away he could never ask for the child. Usually the child takes the name of its foster parents. When a woman is barren and likes children she is usually asked to adopt a motherless child. I know of one woman who adopted five children. Another woman adopted six children, and still another one adopted three children. The adopted children usually think a lot of their foster parents. I know one adopted boy who worked in Chicago, Illinois, after he grew up, and he sent his earnings to his foster mother regularly.

Many years ago young women were so closely watched that they seldom went wrong, and if they have an illegitimate child it was considered very disgraceful. That was one reason the parents married their daughters as soon as the parents thought they were old enough. I can recollect some women that brought disgrace on themselves and had several illegitimate children and would not tell who is responsible for their disgrace, and in that case their children took the mother's maiden name. There was a woman [. . .] that had several children, and never got married legally, nor by the church. Another woman [. . .] also had several children, and she also was never married and I remember one man [. . .] who had children by several different women. He used to take other men's wives away from them and live with them for a short time, and maybe [the woman would] have one child for him; then he would live with another. He was a man that was considered quite prosperous, and that may have had something to do with his popularity with the women. But they used to also say he used Indian love medicine on these women, so that they would leave their good husband and live with him as a common-law wife.

Years ago the children did not know as much as they do now regarding sex. The parents kept everything from them that would arouse their curiosity. They never allowed the children to even see when they butchered a cow or a hog. They did not like to have them see any domestic animal being bred. The reason they did that was because they know that the children play and act out whatever they see. They were extremely careful not to discuss anything in their hearing—any scandalous report of anyone. Nowadays the children know most everything by the time they are six or seven years old. Maybe it is better so that they can discover when temptation comes.

The children were looked after and the parents did everything to make their children happy, and as a rule the Indians parents spared the rod. When the children started to go to school, if an Indian child complained of a stomachache and does not want to go to school, the parents usually let the child stay home. The children learned mostly by stories, and most children believed what they were told. They used to tell the children to be nice to old people and not to be mean to dumb animals nor to take eggs away from birds' nests. The children were never expected to do hard work, but they were told to help. The boys were expected to bring in the wood, haul water, and the girls were taught to wash the dishes, sweep the floor, and make up the beds, and to take care of the baby if there is a baby in the family. The Indian people humor their little children, and they sometimes spoil them, but as a rule they make their little ones mind. There are some Indian children that behave all through the service on a Sunday. White people do not train their children to keep still in church and hardly ever take their children to the church services while they are little. When I was a child if anyone visited my mother, and if the visitor brought her children along, they would tell us to go outside and play while they talked and gossiped. They did not allow us to listen to any scandalous tale. They never let us interrupt anyone talking, especially if they are visitors. In fact, we had to be quiet during meals. We had to go to bed soon after supper. They never took us anywhere at night, and they hardly ever took us to town, only on a special occasion—to see a circus.

When I was going to school, if I was lazy to go to school I would just tell my mother that I felt ill and she kept me home. I used to miss school so much that I never learned anything. I could not understand English, and when my daughter married a white man I wished I had learned how to speak English so I could talk to my son-in-law and understand him when he talked to me. I often regretted that my folks did not insist on sending me to school, because I could never go to the store alone and buy what I want. I always have someone to interpret for me. I sent all of my children to school, so they could learn to speak English and to count. I only know how to count money the way the British count. I know that a quarter equals to two shillings, and half a dollar equals to four shillings, etc. The Oneidas all count with shillings up to twenty shillings, or $2.50. Then they count according to the United States method.

It must be nice and helpful to know how to read. Now I have lots of time to read but I can't read—not even in Oneida—so I waste a lot of time when I could be reading and enjoying a good story. And if I understood English I would enjoy listening to the radio, but I am really annoyed by the sound of the radio. Now if my folks had been real strict with me, and insisted on sending me to school, it would have been for my own good. That is why I think the parents should make the children mind. The children don't know what is best for them and should not be allowed to do as they please.

I always spoke to my children in a kind way but I used to see to it that they mind me, and I never had to use a whip. Most children are afraid of the whip, and I think a little switching does them a lot of good. I don't like the idea of hitting or slapping or spanking them because a little slap might injure the ear, or if you hit their back you might give them too hard a knock. The best thing to use is a little switch and tap them on the legs. It will hurt them, but it will not injure them. The Indians used the red willow for a switch to whip their children. The red willow has a very smooth bark and I think that is the reason they used that. I notice that nowadays the parents punish their children by making them sit still for a long time, or by putting them to bed. I do not approve of a child put to bed without his or her supper because that child is liable to get hungry before morning and may get sick.

JANE CORNELIUS

Mrs. Jane Cornelius, age seventy-five, gave the following interview to Ida Blackhawk on August 26, 1941, in which she recounted the outline of her family life. She speaks of Oneida singing groups, one of the major cultural institutions of the Oneida until today. These groups sing Christian hymns in the Oneida language, and they offer their art on many occasions, especially at wakes.[16]

A Preacher's Daughter's Life

My father was a Methodist preacher, and he never was harsh with any of us. When he spoke to us, he always spoke kindly, even when he reprimanded us. I suppose we were like other children, but we never knew what a good whipping really was. My mother used to threaten us, but she never whipped us. I used to see the teacher whip the children, or hit them with a ruler in school, and I was always afraid of such a beating, so I tried to mind the teacher.

My father used to talk to us and told us stories of the Bible, and he used to tell us some stories of the wicked people written in the Bible. One time I asked my father why God let them write about those bad people in the Holy Bible. He told me it was to teach other people of what will happen if they lead a wicked life. I guess we had so many Bible lectures at home that we all seemed to be indifferent about going to church, but I often recalled my father's old Bible stories, as a girl, and after I was grown up. Whenever I was tempted to do something that I knew would be wrong according to the teachings of the Bible, then I hesitated and was always able to resist it.

My husband is altogether a different type of a man compared with my father. My husband never talked to our children in the way of teaching them anything. I always did all the talking and the training of our children. He absolutely shirked his responsibility. All my children died excepting the oldest daughter and my son. They both went to work in Chicago, Illinois, and are both married to white people. I don't know whether I taught them to marry into the white race. They both seem to get along alright. I never whipped my children, but my son was always hard to mind. At the same time he was always ready to work and always acted like a grown-up man, even when he was just a small boy, and his ambition was always to be doing a man's work. He had no interest regarding religion, and I never could interest him to go to Sunday school, but he knew the difference between right and wrong, because I had taught him at home some of the things that he would have learned if he had attended Sunday school.

I used to spend some time every day talking to my children, and they used to enjoy listening to my stories.

I think that little children should not see all the moving pictures that they see these days. I think that lot of children get bad ideas just from seeing some of the movies. Although it may be educational in seeing some pictures, but a lot of it is too silly for anyone to see. I think it is nice for the children to listen to the radio, to the children's program. There are always nice bedtime stories for them. We always tried to make things pleasant for our children, and I always tried to make things for them to play with. I could not afford to buy dolls for the girls, so I used to make husk dolls for them, and dressed them up, and my children liked their dolls. In the wintertime my husband made homemade sleds for them. The children had just as good a time coasting with the sleds their father made for them as if they had a brand-new factory-made sled. We used to take our children to the circus so they could see the different animals, and when they started to have the Oneida Fair we always attend all the three days. We also took them to Brown County Fair in De Pere.

I always wanted my children to get a good education so they would get a good job and get good salary, but both of my children finished the eighth grade and started the high school and went for one semester and then quit school.

My daughter worked in a hospital in Manitowoc for several years; then she married a German and they moved to Chicago. My son went to see his sister and he looked for a job and he got a job in a hospital as an attendant and he married a nurse. I went to live in Chicago one winter and I did not like it because I did not know anyone. My children lived in steam-heated apartments, and they had a bathroom, electricity, and other modern conveniences, but I was lonesome for my little one-room log cabin, and although I had to fire up my wood stove in zero weather, yet I would rather do that than live in a big city where I saw only strange faces every time I stepped outside of the apartment.

I can understand the English language, but I can speak very little English. My children both speak Oneida and I taught my daughter to write in Oneida according to Mohawk spelling, so she always writes to me in Oneida because she knows I can't read English. I learned how to read and write Mohawk when I went to school. When we first started to go to school we were taught both Mohawk and English, but I could not learn the English spelling, I attended school only a short time as I was forced to marry when I was only sixteen years old. I kept studying the Mohawk language, but I never looked at my English reader or speller after I left school. What little I know has been a great help to me, and I often wish now that my parents had kept me in school instead of forcing me to marry a man that did not interest me at all. But that was the custom at that time, for the parents to marry their daughters as soon as they were old enough. My folks were planning to send me away to school to Carlisle or to Hampton when my husband's parents asked my folks for me. Of course, it was considered an honor to be asked, and if my parents had rejected my suitor his parents would have felt slighted, and would have ended their friendship with my parents.

At the time I grew up the girls were never allowed to go anywhere without a chaperon. The only social gathering we were taken to was to a church dinner, or picnic. Young girls were not allowed to hold conversation with any man, excepting if he is a relative. That is the reason why in many of the early marriages the man and woman involved were strangers. The girls were more pitiful than the young men because a fellow can pick out the girl he would like to marry, then the parents do the negotiating with the parents of the particular girl he wants for a wife. If he gets rejected then he looks for another girl, and so on until he finally succeeds or his parents succeed in getting a wife for him.

My husband never went to school and he is very quiet, but he has no bad habits and when I married him his folks were well-to-do. We never had no domestic trouble until I started to join some Indian singer's society. I always enjoyed music, and I could sing, and the more I sang with a group of good singers the more I enjoyed it. We used to go to different homes to sing to sick people, and we were also called to sing at the "wakes." My husband objected to my going out with the group of people. I asked him to come with me, but he did not want to do that. I kept on going out, and finally he got so mad at me that he left me and went up north in the woods. He stayed all winter and left me alone. My children were all going to school at the time. I managed to live, but I was getting short of funds, so I started to bake pies and cakes and sold them to a bakery in Freedom, a town near our farm. We lived away from each other several years, but we were not divorced, so finally he returned and we have lived together since.

Our children were both grown up then, but they were glad when we got together again. So I have not had such an easy time; even though my husband did not use intoxicating liquor, he was a jealous man, and very stubborn, and I guess I am too. Now that we are old we get along and seem contented.

Another one of the oldest women, Jerusha Powless Cornelius, was interviewed by Oscar Archiquette. This selection includes two short narratives, one about her brief childhood and early marriage, the other recounting her experiences as a midwife. The speaker was born in 1862 and was seventy-eight years old in June 1941. These two pieces were originally written down in the Oneida language and translated literally, then more loosely, and left in draft form. They required more editing than usual. The title is the one originally given. Chapter 6 includes an account of her changing attitudes toward Christianity.

I Was Married When I Still Liked Dolls

I am always ashamed to tell how old I was when I got married because I was so young. I was fourteen years old when my mother told me that I was to get married now. I was brought up by my parents and I was always home. I started working when I was very young; mother taught me how to work. I was always home; I was not like the young girls are now. My deceased mother did not love me; she did not arrange for me to get education. I have been in poverty many times because I am not educated. I cannot ask in English for anything I want. I am able to count in the Indian way.

I was surprised when she said you will get married now. I thought mother had forsaken me. I said I do not want to get married; she said you are going to get married. I cried for one week when I found out I had to get married. I still played doll yet. Our parents were bargaining [arranging] for one week for us to get married. Finally my husband-to-be's mother came with a little bundle. In it was calico and a shawl. I suppose that is what mother sold me for. The calico was not pretty; it had pictures like this on it. And my husband-to-be presented me with shoes. Then they dressed me up. Then my husband-to-be took me and we got married. We were married by Father Goodnough at the same church where I was baptized and confirmed. [17]

I lived with my mother-in-law for one year. She misused me; sometimes she would hit me, and she was continually scolding me. When we lived by ourselves all we had was a washbasin and pie tin. Finally my mother-in-law gave us a table and a beer keg for a chair. I was ashamed to have anybody come because we didn't have anything. One time Captain John Archiquette came there.[18] I pulled out a beer keg for him to sit on; we didn't even have a pillow.

My husband worked out and sold wood for our living, and we used to plant. I made baskets and picked berries. Besides this I used to save corn husk and I sold it for five pennies a pound. I always used to have money. I was not corralled, but mother watched me all the time. I was always at home until I got married. I never saw the man I married before, until we were made to. I did not know anything about married life.

At that time I used to bake bread in or under live coals, and I baked potatoes, and I would cook different kinds of wild greens. I used to like pigweed or lamb's-quarters the best, and milkweed, and there is toadstool which is very good to eat too. And another called wild marsh rose; it is good to eat too. In the fall I always have different kinds of stuff put away for winter, boiled dried sweet corn, beans, dried pumpkin cut into strips, and lots of jelly.

My husband was a drunkard. I will not keep it a secret. One time he nearly killed me with an ax. He threw an ax at me and I just had enough time to duck and the ax sank into the window frame. We had ten children by my first husband, but they are all dead. My husband's name was Thomas Powless. My father was Elas Jordan, and my mother's name used to be Elizabeth Cornelius. They were two years apart.

The first time I watched a midwife take care of a woman, right then I thought I could do the same. When a child is born it is connected with intestine to its mother. Tie the intestine with a string, one and a half inches from the belly, either with store string or number eight sewing thread. The length of string used to tie the navel is about four inches. Then cut off the intestine.

They have the patient stand up and then have her double up her fist and blow into it with strong force. Sometimes this is done twice and the afterbirth comes out. When I took care of myself, I just blew twice and the afterbirth slipped out. It is bad to tie the navel too close to the belly because it goes into the belly and will cause death. If everything goes well the afterbirth should be out in five minutes; some burn it and some bury it. When the afterbirth comes out then the patient lays down for ten days and eats only toast and butter. When I took care of myself, just the next day I got up and was walking around. I must be a beast, and I ate whatever I wanted. I am always surprised that some people have to lay in bed ten days. When a midwife took care of me, I was ready to get up as soon as I gave birth to a child.

When a woman is about to give birth a small piece of cloth is put on top of the bedclothes or between the bedclothes and the patient. When the patient gives birth then all bedclothes are washed good and clean. The afterbirth is called the infant's chair. When a child is born it is wrapped up in a blanket or quilt until the midwife is ready to bathe it in water. The infant is bathed every day for ten days. I bathe my own every day for one year. When the navel is tied then a white cloth with a hole in it is used for a belt for the belly button to come though so it rests on cloth. If an infant is healthy it will get well in eight days. If the afterbirth does not come out within one hour it means death. The body swells in this case.

I have been a midwife since I was twenty. It is worth five dollars to doctor a person. One time a woman gave birth to a child on the road, so she took care of herself and then went on home. It is said her dress was all soup from giving birth. The farthest I walked to a confinement case was one mile. I was always looked down upon; for that reason they would not come after me, and besides they would not pay me for my services. But I always thought perhaps I done somebody good so I let it go at that.

I disliked the first baby I had. I used to hit it with my fist. I got so I had to be watched. Mother used to tell me not to lick or hit the child because it was bad to punish a child. When my child was two years old I loved it so much it was just like it was sitting in my heart. [19]

I never took care of anybody giving birth to twins. One of my ancestors gave birth to female twins. If a woman is going to give birth to twins, the second one is usually born about one hour after the first one. I heard that somebody gave birth to two sets of twins, two male and two female. What they call me doesn't seem quite right. [But] I am not crazy.

Mrs. M. E. S. tells us how she felt about the white people who had acquired Oneida land and had increasingly moved onto their reservation. She gives us a sense of what it is like to live among people whose language one cannot understand. David Skenandore was the interviewer, on September 11, 1941. This selection bears its original title.

Attitudes toward Whites

Well, I tell you the way I feel about the white people. I never did like them. Maybe it's because I can't talk English and I can't understand them. When they first began to settle here on the reservation I used to just hate to see a white coming to the house because I knew well that I couldn't talk to him. Sometimes if I had time enough or think he didn't see anyone around I would shut the door and lock it until he goes away. Especially if there is no one around to talk for me. But my husband he knew how to talk English—not very good but he understood them when they talk to him. And if any of my children or grandchildren are around then I'm alright and I let them talk for me. So that's how I been getting by all these years: somebody else has to talk for me.

The only thing I can say is "yes" and "no" and I don't know when to use that, but I always feel that I answer his question when I say "yes" or "no," or either make motions with my hand if I think he is asking which road he should take to go a certain place. Well, one time one of my grandchildren was with me—he was a little boy about four years old—and a white man came up to us and he wanted to know which way he should go to get to De Pere. Well, I couldn't talk to him so I ask my little grandchild what he was talking about and the little boy said to me in Indian words, he is saying something about De Pere. The white man was surprised that a little fellow like him could talk both Indian and English. So I told the little boy in Indian, I said, tell him to go on that road and go straight and he will come right in to De Pere. Well, we got rid of him anyhow.

So that is the way I have been getting by with the white people for many years. Of course, as the whites became more settled throughout the reservation I got used to them and didn't mind so much anymore if whites [were there] because there is always someone around to do the talking for me. And then as my own children and grandchildren increased and they were able to talk English, which I knew could help me, the more I forgot about the whites because there is always someone to help. And then as I hear the children talking English I got to understand some things in English and was able to say a few words. I often try to talk with the two grandchildren I have with me all the time. Of course, the mother talks English mostly to them, but they could understand and talk both English and Indian. I often wish I could talk English because there are too many whites around us nowadays. Of course, the whites know now that there are many Oneidas that can't talk English so they don't bother them so much anymore.

Now then you ask me about the whites' ways—what I think of that. Well, from what I can see, even though I can't understand English, it seems to me that there must be some that are really nice to Indians and they are willing to help Indians in what they can. And then there are some that are not friendly at all, and you can always see that he or she hates Indians and they will try to make it tough for you if they become a neighbor to you. That is what I could see or say about them. And another thing: if they once get a hold of your land through mortgage or taxes they either foreclose you before time and without much time for you to find another place. Such cases I know have happened to a good many of them here in Oneida Reservation.

First thing you know some white man will come and tell you that he is buying the place through taxes and then tell you that you have to get out. And a good many of them lost their homes by whites getting them intoxicated. They would have the Oneida sign some kind of papers by which they would perhaps loan you a small sum of money. Later they tell them that they have mortgaged their property, which they perhaps wouldn't know nothing about. And maybe they would tell them that they got one or two hundred dollars which perhaps would only be some odd dollars which they might have gotten. And then there were a lot of them where the white man would sell them a horse or team of horses which are about ready to fall, or maybe it is so kicky that it can't be used at all. And if they try and take it back he would be holding the mortgage on their property, which of course is worth a lot more money than the horse or cow or something of that kind. Dealings like that.

I know a good many have lost their home because when a white man is dishonest he is really a bad one. Especially the horse or cattle dealers have played a great deal of dishonest work among the Oneida. And of course not only cattle dealers but many others as long as they had money. So these are some of the reasons why I don't like the white people, because he will try and beat you all he can. And my other reason is because I can't talk English.

That is all I can tell you about white people. And I want to tell you it's no fun when you can't talk English, especially like going to town to do some trading alone. It makes it hard for me because I can't call everything by name. The best I could do is point at what I want. Of course, some of the old storekeepers know the people who can't talk English, so they always try to help us out as much as they can. So that is the way most of us old people had to get along. We have to point at what we buy at the store. But I always thought it's not only me that can't talk English as there are many others as bad off as I am.

I often said to myself it must wonderful to have education or even just to be able to talk English enough to understand others talking English and know what they're talking about. Well, I often wish I had a chance to have gone to school when I was young, even just long enough to have learned to talk English because it means so much when you talk English. But of course we old people didn't have as good a chance to go to school as the younger generation because there were no schools nearby where we lived at that time. And then at that time the parents made their children get married young, before they even got a chance to go to school. It was later that they began to send their children to school away from home. And then later the government put up a school on the reservation where many of the Oneida children went after that and they began to get education. And they were also allowed to go to some other bigger schools like Carlisle, Flandreau, Hampton, and other places. So from that time on they began to get educated and some even got to be lawyers.

Many of the Oneidas got to be pretty well educated, but few that I know made good use of it. There were few that had a little education that was my age. Of course, my younger brothers and sister got a chance to go to school so they all had a little education, but me and my older brother didn't get the chance to learn anything. So oftentimes it comes to me how important it is to have education, when you can talk for yourself regardless of where you are. So when I had children of my own then my husband and myself realized how important it is to have education, so we sent all of our children to school so that they can get education and be able to talk for themselves whenever they meet white people, and not have someone else to talk for them. Because we knew how hard it was to be without education.

Now I think I have told everything about the way I feel about the whites and that I do hate some of the whites because they will try to beat you all they could if they got a chance. And I think I have told what I think about education. Well, I might say again that education is one of the most important things that a child should have in order to get along in this world now.

DIXON SKENANDORE

> Dixon Skenandore feels pretty good about his life, but he does have some regrets, as he told John Skenandore in this July 22, 1941, interview. Regrets—but not self-pity. Dixon was born in 1871 and died in 1950. He was a skilled farmer, knew a lot about plants and herbs used for medicine, and had a reputation for being witty and generous to those in need. For more about him see the next account, by Jane Skenandore, his wife.

One Man's Life

I am seventy years old and have a family of twelve children, and every one of them is still living. Both my wife and I are pretty spry in our old age. First I must talk about my wife. She must be a good mother or some of her children would be dead, but all of the twelve children we have are very healthy and grown up and have families of their own and we have altogether seventy-eight grandchildren. She is a good housekeeper and also does lots of work outside. She is a hardworking woman and very fast in getting around. She still makes baskets in her spare time, and they come in mighty handy sometimes when we are broke because they sell very good. She is also very good with the hoe in the garden, but that is more of my line of work. This garden, as you see it, is one acre and not one horse track you can find in it. I worked every bit of it with my hoe. I start every morning by four o'clock and get lots of work done before breakfast, and when it got too hot during the day I could sit out in the shade.

The potatoes I have here is about one quarter of an acre, and if the weather stays as it is—rain every so often—I expect about forty bushels, and that is plenty enough for my family and also enough seed left for next year. Corn in all of the three different varieties covers very close to half an acre, and that is also more than I need for feed. I have a few rows of highbred [hybrid] corn which I want to use for chicken feed as I have quite a number of young chicks running around here, which I really don't know how I am going to handle as my yard here is too small for a prosperous farmer like me. I am renting this place for five dollars a month and my rent is paid one month in advance, but I should have a little larger place as I am pretty good at crops yet and I hate to be wasting my time when I could just as well be working.

I only have one of my daughters and one grandchild staying with us so there are four of us at home. I am drawing thirty dollars a month from the old-age pension, and my wife is getting ten dollars per month for mother's pension on that one grandchild we have with us. That's the white woman's son from my son's first wife. He is married again and started another family. This time he married his own kind so he left us have the half-breed, and the money we are getting from the pension is plenty enough. We do consider ourselves very fortunate in getting in on that as we don't know what we would be doing if it wasn't for that. I think that is one good thing our government has done when they passed that kind of law for us old devils.

With my crops and the pension we are getting we make a splendid living. I plant every year the old standby corn, the Indian corn, as they call it. This we use for bread and soups and we just can't seem to get along without it, so we always have a good supply of that each year because it certainly cuts the cost of living and we never get tired of it. And sweet corn; we plant a few rows of that too, which we eat all we want green and also dry a good supply of that each year when the corn is nice and green. This is also very good to eat during the winter months. All we do is soak it a day before boiling the corn with pork shanks, and that kind of soup is hard to beat. My wife cans all the fruit we get a hold of during the summer, and we put up pickles, sauerkraut, and all kinds of vegetables. All these are a great help during the winter months.

If I had to choose today's living and fifty years ago I believe I would rather choose fifty years back if the timber is as good as it was and we had all the game we want. I tell you we had fun in those days and had a very easy living and made lots of money. With what I know today I think I could make myself a dagone good living. In those days we didn't think we would ever run out of wood, and look at it today. I have to use little poplar sticks for my fuel, which at one time we didn't use nothing but the body wood of maple trees. We used to use only the part without branches so the wood was free from knots just as if the knots won't burn, and now I would be only too glad to get just the knots off from maple wood. We just left the part with branches lay to rot and time came when we had to cut them down, pile them up, and set fire to them and burn everything up just to clear the land for crops.

I was married by the old-fashioned way without license and without dates. I didn't have my own pick as you boys have now, but just a few days after my marriage there were few couples married and they all had to have license.

We had an Oneida preacher here at the Methodist church, and he was the one that married us. I have said I didn't have my pick, but I had seen the girl before and I liked the girl at first sight so it just happened that my parents got this same girl for my wife. But it was still plenty hard enough to be placed with a girl you have never met before. But we got acquainted soon enough and we certainly got along very nice.

It has been about twenty years since I had lost my property, and ever since I have been renting around, paying in the neighborhood of five dollars per month for a house and garden. But I have been on few places with bigger farms while my children were still staying with me. Then I had contracts with canning factories which we used to make good money on vegetables, and now that we are left alone we only plant what we use ourselves. [20] When we first came this place was full of all kinds of weeds and quack grass so dagone heavy was just like the crow's nest, and now you can't see one and that is the way I left all the places on which I had rented.

I tell you if I only got the same chance again I certainly know just how to go at things, and whenever a white man is nice to you make up your mind he is after something that you have and the best thing to do is not to give him a chance to hook you in any way because just as soon as he gets a hold on what he is after then he is no longer your friend.

When I got married people said it was the biggest wedding that was ever held around Oneida. I was working in Freedom the same day, and that evening when I came home the Big Time started. The reason I was made to marry: I never used to join up with the bunch that's drinking every weekend at my dad's place, but I was about eighteen years old when my mother caught me drunk with the bunch and soon after that she told me that I must get married. I imagine she did that to have me cut out drinking, which did some good. The wedding lasted a whole week, and all they did was dance, drink, and eat. I had money saved up so they did not get hungry, and by the time the wedding was over my wife and I were well acquainted and got along very nicely.

I was well fixed at one time and had two teams of horses working every day hauling pulp and different kinds of wood into town and men working for me. And money was rushing into my pocket from every direction. I sure had the old world by the string! And look at me now!

JANE SKENANDORE

Here is the perspective of Jane Hayes Skenandore, Dixon Skenandore's wife, on her husband and their marriage, and of a very recent change in their life. She and Dixon had twelve children, eight girls and four boys. She was born in 1875 and died in 1955. She was interviewed by John Skenandore on February 5, 1942.

Mrs. Dixon Skenandore's Perspective

I have the best man in the whole world today. You can't find a better man than my husband is right now. For fifty long years that I had been married to him we never separated and all those years he had been a regular soak, and mean when he is drunk, and he scolds with the dirtiest of language as any man can talk it. But each time he sobered off he is just as nice a man as could be found, good to his children and me. He always told me that he didn't remember anything when he is drunk, so for that reason I used to just walk off so that I don't get to hear him and come back when he has sobered off. The reason I stuck it out that long was because I had promised to the minister that I would stay with him as long as we both live. And I only hoped that he would change someday and settle down to real life.

His children are all good to him in spite of his conduct when he is drunk. But one thing, we were never short of anything to eat but always had plenty of everything. He is a good worker and always have money on hand, and at one time we were pretty well fixed on the farm and had everything that a farmer should have. But our troubles was that the property we were on belonged to my husband and his sister so we couldn't do as we pleased. And at one time when we were going so nicely my husband took sick and was sick for a long time, and during that time everything went wrong because he wasn't able to see what was going on in the fields; otherwise he is a very good manager.

It was during hay season that he was sick—in fact nearly all summer—and the hired men we had couldn't have been very good because the hay they put up spoiled on us and we were short of nearly everything for the long winter that was coming before us. So as soon as my husband was well enough to get out he began talking about what he should do since he didn't have enough hay and feed for the horses and cows to pull through the winter and no money saved up to do any buying in the fall when he could get it cheaper than in the winter months.

During this time someone told him that he and his sister could borrow money on their property. So he went to see his sister about that and told her the tough luck he had. But she wanted to sell the property instead. But after talking it over for some time his sister agreed and they borrowed three hundred dollars and each got one hundred and fifty, which they were supposed to pay back so much every six months. He bought up everything he needed with that money and we got along just fine all during the winter and sold milk. We got milk checks every two weeks, outside of selling different kinds of wood. So it was easy for us to keep up with our payments, but his sister didn't pay her share and for that reason they had to sell the property later for very little money or they would have been foreclosed. And since then we were only renting around but we got along just as well as people that has big properties.

We always had money even when my husband drank as much as he did. I often thought that if my husband didn't drink as he did, with the money he has made from crops and working, that we would be pretty well-to-do today. As old as he is now he still can outwork many young men and you can't make him sit in the house any length of time but he's always on the go doing something. He was so fond of drinking that, even if he was sober, just as soon as he got inside of a tavern he would just jump and give a good jig. A person would think he was drunk. And he treated everybody to drinks. That used to burn me up the way he spent his money on other men when it was bad enough with what he drank himself. His boys as they grew up all behaved themselves and none took after him and they were good to him. They all knew how much he valued his drinks so that often when they come to see us they would bring a bottle of whiskey for him and when he got drunk then they would just laugh at him.

We were married by an Oneida minister whose name was John D. Cornelius, a Methodist deacon, and I didn't have my pick like the girls have today. At that time I was staying with my aunt and she was the one that made the agreements with his parents and we didn't know a thing about it until the date was set for the wedding. And we were married without any records of any kind and at John D. Cornelius's place. After we had been married a number of years the Methodist minister then was a white man, and he used to come over to our place and try to tell us that our marriage was not legal and that he should bless our marriage. But we didn't think it was necessary so we never went and only went to church once in a great while.

My mother was a Stockbridge Indian so I am only half Oneida, and my mother spoke only the English language so that is why I prefer talking the English language more than the Oneida. I make too many mistakes in Oneida language and people laugh at me so for that reason I rather speak English. When I was a kid my parents must have been very poor because when they first sent me to school I must have been about eight years old and the other children laughed at the way I was dressed so I didn't like it in school at all, but my mother insisted that I keep on going to school. So mother made me lunch every morning and I went to school, but my aunt lived beyond the school so I used to go over there instead and visit her. She was nice to me and she understood just what I was up to so she helped me along. And after my parents found out what I was doing then they sent me to school in Keshena and there I had to go to school and I went up to fourth grade when I quit school altogether.

I didn't care about staying with my parents so I stayed with my aunt, and it was her idea that I got married and I was only fifteen years old. That was my most amazing moment in my life—to live with perfect strangers, as I had to live with them at his parents' home. The very next day I felt like going home and it didn't seem like I was married. It took us just about three days before we got acquainted enough to say we got to love each other.

But we got along, and as mean as he seemed when he is drunk he never tried to lay his hands on me to hurt me; but he certainly called me down at times when he was drunk. But each time he sobered off I asked him if he meant what he had said to me and he always apologized and told me not to think anything of it as he didn't know what he was saying when he is drunk.

For fifty years I put up with him—as miserable as he is when he is drunk. And now just two months ago we went to one of James White's services at a private meeting, and during the service Reverend White asked the congregation if there was anyone in the house that wishes to be converted—that the time was open. One or two got up and told their story about themselves and were converted by Reverend White, and the first thing I knew my husband got up and told his story and that he now wishes to get on the right path. Why you should have seen the people, how surprised they were, and everyone gave him a hand and it was so touching that it made every one of us attending just cry right out. The shock to everyone of us was so heavy that we just couldn't hold it back, and every one of us just cried right out and I was so glad that he had made up his mind like this that I got up with him so we were both converted at the same time.

From that time on we haven't had a drop of beer or whiskey, and you will be surprised to hear him talk now. The language he used to use before, he also did away with that too. The change it made in our house is something wonderful; everything is so nice and peaceful that I just wish all our people could see it that way too. Since he was too old to work on any job so that we mostly depend on the old-age and mothers pension we get, we used to go broke between paydays. But since we joined the right religion and really put our faith in it, why we even have money right up to the next payday—and all we get is forty dollars per month between us.

I think I have Jessie Peters to thank for this good deed because he is the one that come to visit my husband a lot, and I have noticed that he has been talking religion to him and finally got him interested. And since he joined that religion I don't think there is another man better than he is. We are both baptized over to the Church of Christ as Reverend White calls it. I suppose people do wonder how long we are going to last in church as we were both soaks at one time and everybody knew it. But we really mean it and they even have services here in our house at times and we certainly like the religion we now belong to and it is growing very fast. We are buying a new place for our church over here on the corner of Highway E and H, and since we agreed on this us members have promised to donate so much money every month. Otherwise there wasn't any set price that you was expected to donate each Sunday, but only what you are willing to give to help the church along. We like this religion because there is nothing covered about this religion and the minister makes himself understood plainly, and if there is anything that a person can't understand he is only too willing to explain things to you and he has proved many parts of the Bible where it was never mentioned in some churches. And the church is not decorated up with gold or any shiny things—bell, pictures, or ornaments—and he preaches the gospel with plain clothes on and doesn't want to be honored any higher than any other man. Why, everything is so different than the church we did belong to before.

JACOB DENNY

Jacob Denny was concerned about the changes in Oneida religious life, and he found his own way to deal with these, as he told Stadler King on June 10, 1941.

Changes in the Way of Living

I am not so well posted on the way of living because up until a few years ago I was a working man and most of the time I would be working away from home and I was not married very long. My wife did not get along with me because she had an altogether different disposition than I did. I could not please her with all my efforts. She was a lot younger than I was, so she wanted to be on a go all the time and sometimes I would come home from work and she would not be home. Finally she stayed away for good and I was getting tired of it so I did not bother to try to get her back. I then lived with my mother and father until they passed away.

I remember that we lived a lot on corn bread and corn soup. This was good food, and in fact all the Oneidas did live on that for many years. We also used to have what Indians called *o nu' u•gùhl*ᴬ. This was pumpkins with the peeling taken off, and then this pumpkin is sliced into strips and then this is put in a bunch and hung up to dry. When this is wanted for dinner it could be broken up into small pieces. These would keep all winter, and when this is cooked some kidney beans would be added to this. This makes a wonderful dish. Nearly all the Oneidas at that time lived altogether on this corn bread and corn soup and this dried pumpkin. The Oneidas used to raise other crops for food such as navy beans, potatoes, carrots, cucumbers for pickles. So they used to live pretty good at that, especially some who always raise a pig for meat.

This kind of living went on all through the years until about 1910 when people were able to get money on their lands so they started to live different. They did not bother about corn bread much, only on some occasions. People began to live more like white people—that is, they bought bread and more sweet foods. Nowadays the Oneidas live good with whatever the stores have for food.

I get my old-age pension check once a month, and I am able to buy whatever I want. I pay my rent and still I have a little money left which I used to help my church.

I want to be good now as I am getting old, and with the number of days I have left on this earth I wish to do what is right. I have had many years here on earth, but when I look back it seems that it was just the other day that I was a boy. So it appears to me that we are all here for a little visit. We are here only once; when we go we will never come back. We are brought in this world to work; we must work the kind of work that our maker intended us to work. We must be good to each other, we must love our neighbors, we must do good to others, and we must try to be patient. We must be able to bear all the trials of life and cast off all evil temptations. We must shoulder the cross, and we must say nothing back to what is said of us which may be intended to lead us off the true and only road that enters into happiness after we pass into another world. We live here in this world with all the liberties of choosing for ourself what road we will take. I have chosen the road which I think is the best road.

I was baptized in the Episcopal church when I was a still a baby, and I belonged to this church all through the years, but then I want to change over; that is, I want to drop all the wrong ways of life. I studied all the different churches for some time, and finally I came to the conclusion that I should join the Methodist church because I found that it is particular in many things. I found that if and when a person wants to work the right kind of work they must put aside all the doings of the world. They must not go to a ball game on Sundays, they must do no manner of work on Sundays, they must not take part in any kind of games. The only thing we should do on Sundays is to go to church and worship our maker.

The Methodist church is particular about these things; they would not even allow any dancing. The Sunday is a holy day and a day of rest. I left my Episcopal church because after I had studied I found that they made money on Sundays by having picnics, dinners, dances, raffles, and other games. This is what I found which could not be right if we wanted to be right and honest about the holy day. That is the reason I decided to quit this Episcopal church and join the Methodist, where they do not do those things on a Sunday.

I visited a church some days ago—in fact, I was called to visit the church when they were having a service—so I went in. I like the beginning of it because the preacher asked to have a few good old Indian hymns. After they had sung four or five hymns in Oneida the preacher got up and started to preach, but first he read the Bible and then went to explaining what the reading meant. He had not preached much when he switched to telling about other churches. He started from the Methodist church, the Episcopal church, the Catholic, the Lutheran, and he wound up with the Seventh Day Adventists. He told of the names of these churches when there is no mention in the Bible about names for any churches. He told his congregation that these churches were working falsely and that the ministers are not explaining all that the Bible teaches. He told them that the Bible says that it would be wrong for anyone to add or deduct or misrepresent the teachings of the Bible. When he wound up he said that the only true and right church is the Church of Christ, which he calls his church. He mentioned about the baptism and said that the only true and right way to baptize is to dip in the water and that he was going to baptize people in Duck Creek this July. I felt downhearted, but as I have learned that no one was to quarrel over religion so I took it all in.

I know that it is wrong for people to talk about another person, so it is the same if one preacher talks about other churches. So that is where this preacher was wrong. The Devil himself has much power. He is very wise and would be able to use friendliness and love and in the end wind up in trouble and hate. He has many assistants who help him in the work that he is doing. His work is to deceive, to make hate, to get people to break holy matrimony, to lie, to steal, and all kinds of bad things. He rejoices when he is able to get people to do any of these bad things. His assistants are those who were cast off with him when he was cast from the Kingdom of God. He was cast off because he wanted to have equal rights and power as God, and some other beings who were siding in with him came with him.

I am now an old man and I never went to school, so I have no education. I could not read or write so I could not take a Bible to read, but I have studied all these things that I have said and I believe that the thoughts I have mentioned are given me by God, for whom I am now working. I did live an unclean life, and I have changed that way of living to a good, truehearted, and honest way of living.

I hope you will write what I have said, because this is the change I have made in the way of living. I am glad that I had this opportunity to tell someone what I have in my thoughts because I think it is the duty of everyone to spread good thoughts to all people.

A person does not need education to study what is right and good or what is wrong and bad. My brother William Denny was a great preacher and he had no education but he was able to stand up and preach and he always brought out good and true facts. There were other men like John D. Cornelius and Peter Jacobs and Tim Metoxen and Isaac Denny. All these men were great men. They were constantly working for the good. They have helped so many people to realize how much happiness there is for them who are obedient to the teachings of the minister; also what great and long sorrow it would be for anyone who may not have worked or who were disobedient. We must do as the Bible says, that if your arm is not good and it bothers you, put it away, or if the eye has something in it, take it out and throw it away. This lesson would mean that if we had a wrong in us we should put that aside. The good thing about the Methodist church is that they have men in the congregation who are appointed to have the right to preach to the people or remind them of the sorrows that may come after this life to those who may have not been obedient. All these men I have mentioned were great boosters of the right kind of work and the good word which in fact is the Bible.

John Webster, age seventy-two, was then sharing living quarters with Jacob Denny. He comments on the same changes in morality as others do, but his approach is rather different, as he told Stadler King on November 13, 1941.

A Lumberjack's Life

I am seventy-two years old; I have lived here and there in the south end in the Town of Oneida. I do not have but very little education, but I have picked up lot of English language while I was able to work around. I never was married. I live now with Jacob Denny in the Town of Oneida. I have always worked in lumber camps every winter, and in the summer I would come back to Oneida and work on farms for different farmers. Sometimes I would cut brush by the acre and sometimes I would cut wood, so my work is always with an ax.

What I would say about religion is what I have seen myself while I was a young boy. I was brought up at the Episcopal church, and that is where I went to school for a few winters. I liked our teacher, who also was a minister. He was a real good man. His name was Father Burleson. He used to hitch up his big team of horses and give us kids a sleigh ride. We had lot of fun, and he used to like to see us play as we rode along.

The church in those days was a lot different because the minister was different. You would never see anyone drunk the day before and go to church and take their communion the next day. People seemed to be true to Christianity in those days. If a man got drunk and the people heard of it, he was barred from taking his communion for a month. The Methodist church also had services twice a week at the homes of people. This Methodist church has changed so much too, in a way that long ago the minister was very strict about marriages. He did not allow people who were not married but living together take any part in the church work. He did not allow people to dance, and everything was pure religious undertaking.

Nowadays this is not the case, and I don't say this only because I am not married, but people nowadays who are not legally married seem to be the leaders of the Methodist church. Some men who are living with another man's wife are in the choir, and some men are leaders of the church who are just living with a woman. Long ago this was not allowed by the ministers. Now people can go to dances, ball games, drink, and everything else on Sundays and never even think that Sunday is a holy day. People do not go to church on Sunday, but they go to town, to a show or some other amusements.

All other churches are losing their members. They leave one church and join another; they get baptized each time to join another church, and this is one thing that looks like people are just playing with religion. I have heard that the Episcopal church has changed so much that a person would think that it was a different religion altogether. They have parties, dances, and make money on Sundays. They get drunk on Saturday and on Sunday they are in the choir, and right after the service they go to a money-making dinner or some social.

I have not changed in this because I never was a good church member. I was always rather backward about going to these parties. I have made a lot of money since I was old enough to earn money. Each winter I would go up to the logging camps and work there from early fall to late spring, and many times I would have four hundred dollars in my pocket when I get off the train in Green Bay in the spring. I would buy me a good pair of boots or high-top shoes; I would buy underwear, shirts, good overalls, a good hat or cap, and good gloves and socks, and all these put in a bag. I would leave this in some saloon. I would start drinking, going from one saloon to another. Sometimes I got on a streetcar and went to De Pere. Here I was sure to meet some Indians, and we would drink together and go back to Green Bay again and stay there for the night. I would be drunk and the next day I would find myself almost broke. I would not know if I had spent the money or maybe someone shortchanged me, or maybe someone had been into my pockets. Well, what little money I had left I would spend, and then when I was really broke I would sell some of the clothes I had bought, and when I got enough money I bought a ticket and went right back to where I had been working.

This happened to me not only once but many times.

That is one thing I could say for myself, that I was always a drunkard. But I must have been a good worker because I never had trouble about not finding a job at any camp. I was known in all the camps and was sure of a job if I came there to work. We cut logs and timber all summer many times. Sometimes I would get a job cutting wood or cedar post and sometimes we cleared land. I may as well say that nearly all of my time was spent in the northern logging camps, but now I am old so that they would not hire me anymore, and besides this I would not be able to work at those kinds of jobs now.

I feel rather well at my age, and I am lucky that I am getting this old-age pension. I live fairly good on what I am getting, but I must cook for myself or go without eating. The man Jacob Denny also gets old-age pension, so he and I change off cooking in the mornings. I could not spend this pension money for drinks, so when I get a job like cutting beets or carrots this summer I made extra money and with that I did drink to remind myself what I used to do long ago. I am not ashamed to tell this because it's no lie, and I do not have no one else to look after—only myself.

3.

Working, Earning a Living, and Struggling Through

The following accounts give a more detailed picture of the working and economic lives of men and women. Quite a few Oneidas continued to do some farming on whatever land was available to them, but most became wage laborers. Only a few went into business as storekeepers or tavern owners. They speak of many different kinds of work, sometimes in considerable detail.

Although some men held the same job for years, many went from job to job, even before the depression. After 1929, however, it was a constant struggle for them to find work, as it was for so many millions of other Americans. Both men and women speak frankly of their struggle for survival through odd jobs, relief, collecting wood, selling assets, and moving to less expensive housing. Several talk about the help that they received as a result of the implementation of the New Deal policies.

Guy Elm, once a successful athlete at Carlisle, was an enthusiastic interviewer and one of the most prolific writers on the Oneida WPA projects. Here he gives an account of his peripatetic and varied work history. It may be more far-ranging than most, but is not unusual. He gives us a picture of the labor market for Indian men and a detailed account of a family's economic troubles during the depression.

Report on Economic Conditions before Relief Came into Effect in Oneida

I was married on November 12, 1919, a year after the world war. My wife and I were married in Menominee, Michigan. I was a professional football, basketball, and baseball player at that time. When I wasn't playing ball I usually worked at odd jobs wherever I could get employment. We moved to several cities the first two years that we were married. When a baby girl was born in 1921, then we knew that we really had to settle down to business. Therefore we moved to Green Bay and rented a house. I worked for the Cass company for two summers at forty-five cents per hour.

During the winter months I was laid off, so I went to work in lumber camps in the northern part of the state. My brother did the farming for my father, so when the farmwork was all done we used to work together sawing logs. It was piecework. We were paid either by the log, from twelve to fifteen cents per log, or a cent a foot. We were able to earn from six to eight dollars per day for each man. When the weather was bad or too cold we didn't go out to work.

One winter at Soperton, Wisconsin, we kept the figures very closely. We started sawing logs first part of November and we stopped sawing logs the fifteenth of March. A total time of four months and a half, when we were paid in full. The company totaled the amount we earned during that period. It was figured that we averaged per month $130 for each man after we had paid our board bill, which was one dollar per day each. So I thought that was very good wages for winter work, and so from that time on, whenever I got laid off from work, I always went to the lumber camps and made good wages.

That time I had a small family; besides, my wife also worked in a factory and was a member of a dance orchestra. We were able to buy furniture and furnish a five-room house that we were renting. We were able to have some money in the bank. Every member of the family was insured by the insurance company.

My wife and I both were enrolled at Carlisle Indian School before the world war. My wife is part French and Oneida Indian, and I am also Canadian French and Oneida. I worked for white people near Trenton, New Jersey, for three years, and during this time I learned much from them in regard to ways and means of making a living for a family, so that when I myself got married, I settled down and worked hard to support my family. And I am fortunate that I have a good wife. Whenever I can't make ends meet, then she helps me by going out working during the summer months, when the children are home from school. With her help we usually manage to catch up with our bills. The family is large now; we have five boys and two girls to support. We never knew what poor relief was until the depression struck the nation in 1930. But even then we struggled along until two years later, in 1932.

We had a good car and we had some money in the bank. First we drew out the money that we could, and then we sold the car. Next thing we did was to sell the furniture. We kept getting poorer. We thought that perhaps the times would eventually get better, but it got worse instead. We finally decided we would have to move out in the country to save some expenses. So we did, in 1930. I bought a cheap Ford car that was in a wreck for ten dollars. I repaired the car so that I used it to ride back and forth to my job in Green Bay. I was working on the docks as a longshoreman at that time. I also bought an old house for seventy-five dollars, tore it down, and rebuilt it on my ten acres which I inherited from my father as my share of his estate. I rented a house for eight dollars per month at first, when I moved back to Oneida. I was paying twenty dollars per month in the city. My wife and I cut out the expenses here and there so that we were able to reduce the general expenses to about half of what we were paying in the city. We went without lots of things that we were used to having in the city.

We changed our mode of living considerably—for instance the food. She stopped making cakes, pies, and other sweet eatables. The meat was the same way—no beefsteak, ham, or fresh pork. But instead every time I got a chance to kill wild game I sure did regardless of the season. Eggs and milk I bought plenty for the children. I started to plant potatoes, beans, corn, onions, cabbage, carrots, red beets, and I always plant a big garden for the summer. By doing so my grocery bill was reduced very much. The only time we had extra good things to eat was on the weekends and holidays.

The clothing was worked out the same way. If a garment was torn, my wife saw to it that it was patched up so that it could be used again. When times were good, if a garment was torn or faded slightly it was thrown in the ragbag. I knew that when my overall was ready to be washed I usually buy a new one instead. Now I had to keep it as long as possible; sometimes it had so many patches on it that it looked like the United States map. With careful management we were able to get along very nicely with our family. In 1933 I was able to rebuild the house, but it was not till 1934 that we moved in there to live. I worked on the FERA [Federal Emergency Relief Administration], CWA [Civil Works Administration], and now I am working on WPA.

I can't give the exact figures of my wages from 1919 to 1931. But I would not be overestimating my monthly wages in telling you that usually I was paid anywhere from five dollars to eight dollars per day depending on what kind of jobs I was working at, besides the extra money I earned at playing ball on different teams such as football, baseball, and basketball. A close guess would be about $150 per month for my earning capacity. When the depression came my earnings was reduced to about one-third of that amount. This caused me to reshape my standard of living, but still my family endured much hardship until the relief came into existence. I am very glad to say that I was lucky enough to be one of the millions of men to be placed on the work relief program. I feel as though I earn my living by good, honest work, although we all know that the wages received in doing it is way below the standard of living of those that have large families to support. However, it's better than no job at all. I know for myself that if I wasn't placed on some kind of a job, sooner or later I would have turned a crook for my last resort to get some money to feed my family, regardless of the consequence.

I had made up my mind that I wasn't going to stand there and see my family go hungry when there was plenty of food in the stores and warehouses. Somebody would sure have got robbed in a big way, just as sure as I am writing this story. But don't get me wrong; I'm not a bad man, and I am very glad that I wasn't forced into that kind of living.

I will give you the names of some of the firms that I was employed by from 1918 to 1931. I worked at Hog Island shipyard during the summer of 1918. I was drafted into the army October 25, 1918, and I was discharged in the month of February 1919.

I was home about two weeks, then I looked for employment. I got a job in Green Bay at the Acme Packing Company. I worked there until that fall. I was paid at the rate of fifty cents per hour. I left there to play pro football at Detroit, Michigan, with a team composed of ex-Carlisle Indians, and finished the season with an Indian team at Altoona, Pennsylvania. In November of that year I came back home, got my girl, and took her to Menominee, Michigan, to get married. After we were married I took her along with me back to Pennsylvania. We were there until the season was over. That winter I joined a basketball team of Oneida Indians, a traveling team; we played the city teams throughout the state.

That spring, 1920, we went to live in Beloit. I was employed by Fairbanks and Company manufacturing gasoline motors, scales, etc. My wife was also employed by a garment manufacturing company. We lived there for one year. She took sick, and we were forced to return back to Oneida in 1921.

In August of that year my wife had her first child, a baby girl. That summer and the following summer I worked for the gas company or the [Wisconsin] Public Service Company. And during the winter months I worked in the lumber camps for Bay Shore Lumber Company, Hiles Lumber Company, and Walrick and Son and Company of Shawano.

In 1923 in the spring I started to work for Green Bay Water Works. I worked there until late in November. I was laid off for the winter, and I went to Milwaukee and worked at Federal Tire Company until spring of 1924. I started working for Selmar Construction Company of Green Bay for about four months; then the men went on strike. I was employed at once by Webster Telegram Company putting wires underground. This job was completed in about two months. The next job I had was with Hansen Construction Company of Green Bay. I worked for them until I was laid off in November. I spent the winter in a lumber camp in Michigan.

The summer of 1925 I was employed by G. W. Kennedy and Son, house moving, erecting smokestacks, and moving heavy machinery. Later that fall I went to Milwaukee and worked for Brogan and Shafer Construction Company, contractors for digging ditches for sewer and water mains. That winter I was employed by Northern Paper Mills in Green Bay.

In 1926 I was employed by G. W. Kennedy and Son in the spring
for a few months. During that summer I went to Sturgeon Bay to pick
cherries. In September of that year I was employed by the Steward Construction Company of Chicago, Illinois. The company was building a
grain elevator for Green Bay and Western Railroad Company here in
Green Bay. We completed the job in December of that year, so I went
to a lumber camp and worked for Menominee Indians at Neopit, Wisconsin, that winter.

In the spring of 1927 I started to work for Spokane Steamship Company, loading autos into boxcars for the Northwestern Railroad Company at the Northwestern docks. In September I was again hired by
Green Construction Company, cleaning up the old Northwestern grain
elevator, and we drove pilings for the new grain elevator. In the last
part of October the Steward Construction Company of Chicago, Illinois,
came back to Green Bay to build the elevator. I was again hired by this
company and worked for them all through the winter until their equipment was loaded in the boxcars and left the city for St. Louis, Missouri.

1928 I worked for Spokane Steamship Company. From that time on
I worked on the docks loading cars. And that's the place I was working
when the depression started in 1930. But it was in 1931, sometime in
November, that I stopped working on the docks. I really don't remember just how many short jobs I had until I was placed first on CWA, then
WERA [Wisconsin Emergency Relief Administration], and finally WPA.
I have worked on these projects sometimes as common labor, assistant
foreman at the stone quarry, foreman and timekeeper on the state cover
mapping project, and rechecker on the same project.[1]

For the last two years I have been working on the Oneida Language
Project, sponsored by the University of Wisconsin here in Oneida. I am
very much interested in my work. We are writing all kinds of Indian stories, jokes, and the Oneida history. Someday I hope to see it published
in books so that the people can read it and find out for themselves what
Oneida people really are—bad or good.

Stadler King (1889–1948) was another prolific writer, both in the Oneida language and in English. He wrote a long and detailed account of the many jobs he had held until that time, including his work as a foreman on the WPA cover mapping project. He eventually retired from a job at Hurlbut Coal Company. This selection recounts his experiences on just three of his jobs: in a paper plant, a cranberry bog, and a lumber camp.

Three Jobs

Another job was when I went to the cranberry marsh. I had long been wanting to go to this place and see how they pick the cranberries. A man named Mose Denny came to me and asked if I would sign up to go. He told me about just how things were out there and said they will pay from three dollars up to four dollars a day depending on what a man can do. I told him that I never was there before so I just had to learn to work there so they may not pay me much. He said they will give you a chance to learn and if you can prove to be able to do what the average man can do they will pay you accordingly. I was not afraid to work and to learn so I signed up. So on the day we were to go I was at the railroad depot early in the morning. When the train came I stepped on to it and went inside. Soon as Mose saw me he called me over and said wait here until the conductor comes. The conductor came along collecting tickets but I did not have one, so Mose told him that I was one of them whose ride will be paid by the cranberry company. He put a mark on some paper and went on so I was alright.

We got there about ten o'clock and walked across some marsh and through some woods. We arrived on the place just before dinner. The foreman took names of the men who came and then dinner was ready. After dinner he gave the men the rakes and then told them where they should start. When he came to me he asked me if I ever did rake before, I said no. Then he said well you can help this man haul the boxes to the road. The man referred to was a big Norwegian fellow so he and I went together to the marsh. There was a truck-like outfit by the road and sort of a railroad made on the marsh with planks. We pushed this truck over on these rails and down to where the men started. We waited there a little while when one of the men had filled a box and he carried it to a bank. Then one after another they came and we had our hands full to pick the full boxes and loaded them on our truck. We put on about twenty boxes on the truck, then pushed it on these rails to the road. We piled these boxes on the road and then loaded some empty boxes which we took to where the men were.

We did this day after day, but soon we were so used to the work that we did not have to work hard and the men also rather cooled down. They did not work so fast as they did at first, but they work more steady. When they were pretty well over on the other side it was too far to carry these boxes to the rails, so they put the boxes alongside of a ditch which had lot of water in it. The foreman told us to use a boat to haul our boxes. When we had the boat loaded we would push it from each side with poles. This was more fun. We were just like two kids playing, but we managed to haul all the boxes to the road where they picked them up with a horse and wagon. One day we had bad luck. It was the last load of boxes we were to haul to the road when the men had quit. We had all the full boxes picked up and loaded on the boat. We pushed the boat along nicely, but when we got to the end of the ditch we must have pushed the boat a little too hard so that the end of the boat went on to the bank too high. Our boxes were piled about three high and this went and tipped backwards and a lot of our cranberries fell into the water. We stood there looking at our berries and seemed like we didn't know what to do. The men were going back to the camp to eat supper, and here we were with a lot of our berries in the water. I thought of a plan, so I said we will have to get them out. My partner said, how can we get them out. So I ran to where the men were working and got two rakes, I gave one to him and we started to scoop them out. This did not take so long but we still had to unload the boat so we started on that. Finally we got them all on the road, then we also went to the camp and all the men were done eating but we were given supper.

On Saturday evenings I would draw out seven dollars to send home to my wife. This lasted four weeks, and all this time I was hauling those boxes with my big partner. We became good friends, and the boss or foreman, whose name was William Rush, liked us because we were good friends and worked together so good. He never was around where we worked but he did watch other men, especially the Winnebagos. They live just beyond the marsh, so they worked there every year. Some of them were so big and fat that they would crawl to pick the berries by hand.

When everything was done the foreman called in one man at a time to settle up. My turn came and I went in. He did not ask me any questions but the timekeeper was there, so he told how many days I had in. He said twenty-four days. The foreman said what was his grade. The timekeeper said I don't know because he was hauling boxes all the time. The foreman started to figure and asked if I had drawn any money. I said yes I drew twenty-one dollars. Then he made a check for sixty-nine dollars and handed it to me. I was rather surprised to receive so much so I said did you take out that twenty-one dollars? He said yes I took it out. I am paying you three dollars and seventy-five cents a day. Here I was expecting about three dollars a day. So I just thanked him and I said I want to buy a bushel of cranberries to take home. He said when I am done here I will come out and give them to you. So I waited outside until he came out then he said have you something to put them in? I said I have a bag where my clothes are in; I could take that. He said go after it and I was back there in a few minutes. When he gave me a bushel I said how much is that worth. He said just take them along and don't tell anyone that I gave them to you. I found that he was a good man. Right after dinner we all went to the railroad depot. The train came along at about half past one and we boarded that train back to Oneida. We arrived in Oneida at five thirty.

Another time there was a job in the city of Appleton. We had been hearing about this job and also that the union men were laying low for any workers who may come into town. We heard that one Oneida man had a fight in some backyard when the union men caught him. They were going to give him a licking, but he had a knife and nearly killed one of them. The police took him in, but he was let loose when he told what happened.

Men were going there to work, but we heard that when they got inside of the mills they could not come out. The wages were three dollars a day. Some men from Oneida would sneak out and come home. They would be the ones who told of the job and that they were short of men. This job was at the Interlake Paper Mills. The union men who worked there were on a strike. The company was hiring men from the outside; some were from Chicago. Most of these were Italians. The Oneidas were starting to get into the mills. We had heard that they had their boarding place right at the mills, and a man did not have to go out at all because they had a stand where they kept tobacco and other things like that. They paid every week, so that sounded pretty good. I and another man named Elijah John went there to see if we could get into the mills, so we went to De Pere and from there we took a train. We arrived in Appleton just before noon, so we went to a restaurant and had an early lunch.

When it was noon we went down to where the mills were. We thought that everyone will be gone to dinner at that hour, so we went and as luck would have it no union men were anywhere. We got to the mills, and the street was boarded up so one could not look into the yards; a police stood at the entrance. He could tell that we were not union men, and when we asked him about a job he said go into that office, pointing to a door. You can ask there if they need men yet. We went into that office, and soon a man came to talk to us. We asked him for work, and without asking anything else but our names and where we were from he sent us out with another man whom he told to take us to the foreman. He took us to the mills, and we went through building after building and soon we were brought before a big old man who appeared to be the foreman. He said put these two men to work and the foreman said alright. The mill was running then and men were working here and there. There were sounds of sawing and as of something chipping wood. We followed this man to a place where there was a conveyer coming from below on which came blocks of pulp. The foreman said, here, take these from the conveyer and pile them up right here. Well, we had a job where we long wanted to go. In a little while we had a big pile all along the wall.

The next day the foreman put me at another job and also took my partner away and put him at something else. He took me to a machine and started to tell me how to run it.[2] It was a big machine that looked some like a clock, but the face of it was about four feet round with four blades of knives on it. He showed me how to take the knives off and to put them back on because he said I should change knives every day. When a switch is put on the face of this machine it starts to go round, and when it got to full speed he took a block of pulp [pulpwood] with bark on it and placed it on against these knives, which were going so fast that we could not see them. He held this block and turned it slowly with his hands, and when he turned it clear around the bark was all cut off. I thought I could do this so he let me try, and I did it nearly as well as he did but I put what bark was left against those knives and this took it all off. The boss then let me alone and I went on barking the pulp, and I would put the blocks back on the conveyor which took them to the machine they call beaters. After a little while I was used to this work and able to turn out more blocks. [3]

There was a conveyor close to this machine, so I took the blocks off of that and when I had the bark off I put it back on the conveyor. There were other machines like this on the same line, and what pulp passed me was taken by someone else down the line, so when the pulp got to the end, to the beaters, they were all barked. They were then run into beaters which chips them into small pieces almost as small as sawdust. When this is chopped it runs into some blower which blows it into a big hopper. This hopper is where they put my partner [to work].

It takes some time before this hopper is full, when they put in some strong acids which dissolves the wood. They also turn some steam on it and close it up for a certain length of time. After this hopper full of chips has dissolved, they let down the bottom and they drop it down into a gutter with water in it. This water shock them and it is then like shocked paste bond. [4] It runs in these gutters, about like soup would, until it gets to some drain, and then it is run over some rollers which has some kind of a rigging that spreads them even and a certain thickness. This is then run over other rollers until it comes to hot rollers which makes them into a dry, thin piece of pasteboard like paper. This is still called pulp and must run through other machinery to make real good paper. [5]

I run this machine three days when the foreman came and took me to another machine. This was a bigger machine which they call Green Bay barker. He showed me how to run this. This machine was also run by the conveyor from below. I learned to run this machine easier but I had to have two helpers, one to pick out the pulp from the conveyor and feed my machine from one side. I had control of the machine, so I raised the rollers with teeth-like pegs which is turning all the time, and when this catches hold of the pulp it pulls it through, turning it as it pulls. When it comes out at the other end it is all barked, and I had another man on this side who takes it and puts it on the other conveyor which goes to the beaters. I liked this machine because I only stood there and handled the lever, but I had to know the size of the pulp that's coming and I let down my lever accordingly. This was all I did all morning and afternoon, but I always went and oiled up my machine a little before time to start in the morning and right after dinner. I did not get tired at all, only my feet because I was standing all day, but one of the millwrights told me that I should put a piece of pasteboard where I stand. He said you will see that it will help. The floor was concrete so it was hard to stand on. I did find a piece of pasteboard and laid this where I stand and I noticed that night that I was not so tired.

This was a good place to work because we had our beds in one of the big mill rooms which they were not using. There were two long rows of folding beds each for only one man. This place was always warm because they had steam pipes running through here and there. They gave us clean bedclothes every week. There was also a place fixed where we can take a shower bath. This was not even closed in. It was right where anyone could see the bather, but there were only men there so we were not afraid to take a bath. I took a good bath every other evening because it was rather warm working in the mills and I always wanted to work off the perspiration. I always felt so good when I take a bath and then lay down to sleep.

When mealtimes came we would go into our dining room. There were two long tables so that all the men could eat at the same time. They must have hired some really good cooks because everything was so good. They even had pies and cakes made and we could eat all we wanted to. I gained in weight so much that time because all I did was to wait for meals, my work was so easy. I also washed off all my tan because I washed so often and I was not outside in the sun. I came home twice while I worked there, and the first time was about a month after I went. My wife hardly knew me because I was so white, almost like a real white man, and I was so much heavier. On account of the union men I always went out the back way and walked to Kimberly, which was maybe three miles from where we worked. Here I would get on a streetcar and go by way of Kaukauna and De Pere, and from De Pere I would hire a cab to come out or I may meet some Oneidas who I would get to bring me home. I would have to be back there again Monday morning, so I went back Sunday afternoon.

There were about forty Oneidas working there and about fifty Italians. The union men would come to the gates or entrance sometimes, but the police were always on guard. There was one or two policemen on each side of the grounds, and the only way anyone could enter was at the entrance. One evening two Italians and I and another Oneida sneaked away and went to town. We had no business going there, but these two Italians thought they would invite us along because we knew the city better. This was the first time they were ever in Appleton. We did go along with them.

We got into the main streets easy enough, but soon one man wanted to talk to us but we did not listen to anything he said. We walked along and went into an Italian fruit store. These two men talked for some time with this storekeeper, and I and the other Oneida noticed that there were a few men outside. When we came out these men followed us down the street. We were then a little uneasy, so we went into a saloon where Mr. Brown was the proprietor. Mr. Brown was not in with the union, but he was the paper mill company's friend. These men came in and watched us, and one of them wanted to talk to one of the Italians, but the proprietor told that man to get outside or he'll put him out. The next thing was to get back safely to the mills.

This Oneida who was with us told the proprietor to call up the company to come after us at Brown's place. It was not more than ten minutes, and a young tall man came in the saloon with a billy club in his hand. When he saw us he said come on boys and we went out but he walked behind us. Some bunch of men were outside. They said all kinds of things to him, but he just told them to keep quiet. We got into a car and away we went toward the mills. We drove right into the yards and then got off.

It was some time when the union men were not seen anymore hanging around the mills, and one of the police told us that they were all trying to get jobs at other mills but no one would hire them. They were always told why did you go on strike; you had good jobs there. It was late that fall, nearly Christmas, when we were told that the union had made up with the mills and that on the first of the year they would take their places at the mills. So we all made arrangements to get off the job. We were paid in full and came home. We made good all this time, as they paid us three dollars a day and our meals and lodging were all free.

I also worked up north near what is called Bowler. A man who had worked there for some time came to Oneida to pick up some men to go where he worked. Two of us went along with him, we went early in the morning and catched a train at Anston. We got to Bowler, where we got off and went still a mile into the woods. We passed through some real big woods where the trees were so big and tall that it was actually dark in it. The trees were so big and it was mostly hemlock so the sun did not have a chance to shine through them.

We got to a camp, and a little ways off was where this man lived with his family. We were sent to the camp where these men boarded. We were given bunks to sleep. There was only one room in this camp with double bunks on three sides. There was a big stove almost in the center of the room. There was plenty of heat in this room; there were big chunks of wood on the floor by the stove. Behind the stove there was a bench with a big pail of water on it and a washbasin. Couple of towels were hanging on the wall. I was satisfied with the place and thought here is where I'll make a living for some time.

At noon men came back from work in the woods. They all looked like hard lumberjacks with heavy woolen clothes and high boots. The foreman of the camp came also and found us there with the man who brought us. He gave the foreman our names and then went back to his own house. In another minute a man came to the door and said "dinner." The men began to walk out and the foreman said, come on boys, and we followed him into another building. There were enough places for us too, so we went after the food. There was plenty of meat and potatoes, butter beans, and everything that is good. After dinner we were given a saw, axes and wedges, and a heavy maul. The foreman went along with us into the woods. He seemed to be a good sort of a Polish man. He spoke freely of the events and also asked questions concerning us, such as if we had ever worked in the woods, and he seemed to know where we were from because he asked if there were any more men in Oneida. He showed us where we were to work and told us that what would make logs we should saw them to certain lengths. And after this is taken off we should make four feet wood and what would make what they call body wood, and the top and limbs we should make kilwood [kilnwood], and all the trees that are down should also be made to whatever it would. [6]

There was plenty of work here, but we were not paid very much. We got one dollar and fifty cents a day and board and lodging. This was not bad for that time because everything was cheap in those days. We worked right along and cleaned up as we went. After a month we had worked into some tamarack swamp when we made bolts four feet in length. This was where we cut eight cords of bolts but we had another man to pile up the bolts for us. That's how we found out how much we had cut. The foreman was so surprised when he saw that we had cut that much. He began to like us and every time he had a chance he would talk about it, and the other men were rather jealous of us because he talked so good about us. We also used to catch rabbits in wire snags.

The owner of this land and camp lived in Chicago. He must have been a rich man because he had so much money when he came out. He came out every two weeks and paid us off and also bought some rabbits from us. These were all big jackrabbits. He paid us twenty cents apiece. I saw what they call lumberjack style in taverns or saloons at that time. When we got paid we would go to town and of course I always sent home some money the first thing, but I always would keep some too. Never drank beer in those days so I was just with the bunch.

I saw the biggest fight there one time when one of our gang had a fight with another man who had come from some other camp. This was on a Sunday afternoon when we were there at what they call Joe Neemits saloon. The stranger was the meanest man I ever saw, he was insulting everybody and soon he came to this man from our camp. They did not talk much, when our man said you have been insulting everybody here and now you are going to stop it. He called another man and said you be the referee so they went out and everybody else went out. When they got in the yard behind the saloon they went to it. They must have been well matched because they fought for a long time, but soon the stranger was all blood on the face but he would not give up. No one tried to stop them but let them go. And no one said anything; we were just watching. After some time the stranger went down and the referee said "down" and our man stopped. They let him lay there a while and then the referee and our man helped him up and took him inside and washed his face. He did not say anything, but when he was washed up he came to the bar and said "give the boys a drink" to the bartender, and we all had drinks. He bought more drinks than anyone else. Someone had said that wolves were seen in that big woods so some of us went back before it got too dark, and it was suppertime when we got back.

I worked here all winter, but my partner had come home before. It was first of April when the owner came and told us that he would have all the men cut by the piece [for] logs and by the cord [for] wood. All the men quit right there because the timber was not so good anymore, but it was alright while we worked by the day. We would not make so much by the piece because we would also have to pay for our meals. The camp we were in practically broke up. It was not altogether because we did not want to work by the piece, but at that time of the year most men would be preparing to get some gardens in so the men preferred to quit the job and go home.

It was late in the evening when all the men were settled up. I and another Oneida man got settled up about six o'clock, and there was no train out anymore that day until midnight, but that was what they call a limited train and did not stop at all small places. This train only stopped at Shawano. So this Oneida man and I decided to walk to Shawano and catch this midnight train. This was twenty miles away, but there was not much snow on the railroad tracks so we walked on the tracks. It was dark but we had to do something. We walked and walked until we came to the depot in Shawano and we were there only a few minutes when the train came. It was midnight so we got into Green Bay about three thirty in the morning and then waited for the Green Bay and Western, which used to start out at seven o'clock. I arrived home with about seventy dollars, but I had also sent home money every so often while I was there.

MELISSA CORNELIUS

When Melissa Cornelius (1882–1982) went to school at Carlisle in 1895, at the age of thirteen, she couldn't speak any English. She soon learned, however, and was proud that "we studied Shakespeare and many other things and learned to debate and to express ourselves dramatically" (M. E. Cornelius 1982:64). She took an active part in political and church affairs throughout her life. According to Thelma McLester (1988:113), Cornelius continued her learning through classes at the Green Bay YWCA and was actively engaged in painting, ceramics, and sculpture.[7] In this interview, held with John Skenandore on June 12, 1941, she speaks of her difficulties making ends meet and of her participation as a member of the recently formed tribal finance committee, established under the Indian Reorganization Act.

Trying to Get Ahead

I am having an awful time with myself trying to get ahead. It has been
four years since I had taken this place in full charge. Before that my
brother was running the farm, but he took sick and is not able to do
any more work, and at the present time he is in the soldiers' home in
Milwaukee [Milwaukee Soldiers' Home]. So we are left alone here, my
mother and I, making the best of it. My mother is eighty-nine years old,
so you can see that I have to stick very close to her at that age. She is
drawing the old-age pension, which helps us along a great deal. She
was getting only eleven dollars a month until her eyes got so bad that
she can't hardly see anymore; then she got a raise of eleven dollars, so
now she is getting twenty-two dollars per month.

Between us in the family we are holding the same ninety acres that
my parents were allotted fifty years ago, but in order to keep peace in
the family mother decided to break it up into shares, which cut us down
to twelve acres apiece. But mother and I are holding the best part of the
cleared land, and that helps a lot when we can raise our own vegetables,
grain, and hay for the cows. I have three milk cows and sell milk every
day, and that brings around thirty dollars a month. But my work includes caring for my mother, housework, and care for chickens, cattle,
gardening, and being a member of the New Deal Finance Committee.
People from all over come for applications for loans, and this takes a lot
of my time when I could be resting. People come mostly in the evenings,
and sometimes it takes me a long time to fill in the questions necessary,
and in doing this I am just killing myself as I am not paid for doing this
kind of work and just the same I am losing a lot of sleep by it. Like
meetings we have every so often: one night we didn't break up until
three o'clock in the morning, and just the same I had to get up by five-
thirty to milk my cows and have the milk ready when the truck comes to
pick it up to take to the factory. Just the same I like to fulfill the duties
as chairman of this committee and to show appreciation to the people
that elected me to this position.

Outside of my garden I will say I am very fortunate to be able to get a
hold of such a good worker as the man I have to run this place on shares.
He does a very good job working on all the crops on a fifty-fifty basis and
I only have to see that the cultivating is done, so I do the hiring for that
work. I don't sell much of my products like grain and corn because I

get that ground into feed for my cows. I have found a lot of difference when a cow is grained, so this way I am getting lots more for my grain and corn than I would be by selling it offhand and still buying other minerals to go with it.[8]

I also have forty grown chickens and have just bought fifty more little chickens, and they are getting along nicely. They also have to have lots of attention or I will lose them all. There's good money in these chickens. What I raised through the winter was only forty chickens, but during the winter some of them laid eggs, and picking up a few eggs per day and storing them in the cellar each day, why it didn't seem but a few days and I had enough to haul them into town and they would bring me somewhere in the neighborhood of twenty dollars. That's also a great help. I have a few chick hens setting, and I expect these hens will bring quite a few little chicks and I expect to do better on poultry this year if I don't break down before, as I could just feel myself failing at times.

There are days when I do feel better, but not long ago I felt so bad that I had to go to a doctor, and he told me I had painecious [pernicious] anemia. Well, I didn't know what kind of sickness that is so I looked it up in my book after I got home. And my book told me that a person with this kind of sickness shouldn't expect to live long. It is a good thing to be able to know what kind of sickness you have; then you can prepare for it. For a while I was so sick that I had to hire someone for all of my outside work but I am feeling much better and I am doing my own work again. [She lived to be one hundred.]

Since I have taken the place over in full charge I've been also tending to the orchard we have here, as I remember when my mother used to make money on apples. What she didn't use for her own canning we used to take loads of apples into Freedom and sold to one grocer where we were credited fifty cents on groceries for every bushel, and we used to get all our groceries from that place. Each time we brought him apples he would give us a slip of paper for so much worth of groceries, and we got our groceries as we needed. Sometimes this does not run out until way in the middle of the winter. Each one of these apple trees used to produce around five or six bushels of apples, so with all the trees we have here they should bring a lot of money. But it is the same like all other plants, they need attention. Now I have a big pile of branches out there which had broken off from the apple trees during the winter storms. I hired a man first thing this spring to prune every one of the trees and pile up all the branches by the house so I could use it for wood, but I will still have to do more hiring until I can get it into the stove as they will have to be cut up into stove wood lengths. But now the trees are all in pretty good shape so I expect some apples this summer.

We still have good standing timber, so we don't use much coal for fuel. We use mostly wood, but I do buy some coal to mix in, which makes the fire last much longer. I hire a man to cut the wood for us during the winter and pay around twenty cents an hour, but this is lots cheaper when the wood is ours than it would be if I bought it from someone else.

The orchard which I was talking about has been neglected while my brother was in charge and they were run down to mostly nothing. The apples are of all varieties, early, summer, and winter apples, so if a person took good care of these trees we can have apples the whole year around. I have hired help for chores around the barn, feeding cows, watering them when the pastures are dry, and cleaning the stable.

That's another thing that ran me down before the hired help and the drilled well on the place: I used to haul the water from the creek with a pot and pans, pulling that distance to the pasture. The hired helper also helps me with the milking; he is quite reasonable as he charges me only twenty cents per hour and it takes him only one hour each, milking twice a day, and I consider myself very lucky to be able to hire a boy from the neighbors so that I could depend on him even in bad weather.

My story is very interesting and may be a good lesson for many of us. I worked in Chicago for a number of years and earned good money until my mother got too old to be left alone. I made up my mind to come home and take care of my mother. My brother and his wife were staying with my mother, but they were on a go a good part of the time so I thought it was not safe for her to be alone so much. We got along nicely for a while until my brother got to drinking, as he was still running the farm. He sold a good part of what he raised on the place and drank it up and then come home and give us lots of trouble. He got after his wife and beat her up at times. For a while I couldn't see his reason for his actions until his wife was dead. He came home one day and got after me next and even choked my throat, and at that time he spilled everything he had covered up so long.

As far as I saw he was just jealous that I was so good to my mother, and all the time I thought it was only his ailments that made him act like that. Of course it must have had something to do with it as he got sickly soon after that, but this might have been bothering him for some time and he didn't have enough nerves to spill it until he is drunk. Today he is in the soldiers' home in Milwaukee, sick with cancer in the stomach. I feel sorry for him because I know it wasn't all his fault. He was the youngest in the family and he had everything he wanted and always had his own way from a baby on, and that was just where my parents made their mistake. That is the kind of boys you get when you think you are doing so much for your child. It does look like children brought up like this would have lots of respect for their parents, but it works out just the other way. You bring a boy up where you will give in to him and leave him have his own way, you will find out that he won't have any respect for you at all when he is grown up. My mother was getting an old-age pension, and as soon as the pension department found out that he was sick and living on mother's old-age pension he was taken right away to the soldiers' home as he was a soldier of the last world war. They told us that we can't keep anybody else in that house and still draw an old-age pension.

HERBERT CORNELIUS

Herbert Cornelius, age fifty-seven, was relatively successful in his economic life at the time he was interviewed. His story, as recorded by Stadler King on March 9, 1942, has a different tone from the others. The first paragraph, King's lead-in, is in brackets, as are two additional comments he makes later.

The Blacksmith

[Herbert lives in the center of the Town of Oneida. He was married long ago but is now separated. There were no children in the family. He is a blacksmith and machinist and speaks both Oneida and English real well. He obtained a good education from Carlisle Indian School. He was a Roman Catholic but changed to Methodist twenty-four years ago, and he does not belong to any organizations. Herbert was born and raised in the south end. When he was a boy old enough to remember things, his mother asked him what he would like to be when he grows up. He says that he told her, "I want to be a blacksmith and have a foundry."]

This was what I really wanted to be, and I had this in my mind all the time and actually dreamt of it. I had visions of casting iron and making [it into] machinery. So when I grew up that was what I wanted to do. I went to school where I had a chance to work in a blacksmith shop, and I was so interested in it that I made special efforts to learn the work well. I knew that this required much strength, and I knew that I was able to do the work as far as strength was concerned. I learned how to beat iron so that I could put two pieces together and make it stay. I learned how to make horseshoes and how to put them on the horses. I was not afraid of horses, and I knew that I must take horses according to the disposition of the horse. If he was a good gentle horse I treated him well and was careful not to spoil him by treating him rough. I was kind and patted him and he gave me his foot willingly. Some horses are different so I started on him by being good to him, and when once I got his foot I kept it where I wanted it; he may move and want to kick or step down, but I was strong enough to hold his foot. I must say that there are ways of holding a horse's foot so that he could not jerk it away. After he finds out that he could not take it away from me he would stand still on three feet. I always got the shoes on them.

I have quit shoeing horses because there was more work and better pay by doing repair work on farm machinery, and it is on account of these ready-made shoes that can be bought in stores and easily nailed on. Farmers do this themselves on the good horses, but if they have a mean horse they would not shoe him but would bring him to me. One farmer named George Ebbens brought a bronco here and told me that he had all his other horses shoed by himself but this one was hard to shoe so he brought him to me. I told him if you can shoe the other horses you can shoe this one too.

[I asked how people pay if they are charged for any work that he does for them.] Well, I find that most of them mean right and pay nearly as they agree; that's the white people. I am sorry to say this, but it is just as true as you and I are living that the Oneidas must be born to be crooked. I have done a lot of work for them, and I find that in most cases they come and make good once or twice and this just about establishes a good credit for themselves and then [they] turn away and do not pay. I would not see them even if they promise to come on such a day and pay, but they will lie on that promise too. This has happened many times by many Oneidas, and that's what makes me think that it must be in them to be as I have said. You can ask any blacksmith in town, he will tell you the same thing. White men are better in those things as I have found out; most of them do pay as they agree.

There was one Oneida come to me late one night and asked for a loan of one dollar. His car had gone off the road and by trying to get out he used up his gas, so he wanted to buy gas with this dollar. I did not want to give it to him at first but he coaxed so much and soon he said even if I get the car off the road that would be better than to leave it there on the road. He promised that he would be around to pay me back on such a day that week, so finally I did give the dollar to him. To this day that day has not come yet. He came one time but he was so drunk—he said I want you to forgive me for having you wait so long for your money. I thought he was going to pay me but he said this will not happen again, so I said I know it will not. Then he cried like a baby and stood there. He then went outside and was still crying; then a car came with some men in it. They stopped and took him away, and that was the end of my dollar.

I have worked here in the shop even when it's ten below zero. Now I am making these drags which are for Nick Vandervest.[9] He wants two of those sixteen-foot drags and I make them for one dollar a foot, so a sixteen-foot drag would be worth sixteen dollars for me and he wants two and I will make another one for another farmer. Then I have this trailer which belongs to Schulnig. He has an orchestra and they want it for their instruments so I will have to put a top on this trailer. I also make neck yokes for teams. These are better and stronger than factory-made because you can see that this is the best grade of wood and I make the rings myself so I know that this is the best iron rings for a neck yoke.

I also have my own electric power which has the power to run any machine I have. I run all my machines with my own power. I have this woodturning saw, a band saw, the straight circle saw, and a planing saw; this is the grinding tool and the emery wheel. And beside this I get my lights for this shop and in my house. Then I just bought these two machines in Milwaukee. This is a threading machine. I can make any length of thread on any size bolt. Sometimes a farmer brings in some of these iron hoops for a silo, which need long threads, and this is the machine that can make it. This big machine is what they call a drill press, which will drill any size hole in any iron. I used to do all my drilling with a hand drill. This takes longer, and if a big hole had to be drilled it would be hard to do by hand. But this machine will drill any size of a hole with perfect ease. This machine cost me a hundred dollars cash and the threading machine cost almost as much. These machines I will install where I can use the power and I can make bushings for any size pulley. One of these days I will start to make an addition to my shop because even though there is much room now it will not be big enough for all I want. I must have more room here with all this machinery.

I have just bought some real good timber of all oak; then I had it sawed by Schauman. This cost me thirty dollars, but they are all good timber. I have no room inside so I left them out here. I have these twelve pieces for wagon poles; they are now well-seasoned oak. I get many calls for wagon poles, so I have made a few in advance. You can see these piles of iron, which I can make use of easily for bolts, strap iron for boxes and braces. That pile of iron is worth much to me because I can use it for many purposes.

This Maas from Chicago Corners was here one day, so I wanted to ask him the difference between this high line power and my power. I said, will you tell me the straight goods about those high-power lines? How much does it cost you a month? He said, I will tell you the truth, it cost me twenty-eight dollars a month. He said, this John Vandenberg pays thirty-five dollars a month for lights in his store, house, and dance hall. And my dynamo is run by gas, and this costs me only about one dollar and a half a month for gas. It does not take much to run the dynamo which makes the electric, and the electric makes the power to run any of my machines and also gives me lights. There were two men here twice trying to persuade me to get on the high line and get my power from there but I told them that I was getting off cheaper by having my own power. I told them that if I did they might soak me about thirty dollars a month with what power I use. Then they would be here every month and make out a slip for so much, and I would have to pay them. But now if I don't use the power during the day it would cost me less than a dollar and a half a month.

Johnny Jergerson told me that when he started his garage these men came out and induced him to put in the high line and some of these electric machines. They had him coming for he bought all machines that he needed which were run by electric and this came so high that he had a hard time to pay each month, so there was a time when he could not pay and these same men shut off the current on him. There he was; all his machines ran by the power of the high line. He could not do a thing, so he had to go and borrow money somewhere to pay this monthly bill. He got some money somewhere, because the next night there were lights again in his shop and his machines were running. This is what I would not want—to have someone shut off the current on me. This little dynamo I have runs by gas and the dynamo makes the electric and the electric runs the little motor which turns this shaft and I can attach a belt to any of my machines from this shaft. My electric does not have the high voltage as this high line would have, but I have good lights in the shop and in the house and I also have other appliances hooked to this power, and it gives me enough power to run any of my machines although some of these bigger machines take more current than others do. I do not use much gas to run this dynamo, and it costs me less than two dollars a month. All these machines I have bought and have paid cash money for them, but I am now set so that I can make almost anything I want to make.

This shop is worth about six thousand dollars, so you can see that I have collected all kinds of machinery and installed them in my shop so that I can use them. This shop and my house and one acre and a half is worth quite a bit, and my taxes come to about thirty dollars. I have insurance on both the shop and my house. The insurance on this shop is twenty-four dollars a year, but I have to pay each month because this is more likely to catch fire on account of the forge and this big heater stove so they want this paid every month. But my house is insured for eight dollars a year and this can be paid once a year. I figure on ten more years of work for me, then I will retire. I will then have my shop just in good shape, and I could rent it to some man for good rent. I will then be sixty-four years old, but I may have a little money saved up and also the rent should be enough to give me a good living. My living does not cost me much, so after I get my shop fixed up I will not have so much expense.

I also have about fifty bushels of good grades of shelled Indian corn for making corn soup or corn bread. There was a man who saw me shelling that corn; I tried to sell it to him so he figured up as to the price of feed which he buys and then so much a hundred for my corn, but he said that the corn would come too high. I said, this corn is whole corn and if you get this ground up for feed you would have all the vitamins in it, but this feed that you buy only has leavings or what we would call chaff of the corn. However he did not buy any, but in a few days he came back and said I will buy the corn. But I said no, I will not sell them now because I have made arrangements to sell them all by the quart, which will bring me more than by the hundred. I have them all shelled and can keep them as long as I want. I like good corn soup real, well but I sell some pretty often for ten cents a quart. I am getting to like to plant my fields with corn and potatoes and other garden vegetables. This gives me a different feeling when I go in the garden to hoe my plants.

I like the work you are doing because it gives you a chance to talk to other people and you can go to visit them so you can learn lots of what people are doing and how they manage their work and business. If you come around again sometimes I will have thought of more to tell you, and I am glad that you did come to see me. That work reminds me that I taught this Father Vissers how to talk Indian. He used to be able to say many words in Indian. He could understand almost anything you say. I used to like to hear him because he had such a clear voice and you can tell that he says it so perfect. It seemed to be easy for him to learn, and he will not forget.

I was out to see Peter Smith about some timber some days ago and I saw some real nice houses which were build by the New Deal. I rather like the plan they have about giving allotments to the Oneidas and building houses on the allotments. They have a chance to pay a little at a time but they can pay up in time and when they do they will have a home. They do not need to pay taxes on these lands because it belongs to the government; that is, it holds the title. There are many houses built about the same way. I was telling my brother Jim about these New Deal houses and I rather praised up the plans of the New Deal, but he said yes that seems to be alright but for me, I would not be quite satisfied because these lands and property could not be divided or sold. He said, now we will say John Danforth, who has about twenty acres and a house on it, suppose when he gets old and dies his family may be all grown up. They could not divide this in any way, so if they all get married they will all have to live in that one home and they will be so crowded. They would not know who would be the head of that home, and this may cause some misunderstanding someday. This was the only reason that Jim was not quite satisfied with the New Deal plans, and I never thought about that.

Now I will tell you about what I think of the Oneidas. Of course there are a few exceptions there, but it is the case with nearly all the Oneidas. If I did what they do I too would have nothing to my name. These fellows work and earn money, and when they get paid they go in to those taverns and buy beer or some other drinks. They do not seem to think of what they could have used that money for. There are so many things that a man could buy with a little money, or if he did not need to buy anything he may save his money. But they do not do that; he is so liberal with his money, but when he lays his money on the bar and the barkeeper gets his hands on that money he is going to hang on to it. The barkeeper is not so liberal with anything. A person will have a hard time to get even a drink from him. It would appear that the fault is on the Oneidas themselves that they are poor, because they are so liberal and they spend it for something that will not give anything in return. A white man came here one day and spoke of being in that tavern and saw a bunch of Oneidas lined up to the bar and they kept up rounds of buying beer. They actually were anxious to buy the next beer, and they kept on for the time he was in there. The barkeeper took all the money they laid down and he would not even buy back. Now why should these Oneidas spend so much money for drinks when one may be as good as many?

The Oneidas as a rule do not seem to know the value of money. They should know that without money they could not buy anything, but they will stand there and spend it as fast as they can without thinking of something that may be of value to them. Here I am working every day for money, trying to get more and saving it when I get it. I could not stand at a bar and spent a nickel of what I earn because I need it for something that I could use. I must save every penny of the hard-earned pennies. If this is not worth putting down, I do not know what is. Some people say that money is no more than value received. That would mean that if one had many things that was equivalent to money, then they are alright, so this shop is not money but it is equivalent to much money and all this is brought about by my earning and saving. This is where I find a sad story about Oneidas. They are my people, and I am sorry to say this but it is true and there is nothing that I can, or anyone else can do to get them to stop spending money for nothing worthwhile.

[All through this Herbert was speaking without hesitating, and only a hint here and there by the interviewer led him to tell all of his story. He had a half smile on his face, but at the points when he talked of his people he would shake his head as if not satisfied, and he had rather a sad look on his face and nodded his head as if to prove that what he said about them was true.]

That young man that was boss at your project used to come here sometimes. He [Floyd Lounsbury] is very friendly and I could see that he could understand Oneida quite well and he seemed to say many words in Oneida. I do not know this other man [Harry Basehart], but I hope he will come to see me sometime. Well, be sure to come again. I shall study up some things that's of interest. Good-bye.

JOSIAH CHARLES

Josiah Charles apparently had an entrepreneurial spirit. In this account of the course of his life he spoke of his enterprises and also of recreation, sports, politics, and health. He was interviewed by Guy Elm on June 2, 1941. His account of lacrosse, from the same interview, can be found in chapter 8.

An Entrepreneur's Career

I was born on the Oneida Reservation seventy-odd years ago. I'm a married man but have no children. When I first got married, my wife and I went on a farm and started farming. We had a few stock and a team of horses. My wife started raising chickens; the location of the farm was very suitable for raising poultry. Besides chickens she also raised ducks and some turkeys. Sometimes she was very successful in this venture, so that afterwards she saves some money and I have saved some too. We always kept our funds separate, but we decided to invest together by starting a little store of our own. The farmhouse was a large one, so I remodeled the house a bit and because it was just two of us in the house we had plenty of room for our store. She had charge of the store during the day; after my working hours on the farm, I used to take it over. We managed to run the store and farm at the same time. During the busy time of the year sometimes I hired a man to help out.

The store grew in business every year until we finally decided to quit farming and just have a store to look after. We sold the farm and bought another location at what is called Chicago Corners. I opened a store there and built a small dance hall near it—where the present cheese factory is located. We had this store for about fifteen years. We made good money and we lived good; we didn't have to worry about anything. But I made a bad mistake: I started to loan my money out to some of our relations with no security at all. Besides I invested some money which was a bad investment so that we lost most of it. Then, too, I let the customers have groceries on time but they never paid.

So finally I decided to go into the tavern business. I got along good on this business for a few years. Then my wife got tired of that business. We finally decided to retire. We looked around for a small property. I finally located a three-acre lot in the southwest part of the reservation called Goose Town. I built a small log house on it and some small buildings and I went to truck farming. It was about this time that the depression started. I got an offer to sell the property I had before, but then I made another bad mistake. Instead of renting it I sold it. The times got worse so that the money I had slipped through my hands on bad investments. Finally I was broke; then I was satisfied. They kept telling me that this depression wasn't going to last very long and that the times would be better again. But I see now that I was a fool to listen to them; otherwise perhaps I would have had some of the money left in the bank. They were more concerned about me losing my money in the bank then I was. Well, anyway, I was the loser. I am living on this property of three acres drawing old-age pension and I'm contented.

I do some truck farming in the summer, and my wife helps me along. She has chickens enough for us to eat. They also furnish us all the eggs that we want to use.

I have been on WPA for five years. I was a foreman on a road job. We built a new road about three miles through a swamp one summer, at the north of the reservation. We done the ditching, the cutting of brush, and grubbing of stumps all by hand. So this all took time and hard work. I have found out that the Oneida men are much easier to get along with on different jobs that I have had to work. They don't seem to mind the hard work they are doing. They tell jokes about one another and tell stories—some clean and some very dirty. They do lots of laughing, but they don't loaf on their jobs. They joke about the wages they receive for WPA work. They talk about the form of government we have in this country. They all seem to agree and are satisfied with the kind of government we have in this great country of America.

Their contention is that the government is alright, but some of the men that's running it are no good at all. They don't mention the names. I have been surprised many times hearing them arguing about this and that political party, either against it or for it. They can argue for hours until one or the other gives in and is satisfied that the other fellow is right in his point of view. Around election time is when you should hear these Oneidas arguing who they should cast their votes for. I have also had the pleasure of hearing them argue with their brotherly love, the white man, and in most every instance their white brother came in second best in the argument.

The last job I was on was a stone quarry. The work was heavy, but they didn't work us so hard. It was kind of hard work for me due to my age, and I had never done that kind of work before. I did common labor at that place. I was laid off last November, and soon afterwards I took sick and I am still under the doctor's care. I have been in hospital in Green Bay. They tell me I have what they call sugar diabetes and other ailments that the doctors can't tell me what they really are. My eyes are failing, too; I can't see very good and I can't read at all. I can't walk very far—just about able to get around in my room and that's all. I suppose the old age has caught up with me. I'm taking different kinds of medicine every day, but it don't seem to help me very much, although I feel better than two months ago.

My recreations are fishing, hunting, motoring, shows, card parties, and church. Since I have gotten old I don't do much hunting, but I used to like that sport when I was younger. Going on fishing trips—I still went last summer. This summer I don't think I will be able to do it on account of my health. I have had some good mass of fish several times already this spring. My friends brought it to us.

I never did go to church often, only when there is a funeral, Christmastime, Easter, and other big days. But my wife does go to church and other church doings. We donate whenever they come around for donations. I have nothing against any church, but I figure that as long as I'm not doing anything harmful to anybody and mind my own business, I don't see why I should be going there. I do my praying right at home every morning and night and before each meal.

Mark Powless was the elected chairman of the Oneida Tribal Council at the time of the project, serving from 1939 to 1941 (his son, Purcell, was chairman from 1967 to 1981 and from 1982 to 1990). Like Josiah Charles, he was an entrepreneur, and he and his family owned a variety of enterprises over the years. Although the title of this piece is "Economic Life," when speaking to Guy Elm on September 24, 1941, Mr. Powless spoke about such things as baseball, law and order early in the century, and some of the complications arising from the pursuit of alcohol during Prohibition.

Economic Life

I am fifty-four years old; I was born here in Oneida. My father and mother are both of the Oneida Tribe of Indians. I come from a large family. When I was old enough to remember what was going on, I was about five years old. At that time the Oneidas were well-to-do compared to what they have and how they live today. But then they were not all well fixed. Just like today, some were very poor, others were making a fairly good living, and some of them were really making a good living.

My dad had a farm near the Oneida Village, near the station—in fact right across the tracks. Besides farming, he used to run a boardinghouse and livery stable, and at one time was Indian police here in the reservation. The boardinghouse was for the white people and government officials that used to come here to inspect the reservation, and also the United States Marshal. This United States Marshal used to hire my father to take him around and make the arrest. My father knew all the Oneidas and he knew where they lived, and so he made a good guide for the marshal. He used to make pretty good money for this kind of work, because almost every week the marshal would come here to arrest some Oneida for bringing firewater into the reservation or for some other reason. Anyway, the marshal and my father were quite busy, whatever racket they were in. Besides boarding at our place, the marshal paid my father so much for his trips, and I presume as a bodyguard for the marshal. The two worked together like that for a number of years.

With this job my father didn't do much farming himself; he had a fellow working there just for his keep and a little spending money. We had a nice home, a big house to live in, and my mother was a good housekeeper and first-class cook. The reason for that I suppose is that my mother was raised from childhood until she was a young woman by white people near Brothertown. They were religious people and well-to-do. She could talk perfect English. I didn't know that she was well educated until I was a young boy going to school; sometimes I would ask her about this and that about my schoolwork. She usually told me or explained everything to me.

Besides the marshal, most every white person that came to Oneida stopped at our house, sometimes just for a day and sometimes a longer period. My father kept a small store in connection with his boarding-house. What he sold mostly was candy, cigars, and peanuts as far as I can remember. I know that us kids used to steal his supplies every chance we got, so I suppose he couldn't have made much profit. Well, anyway he had a store.

The horses that he used for driving around were Indian ponies and light buggy. The team that he had could make a trip to Green Bay in one hour or Appleton, twenty-five miles away from Oneida, in three hours.

During the winter months he sold wood—cordwood, stove wood, and kiln wood. I don't think that he did any cutting himself, but he hired a man to do that. Besides, he sold standing timber to the whites.

Whenever the marshal came to Oneida my father let his work go and saw to it that the marshal got his man. The cases were tried in Milwaukee Federal Court, so that the Oneidas got mileage and witness fees. When anybody saw Oneida with some whiskey in his possession, all they had to do was report to the Oneida police, and the police in turn got the names of the Injuns that were sharing the contents with the Oneida that actually had the bottle. These Oneida police would send the names to the marshal. In a few days the marshal would send the warrants out to his Oneida police to serve on the parties that were to be arrested. They also note the date that the marshal would be in Oneida to get them for Milwaukee. When they had their preliminary hearing, if they didn't plead guilty the date was set for their trial, and likewise all witnesses were notified to appear on that date.

The Oneidas capitalized on this setup of the law to the extent that quite often they were the same group making these trips to Milwaukee. The white man was the goat in every case, because all they had to do was prove that he was the seller and he would be convicted, pay a heavy fine, or go to prison, or both, and the Oneidas would go scot-free and look for another victim.

One time it backfired. I will tell a story of what happened to a man and his brother-in-law. These two men, it seems—as I was told—had never been caught drinking whiskey. So one day they were talking about how easy it was to make some easy money by getting caught drinking whiskey or to purchase the same and bring it into the reservation. The younger man said to his brother-in-law, the older man, who had married the younger man's sister and by this time had a family, what do you say we scheme and get caught, too, and get some of this easy money? His brother-in-law was very much opposed to the plan. He said to his younger brother-in-law, but supposing our plan didn't work the way it should—what then? The younger man said, well, I will take the blame and get the rap. Well, said the older man, in that case I'll consent to be one of the parties in our plan to get arrested. Now what is your plan?

The younger man didn't say a word for a long time; he just kept on thinking. Then he said to his brother-in-law, suppose you go to town and hang one on and come home and start raising hell and we fight it out. That ought to do the trick. No doubt there would be plenty of evidence. Yes, said the older man, but that's too hard on the eyes. I have a better plan. Tomorrow you take a load of wood to town. When you get ready to come home, look for a bootlegger named [. . .] and get him to buy one quart of brandy for you, but be careful that no Oneida sees you with the stuff, because I know a friend of mine who is Oneida police and I can fix it with him so that we'll get arrested without much commotion. And so the next day, the young lad went to town to sell the wood and to purchase the whiskey. Everything went alright until the lad got the bottle and started to empty its contents. Before long he was drunker than a hoot owl and started treating every Oneida Tom, Dick, and Harry, and gave full information about where and who he purchased the whiskey from.

The man that he got the whiskey from was told that the young lad was spreading the news about his purchase. Naturally the bootlegger could do nothing but pull stakes and leave the country, which he did, and went to hiding in Canada. The news got around so fast that the Oneida police was waiting for the lad. As soon as he cross the reservation line he was apprehended. He couldn't see his brother-in-law; besides his pal was pretty dry waiting for that firewater. Well they got arrested—both of them—no white man to put on the spot, no witness to testify for them; they sure were up against it.

The marshal came as usual and took both of them to Milwaukee for their trial. When their case came up and they had to face the judge, they were no more redskins but they looked more like the paleface. The judge asked what they had to say for themselves one by one on the stand. The older man went on the stand first and told his story; then his brother-in-law went on the stand. Well, the judge took his glasses off and looked around and asked if the bootlegger was in the courtroom. The marshal told him that he couldn't be found nowhere, that he had left the country altogether. Well, he said to the younger man, I'll go easy with you; ninety days in the correction house for you. And the older man, he looked at him for a long time, he said to him, You old Injun, I ought to give you ten years, but since you got a family I'll let you go free, but I warn you that next time you come here for a case like this one you won't see your family and Oneida Reservation for a long time. Do you understand? The Oneida said, yes sir, judge, Don't worry, I am buying the next whiskey all for myself, and if I ever see that bootlegger, he better have a pair of wings to fly with.

In regards to my economic life there isn't much for me to say. I will say that I was single for a long time. I always was kind of afraid to get married and raise a family. I have been married now about nineteen years. I made a good living until this depression came on. I have been in tavern business, trucking, and farming.

When I was in tavern business I had a baseball club on the side. The best teams that was ever turned out in Oneida. We used to play some of the best semipro baseball teams in the state. One season in particular that I remember very well was 1920. We played thirty-six games; we won twenty-eight and lost eight games, but we never lost a game on our home grounds. I was part owner and manager. We had some of the ex-big-league players on our team that season. The big leaguers were "Chief" Williams, ex–New York Giants; Jonathan House, ex–St. Louis Cardinals and Pacific Coast star; Wilson Charles Sr., ex-Carlisle athlete and was also ex-big-leaguer—he played with Boston in the American league. "Chief" White, ex–Western League player, was our catcher. This "Chief" White is a Sioux Indian. The John brothers, Leonard and Lawrence, were the pitchers; Lawrence was our right-hand pitcher and

Leonard the left-handed pitcher. Sherman Baird, Ben Green, and Corney Huff. All the above names I have mentioned were old-timers. Then I had a bunch of young players just out of Indian schools, players like Hill, Summers, Silas, Skenandore, Metoxen, Cornelius, Elm, and Smith brothers Elijah and Alphius. And there were others that played now and then for me during the season, but I don't just remember their names. This team was the best that I ever owned, and it was a pleasure to be the manager. Let me look in my score book so I can give you a lineup:

> First baseman = William Metoxen
> Second baseman = Alphius Smith
> Shortstop = "Chief" Williams, "captain"
> Catcher = "Chief" White
> Third baseman = Jonathan Johnny House
> Center fielder = Ben Green
> Left fielder = Corney Huff
> Right fielder = Mckinley Silas
> Pitcher = Leonard John

The other pitchers were Lawrence John, Wilson Charles, and Whitney Hill, relief pitchers. The lineup I gave you usually starts the game because they were all experienced players. After we get a good lead on the other teams in runs scored then I keep putting young players in their place to relieve the old player as well as to give the young players a chance to gain experience. These young players were fast, hard hitters and fancy fielders, but they were not dependable as the old-timers in hard, close games. They were inclined to take chances, causing them to make errors on some close plays on the bases.

Some of the young players that I mention played for me until 1931. A fellow named Peterson near Seymour laid out a diamond and hired some of my ballplayers, and I wasn't managing the team any longer. My brother had taken my place as manager, but I was still part owner at that time. Besides, Vans Valley had a team too by that time, and so we decided to quit. I sold the equipment such as bats, balls, gloves, base sacks, and the uniforms. I sometimes wish I didn't quit running a ball club because I used to enjoy myself watching the boys play, although sometimes they made me pretty angry too. We developed some good baseball players during the time that I was running the ball club. Most of them went out and played with outside teams. I couldn't pay them very much, so I always told the boys to sign up with the other teams where they could get the most money for their playing ability.

The most consistent home-run hitters were David Skenandore and Alphius Smith. Many a time these boys came through in a pinch to break up a ball game and get the Oneida team on the winning side. The other players were also good hitters, but they were not as heavy hitters as these boys. Some of the longest home-run hits I ever saw was hit by this boy Skenandore. The fastest runner and fielder was Ben Green, the best catcher "Chief" White. The best place hitters and infielders were "Chief" Williams and Johnny House. And the best pitchers were the John brothers and Whitney Hill. I might say that the Oneidas had great ball clubs way back in 1899. About that time Father Merrill was our priest, and he took a ball club and toured the eastern part of the United States and Canada. Just how many games they won, that I couldn't say.

About the present-day ballplayers, I don't know why that it seems to me the boys don't seem to take very much interest in trying to be baseball players when they could earn big money as professional ballplayers. They have the makings of developing into good ballplayers but they go just so far, then they quit the game altogether, whereas the old-timers kept on playing until their legs couldn't stand it any longer, about forty years old.

Some of the reasons I might say are that the Oneidas no longer are able to enter the Indian schools like in my day. And here in Oneida the taverns have the teams and a player has to be a first-class ballplayer right off the bat to stick with the team. Other reasons are cars: they want to be riding around when they should be playing ball. And too, they can't get together to practice as a team; they are all working at different hours on the projects or in the factories.

That is about all I could say in regards to ballplayers. I might add that I don't know anybody else that knows more about baseball and ballplayers here in Oneida than I do, that is from the time I started running a ball club up to the present time. "Chief" Williams and Johnny House and Wilson Charles were the only players that I know that really capitalized their playing ability to the extent that they were getting several thousands dollars per season in the big leagues.

After I quit the tavern business, I worked on the docks in Green Bay for about two years. The next thing I did was to buy a truck and I went into the trucking business. About this time the depression was at its worst. I sold the truck and went to farming with my brother in partner-ship. Sometime later I got on the WPA project, but I kept on raising cash crops such as beans, cucumbers, and cauliflower. Sometimes I make out pretty good and sometimes I just break even. The weather has lots to do with the kind of crops a person can raise. And I am still at it trying to raise different kinds of crops. With a large-size family like I have a man has to do some things to balance his income besides working on the WPA. I quit the WPA in May, but I suppose if I can't get any other job for the winter months, that I will be able to get back on the project again. Although I would rather work for a private concern.

ISAIAH REED

A common theme in accounts of work by Oneida men is their pride in their qualities as workers and their work ethic. They see themselves and other Oneida men as solid and reliable workers, proud of their skills, and happy to work in the company of other men, especially other Indians and Oneida. This pride comes through clearly in the interview Isaiah Reed gave to Guy Elm on May 13, 1941.

Moving Buildings and Tearing Down Smokestacks

I am over sixty-five years old, but I feel like a thirty-year-old buck. I am well and still can outwork lots of men younger then I am. I think the reason that I don't show my age is that I have always worked hard ever since I could earn wages. I have done all kinds of work; I will tell you about it later in your interview with me. I got married in 1906 to Phoebe Stevens, and a child was born in 1910. We named him Emory. My wife died a few years later, and my son is also dead, so that I am left all alone in this world.

My father, John Reed, was the last Indian police they had here in our reservation. Even after the reservation was divided into two towns, Oneida and Hobart, they had him as constable. When I came back from school, he was police for the Oneida Boarding School. He used to go after the runaways from the school. I suppose he was hired by the gov-ernment to catch these boys and take them back to school. Anyway, he was kept quite busy chasing these boys from the school. Well, it was through his recommendation that I got my work at the Oneida Boarding School. I was fireman at the boiler house and night watchman. I was on night shift. I worked on this job for few years; then when my wife died, I quit and went to Green Bay.

In Green Bay I worked at different jobs such as carpenter work, factory work, for a streetcar company—on a repair crew and just a common laborer. In 1918 I started to work for G. W. Kennedy and Son Company, house moving, erecting smokestacks, moving heavy machinery, and so forth. I have been working for them ever since something like twenty-three years. In the winter months, when the work is slack, I usually go up north until the work picks up again in spring. The work I do requires skill and keen judgment so that there may be no mishap or bad injuries to the men that are working with me. I was made a foreman after I had worked for the company about three years. I have full charge of my working crew, which usually consists of six to eight men depending on the size of the job involved. I raised and moved some very large buildings, including warehouses, barns, stores, school buildings, and other types of houses and buildings, besides erecting smokestacks and taking the old stacks down. We also have done lots of removing old boilers and replacing new ones in its place. Water tanks, transformers, and other heavy machinery—I have had the experience in moving them and in loading and unloading them from railroad cars, so that I am classed as a number-one man when it comes to loading, unloading, or putting them in place in the factories and other plants. I have had some very nice crews to work with. But I like to work with the Oneida boys the best.

At one time I just couldn't get along or get used to working with white men, and so my boss, whenever it is possible for him to hire Oneidas, he hired them at my request. As a matter of fact, I always insisted that he get me an Indian crew when there is a big job to be done. The Oneidas are easy to break them in line with their work. They are careful not to get hurt or to hurt their fellow workers. Besides, they don't mind the work and the dangerous part of the job they are sometimes required to do. They are steady workers at all times.

In raising houses, the first step is digging holes big enough for blockings for the screw jacks to be placed on it, directly under the sills. The blockings that are used on small houses are about three feet long, the size of six inches by four inches, and the plate for the jacks are two feet long, the width six inches, and the thickness about two inches, made out of hardwood lumber. For an ordinary house it takes about ten jacks. The jacks are placed one on its corner, two jacks between the corners on each side, and one jack at each end. Just as soon as the holes are deep enough for the jack to be placed underneath the house, it is best to do so. After the house is raised enough so that square timber can be put in there. Then we block the house by building cribbing on each corner, by turning the jacks back. [10] The house is put on the blockings while we placed the timbers in place; then the jacks are placed underneath the timbers. Each man has so many jacks to take care of. Before we start turning the jacks, I tell the men just how far I want the jacks to turn whether it's a quarter turn at each round or half or two-thirds or full turn. When we are raising larger buildings and heavy machinery or other heavy things, we usually just turn the jack a quarter turn.

I never let a new man work on the jacks until he has learned how to build his cribbing or blocking for the jacks. The blocks that are used on these work are blocks about four feet long, six by six inches, seven by seven, eight by eight, nine by nine, ten by ten, up to twelve inches. When the house is to be moved then we use trucks made for that purpose, and a small Caterpillar for pulling, but if the house is a large one then we got to have more power. About fifteen years ago we used to have a team of horses turning the capstan for pulling the house along. A long cable was used, and the capstan was anchored to manholes along the streets or to trees on each side of the street, just so the capstan was in the center of the street so that the building can be pulled on a straight line. Well, this new way of pulling or moving houses is either pulled by direct power or if necessary by spool or winch, the cable winding around it [while] the power is used from the tractor. When all the cable winds to the end, the tractor goes ahead again and the operation goes on again. We can move a house a long ways in a day. If we are moving a house out in the country then we use direct power. Large tractors or thrashing [threshing] machine engines will do the trick. At least I haven't seen it fail so far.

Erecting a smokestack is a dangerous job, and it must be done with careful supervision on the part of the foreman. We use long poles for this work. It takes a long time just to set up the rigging ropes; cables and guy wires have to be fastened to the stack before it goes up. The pole that is used is about eighty-five feet long, and other poles are about sixty feet. It requires lots of climbing and tying and untying ropes.

Mr. Kennedy, my boss, has depended on me for many moving jobs since I have been a foreman. Most all the big jobs he has put me in full charge of raising and moving houses and heavy machinery. He pays me good wages. When I first started working for him, he used to pay me seven dollars per day, no lost time, and when I went out of the city he paid my expenses, both traveling and lodging. I have worked in all the surrounding towns, villages, and cities from here to Milwaukee south, and northward clear to Iron Mountain and westward to Stevens Point. I have never run into a job, no matter how difficult it was to be raised or moved, that I have failed at.

Sometimes I have to figure just how to go about clearing the trees, poles, and other obstructions in moving the building. When we are on the move with houses it is necessary to get a permit for going through the streets, and when we come across a street that has a streetcar line we have to stop there until after midnight; then the electric company sends a crew out to look after the line until we get through with the building. And sometimes we have to work on Sunday so that we do not stop the traffic too long. Whenever the crew worked at night or on Sunday, they are paid double time for their work. Sometimes it takes a long time to get through; then again sometimes it just takes a short time and we are done. As soon as we are clear of the electric wires then we stop moving until the following day. Sometimes it seems to me a like circus parade— the people will follow us along the street to see what will happen next. One time we were moving a seven-room house along the street. We came to a street that has lots of telephone wires and electric wires, and the house was on trucks. In order to clear the limbs and branches, the street department had to go ahead and cut off some of the branches, so that it took us all day to go one block. But the next day was a different story; we had good going and got the house to its location ten blocks away.

Where the Hotel Northland stands today we moved about eight houses away from there, and some houses were taken down. It wasn't so long before we moved all the houses from there and they started to dig the basement for the big hotel, one of the largest in the city.

The most interesting experience I had since I been working at house moving, placing machinery, and erecting smokestacks was at Shawano, Wisconsin, about fifteen years ago, I was sent there to supervise the job of taking the old smokestack down and putting a new one in its place.

Well, I got down there and just looked for a place to board and to look at the job—what I was supposed to do. I reported at the plant, a sawmill, and I talk to the head man of the company. I introduce myself to him, and other officials were there. I said, I was sent here to supervise the work by my boss, Mr. G. W. Kennedy. He looked at me up and down. I said perhaps I better call up Mr. Kennedy and tell him that I have arrived and I'm ready to go to work tomorrow morning, if the job is ready to be started. He looked at me again; then he said, are you sure that your boss send the right man to us? Well, I said, here I am. About this time here walk in my boss Mr. G. W. Kennedy. The two men greeted each other, then Mr. Kennedy said, here is the man that I sent down here to supervise the work of pulling down your old stack and to put up the new one. All I ask of you is to give him all the men that he may want from time to time. He is my best man for this kind of work. Well, they furnish their own men to help with the work. I had quite a time with them the first day on the job, I suppose on account of me being an Indian. So the second day before we started to go to work, I said to the men, I am going to lay off or fire the first man that don't do what I tell him to do on this job. Any question you men want to ask before we start working? Nobody didn't say a word. Alright, I said, let's go.

That did the trick; they work hard and even come to me and asked me what they should do next. I never had any more trouble with them, until we had the new one standing up ready to be unfastened with ropes and block and tackle. I said to one man, you go up on that rope ladder and release those ropes. He looked at me and said, alright you can fire me, because I just can't go up in the air higher than ten feet. I sure in hell would fall off it if I went up there. Then I asked another man; he too didn't want to go up there. I asked a third man, and he seemed to feel like trying so I said, go ahead, try your luck. Well, he went up about halfway then he look down and said to me, no, "Chief"—nothing doing, and came down. The smokestack did swing a little because the guy wires had not been fastened tight as yet. I said to all the men, what is the matter with you white men? Don't like to go to heaven, eh? And I went up the ladder like a cat and did the job myself.

On June 17, 1941, Wilson Cornelius, age fifty-eight, gave a wide-rang-
ing interview to Stadler King in which he touched on some key issues
for the Oneida: the loss of their land and political attempts to improve
the land situation. He also offered general thoughts about such matters as cooperation and enterprise. "My Old Plantation" is his own
title.

My Old Plantation

I have lived on this little farm ever since I got married. My father bought
this land long ago, and he had this house built here for me and my wife
to live in. So we had a home right from the start. I have kept it up and
I have planted crops here all during these years. I always raise enough
for our own use and sometimes a little to sell for cash, like the canning
beans. I have a big family, so it is no trouble for us to handle an acre
of canning beans. That is what I have planted again this year. I always
raise a lot of chickens because that is one thing that you can always sell
if you need cash. Just the other day my wife and I went to town and sold
three roosters and we got almost three dollars and fifty cents. We have
quite a few chickens left yet, so we could say that we are not broke. We
have plenty of squaw corn so we can make corn bread. We make a lot of
corn bread and sell it all around; this is a good way to make cash money
because everybody will buy good corn bread. We have went out selling
corn bread and made as much as five dollars. I have planted as much
corn as I usually do this year so that I will have corn next winter. In fact
I am all set because I have all my crops planted, but now I must work on
them so that they may not get too weedy.

I do not work out anymore—that is, to work steady—but I did make
a long fence for my neighbor where I and Marshall Denny made nine
dollars apiece. That is all the work I did away from home. I was sick
last year and I did not think I ever would get well the way the doctor
said. He said my blood was sweetening—he called it diabetes—so they
sent me to Madison Hospital, but they did not do anything; they did
not give me any medicine. About all they did was to give me a rest, so
finally I came home and I doctored myself. I knew of a medicine that my
father used to make which has helped many people, but this is more for

women's blood. But I thought if it was my blood that was not right it might help me too. This is a very valuable remedy, and I could not give it away. I went into the woods and picked all plants that goes together to make this. There are twelve different plants which I put in to make this medicine. I took this for about two months. I did take three gallons of this medicine, which made me feel like a new man. I thought I was completely well from this, but now I feel that it's coming back on me, so I will go again this afternoon to get the plants and try to check it before it gets too bad. This same medicine has been used by women who may have got cold during their periods and it has helped them. The doctors do not seem to know just what to do for cases like that, but this medicine is sure to help anyone whose blood is not perfect.

I also have known that it is good for rheumatism. My wife had that in her joints, and it pained so much that we had to go to Seymour to see Dr. Hittner. He told us that it was rheumatism of the blood. He gave her a small bottle of some kind of medicine, but this did not seem to help her, so I went and got some of these plants and made medicine. She used two gallons of this and she got rid of this altogether. I make this and have some on hand all the time, and it can be taken all the time same as water would be taken—that is, it could be taken any time and any amount.

When I was a little younger and my eyes were real good I made a violin. I studied how I could make this for some time and I was sure that I could, so I got me all the things like glue which would hold wood together and I started to carve out the wood for the box or body of the violin. When I had this all made and fitted, I put in the post which would hold the bottom and top of the violin in place; then I put on the sides and the neck which I glued on. I could tell then that it was going to be a good one. I put on the long outstanding neck on which I attached the strings of the violin. I had the tightener on so that when I got the strings on I could tighten the strings as I wanted. I got this gut string which makes the best strings. After I had it all put together I tried it out and I saw that I could tune it just the way I want it. I started to play on it and my brother Isaiah, who was at a neighbor's house about a mile away, said that he could hear me playing, so the sound of this violin seemed to carry a longer ways than other violins. I know that this violin and another one which was bought were played together and one could not hear the other violin. I took this violin to the fair and I got a prize for it. Then one day I thought I would sell it so we took this violin to Green Bay and I asked how much they would give me for it. This was before I had it varnished. I was offered eight dollars for it, but I thought it should be worth more than that, so I did not sell it and I kept it all this time. Someone must have dropped it, which cracked the bottom, so I just glued it together again.

I have also made moonshine while there were moonshine days. I made quite a lot of money because lot of men liked my whiskey. I sold a lot of it every week. It was because I live a little off the road that no one never bothered me. I never went out to sell moonshine. The men who wanted my whiskey would come to my place to get it so that there was hardly anyone else who knew of me selling, and that was why they never bothered me.

This home was given me by my father, but there were never any papers made to that fact and he died without making a will. It was not the custom of the Oneidas to make a will of their property to anyone, so that what property there was would be divided by all members of the family. It seems now that an agreement was made by all our brothers and sisters that we give our brother Joe the right to use and live at the old homestead, and we all signed to that agreement and now it seems that he owns the whole estate. If this is the case he owns my place too. Those papers which we signed were papers made by a lawyer who may have been hired by Joe to avoid telling us that we signed off the whole estate to him. Sometime later Joe came to collect rent from us, so I investigated and that was what I found, so as long as we all signed off and there were so many of us but no one knew of it, we have let it go, but I am making plans by which I could buy this place from the party that has the mortgage. There is a mortgage on the whole estate, and I am sure that Joe will never be able to pay that off, so in time he will lose it all, but if I buy this piece where my house is, and a few acres with it, I will still have the same home. But if I wait until the holder of the mortgage gets the place then I would surely have to pay more for it because he may not want this place taken out of it. Joe could not stop me from buying this piece of land with my house on it.

Well, this shows that people must look out for themselves and never sign anything unless it was to their benefit, but it must be sure that they know what they are signing. This is what I have learned for myself, because I thought that Joe was my brother and that he would not do anything that may not be good for me, but I have found out different. It would not make any difference who it was, whether it's your brother, you must watch out for him so that he would not get a chance to beat you out of everything you have. The land that was allotted to me by the government I sold, and the money I got for it was invested in this place so I would be losing not only my father's property but some of my own. I know that it has been the case with other Oneidas who were beaten by their own relatives. And take men who got good education and were smart: it looked like they should have instructed their people in the better ways of living and protected them from losing their homes, but instead of that they were just the other way, they went and beat everybody that they could.

My neighbor is a white man, but he has ways like the Oneidas. He would joke and make fun of anyone. He always came at nights to talk, so one year he saw that I had a nice field of potatoes but he said there is only one stem in each hill. He said you ought to see my field, it is just full of vines. That fall he dug his potatoes and he got fifty bushels from half an acre; he had all small potatoes. I dug mine and I got forty bushels from quarter of an acre and all mine were big round potatoes, so he wondered where the difference could be. He thought that I must have better ground, but I said no it could not be better than yours. Then I said what time of the month did you plant yours, so he told me and we looked at the calendar and found that he planted his during the new moon period. Then I told him about the way I plant after the full moon. I said when you plant in the new moon you will have lot of vines but hardly any potatoes. And I said when you see the white blossoms of the wild plum trees, you look to see how the moon is; if it's full moon or after full moon you can plant then. I also told him that the best way to cut the seed is to have only one eye in each seed. This makes only one stem, but there are always two or three great big potatoes. So after that he did not make fun of me because I told how to plant to get good crops.

It seems funny that crops should be planted at certain times, but this is true with all crops that yield crops in the ground like potatoes and carrots and onions. But I have always kept this rule also for corn and grain crops. The moon surely has something to do with this just as much as it has something to do with people. My father always took notice of the moon when he was planting crops. If it's new moon he would not plant anything even if it was nice weather for it. I have heard that Oneidas have always kept this rule.

I joined the church they have at Chicago Corners, which is called White's Church of Christ. I did belong to the Methodist church when I got married, and a short time after this the Seventh Day Adventist came to Oneida and started to organize a church and my father was for it at once. Well, we all joined that church although my wife was a Catholic. She had went to school at Keshena so she joined it while she was there, but she always went to the Methodist with me while I belonged there. We belong to this Adventist church for many years, although they do not have a church now. We did not return to the Methodist, so when we came across this man White, he told us how he was starting a new church and he wanted all Oneidas to join. He said he already had quite a number of people, so we decided to join his church. Mr. White is a Sioux Indian and he married on Oneida girl who was a sister to this William "Fat" Skenandore.[11]

The first time we went to his church he was very glad and he spoke good for us. He preached so much and everybody was surprised that he could preach so good. What he said must be true because he read from the Bible. He said that by rights there should be no other, but only the true church, because the Bible says that churches do not need to have names like the Lutheran or Methodist. He said anyone could look all through the Bible but they could not find where it says the churches must have names. This looks to be true, so my wife and I decided to join. He wants all my family to join so that we will all belong to one church. I liked the church because they sing so much in Indian. I like to hear them sing in Indian because they seem to have such nice words.

It seems queer that trees grow so fast now; when I moved on this place these trees were all small and now they are such big trees. If the business of ours would grow so steady and big we would now all be millionaires. But that has been the case with white people. Now that company Sears Roebuck had their fiftieth anniversary last year. That must be that they started business fifty years ago, and see how much they have made in that length of time. Now they have the biggest store in Chicago and they have stores in all of the big cities like Green Bay, and they are all over the country. Now how could a company make so much in fifty years—and look at the Oneidas: they lived here more than one hundred years and they are just as poor as they were when they came here from New York. In fact, I would say they are worse now because when they came here they still had lots of land and plenty of game such as deer and bears and rabbits. But now there is none of them left but we have gotten nowhere. The white men are smart and wise in dealing. They made big deals, and when they make money they save it to buy more things. They must do lot of planning. They sell all their goods for cash; they do not trust out their goods like I did when I was selling moonshine. I trust so many men and I still have money coming from some of them—and they also did not get rich even if they did not pay.

That is the trouble with Oneidas: they never could work together for the benefit of all. Each man wants to be sure that he does not lose anything, and never mind the other fellow. My father used to say that it was always that way. When they had chiefs here the chiefs looked out for themselves and they got all the proceeds that came to Oneidas in all the claims from way back. One of the chiefs built a great big expensive house—they say that the inside of this house had gold trimming on posts and stairways. This is what built from the money he received from some deal or claim the Oneidas had with the government. No one knows how much he received, and he surely kept it all when it should have been divided among the Oneidas. At one time my father was telling of how the government sent farm machinery and all kinds of tools to the Oneidas to be distributed to them by the chiefs. All the chiefs got machinery like binders and mowers and cultivators, and some of this went to the relatives of the chiefs. If a poor man who was not a relative came along he got a hoe or an ax or a corn knife, which may be worth not more than a dollar, but the chiefs and their relatives got over a hundred dollars' worth of machinery each.

The only time this did not happen is now when the New Deal started to give out land to Oneidas. It seemed that it was given to anyone who really wanted it, so they applied for it first. It is going just as the names have been taken down. This is the best it has ever been done. Also, the houses that have been built was according to the way names were handed in: the first one applied for it was the first one for whom the first house was built, and so on down the list. It almost started out like that [the old way], but just at that time they had an election and got another man at the head of it and this stopped right there. The man who was the chairman was going to work that way and everybody caught on to it. He gave land to his brothers and other relatives and built houses for them, but after the election another man was elected for the office of chairman and new directors were elected so everything took a change. The new officers took the list of applicants, the first come, first served. It made no difference if he was related or not. He was given land and a house was started for him. Everyone seems to be satisfied the way things are going. I have been thinking of asking the New Deal to take over my plantation so that I will know that it's safe for my family. But I will see first if I could not buy it from the man who holds the mortgage.

MARY HILL

> Mary Hill's family was one of those that received aid from a New Deal housing program. In this June 25, 1941, interview she told John Skenandore about her current situation as well as a bit about her childhood and youth.

Present-Day Living

I am forty-five years old, and I am just now getting started to live where I could call my home. Both my husband and I were born after the land was allotted to the Oneidas here in Wisconsin, so since our parents died we had been renting around here and there, paying around five dollars a month for house and a little garden. My husband works on wpa and with what money he makes does not meet our everyday expenses, as we had five children to support up to a few days ago. But since three of the oldest children went out to work for wages I have noticed the changes in our expenses.

Early this spring we moved into a little shack we are now allotted on New Deal land. We managed to squeeze into the little place just so we do live in a place we can call our own and stop paying rent. And since the place is so small and the older children wanted to work out and make money I told them to do so, but I will expect ten dollars from each one of you this fall, as the material for a new house we are putting up will have to be part paid and it is a benefit for every one of us. They all agreed and started out, and now that my husband is working on wpa he doesn't get much time to work on the new house. We borrowed $350 to buy the house material, and we are putting it up ourselves.

During the day I am left alone, but I am never lonesome even if the place looks that way. I don't have any time to get lonesome as I am working every day cutting brush. Just the way you see, there is about two acres around the place cleared or thinned out. I did it myself during the day when my husband is gone to work on WPA. People that comes here to see us gives my husband all the credit for my hard labor swinging the ax. Well, he deserves credit right enough as he is a very busy man. Right from his work on WPA he would switch over to his house next and pound away until eight o'clock at night when he can't see the nails very good anymore. I figure that just as soon as he will cover those rafters on the roof I would shingle it during the days, and now in my spare time I spread that pile of boards to dry so that when it is nailed on the wall it won't leave any cracks. I am so very glad to have a place I could call my own that I don't even get tired no matter how much I work. I have planted a few things where we have cut and filled in low places and everything is coming up good so the soil must be good.

The people living around nearby are very good neighbors. They come to see us often and offered us help if we needed. One of the men offered to come over with his team and plow a place for us so we can plant at least a small garden, so we are expecting him anytime. All those things are very encouraging, and I just can't rest until I get this place all fixed up. Most people that come to see us think that we have a lonesome place, but we couldn't be any happier as we are and we are both very interested in our work so we must be going someplace.

A few days ago on Sunday we were surprised by a big company [group] that came to see us, and we had a very jolly afternoon under our many shade trees. And while I was telling the group how far we had to go for water, I said as soon as I get a chance I am going after Thomas Elm to find me where I could dig a well. One of the ladies said, I can find that for you if you will bring me a willow crotch about two feet long. Then I asked the menfolks to go and find one in the woods so we can have some fun. Two of them went, and it took them quite a while before they came back with the willow crotch—I imagine I was too anxious to see this done. Well, this lady is only thirty-seven years old, and neither one of us believed that she could do anything like that. I have heard that some old men are good at that, but I never heard of a woman doing this kind of trick.

She took the crotch end on each limb and held the butt end up in front of her and started to pace off where we thought would be a good place for a well. All at once she stop and said, now it starts, and we measured from the place where she said it started to work to the place when she couldn't hold the butt end up any longer and stopped. And she said, here you will find a water vein if you dig ten feet deep. She tried this from a few different directions to that point where we stuck a stick for a mark, [and] each time she came to that stick the butt end of the crotch would work itself down. Yes, she said, you will find water here in ten feet. Then Oscar Archiquette, one of the menfolks, said, let me try that stunt and see if that will work with me. So they gave him the crotch and he started to pace in the direction where the stick was placed and he never felt the crotch to make any effort to turn down and he walked right past the stake. Now this goes to show that it isn't everybody that can do this, and we watched that lady as she paced along and saw that she tried her best to hold the crotch up but she just couldn't hold it at that point.

We thought that ten feet was kind of deep as we didn't want to put too much time on that for now, so we asked her to try a little further back. And she did the same thing back there, but she told us that she found a place where the water is only five feet from the surface and we drove another stake there. We just couldn't rest until early Monday morning when my husband started to dig on the place where it was supposed to be five feet deep. He dug the hole about four feet across and went down about four and a half feet and struck a vein already. The water came rushing in so fast that I had to help him dig water out, but he just couldn't get down any deeper and the water came up to about two and a half feet from the surface and it is very good water. This is a great help because if we dug the well wherever we think is best we may dig twenty feet and still can't get the water. This way it only took my husband a couple of hours and hit the vein of good water and now we don't have to haul our water from a mile away and we don't have to worry about running out. With the force the water vein has, and all the wood we want for the winter months—and even pheasant and partridges are plentiful in our woods.

Look at my boiler here. [12] Every time I look at that fireplace with the iron kettle hanging there it makes me think of my grandmother about forty years ago. When I was five years old I used to stay with my grandmother a lot. I don't remember today just where the place was. Anyway, she used to bundle up some dirty clothes into a big bag about once a week and go washing. She used to fasten the big bundle of clothes on her back and carry an iron kettle and wooden tub in each hand and walk through the woods to some waterfront where she had a place fixed something like this for boiling the clothes. Only she had a bigger kettle than that.

Well, the reason why I always think of her when I look at my fireplace is because I certainly hated the trip—when she first asked me to come along with her, and she had me carry the big iron kettle for her—which seemed to be so heavy that I just had to stop every little ways and rest up. How she hurried me along when I was overloaded—that is, I tried to make her believe I was; I was just lazy. We finally got there and she told me to pick up dry sticks and start a fire. How I made up my mind to disappear from her and come back home: I made her believe I was gathering dry sticks and kept walking away from the place slowly, and she catch me at it and told me to come back and I just stood in one place and she kept walking closer to me until she thought she could catch me by running after me. So we ran a race but I happen to lose out on the race by tripping myself on sticks so she got a chance to catch me and didn't she ever gave me a good licking and then brought me back to the fireplace and I had to make the fire and dip the water from the pond and she watched me very close after that. I spoil the whole day for myself trying to run away from her.

This also reminds me when my grandmother used to tell me how they used to plant before the land was cleared of trees. She used to tell me that in between trees they used to work up the dirt and plant their corn like that. That is just what I am doing now; every time I see a little dirt scratched up I would plant a hill or so of potatoes and other vegetables.

When we first settled in this woods we just made a little opening big enough to put up our shack in and also put up a little tent for the menfolks to sleep in at nights. I said to my girls, here you have a chance to learn to cut down trees and cut them up into stove wood lengths as you can't never tell what kind of husbands you are going to have. You may have to cut your own wood, so if you learn now it won't be so hard for you.

They were all quite game and helped cut brush and even good-size trees, but they sure leave the stump like a beaver had cut the tree down. What you see thinned out is about two or three acres. I did most of that myself, and that is where I pass my time away during the day, and in the evenings when there are lots of mosquitoes we just set fire to the brush piles and smoke them away, so even the brush helps us in getting a start. It seems discouraging at times to think that we are just now getting a start at our middle age. But after we have paid out so much money for rent and have nothing to show for it, now that we have a chance to get ahead—why we just don't get tired anymore because everything we do now will show. And it will be here forever as we won't have to pay no taxes on this New Deal land and we only have to pay for the material for our new house on a very easy installment plan, which I think we can handle very easily—more so if the children would help in making the payments. We appreciate greatly this chance the New Deal officials gave us and I think this is one good thing the Oneidas did when they organized the New Deal in our settlement, as this gives us poor devils a chance to live in a place we can call our home. Maybe in time we won't have to depend on WPA.

My oldest girl started to work out this spring and the oldest boy is working in Sturgeon Bay and the next oldest boy is working on the farm not far from home. Now if these children got together and help us along on building expenses it won't take long and we would be on a level. I certainly do my share at home every day, and someone has to stay home to do the cooking—but I do lots of work outside of cooking. I even do carpenter and lumberjack work.

In this July 2, 1941, interview with John Skenandore, twenty-eight-year-old Mrs. James Skenandore makes it clear how much she and her husband depend upon the New Deal for their survival. She also gives us one of several accounts of the workings of love magic as well as a vivid picture of a poor family.

Struggling in the Depression

At the present time we are living mostly on WPA wages. My husband is working in a stone quarry getting forty-eight dollars a month, and we have to watch very close and earn all we can get to make ends meet. We have three children to support and are paying five dollars a month on this place, until it is paid, for the material that is used to build up this place. We appreciate a lot getting a chance to own a place this way because if we were to pay cash for a place like this we certainly would never own a home. The New Deal is certainly a good organization for us poor people. Before we got this place we were paying around five dollars per month, but there was no sign of ever owning the place even if we lived on the place for a hundred years. And here we have a new house, a good drilled well, and are paying only five dollars per month, and the principal is getting smaller every payment. We owe about $750, which we think will be paid up in time.

Just now it is hard to make any money on the place because we have no tools and power to work with and the place is full of quack grass. My husband is thinking of getting one horse to start with so he can cultivate his crops with it. We have twenty acres of land and all of it is clear, but since we are only beginners and don't have power to work with as yet we only have eight acres under cultivation this year. We have about five acres of flint corn and half an acre of contract beans and half an acre of cucumbers, and since my husband is working for WPA during the day then I do all I can, weeding and hoeing the crops in my spare moments. I have three grown chickens—two hens and a rooster—and few little chicks, and that is all the domestic animals we have yet, but we figure on doing better in time to come.

I do a lot of canning also—mostly wild fruits: raspberries, blueberries, strawberries, elderberries, black raspberries, and the tame peaches, apples, cherries, and some straw- and raspberries. I also can vegetables like sweet corn. I always get good results by first boiling the corn with cobs for three minutes, then take the corn and cut the kernels off with a sharp knife and fill up your jars and place them in big kettle with covers on loose and than add hot water in the big kettle up to about half an inch from the top of the jars and let boil for three hours. After that take the jars out and tighten your covers; then it is ready to keep as long as you like. This could be done with most vegetables. I can also can different kinds of meat.

I have learned these quite young, as I have started to work out for wages when I was only thirteen years of age to do housework as my parents have a big family. There are thirteen of us children in the family—four boys and the rest of us are girls. My father is only a laborer, so he must have had to scratch to keep us fed and I can't place him as a farmer because he didn't have much cleared land. What little we use to plant is only a garden, and us children had to do all the work on it as he was always working out for someone else.

Mother never preached to us children not to do this and that, and she never worked but made us children do all the housework she had, and she was always on a go and hardly ever home. She was a wild one and father got disgusted with her many times, and at one time he was going to leave us and get a divorce from mother. He had been to court in Appleton for advice and they told him to give her another chance to change, and so from that time on she behaved better and now they are both good Christians.

We belonged to the Methodist church, but lately we are joining up with missionaries that come from Stockbridge, Wisconsin, every Tuesday evenings and hold services from house to house. And sometimes they hold service at my dad's on Sundays. They are really nice people and they don't ask for money like some other churches do and they certainly teach the gospel. We had been going to these meetings nearly every Tuesday, and I certainly hoped that they would open my husband's eyes to do better, as he sure likes to drink every chance he got. I had many tough times in my days since my folks had so many children, and I happen to be one of the oldest ones and mother always want to be on a go, so I had to mother my brothers and sisters and did the housework, washing, baking, making corn bread and also corn soup, when I was only nine years old. At the age of thirteen I was allowed to go out and work for wages and worked around until I got married. I was then twenty-three years old and married a boy eighteen years old. We got along nicely the first couple of years. He worked for a white farmer who furnished us a small house to live in right on the farm and we made a nice living. He gave us one acre of land to plant whatever we please.

One of my sisters was married to a Menominee boy, and we used to wonder how she can put up with him the way he carried on drinking and leaving her home alone at nights, and when he did came back home everything was just fine with her and not a cross word he would hear. The Oneidas got suspicious about this and thought that he had used what they called love medicine on her, but there was nothing we could do to make sure for some time until one day they came back to my father's for a visit and while they were there he got on a big drunk and came back to our place like that, and while he was falling all over we noticed something dropped out of his pocket and mother picked it up. And when he fell to sleep then mother showed us what he had dropped on the floor. It looked like a glass tube, and inside of this tube looked like a small stick on which my sister's hair was wound, and packed in with some kind of stuff which looked like small pieces of crushed rock. I was going to take those things out of the tube and my dad told me not to touch it, as we don't know what effects it would have. But mother just couldn't leave her daughter's hair in it so she open the tube and poured the stuff out and got all of the hair off and then burned the rest of it up.[13]

And once before this same sister took sick. We just couldn't make out what was wrong with her, and the way she suffered was very pitiful. Her husband at that time took something out of his pocket and put a few grains of it on a knife and gave it to her to eat. Soon after she had swallowed the stuff her pain stopped. And mother was very sure that it was the same stuff that was in that glass tube we found later. Anyway, she was never bothered from that same sickness again, and not long after that she left him for good and [it] seems like his control over her was all off. Well, this proved that there is such a thing among the other tribes of Americans outside of Oneidas. I can't say if this kind of stuff is still going on among the Oneidas, but I have heard that it was done.

I married a boy whose parents had a very bad habit of getting drunk, so the boy was naturally more like his parents. And we had to stay with his parents when we were first married. I had to put up with lots of misery as every time they got a hold of a little money and they went out on a big drunk and would come home unruly and start giving my husband drinks and would even offer me to drink and because I didn't drink with them they thought that I was just stuck up and said lots of things about me when they are drunk which they never would say when they are sober. They are very nice to me otherwise—that is, when they are sober—so I toughed it out and finally they got me to drink with them. At first I only took just a little just to satisfy them, and at first they were satisfied with just a little, but as time went on they got me to drink more and more until they finally got me drunk with them. It wasn't that I liked it but just to please them. Well, I finally convinced my husband to move off to another place so that he might slow down on drinking, which he did, and we bought furniture every time we got a little spare money. He still drinks, but he always bought his groceries first so I can't say he is as bad as some which would drink up a full check and not think about their family at home. I am quite sure we will do very nice after we get a good start. Of course right now he has nothing, you might say, to work with, so it is very hard to get anyplace. My husband is a very good worker—if he had something to work with—and he is very nice to the children and me when he is sober, and plays with us like a kid.

I can't speak my own language, but I can understand it very well and I certainly wish I went to those Oneida language classes when they had them. I think I could have learned very easily, as I do understand the language quite well, but my children kept me from going as they were quite small and I could not leave them so I just missed my chance.

Stadler King gave this account of the problems involved in getting relief from the local authorities before the New Deal took on that task. Relief had been the obligation of the federal government through the Bureau of Indian Affairs, but from 1910 Oneida was no longer considered a reservation and the bureau had abandoned most operations and services there. By the early years of the depression the township government of Oneida was largely in the control of whites.

Distribution of Town Relief

Relief in the Town of Oneida was started at the same time that the townships were started, about 1910. I remember the first town board. All the officers were Oneidas. There may have been quite a few white people, but the vote was mostly Oneidas, so they were elected. At these first elections and town meetings the officers spoke in Oneida because there were not many white people. I remember so well when the question of relief came up before the town meeting. The officers understood that they were obliged to give relief to people who are poor and unable to earn their living. I remember the first town chairman, Nelson Metoxen, when he was asked just how poor must a person be to be entitled to town relief. The chairman himself did not know, so he only said that they must be poor. I remember that this caused laughter by all at the gathering. There were two older men as supervisors whose names were James W. Cornelius and Wesley Cornelius. James, after the chairman was done speaking, got up and explained that it is for when a person is sick or unable to work to earn his living, and when he has no close relatives who may be able to help him. This gave a better idea to the people and to the town officials.

This was the beginning of town relief in Oneida. This was thought to be a good system because there were some real old people who could not work anymore, and their relatives were not fixed so they could care for them for any length of time. We heard afterwards that certain old people were getting relief. The Oneida officials did not give much, but the old people could live without depending on other people. Some of them were given to the care of some other people who were paid a certain amount for the care. There were not many of these people at

Working, Earning, and Struggling Through

that time because Oneidas hated to be classed as being supported by the town. As the number of white people were increasing in Oneida, this relief became greater and greater because white people knew the laws and some of them brought old people along when they moved into Oneida. I would not call it relief when at that time there were many new roads that were built and this was done by strong, able-bodied Oneida men. This would be considered as labor. There really was not much relief given to Oneidas in the years between 1910 to about 1920, when the effects of the world war were felt in all parts of the country. Wages were good during that war and a couple years after, [until] the presidential election changed back to a Republican president. I remember that after the election of Harding everything such as labor and circulation of money were just like it froze in one day. Coolidge and Hoover did not better the conditions, so these were the years of much relief from the towns.

The towns themselves were short of funds, and there were times when they were obliged to borrow money from county funds. Farmers did not have money to hire labor, and many construction jobs failed. It was noticeable that almost every other store or shop in Green Bay was vacant, and many windows were used to display advertisements of some big companies. There were no saloons or taverns, which pay the biggest part of revenue to county, state, and federal government. So the whole country was on a downward trend. There were many hobos in what was called jungles along railroad tracks. I saw poor city people in the junkyards looking for shoes and other things that they may be able to use. The worst of these years were when Mr. Hoover had the chair. These were surely hard times, and everybody wanted some relief. The towns did not have money, but they were able to give orders for groceries and paid it later.

It seemed easier for white people to get relief than Oneidas. The towns gave jobs like cutting brush or cutting wood or working on roads to the Oneidas to pay for groceries that they were given. That is, the Oneidas had to work for the relief they got from the town. I remember that the Town of Oneida, when it gave jobs to men who asked for relief, these were such small jobs that one could hardly live on what he was allowed to make. The white people—men like Bill Ness, David Ketchum, and Joe Stick—these men had big families and sure needed relief but they did not have to work at any of these jobs, but they got relief, and more, too, than Oneidas—even though Oneidas had to work for what they got. The chairman in Town of Hobart was John Roels, and Pat Garvey was chair of the Oneida Town board for so many years.

The first time I ever asked for relief was in 1930. I had been working in Green Bay up to the fall of that year. The depression had then started, and I was hurt on the railroad job that I was working on and was laid up. I was getting less and less chances of making a living in the city, so I moved back to Oneida and I did not work anywhere for a month or so until I was just about completely out of money. I went to Pat Garvey and asked him for relief. He said, I will be at your place tomorrow and see you, so the next day he did come. He looked around the room and then began to ask a few questions. He said, you have always worked and this is the first time you ever asked for relief, and you would have been working now if you did not get hurt. I said, yes I would, so he pulled his chair to a table and made out an order for twenty dollars. He said, this will hold you for a while and if you still have no job when this is gone I will give you another order. This was then late in the year and almost Christmas, so I went to the farmers' store and traded. I had so much groceries that I felt I was rich.

It was toward spring in 1931 that I asked for more, and sure enough he kept his promise. He gave me another twenty-dollar order. That spring I went and helped him to get elected because he was my friend and he saved me. That year about planting time I needed seed and other things like plowing, so I goes again to ask, but this time he gave me a job to cut brush for Van Kawenberg at five dollars an acre. I finished two acres when I went to Kawenberg for my pay. This was all [the work] he had because other men had certain strips so we were done. He paid me ten dollars and then I was able to get my plowing done. This was not bad [yet] because men did work for what relief they got. If Pat was alone on the town board things may be better, but there are the supervisors who have much to say about giving out relief. Pat has always been good to certain ones, and some could not get much from him. These supervisors were against giving relief to Oneidas, and they were able to cut down very much on relief.

It was the fall of 1931 and on to 1932 that was the hardest for me, and it was the same with others. The farmers too were so broke that none of them hired men, but I was able to get a job at fifty cents a day and dinner and supper and a small pail of milk a day. The farmers only got fifty cents a hundred for their milk. That was the year they organized what they called a milk pool and they went on strike. They would not sell milk, and some of them made butter and some gave away cans of milk to some people. The farmers stopped anyone who wanted to sell their milk. In spite of the strike some trucks were sent out by big factories to get the milk, but they were stopped by farmer-pickets. They had a big fight near Shawano, so some state guards were sent there with regular guns and tear gas. They put these farmer-pickets in a garage and locked them up. They were kept there about three days on skim milk and crackers.

This same time some Red Cross flour was brought into Oneida and distributed by the chairman of each town. There was a big truckload of flour brought to the parish hall. John Roels had told Father Grant that if he [Roels] did not come on a certain day, Father Grant could give it out, but to take names of those who got it. Both Father Grant and Fred House were rather drunk on that day, so when the time came and John Roels was not there, Father Grant said to Fred give it out. All he did was to unlock the room and everybody helped themselves. I was there and I took one bag to Father Grant's and left it and told him that I will come after it that night. I was only able to take one along home, but I got two bags. When John Roels came, the flour was all gone and no one had records of who got the flour. After this the flour was taken to Joe Kyesik, the town clerk, and then white people began to get this Red Cross flour.

The towns also got things like meat, lard, tea, sugar, coffee, and some other stuff which they gave to both Oneidas and white people. The white people did not seem to care if the Oneidas got it because it was all Red Cross stuff and this was meant for the Oneidas, but when the towns got a hold of it they gave it to both whites and Indians. Pat Garvey also had this flour and it was said that a big load of it, which was supposed to be only for white people, was taken to the farm of one McCormick. A whole lot of this flour was spoiled because it was put in a damp place.

I did not have a permanent residence, so I got flour from Pat Garvey and some from John Roels. Just about this time some clothes were sent out here to each town, so I went to the Town of Oneida and got an army overcoat and other clothes. The next time they gave clothes was at Henry Schmitz in the Town of Hobart, so I went there, too. I got another coat and some yard goods for dresses, towels, army shoes, socks, stockings, and other things. I was not going to be left out. But after everything was given out they found out that some of us had been to both towns, so they made [declared?] permanent residence for some. However, they could not keep families from moving from one town to the other.

There were not so many white families that were poor enough to come under the relief class. Most of the whites had farms and cows so they did not get relief, but there was quite a number of them just the same. Nearly all of the Oneida families were entitled to relief because most of them did not have homes or stock, so they received more relief than the whites. This included the flour, meat, lard, dust tea, coffee, and sugar that the towns had. [14] The meat they had was thin pieces of salt pork; the tea was all dust tea with a picture of a red rooster on the package. This Red Cross flour was fairly good flour, but it seems that it must be made from wheat that was not dried out. But if the flour was kept in a dry place it was fairly good flour. Some of the Oneidas were said to have made inside pants out of the bags because some people saw the pants on the clothesline with the writing "Red Cross" and "Not To Be Sold" still on it.

I was rather lucky to always have a good boss because when it was time for me to go and get this relief, the boss would always volunteer to take me there and back with the groceries and then he would bring me home in the evening with them. This saved me a lot because it would be a load to carry all that home. He would not charge me anything for this. It was during this time in early fall of 1932 that I did not have any wood and no money to buy coal. I went out looking for a place to get wood from. I saw John Houcks who had some wooded lands, so I asked him if there was any way that I could deal with him for some wood. He said yes, but first I want some stump land grubbed out and you can have the stumps and all that you pick up. You can pile them up so you can haul them out before I plow the land and I will also give you some wood to cut afterwards. I will give you a pig—any one of those in the pen—for grubbing three acres. We went and saw the pigs; they were all over two hundred pounds, so I thought either one would be worth fifteen dollars.

I agreed to do the work so I got an ax, shovel, and grub hoe and made a strong pry. Most of the stumps were old and gave way easily. I kept my two boys from school to help me so we could get done quick. It took us nine days to finish it. We then went to his place and told him that we were done. He came with us to see the job. He was satisfied with the work so he says well we will go and butcher the pig you choose.

He had two grown-up boys who helped him catch the one I chose. He was a quick butcher, for in a little while he had the pig hanging there. Then he said I will take it home for you, and you can ride along. He got a small truck and backed it up to the hanging pig. We loaded this on the truck and we jump on. When we got home we hung the pig outside to let it cool off. I put it in a shed after it got cool off and I cut a few slices of real genuine meat. The next day I borrowed a team from Mrs. Ben Doxtator and hauled my stumps and pieces that I had picked up. I made three trips, so this made quite a pile of dry stumps and roots and pieces. Then I went and cut some wood which he had promised me. I was able to get three loads of this, so I had quite a pile of wood.

Well, we had a lot of meat but not much of anything to go with it. My wife went to see Sister Amy and told her how short we were.[15] Sister Amy said I'll see what I can do, so my wife went home. She had just got home when a big truck came and went into our yard; it was Mr. Morgan with a load of old bolts that he did not sell as bolts. He unloaded these bolts and then brought in a big box of groceries. When I came home for supper, while I was still outside I smelled good things to eat, like hot biscuits. She had things on the table like butter, milk, tea, potatoes, sugar, and of course meat. She said Mr. Morgan brought it over on the orders of Sister Amy. She said God will not let us starve.

This then was in the fall of 1932, the year of the presidential election. Mr. Roosevelt was elected, and soon as he took office all banks were closed and no one could get the money out. And then all the gold was called in. There was a limited time given after which any gold that's out would be considered worthless. After this was all settled, banks were opened and the New Deal government came into effect. Relief agencies were established all over the country. Miss Nona Nelson came to Oneida and started the relief agency. This was the end of hard times and of town relief.

4.

The Lives They Led

As with the recollections of the elders, these autobiographical accounts cover a wide range of experiences. There is a woman who served as a nurse overseas during World War I, and a thirty-year-old farmworker who could speak no English. There is a former professional boxer, a musician who once toured with Gene Autry, and a man with one leg who "ran away" from boarding school in Oklahoma. Others speak about school, their families, and growing up, and one woman speculates about the soul. What they share is a willingness to speak frankly of the events of their lives and of their feelings.

This autobiography was originally written in the Oneida language in May 1940 and translated into English. Oscar Archiquette was energetic, outspoken, a noted orator, and an enthusiastic advocate for the use of the Oneida language. He successfully pursued the compilation, transliteration, and publication of a hymnal in the Oneida language as well as a translation of his father's diary (1869–74). He served for a while as the timekeeper for the project and was prominent in Oneida politics, serving in various elected posts, including tribal chairman and vice-chairman. After World War II he lived in Milwaukee and worked as a mason.

Autobiography

I will start to tell you about myself from the time I was born. The building near the big stone house known as the hospital is where I was born in the year 1901, at the time when raspberry blossoms, June 15.

My father was Captain John Archiquette. His parents were Martines Archiquette and Phoebe (Hoynost) Archiquette. Both came from Oneida Castle, New York. My mother was Christine (Hill) Summers Archiquette, and her parents were Jacob Hill (chief) and Sarah Cornelius Hill, who was also a daughter of a chief. These people I mentioned all believed in Christianity and they were members of the Episcopal church. My father volunteered in the Civil War of 1861 when he was fourteen years old. [1] My mother worked in the house; she was of the Mud Turtle clan.

Our living was through my father getting a pension for being an ex-soldier, and he also planted and was captain of the Indian police force here where we live, so that was another way he got money for our living.

About 1903 my father built another house. Our house is located about two miles south of the big stone church. Our house is a log house, but it is fixed up like a white man's house. It is twenty-four feet wide and thirty feet long and two stories high and there are lightning rods on it. There are four rooms and a cellar.

Our farm is ninety acres, and there is about sixty acres under cultivation. The apple orchard is about three acres. There is also a barn, granary, well, and shade trees. The whole farm is fenced. We had all kinds of farm machinery and we had horses. We usually have about eight head of cattle and pigs, chickens, dogs, rats, and mice. There were four of us from my father's second marriage. There are two of us living.

I was about two or three years old when I started to remember. I remember well when my mother was scrubbing the kitchen floor and she tied me to her back while she was scrubbing. I was five years old when I was of some use such as to go after thread or something else. I was seven years old when I started—or tried—to milk a cow. I was eight years old when I could milk a cow. Father paid me three cents every time I milked one cow, so when I got to be a good milker he paid me less.

I would run away when I saw a white man coming. The reason why I was afraid of them is that I used to hear conversation about how bad the white people were and that they kidnap children. At that time I did not know one English word.

Once in a while Julius Summers would come and visit for one week, and he used to help me feed the stock. When we got through we would play. We usually played in the barn. We would climb up somewhere in the barn and then jump down on the hay. I had lots of friends. These are their names: Robert Luther Hill, Ellen Hill, Wilfred Webster, Abbie Dora Webster, Albert John (deceased), John Webster, Cora Webster, Grace Swamp, Albert Swamp, Rose Swamp, Guy Metoxen, Rose Baird, Mariam Hill, Gilbert Metoxen, Lambert Metoxen, Louis Elm (deceased), and two Stockbridge girls (their names were Doxtator), and one family of white kids by the name of Deboth. We played all kinds of games. They were hide-and-seek, tag, drop the handkerchief, the farmer in the dell, London Bridge is falling down, "button, button," blindfold, croquet, fox and geese, and baseball. In the wintertime we would skate and coast downhill with a sleigh and jump in the snowbanks. [2]

As long as I remember my father always prayed just before meals, and every Sunday he would go to church. He taught us lots about religion—which is to believe in Jesus and his laws. And about the forbidden things: not to steal, not to be liar, and not to hurt other people; not to commit adultery, never to take God's name in vain, and to be true to your word. These commandments I have heard since I was a little boy. And the laws of the land he told us about in order that it might help us as long as we live, and that is not to drink, cheat, and not to lie. To think of the future and see just how you are going to live. He used to say "use head work" and be careful with your money and always try to have a little on hand, and to take good care of what you might have.

My mother was also very interested in me—to learn what is good. She did not go to church very often, but she often read the Indian Bible, which is written in the Mohawk language. One time I did something wrong and my mother caught me and she started to whip me. Just then her skirt dropped down and she could not help but laugh, so she couldn't give me a good whipping.

Finally I wanted to go with my father to church, so my mother got me ready and to my surprise mother started to wash my face and that was one act that I hated. She had a hard time to wash my face every time father and I went to church. That is the time when I started to learn how to read the first reader. Phoebe (Elm) Webster and Lilly (Elm) John taught me how to read. They worked for us. By the time I started to go to school I knew how to read. I was nine years old when I enrolled in the Oneida Indian Mission School [Episcopal]. Mabel Thorn, daughter of Reverend Father Thorn, was the teacher. There were many of us attending the school. All those things worked together to keep me busy— going to school, going to church, working, and playing.

My work was to feed the cattle and milk them twice a day. I started to drive a team out in the field with a spike-toothed harrow, and from that time on I kept on learning how to work. One thing I learned rather fast was to obey. That was one thing about my father; when he said anything he meant it. He never told me more than twice to do something. If he did then I would be yelling, "ouch, ouch" from a whipping.

I was twelve years old when I first plowed with a walking plow, and I was now really interested in my work, or I might say I enjoyed the work I done.

One time I wanted to sell logs at Seymour, so I went and started to saw away on a great big piss elm tree. I was thirteen years old then and it took me about four days to cut it, but when I did the tree did not go down. The tree was three feet in diameter on the stump. About three days after, my father went and saw the elm tree I had cut. He went around the tree and saw that it was cut through, so he started back for home. He had walked just a little ways when he heard noise and he looked back and to his surprise he saw the big elm tree fall over and it just missed him.

At this time I became an altar boy in church and my schoolwork come easy for me—especially arithmetic. I was fourteen years old when my father gave me the responsibility of managing the farm. I was able to work as much as a grown man. When there was anything about farming, father and I always discussed it and found out what was best to do.

I was at this age when I started to chew tobacco and also started to like girls—I mean their looks—and I didn't have anything to do with women. I suppose my father noticed that I started to like girls. I was surprised when he said, "You go to West De Pere and buy yourself a suit at Risdon's store." It was just what I wanted. The big or important days of the year when father took his whole family were New Year's, Easter, Memorial Day, Bishop's Day, Thanksgiving, Fourth of July, circus, fair, Christmas, and to the moving-picture show in Green Bay. My parents were pretty old then. My father was born in 1847 and my mother was born in 1865.

I got a notion to go to school elsewhere. I made it hard for my parents, but they consented for me to go to Flandreau Indian School in South Dakota. I was fifteen years old when I went. When I was leaving I shook hands with my parents, and that was the first time I was kissed by a female. I let my mother kiss me good-bye. It was in September 1916 when we left. I got in the coach here at Oneida, on the Green Bay and Western, at 7:30 a.m. We ate dinner at Winona, Minnesota, and sometime after dinner we went on. While we were going on I saw stacks of oats and perhaps wheat. This was in Minnesota. Some places I saw forty stacks of grain in one group. They planted corn as high as forty acres of it. Finally we landed in Flandreau. I was surprised to see so many different tribes there. I was busy all the time seeing things I had never seen before. All of a sudden I heard a bugle which meant for us to line up for supper, and then we marched to the dining hall and kept time to the sound of a snare drum as we marched.

The next day I was put in the fourth grade, class B. Then I started to go to school. I got lonesome, and sometimes I would be by myself somewhere crying. On top of it I got a boil on my face, and that made it worse for me. Finally I got over the boil, and then I was troubled with my tonsils and I got lonesome again. I wrote to my father and told him I was lonesome and I would rather go home. I got an answer in about four days, and father said, "If you want to come home I will see about it." By that time I was not even thinking of home anymore as I was enjoying myself by playing ball and other games. There were good-looking Indian girls, and if you look at a girl and she smiles it means that she is one of your girls. It was not long before I had several girls. On Sunday at dinner the girls would send over their pie to their boyfriend. I used to get several pies and biscuits, and that made me happy. By the time we came out of the dining room I would have a big belly on me from eating all the pies and biscuits. Every now and then I would get a letter with a dollar bill in it from father.

My life in school was the same as at home; that is, I was going to school, playing, working, and going to church on Sundays. There was a very good chance to learn a trade because the school had the following: farming, dairy, gardening, shop, carpenter shop, blacksmith shop, shoe shop, harness shop, printing shop, tailor shop, mason work, firing, steam engineering, and paint shop. Recreation is the band, dancing, and games; during the winter it is skating and a game something like golf. It is played with a ball and clubs.

Our living quarters are in a big building where there are over one hundred rooms. There are three to four boys in each room, and they are subject to keep the room clean every morning just before we go to school or work. We would go to school for four hours and work half a day. We had to brush our teeth every day and take a bath on Saturdays and change our underwear. During the winter every morning we would have to drill like soldiers.

I specialized in steam engineering and firing steam boilers and to play a tenor saxophone. I was enjoying school life. I was in the fifth grade, and I was the best in arithmetic in my class. I was sorry when I left, and I had to leave before vacation time on account of the war abroad; father needed my help in the fields.

In 1917 any man could volunteer for the war, so the Indian schoolboys enlisted. Father got a letter from the superintendent of Flandreau school asking for my parents' consent for me to enlist. Father said, "No; I know what it is to be a soldier." I was fifteen years old then. I came home in May 1917 and started to work out in the field in the same afternoon.[3]

My mother was sickly, and she was that way all summer. When it was time for me to go back to school my mother was worse, so it was decided for me not to go back. It wasn't very long when my mother died in Green Bay hospital. We had a wake for three nights for mother according to our custom. The early part of the evening there were speeches by different Indians about religion. The speakers alternate with the Indian singers, and at midnight lunch is prepared for them to eat.

The Bible is translated into the Mohawk language, and from this spelling the Oneidas wrote Indian songs or hymns, which they sing at a wake. When the speakers get through just the singing takes place until just about daylight or dawn. Then we buried my mother. I was sixteen years old then. My sister cooked for us until May 29, 1919, when father died. There were lots of people that came to father's burial. He was well respected by all—I suppose because he was so true to his church and also true with his people.

By 1920 I was on the bum. My brother took over the farm. I was twenty-one years old when I first got drunk. I worked on a highway job, and from it I learned to set steel forms for concrete and to read blueprints, and I also learned to operate different kinds of road machinery. I got one dollar an hour for my work. I was making good money, and after a while I would get drunk every chance I got and I lost interest in girls. Whiskey got the best of me. I was never running away from a girl on account of her getting an illegitimate child. I suppose it was because I was a drunkard and homely looking.

In the wintertime I would work up north in the lumber camps, cutting trees of all kinds. Going from one place to another one was hard for me as I was not used to being on the bum. In 1924 I went to Oklahoma. It wasn't very long before I got a job setting forms in Keystone, Oklahoma. I set forms for three months, and then I was promoted to grade foreman. I was well liked because I was a good worker and I really worked hard.

I noticed the difference about women there. The first thing I know I had a white girl. The girls were not bashful, and most of them were good looking. My drinking did not bother them, nor my looks. I had an automobile in which I used to take my girl out for a ride. One time we were out riding and I asked her if she and I could have some fun. She said, "Have you any disease?" It did not take me very long to say "No," so we went to it. We liked it so well that her and I were just about breathing in a little while. Finally I had several white girls.

In 1927 I went to Texas, and there I became the general foreman. I boarded with a German lady who had two daughters. Finally one of them fell in love with me, and after a while she got so she wouldn't eat until I ate. One morning I woke up and there she was kissing me. Her mother was very nice to me and I suppose she figured on me marrying her daughter, so one time the old lady said, "You two go after lumber that I bought which is about fifteen miles from here." The girl and I hooked up the mules and we started after the lumber. I suppose the old lady had formed this plan to get her daughter and I out by ourselves. On the way the girl kept asking me all kinds of questions and also asked me what kind of songs I liked. I told her and to my surprise she sang it every little while and then she told me she had ninety acres of land and one hundred head of horses roaming.

When we were coming back she said, "Chief, will you marry me?" I said, "I don't know; I haven't anything and you have property." She said, "Whatever I've got, I will put it in your name and then will start raising chickens." So I said, "You wait as I have to go back to Wisconsin because I loaned my brother one hundred dollars and he will be of age soon at which time he will get one thousand dollars." I was not thinking of getting married anyway, and it seemed to me Texas was a long ways for me to get married there and I live in Wisconsin. Finally we got back home. I suppose the old lady was anxious to know just how her daughter came out with her marriage question. I did not know that these German women wanted me to marry the daughter.

Every night we would play checkers, so this night we played checkers until the two women were asleep. Then I said, "Let's sit out on the porch." We did and then I asked her to have intercourse with me. She said, "I am afraid you might got me in the family way." I said, "I'll watch out for that." She said, "Can you?" I said, "Yes," and there is no ending to other promises I made so she consented and I wanted it bad. We just moved around a little bit and I got the tickling sensation and my girl started to breathe fast so just when the fun started I quit right there. The next evening she came into my bedroom and laid with me 'til midnight; then she went back to her room. This took place for some time. One evening I came back home drunk and we went to bed, so when I felt the tickling sensation coming on I just held her closer. I did not know that it was just what she wanted because she wanted me to marry her. It was several days after before she said to me, "You've got me in the family way." I said, "Just put your foot in hot water." It was a few days from that time when she told me the hot water was no good. I still did not realize that she wanted to hook me. I said, "Give me some money and I will buy some stuff at the drugstore for you to use." She gave me the money. I had made a bargain with a white man before this time that I would come back with him to Oklahoma, so that was when I left to buy some medicine.

I found my brother in Oklahoma, and we bummed our way back to Green Bay on August 20, 1928. My brother drew over $1,200 and he paid me back the $150 I had loaned him. From 1929 to 1931 I worked in Milwaukee as a form setter getting one dollar an hour, but it did not do me any good as my money was going for whiskey which is made by the white man.

In 1931 I went to Sturgeon Bay, and that is where I got hooked again and this time I couldn't get to buy medicine. That is the time I married my wife—at the time when Colonel Lindbergh's son was kidnapped in 1932. I thought maybe we will die of starvation since I doubled partners because I had a hard enough time to live while I was single. That is the time when I started to live right. What I mean is I had plenty to eat and always changed clothes once a week.

I was the first Indian to become a foreman on the WPA in 1934. About two years later I was demoted; I did it myself because I shook a WPA official by the collar. In 1937 I was foreman again; this time we were cover mapping for the state of Wisconsin. I lost this job too because I got drunk and I did not report for work. In 1938 I worked on WPA again as a stone mason for a while and then we went on a stone crushing project; then I got a job as a stone driller. On February 6, 1939, I was transferred to the Oneida language project. Mr. Swadesh started this project, and it is carried on by Floyd Lounsbury. His Indian name is Adˆná•tsle [Lunch]. He is very ugly, but what keeps him down is that he knows us Indians scalp a person if they make us mad. It is through the intelligence of white men and the first-class training by Mr. Adˆná•tsle that I am able to write my own language.

When I got married I started to attend the church again where I went when I was a boy. I always asked Jesus to give me power to do away with bad things and to get even a little religion in my head. I hold religion above all things on earth.

William Metoxen also worked on the Oneida Ethnological Study for a while. This autobiographical sketch gives an account of his experiences in schools, including the Haskell Institute, as well as his days as an athlete and his various attempts to make a living. His wife, Evangeline Wheelock Metoxen, whom he met at Haskell, was elected and served as treasurer and then clerk for Oneida Township from 1942 to 1953 (McLester 1988:119–120).

My Life History

I was born on May 10, 1896, on the reservation where my parents were allotted. We lived in a log house built by my father when they first settled, a two-room house, one downstairs room about eighteen by twenty-four feet and one room upstairs where we slept.

My father cleared some land for the meadow and cornfield. We had two dairy cows. Mother used to make butter with the churn; she would have a little to sell. Also had a team of horses which father used to haul cordwood and pulpwood to Kaukauna [to sell] for our clothing and food. I remember well how us kids would wait for Dad to come home from town expecting to get some candy; sometimes he would bring one big box of crackers. That was a treat for us. He used to pay ninety cents per box, and that was one of those large boxes.

My parents used to raise pigs. They had them fenced in with rail fence, and one day my sister and I were going after my father, who was working in the field, but we cut across the lot into this pasture where the pigs were, and one of the large boar pigs took after us. We ran but were not able to run fast enough. The boar caught us, knocked us down, and started to chew on my sister's leg, and every time I would get up to run he would just knock me over again. Then finally Dad heard us crying and he came running over to where we were with his whip and chased the pigs away. If he had not heard us that would have been the end of one of us. It seems like the hogs were more wild those days than today. These pigs were fenced in the red oak grove, and they used to eat the acorns in the fall. Kept about twenty in that grove—about eight acres. Dad would kill one every time we are out of meat. That kept the wolf away. There were eight children in our family, and it took lots to supply us with food and clothing as those days there were no such a thing as town help or relief, so our folks had to make our own living by what they can sell.

Mother used to make baskets to sell to the market; that also went for groceries. There is quite a lot of work to make these baskets. One can complete about six baskets per day and get maybe fifteen cents each.

My great sport was to fish and hunt rabbits every time I got a chance. I would run to the creek and catch a few fish; that makes a real meal for us. And in the winter I would snare rabbits with a light wire, but the owl always got ahead of me in the morning to eat some of the rabbits, mostly the head and inwards.

About this time we got a new neighbor. They were white people, Seventh Day Adventist people; kept their Sundays on Saturday. Well I got acquainted with them, only we had one trouble—I didn't know how to talk English. But in time I learned a little so I could say a few words. They had a little girl about my age, I being about seven years old about that time. We used to play together just like brother and sister. Finally I knew a few words. She used to teach me until I was able to talk with her. We were playmates then.

The people started a school at their house so I went to their school to learn the ABC. I used to think it was so hard to remember the different letters. This little school turned out to be a boarding school, so there were now about twelve boys and girls going to that school and we used to play games in the evenings. Most of the children were Indians that belong to that church. I never joined the church but kept my own Sundays. In the winter we used to play a game in the snow, called fox and geese. That was a great game in those days.

From there I went to the boarding school. There I was punished many times for talking Indian language. There we were taught to make our own beds, roll our clothing just so, so that in case of a fire you can just grab the bundle and beat it. We also had to scrub on our hands and knees. They showed us how to keep the rooms clean and to take a bath once a week. Our clothing was furnished by the government. The larger boys did the farmwork and took care of the milk cows. They had instructors to teach them to farm and how to take care of dairy cows. The girls there were taught to cook and bake bread.

I never forgot the first stage play we had. I was chosen to be a king, and a girl was chosen to be a queen. How hard it was for me to memorize the little verse I had to say when the curtains on the stage were raised. I just forgot my verse that quick, and my queen had to tell me what to say. We were both dressed in snow white with crowns on our heads. We had rehearsal nearly one month; still I forgot mine by being stage frightened seeing all the people in front of us.

Our pastime game there was marbles. We would make a ring on the ground and each put in ten marbles, then try to knock the marbles out of the ring by snapping one marble with your thumb. Some were real good at the game, and each good player always carried all the marbles in his pocket, showing that he was a good player. I remember how our hands were chapped; we didn't like to wash our hands. Sometimes the teacher would send us back to the building to wash. How it used to hurt, but the orders were to wash.

One day I had a little fight with one of the boys. It happened that I got the best of him, but I had in store one good whipping from the matron. I didn't like that idea so one afternoon I ran away from school. I walked all the way home—it was about nine miles to go. The policeman was there twice after me, but I always jumped in bed when I saw him coming and made believe I was sick. That went well. So I stayed home. Then I next went to the day school. This school was about one mile from home; there was about twenty children going to that school. This school was also run by the government. It was located up on the hill, and in the winter we used to go sliding with our handmade sleighs every noon hour and during recess.

There was one big day for us kids to go out in the winter, and that was the old custom on New Year's Day. [4] We would bunch up and go *Hoyan*. That was, we would go to every house and say "*Hoyan*." That calls for something. The people would give pie, apple, or cake, or whatever they had that was sweet. We would carry small logs. This was an all-day affair, and we would be all tired out in the evening when we came home.

My father used to tell us about the way they used to go out New Year's Day. It seems like on the reservation the Indians were divided in two classes, about half on the south side and half on the north. He said that the kids would meet about noon somewhere and they would start fistfights and all the stuff that they had would be lying all over the snow. Finally they would stop fighting and go home, some with black eyes.

Well, I stayed at home that year. We were now living in a six-room frame house. My father had some logs sawed at the mill for lumber to build this house. One of the Oneidas had a sawmill of his own, and he did all the sawing for the Oneidas to build their houses and barns with. He also used to buy logs from them. I used to enjoy going along with Dad to the sawmill and watch the men work rolling the log to the sawyer. Then the logs would go forward and back, taking slabs of board and sending it to another department for trimming to the size we want. We used to bring the lumber home and pile it in a three-corner pile to let it dry. We were now trying to get enough lumber for a barn.

This was in the fall of 1909, and I went to school at the Tomah Indian School [in Tomah, Wisconsin]. This was the first time that I was away from home that far. I remember how lonesome I was to get into a strange country. I was thirteen years old. There we had to get up by the bugle call in the morning and we had to learn to drill. There were two companies, A and B—about forty-eight in each company—and one band. I belonged to A company. I didn't know how to drill, and one Sunday afternoon we were drilling and the captain gave the command of "squad left" and I was number four on the squad. I turned my squad right and got the company all mixed up. The captain came over to me and gave me a bat on my face. I got a nosebleed but kept right on drilling. How I would have [liked] revenge but had to take it.

I worked in the dairy barn when I first went there. I had to milk cows. We used to get up at 5 a.m. to get to the milking, and had to be through before breakfast. Then from there I was transferred to the bakery where we used to set dough in the large tubs—about five of them—in the evening. Then at 4 a.m. we made the dough and about 9 a.m. we would rework it and then put it into pans, then after it raised, bake them. We had to keep the floor just as clean as we can, scrubbing on our hands and knees to keep the floor white. I worked there about three months and then was transferred to office boy. I had to keep the disciplinarian's office clean. I used to take the little kids to clean the lawn, and on Thursdays I would take orders from the different departments. Whatever they need they had to order. On Friday and Saturday, at the warehouse I would weigh everything to be delivered to the different places. Soap, rice, potatoes, sugar, syrup, flour, yeast, prunes, salt were some of the things to be delivered. I used to get the mail at eleven o'clock every day and take some to the girls' building and to the boys' building—letters from their homes.

There were over 250 students going to school there. I never forgot one time two boys were punished. They had to wear girls' clothes coming into the dining room; after we were all seated they would come in all by themselves. How we laughed at them: one would be crying and the other laughing.

We used to steal corn from the farmer and then parch the corn in the woods. We would fill our pockets up to eat. One night a mouse got into my pocket and ate the corn and also chewed my pocket up; made a big hole in it.

The school used to have a football team, and we used to enjoy watching the game when they would play home games. Also a basketball team, and they had winning teams in both. They had socials every other Friday night for the older children. Sometimes dance music was furnished by the school orchestra. We would pass the evening away that way.

One fall on Sunday four of us was going to run away from school, so we started walking to town called Tunnel City. We got within a few miles from there, then got cold feet so we started back. But the officers at the school didn't know what we was up too so we didn't get punished. We told them that we were lost in the woods, and our story passed. Some of the students used to go home every spring after the school closed and I didn't know if my folks would send for me, but when the names was called who was going home I was one of the lucky ones to go also. Talk about surprised—I was. Came home on train and then I didn't go back to school that year. I had to help my folks at home that summer. I went to day school in the winter. I had to walk four miles every day to school.

There were lots of changes in the reservation. The roads was laid on section lines, while before they had just trails, and wherever it was muddy they had brush on the road.[5] It used to make the buggy rock up and down when you drove over it. But now they had wooden culverts made when the roads was muddy to let the water pass; and the roads was graded up so if there was any water to pass that it would run on the side of the road. Also my folks had improved their home, had built a barn thirty by forty and they had gaslights installed in the house. We had now eight milking cows and mother made butter to sell to the market every week, from thirty to forty pounds per week. They made enough to buy the groceries. Timber was already too scarce to sell, so most of them depended on cows to live off.

The community used to have socials to raise money to build a bridge across Duck Creek. By this time they had raised enough to build one. The labor was furnished by the men who all donated. This bridge was built with planks and large timber across. Otherwise it was awful hard to cross; in the spring when the water was too high [it] was impossible to cross.

The older Oneidas were great people to get together on some project, like when they want anything built they just estimate what it would cost, then start to have parties and socials. The ladies would get together to furnish the eats. They would have supper somewhere in the community, charge so much to eat, and if anything is left over the leader would auction it off. Sometimes they would clear seventy-five dollars or more.

In the fall of 1912 I went back to school, this time at Haskell Institute, Kansas. It was nearly a real military school. There we were taught to drill with guns. We had to drill before school every day, sometimes three times a day. The student officers were respected same as in the army. There were over eight hundred boys and girls going to school—all Indians from about sixty-three different tribes. We got up by the bugle calls, and whatever we had to do was all to bugle calls. To go and drill was called by bugle, etc. They had six companies of boys; each company would have forty-eight boys. We also had one large band. These companies were divided into two battalions. We would have dress parade every Sunday afternoon, and the people from town used to come over to watch the parade. We wore uniforms, all blue, and the officers had white stripes showing the different staff they belong to.

The school was a place where you could take any trade, besides studies, like mason, carpenter, shoemaker, harness maker, wagon maker, blacksmith, painter, dairyman, farmer, electrician, printer, and drafting and blue printing. They sent you to school half a day and half a day you work at your trade. The course was from grade school to business course. We all slept in the dormitory for our sleeping quarter—about thirty beds in each dormitory. The buildings were three story high, all made of stone.

I took the carpenter trade, which was very interesting. We used to make chairs, tables, cabinets, and frames, and once a week I would take drafting and woodworking. That's where we draw the work we are supposed to make at the shop.

My first experience in carpentry came one day when my instructor told me and another student to put a porch on one of the cottages. So we went, not knowing how we were to start. He sent us five two-by-ten planks. Well, we figure it up and finally we laid the plan. It was alright, and then we nailed the flooring on next, but it was fun to figure everything.

I must tell a little about this school. It is located two miles south of Lawrence, Kansas. The streetcar used to turn around right at the school grounds. It contains a thousand acres, all under cultivation. The school buildings were up on the hill and the farming land was on low land. The farmers raised nearly all the vegetables for the school. The dairymen used to milk forty Guernsey cows. The school had about forty cottages for the employees, all located on the school grounds. The girls learn to sew, cooking, and domestic arts and science.

The school had a wonderful football team in 1912. They played twelve games and only lost one—by the score of 7 and 6; that was to Nebraska University. The students used to get together before each game to give the school yells. That would pep up the game and the team. We used to take long walks to Breezedale and Woodland Park. At the park they have what was called "jackrabbit" ("roller coaster" is the right name). We would ride that until we are sick. It cost a nickel to ride. On Sunday we would go to Sunday School, then to church in town, and to chapel in the afternoon, then YMCA in the evening (the girls to YWCA), besides dress parade at 4:30. On Sunday we were kept busy all day.

Every spring in June we would have competition drill by six companies to see who has the best company in drilling and manual of arms. There would be three officers from West Point for judges, and the grades used to run from 94 to 99 points perfect. The winning company would have a banquet furnished by the school, and the officers would each get a saber with their names carved on it. The school also used to have societies.[6] The boys had Lincoln, Webster, and Invincible and the girls S.A.B. and Montezuma. We had these meetings every Friday. We used to send a scout to one of the societies, and he would report to us at the next meeting. We had debates against the other societies and lots of other activities. Then at the end of the year we would invite the girls to a big feast. Then they would in turn invite us to their feast. We would make some blind dates with the girls and never know who a partner was until you see her with the same ribbon on as you have on your coat.

We used to a have YMCA stag party where the boys would think of some tricks to play on the new members. One time there was one bushel basket full of apples [that] was supposed to be thrown in the middle of a gym where everybody was lined up. The lights were turned off at the same time and everybody grab all the apples he could and when the lights were turned on again these apples were potatoes and everybody had potatoes.

In June the school closed for the summer and I was lucky enough to go out to Mayetta, Kansas, where my cousin lived, and on the way we saw Topeka, the state capital. There in Mayetta nearly everybody rode saddle horse. I remember the first time I rode six miles and thought I would die I was so tired. But in time I got used to it. We used to ride ten to twenty miles a day and didn't get tired. I well remember that first time I rode a bronco bucking horse; I thought my stomach would turn inside out. The boys thought they would die laughing at me, but I stayed on.

During the summer in July I used to hear the tom-tom from the Indians out there every evening. I would hear it just like if it was only a mile from the place, but one evening we started to go to see the dance and we rode for ten miles and didn't get there. We met some going home and they said it was all over now so we had to turn back. It must have been about twelve miles. I was disappointed, for I wanted to see how they dance the powwow dance.

This cousin I stayed with, they had four boys about from twelve to eighteen years old and we got along just fine all summer. Only one time in August one of their dogs went mad or got hydrophobia [rabies] and he bit one of the boys and the boy had to be sent to Kansas City for treatment. But it turned out alright. The dog was killed, and his head was sent to Kansas City for examination.

The weather was so warm that year that we used to cultivate corn in the night. The moon would be so bright that night was just like daytime. One day there was a picnic in Circleville, Kansas, so we went down to the picnic. There was a baseball game between a traveling team composed of all Negroes that played against the Circleville city team. Luck was that a pitcher was back for a few days from the National League, visiting his folks. Well, they had hired him to pitch against the Negro team. It seems like it was impossible to hit him. Sometimes he would let them fill the bases, then strike out the next three batters. This was my first experience seeing a good pitcher. After each inning when the pitcher would walk towards the bench the people would throw money at his bench. It was a day that was enjoyed by us.

In the fall I went back to school. About this time my room was just across from the disciplinarian. There was seven of us rooming together. One night two of the boys ran away to town for some eats. We had collected some money together when they came back about eleven o'clock at night; then we ate the lunch, and when we got through eating we were not sleepy anymore. The lights was out so we got to playing, throwing our pillows at each other. Then all at once the lights went on and the disciplinarian rushed into our room. We made believe we were asleep, but that didn't help. He made us get up and get our guns and we went out and he made us drill for one hour. We were sure tired then. At the end of the hour he asked us if we thought we could sleep now. We told him yes so he let us go to bed. I was than made sergeant in Company D and got a different room. There was only three of us that roomed together, in another building.

At the carpenter trade we would tear out the old buildings and then rebuild them into a later model; that was learning the trade by experience. One night about 11:30 I woke up; it was raining and there was a big fire in our carpenter shop. About this time the bell rang and everybody had to get out of bed and get into their respective company, then call roll to see if anybody was missing. Only Company A were excused because they were suppose help the fire department. They had called the city fire department by then. At that time they use only a team of horses to pull the engine and hose. I remember this was a two-mile run, and when the horses got there they were all tired out; they made it in five minutes. But one had very hard luck. The electric wire was lying on the ground and one of the horses got electrocuted and died right there. I saw that when it happened the horse made one jump and fell over dead. The other one was alright, but one of the men, when he took a hold of the lines was shocked enough that he also fell. But he was lucky enough that it was just a light shock. Our carpenter shop was badly damaged, but they got the fire out. But there was lots of work cleaning and repairing the shop. Nobody seems to know how the fire started.

Towards spring now I put my application to go out working in the summer. I was lucky; in June I got a job on the farms. The people I work for were very fine. They took me in just like their own son. I received twenty-seven dollars per month, of which two-thirds of the money was sent back to the school and one-third I used.[7] They had 260 acres, nearly all under cultivation. Everything went fine until silo-filling time. The cornstalks there was about ten to twelve feet in height—to load on the wagon after it was cut green was a man killer, but I stood it. They raised my wages to $1.50 per day while filling silo. This lasted three weeks.

This man that I work for had seven horses, and when I first went there he told me that was all I had to do was to take care of the horses, so I did. He told me to feed them just the way I wanted to. The first thing I did was to curry them twice a day; they had long hair. In a month time he didn't know his own horses—shiny and lively as can be.

They raised mostly alfalfa hay we used to cut four times a year or season. We had a cornfield and on one end of the field there was a peach orchard and in June when I was cultivating corn the peaches were dead ripe. I sure used to eat my share. They could never even just let them spoil out there on the ground.

One day my boss and I were in the haymow and found a hen's nest, nearly three dozen eggs in it, so we filled our pockets up and started down the stepladder. I was ahead of him when I got down on the ground. I looked up at him and saw his hip pocket full of eggs; it was too tempting. I just hauled off and hit him where the eggs was, then ran. He came down and started chasing me at the same time he was throwing eggs at me until finally he hit me right back of the ear. It splashed all over my neck; we were even then. If his mother ever catched us for what we were doing she would have murdered us as she was a real miser for eggs.

Where I worked was only six miles to school, and on Saturday he used to take me back. Sunday I would visit the school friends. He also had one saddle horse which I used to use anytime I wanted. I used to visit the young people around the neighborhood where I got acquainted. There used to be lots of coyotes, and during the hot weather I used to sleep outside on a hammock. It used to give me the chills when the coyotes would be howling right by the house. They used to try and steal chicken or young pigs, but around there we never missed any.

In the fall I went back to school. I had saved up ninety-three dollars in the bank, and that was the first time I had any money while in school. That lasted me all winter, and I bought a new suit of clothes.

I went in for drafting and tracing in manual training. I drew up the plan for a new domestic science building for the girls. It took me three month besides my studies in school to complete the drawing. I had to have the four different elevations and all the specifications of the house.

It was interesting all the way through. Then everything was blueprinted. The carpenters started to build some cottages that could be taken apart in sections and bolted together, that were to be sent to other Indian schools for the employees to live in. They also started building sleeping porches, as we were getting too crowded in the old buildings. At this time they enrolled about one thousand students.

In the spring during the baseball season we had a game between Oklahoma Indians and Haskell. We won, so in the evening after supper they had a social for them and the band was supposed to give a concert. The band boys didn't like that, so they went on strike. So they took all the band boys to jail and kept them there until they had to apologize for what they did. Finally they did and were turned out again.

In the spring of 1915 they had floods all over. The railroads were just about tied up, and that was the year I was supposed to come home. Well, it was June when I was supposed to go. I packed up all my clothing in the trunk. I didn't know if I would ever get home, as when I went on the train some of the places were flooded up to the second steps of the coaches. Some of the station platform was under two foot of water. The train would just about be moving water over the tracks. Seen lots of farmhouses standing in the water up to the window; some buildings washed away. Well, finally we got to Kansas City, and from there it was all night riding. Didn't see anything until we got to Chicago, where there were so much changes made in three years. When I went the first time we rode on the transfer by hack-drawn horses from one depot to the other; now we came down in the basement of the Union Depot and you walk upstairs to change trains—Santa Fe to Northwestern. I waited from 5 a.m. until 10 a.m. for the Northwestern, then came back to De Pere, our hometown. I wrote home telling my folks what time to meet me, but I was ahead of the letter. So I had to walk home about ten miles, surprise the folks at home.

Being away three years, there were quite a few changes made all over. Better roads were laid; the woods was pretty well all cleared off. They had more land to work on. My parents were now in the dairy business, milking ten cows and selling milk to the cheese factory. We now had five horses, two teams of working horses and one colt. So they were really farming. My brother was staying home helping with the farm while I was away. They had by now about thirty-five acres under cultivation and raised corn, grain, and hay for the cattle.

A few things I learned while in Kansas was how to plant corn, although the weather was lots different. When I left Kansas the corn was three foot high, and here the corn was just coming through the ground and some were just planting. I learned that when the corn is first planted one can drag the whole field. That can be kept up once each week until the corn is about three inches high; then there would be no weeds to hoe. Otherwise we used to hoe the whole field before. That saved lots of time and the corn grew much better. Some of the older Indians saw me dragging our cornfield and told me that I would destroy the crop, but I told them that where I work the last three years I always did that. Well, that was quite an experience for them. In the fall the field was better than any one of my neighbors'. From then on the rest tried the same method with the same good results, and that saved lots of hoeing by hand. After dragging is done the riding cultivator is used until the corn is three feet high, then left alone.

They were making new roads here and there, so I had a job with my team working on the road. We kept one team on the farm and the other on the road, working. My father had bought farm machinery by this time, such as grain binder, hay mower, rake, cultivator, plow, harrow, disc. I worked at home all summer until fall. I had a job in Detroit, Michigan, in the Maxwell Motor Company, so I went to work there. This was in 1915. I worked as a drill press machinist, and that same fall I played football on the factory team. We used to work half a day, every day, then practiced football in the afternoon—and got our pay just the same. Then I was promoted to inspector in the stockroom.

We traveled all over playing semipro football; I played right end. I remember one game in Pontiac, Michigan. We were playing for 40 and 60 percent of the gate receipt, and I was the lucky one to catch a long delayed pass to make the only touchdown, the score being 7 to 0 in our favor. That was a great day for me. It was the Thanksgiving game. We had a big feast for supper that time.

The most interesting place to go in Detroit was Belle Isle. It is an amusement park with a zoo connected—a very beautiful place to visit. It's an island by itself, and one has to go on a bridge to get to there. They have all kinds of animals and flowers of all kinds. In the summer it is always cool there; they have band concerts there in the evenings, and the amusements are roller skating, roller coaster, and many other things—nearly like the carnival. They got a place where you can walk inside for hours looking at the flowers from all over the country; the climate in each room was just the same as where the flowers grew. Also there you can find all kinds of fish in the place called the aquarium. That was also very interesting to visit and the most beautiful place to see.

I used to get lost nearly every time I went to the city, for the longest time, before I got used to the streets. One time I took the streetcar back from the city and I didn't hear the conductor call my street, so I stayed in until the end of line. They were going to take the car into the barn for the night—that was about one o'clock at night—so I had to get out and then walk about three miles to my rooming house; it was nearly 3 a.m. before I got back. After that I kept my ears open for my street.

In the winter I took up boxing, basketball, and physical training in the evenings. That was to keep in shape. In the spring of 1917 I came home. It was rainy in Detroit when I left, and when I got home there was about three- and four-feet-deep snow around here. I came home because of the draft. I was going to be twenty-one in June of that year, so I thought it was better to register at home. In June of that year my brother and I were called to register at Kaukauna, took our examinations, and both passed for the army. We were in class I. Then in July my class was reclassified in III. My brother went on July 22 to Camp Taylor, Kentucky. We first had a family reunion at home, had a big feast supposed to be for the last time together—which was true as he died in the service. That left me to help my parents, as they were pretty old by now, so I stayed home to farm.

On Sundays I used to play baseball. We had a team composed of all Oneidas. One summer we played thirty games and only lost four. We had a winning team. We used to draw a good-size crowd every game, and in the winter we used to play basketball. We also had a good team about this time in the fall of 1920. I was hired to play football on the De Pere city team. We used to play every Sunday. We played thirteen games that year and won thirteen. This was the American Legion team. The last game on December 2 we were supposed to play the Green Bay Packers, but on account of the bad freezing weather we canceled the game.

We had three working horses and a colt about this time, and we bought a car. The roads was still bad for cars, but every year we would do some road work, hauling gravel on the road. It was hard to go anywhere after a rain. We were now citizens; we had to pay taxes on personal property and on real estate every year, so we used to do road work to pay the personal property tax.

Our pastime at this time was roller skating at Epworth Hall every Friday night, and dances at Oneida on Sundays. There is where all the young people would enjoy the evening. The fall of 1921 I got into a traveling basketball team. We had our headquarters at Plymouth, Wisconsin. I left early to join, as we were supposed to practice about a month before the season starts. Our hotel bills were paid by the manager, so I stayed there. I hired a man to look over the cattle at home. We used to practice every day until the season opened. Our first game was Sheboygan, Wisconsin. They had 2,200 people to see the game: we lost by the score of 19–23. Then a game with Plymouth and we also lost, 19–20. The games were all close but always interesting. Well, we traveled all over the state meeting all the big teams and drew a good-size crowd. This team of ours carried six men and was composed of Indians from different tribes, all from Wisconsin. We were playing nearly every night except Sundays. They always had a dance or roller skating after each game. That way we got acquainted quite well wherever we went. This team I played for were all from six foot tall and up. We wore orange jerseys with green trimming.

In February I came home but kept right on playing here and there. I would get hired to play in different towns until spring; then I stayed home again. On Fourth of July evening at the dance I met the girl that I married later. We played a baseball doubleheader on that day—one game in the morning and one in the afternoon—at Oneida, where our ball field was, and they had stands all over. A real Fourth of July celebration for the Oneidas. We won both games that day.

I will have to go back to 1920. In August at De Pere the Oneida Indians celebrated the one hundred years since Oneidas came to Wisconsin. We had doings like the olden days, like when they first settled in Wisconsin, such as making baskets, making corn bread, men making ax handles. Anyway, they had all the old ways and it lasted for three days. I remember well. I had a horse or pony that raced at the fair or centennial. Well, we young men each had a pony, about ten in all, and these three days we had horseback races. I got quite a thrill as my pony won first place. This pony I had was an Arabian horse, spotted bay and white, a very pretty horse. I had a new saddle and bridle with red-, white-, and blue-ribbon trimming. One does not realize how thrilled you could be if you own a horse that would win in a race. I had a rider, so I was able to be at the grandstand when the race started and when they finished. I was standing on the top of my seat. It was a close race because my horse got a poor start. She was too lively. When the starter gave the signal to start my horse just stood up on her hind legs until the rest were about twenty feet ahead before she started. But as they went around the track she gained and would pass one horse, then another, until they came on the home stretch. Then she took the outside track and passed all the rest. She was about fifteen to twenty feet ahead when they went by the line. It seems like I forgot there was anybody around about that time—I was so excited.

The Oneida baseball team played every day in the morning. We played against other tribes of Indians—the Chippewa and Menominees. At four o'clock in the afternoon, the long-distance runner—his name was Tall Feather—challenged any four men to run against him for four miles. He would run all the distance alone, and they would change the ones that would run against him every mile. Well, Friday the runners from Green Bay tried and were beaten; then the Menominees tried on Saturday but couldn't make it. So on Sunday we challenged him, four baseball boys. I started the first mile and made it and then the others took the rest, one mile each, and we beat him. We got one hundred dollars for winning. We had people come from all over to see the centennial. A large-size crowd attended every day.

Back to 1922. In the summer I went with my girl steady now. In the first part of July, after the Fourth, she went to the cherry orchard. I went there once to see her. She used to have a chum that she thought was my girl because I used to treat them both the same so they really didn't know which was which. But every time I would invite one I would take them both. In September I went to the cranberry marsh in Wisconsin Rapids to work. They were paying good wages there.

I made good [money] then, but the season only lasted about three weeks. That following fall she took the civil service examination for a government job and she got a position as clerk in Pipestone, Minnesota. She worked for one year, then the superintendent of the school also offered me a job as head farmer there, but I had to turn it down because I was taking care of my parents. So that following spring she came home and June 27, 1923, we were married.

We lived with my parents for two years. Then I bought a house and moved it on the farm so we lived by ourselves. Then I did the farmwork. The income on the little farm of fifty-six acres was so small that I had to work out part-time for the two families. Finally in 1926 I got a job in Menasha Paper Mill, so I hired my brother-in-law to run the farm. I worked there until 1929 when the depression came on. We were only able to work two days a week, so I thought it was best to move back on the farm. By this time we had three children. I always kept about nine or ten cows, and by this time the milk was only sixty-eight cents per hundred. That was discouraging for farming. Even the weather was so dry that some years we could hardly raise enough feed for the cattle, but I stayed with it.

When land was not worth hardly anything I managed to buy a two-acre lot with a house on it which cost only $175, paid by the month. I rented the house for about two years, and when I had the place paid for then my folks had a chance to sell the farm. I told them to sell it, which they did; then they bought one acre with a house on it and a well. There they lived and I moved on my two acres. We would raise potatoes and garden. The rest of the time I worked out on some farm by the day. We had hard going trying to make ends meet.

In the spring of 1934 I thought I would try and run for public office as town treasurer. There was four of us then—three white men and I, the only Indian. I won the election by seventeen votes. That helped me, with the little salary I got, to get along a little better. I always kept one cow on my place for making butter and milk for the children. Every year we would fix up our house a little.

We try to educate our children. They always start school when only five years old. The district schoolhouse is just one mile from our place. I know how it is when you are held back from school by your parents; that is one reason why I didn't have much schooling. So I always said I am going to try and educate my children so when they go out into this world by themselves they can always find some kind of a job.

This district school has a little story by itself. When it was first built, I was the district clerk and Joel Cornelius was treasurer. There was mostly Indians going to school; the white children there were going to Catholic school. Therefore the white people didn't want us to build a new schoolhouse. They thought the old one that was there was plenty good enough for the Indians, as there were not enough Indian taxpayers in our district to help much. But we thought that our children were just as good as any other children, so we Indians in our district stuck together on this plan. We had lots of trouble, but we were just a little ahead of everything. I wrote to the state about our troubles and the condition of the old schoolhouse, and they in turn sent an inspector to our district. Well, he condemned our old school and gave us one year to build a new one; otherwise our state aid would be taken away from us and [they would] raise everything on taxes in this district for maintaining it. We were just lucky that we had a majority of Indians in our district so that when we had a meeting—well, we had it our way and we had our new schoolhouse built. It is a two-room school although they only use one room, but in time we will need both rooms, as the Adventists will soon close their school and about twenty children goes to that school.

We borrowed the money from the bank, and in a year we got the loan from the State Trust Fund in a fifteen-year installment plan. It cost about nine thousand dollars at that time, as materials was high then. There was always a little friction in this district between the Protestants and the Catholics at that time when we built the schoolhouse. There was more Protestants there. But this grudge finally wore away; we now agree in nearly everything that is suggested at the school meetings.

We built a kitchen to our house and also made a cellar sixteen by fourteen feet as our family is getting larger so we had to have more room. About this time nearly all the Oneidas have sold their land on this end of the reservation. I am about the only one left in this corner. The road where I live is now turned into county highway, so the roads are open all year round. In 1938 I started to work on the WPA, having a hard time to live on what little I can earn, and that helped us along very much as I have six children now and our income is very small. I have one girl going to high school, and the expense is much higher now.

The government has stepped in to help the Oneida start building houses, and they in turn have years to pay the government back. Also a relief unit has been added in the community to help us with the groceries and commodities. All these things help us so much to keep from not having enough to eat. I have been in town office that many years now and I know nearly everybody in the town and I get along just fine with the white people as well as the Oneidas.

We always have neighbor gatherings maybe once a week just to past the time away and play games such as Chinese checkers—mostly young people in our neighborhood. And our kids would give parties, such as birthday parties, every so often. My neighbors here are all white people, we being the only Indians. We get along just fine, and my children get along with the neighbors' kids. The only thing that is hard around here is the water. We have no well and have to haul all the water.

There is a new electric power line that came through by our place, and we got our house wired up so we now have electric lights in the house. We are to pay four dollars per month for three years, then after three years we pay by the kilowatts we use.

This Sunday afternoon the Methodist church choir went to the insane institute to sing for the poor people that are in there. It's a pitiful sight, although they came to the hall where we sang and behaved well. Still, I was wondering whether one would get the spell or not. We sang there for one hour and then went to see some of the worse ones. It is something one does not forget for years. Our choir goes to the sanatorium to sing once in a while also. We have choir practice every Friday evenings. Sometimes we broadcast at the Green Bay St. Norbert station. I never forget the first time my wife and I broadcast. When I got to the mike for our song I had forgotten the tune of our song. I stood there a little while, and then I remembered the tune so we sang our part. The choir generally visits other churches to sing because the people want to hear how the Indians sing. We always add two or three Indian songs with our program; that is what most people want to hear.

This fall my wife and I made a trip up north to Ashland, Wisconsin, where my sister lives, to hunt deer. It is great deer country right on the reservation. I was allowed to hunt. The people there can kill anything all year round. The first day we looked over the country—this was before the season opened—so we will know where is the best place to hunt. I found out that it is very hilly country, ravines all over, and there is thirty-five miles of timber and brushland where we are supposed to hunt. Well, the next day the season was open and we were at the starting point by daylight. There were eight in our bunch. Two of the sharpshooters went ahead to a place where the deer were supposed to cross and we went in the woods to drive. The first day was Saturday and no luck. So on Sunday before daylight my brother-in-law and I went alone at 9 a.m. We got two deer. I stayed and he went after for help to get the deer out of the woods and to the road. By noon we had the two deer at the car. That was a big day's work for us.

The next day I went alone. This was on Monday, and I was in the woods nearly all day, until three o'clock. I was standing on a runway, and all at once a great big buck jumped about fifty yards away from where I was standing.[8] He started to run up a hill, and I took good aim and shot him and got him. Just broke his back, but that was enough to down him. Well, I got some help and took him to the car, and that was the end of my season there. Took him back to the house, and my wife and I left for home. When we hunt we always stay at my sister's house and eat doe meat all the time. That meat is better than the buck meat, so we always eat all we want while we are there.

I also went there once for duck hunting. That was fun—right in the rice fields, and plenty ducks too. We always go in a boat with a little gasoline motor attached on the back, which travels very fast. I got seven ducks in four hours the first day, until it rained and we had to leave for home.

I always like to go rabbit hunting in the fall; that is my sport. We always go up to Shawano, Wisconsin. The fellow I hunt with has rabbit hounds, and all you got to do is stand somewhere and let the dogs drive the rabbits. We always get about ten every trip, in just over a day.

I am going back to 1933 when I first went deer hunting. Well, money was not plentiful at that time, so after I got my shells and license I only had $2.60 left for my trip. My partner said that I didn't even need that much, so I took his word for it. We packed our food together—enough for one week supply. He bought a four-dollar Model T Ford truck. We took blankets, filled the tank full of gas, and carried five gallons extra. He said that would be enough to bring us back. We started for Argonne, Wisconsin, about 135 miles north. I bought the gas with the rest of my money and only had sixty cents left. When we got there he drove right in the woods where we were supposed to hunt. We located ourselves about two miles from the highway. This was Sunday afternoon.

Well, he said, now we will build our log house. We got the logs together but could not build that day, so there was a little roofing-paper house by where we were building. We fix that up to sleep for the night— no door on it. We cooked supper and made our bed. About eleven o'clock at night I heard wolves; they kept coming closer and closer. Finally it seems like they were right by the door. About that time my hair was standing up scared, but we kept lantern lights burning. I suppose they saw the light but they went away again, but I'll never forget that.

The next day we made our log house, ten by eight, very small one. We was all finished by the afternoon. Then we cut wood to last the season. It was a cold house, but we were tough by now. And there we settled for the night. Tuesday was the opening date for deer season. Well, that evening, Monday, I saw the first buck right by our log house but could not shoot it because the season was not open yet, but I thought, I'll get you tomorrow. And the next morning I was at that spot before daylight but was disappointed—my buck was not there. So I started walking to look for another one. Along about eleven o'clock there I saw another one but was a little excited. I shot three times and could not down him; he kept right on going. But I saw blood all along the way where he went, until I heard four more shots; I said, there goes my deer. So I went back to our house, disappointed a little.

After dinner I went in another direction, in the swampland. About three that afternoon I saw another buck; this one gave me a little more time. I took one shot and he was out of sight, so I went where he went, to about two hundred feet from where I had shot him, and there he was lying dead—my first buck. Well, we fixed him up and drag him back to our shanty and hung him to a tree. Went back and my partner shot another just as we entered the swamp. But we could not get him that evening, so early the next morning we took the track again for nearly half a mile; there he laid dead. And there was another man there trying to put the tag on our deer, but he didn't know how so we just told him that was our deer and took it.

Well we left on Thursday morning, Thanksgiving Day. We ran out of gas about forty miles from there and only had sixty cents left, so we bought gas with that. Took us as far as a place called Lilly. There we got trusted for five gallons and at Shawano got used oil to take us back home. We got home with my first buck when my parents were eating Thanksgiving dinner at noon.

In the fall of 1938 my wife and I took another trip to Odanah, Wisconsin, about three hundred miles. We went after my sister to help with the housework as my mother was sick. We went down to Wisconsin Rapids where I used to rake cranberries. I showed my wife that country; it is all swampland there. Then went to the place called Castle Hills and on the way we saw lots of CCC [Civilian Conservation Corps] camps along the highway. We got there and found my sister home. So we . . . stayed two days, then came home. I was working now in the Robert Murphy quarry, a timekeeper on a double crew. I worked there all winter until spring. Then our project was finished so we were transferred to Kaukauna, on a dam. I worked in Kaukauna as a pipe fitter. The following winter my mother died; she was eighty-seven years old.

We had quite an excitement one day at the dam. Somebody got drowned there and so they closed all the locks on the river to try and find the body. When the water was drained one fellow worker there saw a great big muskellunge fish so he chased it until he caught it, but there were so many game wardens there that he could not get away with the fish. The man was taken to jail for killing fish out of season. The muskie was forty-two inches long, but this man was let go without any fine. And they also found the body that day. There was a hundred-dollar reward for finding the body, and the crew from the boat found it.

While I was working at the dam I learned quite a bit about pipe fitting. The boss there was a pipe fitter all his lifetime, so he was my instructor. I used to repair the jackhammer, take it apart and clean it, put new parts in it. On the project we used twelve hammers. They used to run twenty-four hours, six hours to a shift. They are starting to put a new electric plant there. The lights are going to be for the city of Kaukauna and the paper mills.

At the present time I think our downfall is the cars. Everybody has cars, and the expenses on the car just about take half of the wages. The gas is too high for running purpose, and it seems like one has to have a car because the jobs are too far away from home. I know for my part I drove sixty miles a day for one whole year before I was transferred back to the closer project; getting $2.88 per day is not much to clear driving that distance. It seem like I never can pay up my groceries; the prices is too high and the wages too low. I now have two children going to high school and three in the day school. The expense for clothing and groceries just about cleans me up of all the earnings I can make, but I will still educate my children. I hope someday that they may realize how much I had to sacrifice for them while I was sending them to school. In 1940, this spring, I bought some more land joining my two acres, sixteen acres, which would make one [piece of] eighteen acres by my place. On contract I am raising three acres of oats and one acre beans and corn; the rest is pasture for my two cows. I also have ten acres that my wife inherited with a house on it. I have a renter on this place. I had to make new fences on my place all around. What I need is a well now; I hope soon I can have one drilled, as I want to milk about four cows to help with my expenses so I can catch up with the bills. I have to build

1. The family of John Quincy Adams outside the Episcopal Church of the Holy Apostles, ca. 1910. Courtesy Wisconsin Historical Society, Whi-25835.

2. Classroom at the Oneida Indian Boarding School. The girl at blackboard on right is Cora Elm Sinnard; on left is Amy Skenandore. Courtesy Wisconsin Historical Society, Whi-25836.

3. Oneida students at Hampton Institute in Virginia. Josephine Hill Webster and Hyson Doxtator are in back row, sixth and seventh from right. Courtesy Oneida Nation Museum, vs76.81.

4. Oneida Welcome Society Choir. Courtesy Milwaukee Public Museum, 405815.

5. Oneida National Cornet Band. Tom Elm is second from left in the front row. Courtesy Milwaukee Public Museum, A621-2L.

6. Oneida professional football team, 1901. Johnny House holds the ball. Courtesy Oneida Nation Museum, VS76.134.

7. Writers on the Oneida Language and Folklore Project. *From left: David Skenandore*, Floyd Lounsbury (supervisor), Lester Skenandore, *Stadler King*, Alex Metoxen, Louis Webster, *Dennison Hill*, *Guy Elm*, *Andrew Beechtree*, *Ida Blackhawk*, *Oscar Archiquette*, Rachel Smith Miller, *John Skenandore*, *Tillie Baird* (names of those who also worked on the second project are italicized). Courtesy Milwaukee Public Museum, 5061.

8. Stadler King writing in a project notebook. Courtesy Betty Skenandore.

9. (*Top left*) Ida Blackhawk. Courtesy
Milwaukee Public Museum, 5145.

10. (*Top right*) John Skenandore. Courtesy
Milwaukee Public Museum, 5222.

11. (*Left*) Guy Elm. Courtesy Milwaukee
Public Museum, 5159.

12. (Right) Andrew Beechtree. Courtesy
Milwaukee Public Museum, 5083.

13. (*Top left*) Oscar Archiquette. Courtesy Milwaukee Public Museum, 5082.

14. (*Top right*) Tillie Baird. Courtesy Milwaukee Public Museum, 5199.

15. (*Left*) Harry Basehart, supervisor of the Oneida Ethnological Study. Courtesy Maxwell Museum of Anthropology, University of New Mexico.

16. (*Top left*) Ida Baird and Hannah Cornelius. Courtesy Milwaukee Public Museum, 5096.

17. (*Top right*) Mark Powless. Courtesy Milwaukee Public Museum, 5072.

18. (*Right*) Tom Elm with Mrs. Elm and his cornet. Courtesy Milwaukee Public Museum, 5140.

19. Dixon and Jane Skenandore.
Courtesy Cinderella Koepke.

a small barn on this place. If I had one hundred laying hens and four cows then I will get out of debts in two years. Some trouble with my youngest boy: he got burned on his neck and infection set in. We had to take him to the hospital; he stayed two weeks—another setback on my debts—but he is alright again, healthy as before.

Well, this spring I went in again as treasurer for the seventh year. That helps me to pay off my bills and debts on the land. I got 260 bushels of oats from my five acres; sold 200 and kept 60 for my feed for cows and chickens; 200 bushels of corn, also contract beans, cleared about a hundred dollars on one acre. But I had hard luck with my potatoes that nearly all drowned. At the present time I have three cows, a tractor, some machinery, but still no well. I hope I can have one drilled soon. This about ends my life history to date. I am still working on WPA. I hope someday I can be self-supporting on my little place, but it will be a few years yet.

CLARA WEBSTER

Clara Webster, age fifty-five, gave this genial account of her life to Ida Blackhawk in August 1941. This is the second part of an interview that began in another book, but that book has yet to been found. She lived for some years in Milwaukee and was the mother of William Webster, a professional boxer, whose own account appears later in this chapter.

Growing Up

There is nothing for a returned student to do on the reservation but to help on the farm, so I stayed home all summer and helped my mother. There were a few parties held at different homes for the young people during the summer. It was usually given in the evening, and the young people played games, etc., for amusement. A light refreshment was usually served at eleven o'clock. The parents usually gave the party to celebrate the return of their daughter or son from school. The social center at that time was the mission. They gave parties frequently for the young people, but usually the parents went too. There were no taverns or saloons on the reservation, and it was considered common ["cheap"] for a girl or woman to go in a tavern. Women that frequented taverns were not considered respectable, so the women were very particular about going in a tavern. The Oneidas who belonged to the church was restricted from dancing, so the young people did not dare to be seen at a dance. A few years later, however, the young people started to dance, and after the parish hall was completed the bishop gave his permission to use the hall for dinners, parties, picnics, wedding receptions, tribal meetings, and for dances. The bishop made a rule that the hall be closed at eleven o'clock at night. Since then the young Oneidas have been attending the dances, and the old people no longer considered dancing as a terrible sin.

After I was home three or four months, I started to work in De Pere as a housemaid. I worked there all winter, until I got sick. Then I had to quit and go home. After I felt better I started to work for the Sisters of the Holy Nativity. I worked for the sisters until I got married.

I was married on October 10, 1906, to William I. Webster. Immediately after we were married we went to Lac du Flambeau, Wisconsin. My husband was working in the government sawmill there. We stayed there one year; then we came back to Oneida and settled on my husband's two-and-a-half-acre allotment. He built a frame house, and before it was completed we moved in. We sold my land, and we bought a team and started to farm. My husband cleared several acres of land in a year. In the summertime he worked at the Larson farm besides planting some garden stuff on our land. We had two hens and a rooster to start with, and one day both of the hens disappeared and we thought they got lost in the woods or someone stole them, but one day they both came back, and one had twenty little chicks and the other had twelve. My father gave me a cow, and we bought a pig.

We seemed to get along fine, but I was lonesome, staying home alone all day in the woods, although we had our little boy to look after. We stayed there about four years, then we decided to sell out and move to Green Bay. It seemed as though my husband made more money working out than on the farm. After we moved to Green Bay we found out that our living expenses was much more, but we continued to live in town. I liked it better than living in the woods. After we had six children, and my husband had joined the longshoreman union and was getting a dollar an hour when he worked, he still had a hard time making our expenses. When our children were old enough to go to school we sent them to

Tomah, Wisconsin, an Indian boarding school. That helped us a lot.

We had white neighbors, and there was one little white boy who used to come to play with our little children. We used to always talk Oneida to our children, so they spoke Oneida fluently but could understand English a little. My husband said, "Let them play with the white boy, so they will learn how to speak English." One day he overheard them talking, and to his surprise the white boy had learned to speak Oneida. After the children started to go to school with white children they soon forgot the Oneida language altogether. They understand some, but they cannot speak Oneida.

We lived twelve years in Green Bay, then one winter we went to Milwaukee to look for work. Our children were all in school, so we both worked. I got employed in a hospital, and my husband found work in a foundry. We had our household goods moved to Milwaukee, and we rented a house and had all the children home for the summer. In the fall the girls went back to Tomah, but one of the boys started to work, and one attended the high school in Milwaukee. My husband started to work for the city of Milwaukee as a common laborer, and he is still working there.

When the saloons closed our white neighbors started to make home brew. They showed us how to make beer and wine. They invited us to their house parties, and they served either beer or wine. In that way I learned to like both beer and wine. At this time there were lot of Oneidas and other tribes in Milwaukee. The Indians started to give either wine or beer parties. The people that came to the party brought the beer and wine they drank. Sometimes they played cards and sometimes they danced quadrille. Most of the Oneida women in Milwaukee started to drink. When the taverns were opened up again they went in the taverns and drank at the bar same as the white women, and no one complained about it.

My husband has been working for the city about seventeen years. We were able to take care of ourselves during the depression, although he worked shorter hours at times and got small checks. My husband gets $120 per month. Both of my sons were laid off from steady employment, and they have been making their home with us. Both of my sons have been injured in accidents, so they were both rejected in the army. One of my sons was a lightweight boxer before he got hurt.

When I was a girl, if we made any money we gave the money to our parents, and if we worked at home we never expected to get paid for what we did. Nowadays children demand their pay if they do any little work at home, and if they made any money away from home they spent their money as they please. I think the children are better off today than when I was a child. We hardly ever went to town when we were small, and we never cared to go unless we knew that there was a circus in town. We did not seem to care to play with other children. I guess there were so many of us that we were company to each other. I know my grandmother used to take me home sometimes, but in a few days I would want to go home. We were happy, although we did not have everything we wanted. I know I used to appreciate if I got a new pair of shoes. I used to like to hear my shoes squeak. I thought it was a sign that it was a good pair of shoes. When my mother bought some dress goods, I used to ask her to cut my dress and make it right away. It did not take long for my mother to make a dress, although she sewed by hand. My mother was always busy, but she hardly took care of the baby. All she did was nurse it and bathe it, and my sister and I took care of the baby.

We always had one or two cows, and in the summer they always milked outside by the fence. We used to take a cup and drank some milk as soon as they milked, and I guess that was the reason we were all healthy and strong. Only one died in infancy. It died of whooping cough. As I recall we were never sick unless there was an epidemic of chicken pox or measles, etc. My mother used to give us castor oil if we seemed dull, and if we have a cold she gave us some essence of peppermint with sugar and water. We never had sores of any kind, and we did not know what lice was until we went to school. My mother used to see to it that we bathed at least once a week. She used to have Friday night for bath night. She bathed the little children and put them to bed as soon as she was through. She had to heat the water for us all, and it must have been a job, but my mother was a quick worker. She did most of her sewing in the evening by lamplight; I often wondered how she even did so much work.

She certainly was glad when she got a sewing machine. I was about seven years old. I remember that my sister and I used to sew on the machine every chance we got. One day we broke the needle and we did not know how to put the new needle in and we had put it in crooked, and my mother noticed that we had been meddling with the machine when she was not home. She decided to let us stitch on the machine when she could help us. She was surprised to find out that we already knew how to stitch, and my sister could even use the attachments. After that we did all the hemming and straight seams for my mother. After a while all she had to do was to cut out our dresses and our sisters' dresses, and we did the sewing. My mother used to cut out our dresses without a pattern. Sometimes she took an old dress for a pattern.

One time the Oneida farmers took contracts with the Larson Company to plant peas for their factory. At that time they hired help to take the pods off the vine. My mother took eight of us to pick peas. The smallest one was three years old. I don't quite remember how much we got for a bushel of peas in pods, but anyway at the end of the week my mother drew the biggest check of all the pickers. We made quite a lot of money that summer. Sometimes my father would pick peas with us.

In 1905 the Oneida got their first payment from their Kansas claim. The government paid them ninety-five dollars a head. There were eight of us under age, and my father got our money. He got a check of $950. For years he had been planning to build a larger house, as we were crowded in our log house. Every winter he would cut his hardwood timber and haul them to Joe Smith's and had the logs sawed into lumber. So with the $950 he was able to build an eight-room house. In that way we all got some benefit from our money. We certainly were happy to have such a good home. I think we all appreciated the comfort we got whenever we came home. The house burned down about fourteen years ago. My father had $1,500 fire insurance on the house, so he was able to rebuild another house immediately. When my father died he was still on his farm and had no debts to amount to anything and left a will for his survivors. There were seven of us left, the others having died before him. Two of my brothers had an accidental death, and my oldest brother died of dropsy.[9]

My father and mother wanted us all to take advantage of the education that the government extended to the Indians, so they sent us all away to school when we were old enough to go. One of my sisters and one brother graduated from the Hampton Institute, Virginia; one sister graduated from Haskell Institute, Kansas; another sister was graduated from Carlisle Indian School, Pennsylvania, and later from the Episcopal Hospital in Philadelphia, Pennsylvania. She was an army nurse during the last world war and was overseas for eighteen months. She is now in Chicago, Illinois, doing private nursing. She is not very well and was a patient at the Veterans Hospital in Hines, Illinois, during the winter.

My father and mother were both conscientious church workers. They helped build the stone church as most of them did who belonged to the Episcopal church. They were very active members of the church. My father served on the vestry for about thirty years, and my mother was in the church auxiliary and was the president for a number of years. She made a good president, and the auxiliary never went in debt while she was president. At that time the church vestry and the women's auxiliary worked together, and when they gave a dinner everybody came and they used to make at least a hundred dollars or more. When they have a church bee they both went and stayed all day. It used to be a social event as well, for the women visited while they cooked for the men, and at noon hour the men sat around and different ones made speeches. The old Oneidas were good orators; they advised and encouraged the people to help the church. My husband's grandfather was a Methodist preacher, and everyone knew that he really was a good man, but for some reason my husband never took any interest in church work. We hardly ever go to church, and after we moved away from Oneida we never went to church. We sent our children to Sunday school, but we stayed home. My husband always says that ministers are doing that kind of work because they want to make easy money. I like to go to church, but I believe that God will hear a prayer even if a person prays in prison or wherever one is. My children are all baptized in the Episcopal church and are confirmed. My mother was such a strict Episcopalian that she believed it was a sin to even visit another church.

Last winter my husband broke his leg while at work in the night shift. He just started to go back to work last week, so I will have to go back to Milwaukee and cook for him. Milwaukee is our home now, but I still think that there is no place like Oneida, and I like to visit Oneida every chance I get. I always go to the cherry orchard during the cherry season. I go mostly for the outing. I enjoy the cool lake breeze in the afternoon and the chance of visiting my old acquaintances. I am always able to make a little money, and this time I have my little grandson with me. He just followed me here. He was bound to come to Oneida, and although he has always lived in the city he has that roaming inclination. I guess he gets that from his ancestors who used to roam through the woods about five hundred years ago. He liked the farm life too. He gets up early and wants to help in everything. He even tried to milk, and the boys let him ride the horse while they cultivated, and he thought that was great. He seems to be enjoying himself very much. I hope he likes the cherry land too, because I want him to help me pick cherries. When we left Milwaukee his mother told me to send him back if he got lonesome, so after we were here a few days I said, "Shall I send you back to Milwaukee?" He said "no" and the other day he said, "I may not go to the cherry orchard because I have to ride the horse when they cultivate." I am afraid I can't get him to go home when the time comes for us to go. I think that it is nice to have children and grandchildren, even though they bring so much worry. They surely brighten a home. I am getting old and I don't enjoy going to any doings, and so I stay home with my grandchildren.

ANONYMOUS NO. 1

This eventful account focuses on the narrator's childhood and youth. He was fifty-seven years old when he told the story to John Skenandore on December 12, 1940. In the notebook he was called "Anonymous," and all the other personal names in the text were blacked out and replaced by numbers. Part of this story was in the newspapers at the time of the events he talks about, and it must have been widely known. It seems a shame to deny him the recognition such an account merits.

An Oneida Odyssey

I might have been about six years old when I first saw light and began to realize things happening. For instance, when our house burnt down— I never forgot that; it was so pitiful. My uncle used to come and stay with us at times as he never had a special place to stay. His legs were crippled up and can't walk, but he got around by creeping hands and seat. It was during the time he was visiting us that my parents took my brother Bill and I along to my grandparents' place and left him home alone. For some reason we stayed overnight, and on our way coming home the next morning we met a man who told my dad that his house burnt down the night before, so my father drove his horses all they were good for just in case we were able to save anything yet.

We came home and found our house burnt up with very little of the stuff from inside saved and my uncle would have burn up with the house if [. . .] didn't come along and carry him out of the house just before the ceiling came down.

Father made a living by selling wood, and hoops. He used to haul his hoops to the barrel factory in Menasha and Mother used to make baskets, and I'll never forget how my grandpa used to come every so often and ask Mother if she has anything for him to do. She used to have him make basket handles for her, and I was never so happy as when he told me that he was going to make me a sleigh. He got two sticks for runners and curved them on the ends and dried them that way, and after they were dry enough then he put the other parts together. I just couldn't rest and kept watching him all the time he was working on it.

And another thing I never forgot was the time when our neighbors gave me a little puppy which made me so happy and I did everything to make my little dog happy too. He grew up and got so he wanted to go along with everyone from our house if they went someplace, and for that reason my brother and Father didn't like him anymore. And one day Bill went to Menasha and my dog followed him and Bill couldn't get rid of him and the dog followed him right into town. While they were in town some white man offered five dollars for the dog and Bill sold him. But in a couple of days the dog came back home and I was certainly glad to see him again, but within a few days my dad sold him again but that time he sold him to a hunter, who chained him down so he can't get away. That time the dog was gone for a few days but he came back home again, so after that they didn't try to sell him again.

Not long after my dog came home my father ask them all to get ready and they would all go to some woods where he said Bill and I will cut hoops and you women can get some splints for your baskets. I might have been in the government school then, as I didn't remember seeing the bears they killed at that time. Anyway, Grandmother was staying with my parents then and she went along in a lumber wagon. Father had put lots of hay in the wagon box so that the women can sit right in the box and be comfortable. When they got to that place where they were headed for they unhook the horses and tie them to the wagon and let them eat the hay in the box. And the men cut some black ash trees and saw them up to certain length for the women to pass away their time on while the menfolks are cutting hoops. My dog of course had to go along, and while the men were busy cutting hoops the dog started to bark a little ways away from where they were working, and Bill wanted to go and see what he was barking at but the old man said, "Oh, he doesn't know what he is barking at," so Bill didn't go. But the dog kept on so finally Bill sneaked away from his father and went to see what the dog was barking at, and as he got to where the dog was he saw a big bear's head sticking out of a den and the dog was barking at that. So Bill came running back to his dad and told him what he saw, and then back to the wagon after the musket he brought along; then they both went to kill the bear.

The old man said, "You better let me kill him with my hatchet," but after they got there the old man saw the big head that was sticking out of the den and he changed his mind and left Bill shoot the bear, and just as he shot, two other bears came out of another hole back of it. These looked like they were young ones so they got one of them too, but one got away. If it wasn't for my dog they would have never got either one of those bears. So Bill ran back to the wagon and told the womenfolks to come and see the bears they killed, and on the way going through the rough forest Grandma fell while stepping over logs and didn't try to get up anymore on her feet. Bill asked her if she got hurt but she said, "No, I am afraid of bears anyway. I'll rest here; you can go and I'll sit here until you come back." So they left her sitting there. Bill and the old man had a tough job pulling the big bear out of its den, as it died in the hole as he shot it.

After they got the big bear out, then they tied the two front legs together and the hind legs the same way and then ran a dry tamarack pole between front and hind legs with ends sticking out long enough for shouldering. Then they fasten the little bear on my ma with front legs of the bear tied together, and the men put the front legs over Ma's head and she carried the bear on her back while the men shouldered the big bear back to the wagon, and on their way back they came to where Grandmother was sitting, still in same position. So the men offered to help her up but they found her leg broken, so they had to take the bear back into the wagon first until they came back after her. And they had to prepare to come right back home, and as there was quite a little hay left in the wagon box and Grandma can't be sitting up on the way back as the wagon was so rough, so they decided to lay Grandma between the two bears so she won't have to be rolling all over the box. But she was terribly scared that the bears might come to.

The next morning Father and Bill took the bears into De Pere to sell, and the first man that saw the bears offered forty dollars but they won't take it and took the bears to a butcher but he only offered forty dollars too so they decided to sell them to the butcher for forty dollars. And after that they thought the world of my dog and never got rid of him anymore.

That same dog was with my younger brother when he got lost, but the dog came back the next day and the boy didn't. On the third day Father went to Green Bay to put an ad in the press about the missing boy and came back by the way of De Pere, and as he was coming out of town a train hit his team, wagon, him, and another man who was riding back home with him. All were killed instantly.

And that afternoon at three o'clock my brother was found in an old well in the woods which had a hollow log sunk into a spring of water and the center dug out. My brother was in that hollow log full of water head first, and the same evening we got a message that my father and another man was killed at De Pere railroad crossing when a train hit their wagon and team of horses. This must have happened in the fall of 1898, as I was hurt in government school that same fall. We were clearing land for the school at that time, prying stumps out with long poles, and while moving from one stump to another carrying the pole I fell and dropped the pole on my foot and infection set in and doctors and nurses couldn't seem to help me any and the wound kept opening into running sores. And finally Mother took me into Green Bay hospital and got treatment from doctors up there, and as soon as [. . .] found out he told my mother that he wasn't going to pay the doctor bill, so they brought me back to the mission hospital where they later cut my leg off. [. . .] paid the doctor bill with Mother's money which she got from the railroad company when my dad was killed.

My leg was cut off five times before they stopped the infection and left me with a very short stump of my leg. This happened when I was thirteen years old in the year of 1898. My mother took me out of school, and I stayed home and was going about on crutches until I was about nineteen years old when I thought of making myself a leg, and after planning different types I started to make one out of cedar and succeeded and was able to use it. Of course I had a very tough time since I lost my leg, as it was hard for me to get around even after I had my homemade leg. I learned one thing, that after I had the leg on I had to saw it off and wear it shorter than my real one or I would keep tripping over little things because I can't bend that leg.

I got along very well after a couple of months and got so that I was able to work and walk around without crutches. It certainly felt nice to think of walking again without crutches, and within a year I felt like going to school again and finally got myself with a gang which was going to Chilocco, Oklahoma, in the year of 1906. I was twenty-one years old then and was very glad to think that I still had a chance to learn, but after being there a couple of months I found that altogether different. When we first got there they gave us good meals, and it seems to me as the time went on the meals kept getting worse, and we were getting lousy [with lice], and I was ashamed of myself to think of going to school with children so much younger than I was so I decided to come back home the first chance I got. I didn't tell this to anybody and just went on my own hook.

When I started off I had twenty-five cents which I thought I could live on until I got far enough away. Then I could hire out and earn money for my fare back home. I hadn't gone far on the first day after leaving school when a man caught up to me with a team of horses and a big wagon and asked me if I wanted a lift, so I rode with him for twenty miles until he got to the place where he was going so I had to walk again. It was getting towards evening, but I kept on walking until it started to get dark. Then I went to an old farmhouse near the road and knocked at the door. An old lady came to the door and asked me to come in. She said the old man is in the barn milking; he will be back any time now and offered me a chair. She was a nice old lady, and I felt quite at home.

The old man came back in a little while, and he too was very nice. He seem so glad to see me, and we had quite a talk before the old lady got supper on. Then we ate a real old-fashion meal and they kept encouraging me to eat more. As soon as we got through eating the old man said, "You must stay overnight as you have too far to go so you might just as well take your time." Of course I had told him before supper that I lived in Wisconsin, and he got interested about that and asked me lot of questions about Wisconsin. We sat up until near midnight talking about our countries and then they showed me the room I was to sleep in. It had a nice old-fashion bed in it and a thick husk mattress on it which I almost disappeared in when I got into it. Nice clean bedclothes: I was just ashamed to think of me in it with all the lice I had with me, but I didn't want to spoil it for myself by telling them what I had as they were so nice to me.

I slept so good that night I didn't even notice the old people were up until the old man called me and breakfast was ready. And after breakfast I asked them if they would sell me a nickel's worth of lunch for me to take along on my long hike. The old lady said, "No, you will need all the money you have on your way back home. I will give you the lunch and you won't need to pay for it." Just as if she knew I only had twenty-five cents. Well, after breakfast she hand me a big bundle of lunch to take along and bid me good-bye and told me if I am ever around that way again to be sure and stop off.

Then I started off again and walked all day and didn't get no ride, but the lunch Grandma made for me sure came in handy and the second night I didn't try to get a place. I just went in a cornfield and fix myself a bed in corn shock near the road as I had enough to eat to last me all of the next day yet. Early the next day I started off again and walked all of that day until it was getting dark and I happen to come to a farm with a good-size orchard back of the house. So I walked up to the door and knocked and a man came to the door and asked me what I wanted and I told him I was looking for work. This happen to be a bachelor's place, but he didn't seem to be very good as he gave me the answer no right off. He said, "I am through with you guys traveling the highways. As many as I have hired, guys like you left early the next day. All they want is a good meal and place to sleep during the night." Then I told him that I was not one of them as I have a home in Wisconsin and like to earn enough for a railroad fare back home. "Well," he said, "I can try you out." And wasn't I glad. He offered me twenty dollars a month, and I jumped at the chance. We ate supper, and after that he showed me my room. I was rather glad that he was a bachelor. Then I had a chance to get rid of my pets [lice], and as I didn't have any working clothes he gave me some old clothes the next day to put on and left the clothes I had on outside.

Early the next day he asked me if I ever husked standing corn. I said, "No, we don't harvest like that in Wisconsin, but I can learn." "Well,"

he said, "that's just what I want you to do." And we got a team of horses
ready and hook them to a wagon with one side of the box much higher
than the other and drove out in the field. As we got to the cornfield he
said, "Now this is fifty acres, so don't try to get it done in one day," and
he started me off and showed me how he want it done. Then he went
back home and told me to bring back whatever I would have picked by
noon. Noon came and I wasn't near loaded and I certainly worked hard
to fill the box. I took what I had back to the house and was rather scared
that he would be disappointed. As I got back the first thing he did was
to look in the box to see how much corn I had and I felt so cheap when
he asked me if that was all I had. But I said "yes" and I worked hard
to get that much. "Well," he said, "you keep on and you will learn in no
time—I can see that already." So I felt better and saw that my job is good
and did all I could to get him to like me.

I started to work for this man on Wednesday and by Friday he asked
me if I could get along if he went away and came back the next day. I
said he didn't have to worry—I'll get along. So he left early and I went
on with my work. Noon came and I went back home, fed the horses,
and picked myself a bite here and there, and out into the field again. I
did all his work in the evening and got supper for myself and sat around
for a while before I went to bed. Early the next morning I got up and did
the chores at breakfast and out in the field again with my team of horses
and put in another good day's work. Late in the evening my boss came
home, and he was certainly surprised to see me home and all the work
done. Then he told me just why he had to leave sometimes and told me
that if I did good work for him all the way through that he would find
me a good job whenever my work was done at his place. He told me that
he had a girl in the next town who he went with for years and he has to
go and see her often—at least once a week. And the following week he
wanted to be gone two days and asked me if it would be alright, and I
was only too glad because that gives me a chance to get rid of my pets
without him knowing.

We got along very nicely, and in a couple of weeks I was able to husk
120 bushels a day. I worked for him just six weeks when he told me that
he had found a good place for me to work and told me that the party
was coming over to see me the following Sunday.

She was a widow and running a farm, so she has to have hired help at
all time. Sunday came and sure enough a woman drove up with a nice-

looking team of horses and top buggy and she was also good-looking. My boss told me to go along with her and see the place, so I did. The farm she had was up-to-date and had a very good location, but how foolish a man can be when he is homesick. I had to turn it down. If I worked for her then maybe you people would have never seen me here again.

But I drew the money I had coming and bought a ticket for railroad fare back home. And as I didn't know anything about traveling, I got lost on the way coming. I stayed in the train where I was supposed to change cars, but I was lucky the conductor didn't charge me any more than what I had already paid, which was over twenty dollars, and I only had ten dollars left from my pay. I finally got back in De Pere on Saturday and met some of my relations there and came back with them and stayed overnight with them and came to church the next day and met my mother there. She was certainly glad to see me back again, as she had heard that I left Chilocco and I didn't once write to her while I was on my way.

In the year of 1910 an agent from an artificial limb company came to see me and talked me into buying one of their make and took me into Milwaukee to their headquarters and like a fool I bought one for $150 and I just couldn't learn to wear it as I had my own make on for so long and got along without making any movements on my shoulders. I tried hard to get used to it, but every time I forgot to give a jerk on my shoulder the joint on the knee would give and I would fall over and sometimes hurt myself. So I got mad at it one day as I fell with my arms full of groceries as I came back into my house when I had been to town. I nearly bump my head on the stove, and I didn't even try to get up anymore and took the factory-made off and put my own make back on. Since then I never tried to put the factory-made limb on again. I never got a cent towards my injury from the government, which I would appreciate a lot if there is any justice.

Andrew Beechtree, born in August 1895, produced the fullest account of his life and thoughts of all the WPA writers. He apparently loved to learn, analyze things, and write. This short selection deals with his experiences while he was working at the Ford Motor Company in Detroit during World War I. He was elected tribal chairman in 1951 and 1952. There is a longer account of his time at Carlisle Indian School in chapter 7.

Life in Detroit

When fall came I went again to Carlisle. I signed up for the period of three years. When my time was up at the end of three years, I had one more year to go to school before I could graduate. . . . I went back to school again [because the Carlisle school] had made an arrangement so that a student could go to work at Henry Ford's automobile factory at Detroit, Michigan. And so a few of us took up training for mechanical arts, a six-months course. At the end of that period, we had fulfilled the requirements for us to get this job. A man took us to the big city. I was to make my own living.

It was December 13, 1917, when we arrived there. Oh! snakes it was so cold. If I had money then I surely would have went home.

This here place where we were stopping, a great fire took place near there. The firemen were doing their best to get it under control. Whenever it got wet it would freeze at once. Every now and then the firemen who were holding the water hose would be dragged along and sideways with it.

We were with the Indian boys who had gone there for some time already. We were treated very kind by these fellows. I worked only five days at common labor. Then I was promoted. I was placed where I had to go through instructions and learn what kind of work is required in the factory. It was required that we spend a certain length of time studying at different departments to learn how different parts are made. It went like this until we went through all the departments and knew how all the parts of Model T Fords are made.

I was scared when they sent me to a department where they make the magneto unit (it seems that's its name), where they do assembling work. I was late in getting in there. To my surprise, here and there were white girls working in that department. Now I felt funny and had a hard time of it. It was several days later that I was forced to ask somebody about something. Now then I spoke to one of the girls, and I said something to her; she just went like this: she raised her shoulders and made motions with her hands like a Jew when he is trying to sell something to the people. I was so surprised I just stood there looking at her, I could not make out what she meant by her actions. I also thought maybe she wanted to make friends with me. It was some time later that I spoke to her again, and she done the same thing that she did before, and besides she said "I don't know." I finally found out that her nationality was Polish and that she couldn't speak English.

Many times afterwards I used to see them, that kind of women who could not speak English. But then they were very good workers. It went like that; I was placed in different departments throughout the plant. Sometimes, now and then, we really went to a schoolroom for lessons. We used to work eight hours per day at daytime. Others that were already working in the plant, they worked for two weeks and then their time would change. There were three shifts, or groups, working.

In the spring, then, they told us that they were going to give us a banquet. Naturally I was such a big Injun I didn't catch on what they were planning to do. Now it was time for us to go to a large hotel. We went in there and went through several large rooms. This here was at night; finally they took us in a banquet hall, and to my surprise it was a swell place, and everything was fixed up so nice. There were rows of lights along the tables, swell chairs were around the tables, and the tables were decorated with all kinds of flowers with bunches here and there all along the tables. The dishes that were on the tables were all shining brightly and the knives, forks, and spoons were made of silver.

So we all set down around the tables. Now there was another door, and from it came black men who were also dressed up in black. But they all had white collars on them. They were even running a bit with their trays, and they started to serve us. First they put chicken soup on the tables. Now then the noise started with our lips as we all started eating soup. I ate all the soup that was in my dish; it was so good to eat. After a little while then they took the dishes off the tables and replaced them with other dishes. Now it was the bread, butter, potatoes, celery, olives, lettuce with different kinds of flavor on it. The main item was the meat. They brought in three different kinds of meat—chicken, beef, and ham. And then the forks started to go after the food that was within our reach. I used to hear the priest and the Christians talk about heaven, how everything was fixed up so lovely, and I certainly thought I was there already.

It was now that I was filled up to the limit. However, they still brought in pies with ice cream on it and set it on the tables. I just took little of it. Shortly afterwards then they took the pie dishes off, and they brought in the finger bowls. Well then I drank the water that was in there, to wash my throat. At once I noticed different fellows started to look at me, and sort of had a smile on their faces. Later on I noticed they seem to be dipping their fingers in it, and they wipe their fingers on table napkins. And now it was time for speech making, and so they had four or five speakers for the evening. And too we sang some songs. Now it was over and we all started for home. We sure enjoyed ourselves very much.

I worked for two months and my wages was three dollars per day. From there on I received five dollars per day. One-fourth of my wages were sent back to Carlisle, where I came from, and there it was deposited at the bank.

I had made up my mind not to drink. It wasn't very long, and now my friends invited me to go and take a walk down the street just to look around. As we were strolling along we came to swell building, lights were all lit up with all kinds of colors all around it, and swing music was going on in that building. Now then they said, let's all go in here, and so we all went in there. I refused to take whiskey and beer. They said this here is not a strong drink. It was Rock and Rye whiskey [a sweet liqueur], and so that's what they put in my glass, and I was sure surprised it tasted so good to drink. I drank that same kind every time my friends bought the drinks. After a while I noticed I was getting drunk. Now then we all started for home. We were just about able to get back. Every little ways it seems the earth would be coming up to hit me. It was the first time that I was intoxicated. I certainly paid for it; I suffered so much the next day.

At first I used to eat at a boardinghouse, but I got tired of it. The meals were served at a certain time, and if I wasn't there when it was served I couldn't eat at all. So I stopped eating there and I had my meals at a restaurant. Now I could go and eat anytime, and also I could order anything I want to eat. So I ate lots of hard-boiled eggs.

It was during the World War I at that time. We used to like to take in the shows. This here where we used to go was mostly burlesque shows where we used to see the pretty women do all kinds of dances, singing and jokes. The whites call it the burlesque shows.

The policemen used to be waiting outside when the shows were over, and the menfolks went out. They used to arrest them as "slackers." So one time they got me and they took me along with the rest. I was caught by the hair too. We were jam full at the jail. One by one they took the men in another room and questioned them. I didn't know what were the questions. Some of the men they brought back, and others didn't come back. There were so many of us fellows that it was towards morning, and now they took me in there too. There was this room and all along were these police—great big ones—lined up. The first thing they asked me what is my name, and so I told them. They also ask me why was it that I hadn't joined the army yet. I told them I didn't know the reason why I hadn't joined or enlisted yet. They also asked me if I had registered anywhere, and again I said I don't know. Well they questioned me all kinds of ways, and usually I said I don't know. And finally now he asked me what kind of nationality do I belong to anyway. Now then I thought here was my chance to say something to praise myself, so I stood erect and I had a little smile on my face. I said to him I am Oneida Indian, that's what I is. So for a little while he just kept looking at me. It showed on his face that he was very much in distress. And finally he said to me, I suppose that is the reason you don't know anything. And now he turned around, and for a while he talked with his fellow officer. Now they told me that they would write to where I registered, and in one week's time I should report back there again to find out what was to be done.

When the time came for me to report, I went back there. They had not received the reply to their letter as yet. So in another week I should go back there again. This went on for about three months. So finally we got to know each other at this here place where I used to report. They just used to say hello chief of chiefs, how goes it? Nothing doing today; come back next week. After a while I got tired of this business, going over to see these kind of looking men every week. I said I think it's best that I enlist in the army instead of coming over here. What procedure would we take to that effect?

It was also this reason that I want to enlist, because almost all the Indians had enlisted and were gone; just few of us was left, and it was getting lonesome around there without these fellows around. So we agreed that they would send me a card telling when and where I should meet a doctor for a physical examination. A little better than a week, then, I received a card stating I should be at the Ford Emergency Hospital at a certain time to meet the doctor. I went there; he started to examine me. First he examine my eyes, nose, my ears and he looked in at all the holes in my body, also my teeth, my throat, and he also used a instrument stuck against my chest and he listen how my heart was beating.

He kept coming down until he came to my feet. There was a table there, so he had me get on top of it. He had me standing there like a doll or a fan dancer. In the meantime while I was standing there he took a flat stick what the doctors use for examining a person's throat, and he tried to stick that underneath my foot, but he fail to do so. And so he pull the stick out and kind of tried to look in there. Then he said seems like you got legs and feet like a gorilla, the largest animal of ape kingdom. My gosh man. Then he asked me if I ever had any trouble with my dogs or feet when I do lots of walking. I said that's the reason I quit trying to be a big farmer. It seems that it aches like it wants to break underneath my feet. He said that's what you call flat foot, the kind of feet you got. He said I guess you can't be of any use if you did join the army, the kind of feet you got. You would be just in the way and bother those fellows. He said, the only thing you can do is play with the womenfolks. I will put you on a limited service, A number one. And now he made a slip or a report card and that's what he wrote on it, limited service A number one. Well, I thought that was that, so I went home.

So afterwards I kept wondering why was it that they never got an answer to their letter as to what should be done. I have found out that the United States cannot force the Oneida Indians to fight in any war unless they themselves want to enlist and fight. [In fact, Andrew Beechtree did enlist late in the war and go through training and a brief period of service.]

A musician by profession, Morris Wheelock was very active in Oneida politics during the 1930s. [10] In 1936 or 1937 he was elected the first tribal chairman of the Oneida Tribe of Indians of Wisconsin, the reconstituted governmental system created under the Indian Reorganization Act. He had lived in Milwaukee before the depression and returned there after World War I, becoming a prominent member of that city's Indian community. He worked for this WPA project briefly and wrote this account of his life.

Autobiography

I was born in the city of Morris in the state of Minnesota on May 29, 1900, of parents who were full-blood Oneida Indians. I was raised in a Christian home, my father being an Indian local preacher, and my mother was interested in church work. And every Sunday my brother and I were made to attend Sunday school of the Methodist church of which we were members. My mother would make us scrub our neck and ears early Sunday morning, and she would comb our hair, parting it in the middle, and we did not dare to scratch our heads, and the last thing she would do before we left the house was to place our caps or straw hats on our heads. I wore knickerbocker pants, black cotton stockings, button shoes, a white blouse (á la Lord Fauntleroy) with a three-inch-wide red ribbon for a necktie. [11] With my hair combed and parted in the middle and my cap or straw hat right on the top of my head, I was so stiff that I didn't dare to look around very much. And when I took my cap or hat off, I had to lift it straight up and carry it in front of me.

There I sat in church, stiff as a board during Sunday school and the regular services, listening to an old, dry preacher. If my mother or dad were unable to attend church, my brother and I had to tell them about the announcements that were made, and what book of the Bible did the preacher take his text from, and the sermon he preached about. In this way my parents were able to know just how we behaved behind their backs, and believe me, we tried to remember everything, as the penalty was terrific if we did not, or if our memory failed us.

I do not remember just how old I was when I started school, but when I first remembered school I was attending a little red schoolhouse located by the Methodist church cemetery. This was about 1905, and I always wore clean clothes to school and church. My mother saw to it that I had a clean change of clothing twice a week for school, besides Sundays. My brother and I were never allowed to attend school or church with soiled clothing, much less dirty clothes. All my brothers and sisters, of which I have two brothers and two sisters alive, were brought up the same way.

It was never possible for all of my brothers and sisters to be home at the same time, as they were away from home attending school at the Carlisle Indian School, so it was my youngest brother and I that were most of the time with my parents.

My grandfather on my dad's side was married four times; therefore I only know the fourth wife, who is still alive. His name was James A. Wheelock—a well-known Indian, he was the interpreter of the Methodist church for a long time, right up to the time of his death.

My grandparents, Mr. and Mrs. Henry K. Cooper on my mother's side, were well known, and granddad was also an Indian interpreter. He handled quite a lot of Indian claims for the Oneida Tribe, making personal appearances before the secretary of the interior and commissioner of Indian Affairs at Washington DC, where he had quite a number of friends among the members of Congress and Senate of the U.S.

I lived on a farm which my dad operated, and I had to help with the farmwork after school and Saturdays and during the summer. My parents had set up chores for me to do every day, and it became a part of my daily work, such as cutting wood, haul water, clean the stable, get the cows from the pasture, and help with the milking.

It was in 1906 that my dad received his appointment for employment in the Indian Service at Mt. Pleasant Indian School, Michigan, as night watchman, and a few months later we moved to that locality as our farm was rented out. I attended the Indian school at Mt. Pleasant until 1907, when I went to Canada with my mother for a visit on the small Oneida reservation between St. Thomas and London, Canada. It was here that I first met a group of Indian children of my own tribe who were unable to speak the English language, so it was after a lot of hand motioning that we were able to play with each other. In time I learned to understand the Oneida Indian language and they learned to understand the English language, but neither side was able to speak the language we understood. My parents never allowed me to speak the Indian language, and the Indian schools I attended never allowed us to speak our native tongue.

In 1908 I entered the Carlisle Indian School, Carlisle, Pennsylvania, but was there just a short time when a new order came out from the Indian Office prohibiting children under the ages of fourteen years, and in the fourth reader grade, to attend school at Carlisle. As I came under this so-called Act, I had to be transferred to some smaller non-reservation Indian school, or go home, so I elected to go home. My dad came after me July 1, 1908, and we went to Canada by way of Niagara Falls to meet my boyfriends on the Oneida Reservation I had met the year before. But it was the same old story: none of the kids could speak English or understand it, and it appeared to me that they made no effort to remember the English language they had learned from me, and it was quite an effort to make friends with them, more than the year before. And to make matters worse, I spent the Fourth of July in Canada, with pockets full of firecrackers, and nobody was celebrating. Dad and I left Canada a few days after the Fourth of July, and it was one of the happiest moments of my life to leave a so-called foreign country for my home in Wisconsin of the U.S.A.

The fall of 1908 I started back to the little red schoolhouse again, together with my kid brother and my many friends both boys and girls, and also I was back on the farm again as Dad decided to operate the farm again. We had three horses, nine cows, pigs, turkeys, and chickens.

Dad let me use a plot of ground, and so on Saturday I plowed it up, and after school I dragged it next, until I had the soil worked up good. Then I had all my boyfriends help me plant white navy beans after school. We completed the job in about two hours, to plant an eighth of an acre, and on Saturdays the boys would come and help me hoe my field of beans. After we got through then we would all go fishing or swimming, and some of the girls helped out in my field also. Anyway it was fun for us, as well as helping me in my first venture as a small-time farmer. During the time I attended the little red schoolhouse I never had any serious fights with the boys. Of course I had a lot of arguments, but never turned out to be a McCoy-Hatfield feud.

There was a girl who attended school at the same time as I did, but she didn't stay very long as her parents were Adventist, and she went to an Advent school, but one day at this red schoolhouse I went up to her and threatened to strike her for no reason at all, just to be smart. I never realized at that time that fourteen years later she would become my wife.

In 1910 I entered the Indian school at Wittenberg, Wisconsin.[12] I went to school half a day and worked in the laundry the other half of the day. So it went day in and day out from September to June 1911; then I was transferred to another Indian school, at Tomah, Wisconsin, and again I worked in the laundry, and I was beginning to think that was going to be my vocation in life. I left Tomah in June of 1912 and came home for the summer. During all this time my parents were employed in the Indian Service, and we lost part of the farm to satisfy a mortgage and taxation on the property. I stayed on the old homestead with one of my sisters and kid brother until my parents came back a few weeks later on their vacation.

During the summer months I worked for a farmer by the name of Joe Smith at fifty cents per day. By this time a district school was organized; the little red schoolhouse was a thing of the past. So I attended the district school, and after school on weekdays and all day Saturdays I worked in the sawmill where logs were made into lumber. About this time my parents were thinking about going back in the Indian Service, and I had made my application for enrollment in the Wahpeton Indian Boarding School at Wahpeton, North Dakota. My application was accepted and so I entered the school there, and again they had me booked for the laundry. This time I really refused and was placed on the farm as a teamster, as I got there about two weeks before school started and all the farmers were harvesting their grain.

I had just started school for about a week when I took sick with typhus fever. I stayed in the hospital two and a half months before I was allowed to resume my studies. I did not go back to the laundry or farm, but was placed in the tailor shop for six weeks before I was transferred to the superintendent's office as an office boy and mail carrier.

I came back home in June and again I worked on the farm, and during the winter I went back to Wittenberg to attend school and try to learn a trade. Following that I made my home with an uncle, Dennison Wheelock, attorney-at-law, who resided in the city of West De Pere, Wisconsin, and as he had a wide practice I drove his automobile for him on all his trips. During this time my parents were in the Indian Service at the Shawanee Indian Mission School in Oklahoma [then Tecumseh, Indian

Territory] with my kid brother who was attending school there and later enrolled at the Haskell Institute, Lawrence, Kansas.

The middle of July of 1917 I went to the cherry orchards in Sturgeon Bay, Wisconsin, with a group of Indians to pick cherries. We arrived at the orchard in the evening, and it was not until the next day that I was introduced to my new job of picking cherries. It didn't take me but fifteen minutes to learn that I was not going to earn my salt picking cherries at so much per quart, and I had just about made up my mind to quit and go back to my uncle's home when the field supervisor came around and asked me how did I like my job. I told him I could not earn my salt with that kind of a job; then he asked me if I was good on figures. I told him fair. "Well," he said, "I have another job for you, which I think you will like better. Turn in your pail and come along with me." It didn't take me long to turn in my pail, and the job he gave me was field checker, and I did not have to pick a single cherry. I worked at the orchard until the first week in September.

Then I came back to the home of my uncle in West De Pere, which I called home. My aunt and uncle were both very nice to me and treated me like I was one of the family. They gave me spending money whenever I was in need of funds. But this time I had money in my pocket, as I had just come back from the orchard.

The day I left the orchard I told the manager of the orchard I was leaving to enlist in the army. He gave me an extra twenty-five dollars and on September 21, 1917, I enlisted in the U.S. Army for the duration of the war. My aunt and uncle gave me twenty-five dollars before I left for Jefferson Barracks, Missouri.

Due to the fact I was a couple of pounds underweight I had to undergo a physical examination at Milwaukee, Wisconsin, Chicago, Illinois, and two rigid physical examinations at Jefferson Barracks, Missouri, before I was able to take the oath to become a soldier of the U.S. regular army.

I enlisted at the age of seventeen years, but I told the recruiting officer I was eighteen, and it was a good thing he didn't ask for my birth certificate.

As I was sworn into Uncle Sam's armed forces, it was the beginning of a new life for me. . . . I was fitted out in a new uniform and had a hard time getting a pair of shoes small enough to fit me, and when I did get the shoes it was a size larger than my civilian shoes. Right then and there began the process of bodybuilding. I was vaccinated and given a prophylactic injection in the right arm. The meals were perfect; all I wanted to eat.

I was assigned to the Fifteenth Recruit Company, and stayed there for about two weeks before I was transferred and reassigned to Company C, Sixty-first Infantry at Gettysburg, Pennsylvania, as a buck private.

At the age of ten my dad taught me to play the cornet, and as I progressed in music I used to play with the Oneida Indian Band. As the Sixty-first was a newly organized outfit, being composed of men from the old Seventh Calvary, and I being one of the recruits assigned to this organization, it was a couple of days before we settled down to hard work of drilling, and in the meantime there was an opening for a bugler in our company, which I applied for and got. I was excused from all drilling as I had to attend school for buglers to learn all the bugle calls of the army.

During the time I attended the Indian schools we were taught to drill, and at Wahpeton, North Dakota, I drilled once a week with the North Dakota National Guard. There I was taught the manual of arms. This military training I received once a week I passed on to the students of the Indian school I attended.

At Jefferson Barracks we had to drill every day, and my first day out on the parade grounds I drilled with the recruits for about an hour when one of the officers asked me if I had been in the army before. I told him no. He said, "Where did you get your military training?" so I told him about the training we got in the Indian schools. He was very much surprised, and right then and there I was excused from drilling, as he said I did not need the training there and would get plenty of it after I was assigned to some organization. But it didn't work out that way as I became a bugler and did not have to go out and drill unless I wanted to. The men from the Seventh Calvary were all old-timers—they had fourteen years' service in the army or better—and soon I had many friends among them, and they taught me all the tricks of the army and I got along just fine.

So it was, camp life, inspections once a week, and sometimes twice a week for general inspection, and every ten days I had to see the army doctor for a shot in the arm and each time it nearly made me sick.

About two weeks before Thanksgiving my regiment was transferred to Camp Green, Charlotte, North Carolina, where we had our Thanksgiving and Christmas dinner. We had so much to eat that we had plenty of leftovers from dinner for supper. We were finally ordered to move to Camp Merritt, New Jersey, and just about that time we began to feel that it won't be long before we would be on our way for "Over There." On April 8, 1918, no one was allowed to leave his quarters, as we had received orders to be on the "Alert." At 1:30 a.m. on April 9 we were ordered out for inspection and ready to march. Where we were going we did not know, and at 4 a.m. we were getting on the boat, and still we did not know what our destination would be. Of course there was a lot of rumor about where we were going, and that had been going on for quite some time before, before we arrived in Camp Merritt.

Before we got on the boat we were given franked postal cards, and on the back of it was printed "I have safely arrived overseas." Each man was ordered to address the card to his parents and sign his name to it, and as we passed over the gangplank there was a mail sack hanging there, where we dropped the cards. This mail sack was held at Hoboken, New Jersey, the port of embarkation, until we arrived overseas.

We arrived in France on the morning of April 28 at the port of Brest, safe and sound, with a wonderful ocean trip behind us. After a rest of a couple of days to get our sea legs back to normal, we started in what is more or less a human endurance against the elements. Rain one day and sunshine the next. I took in five battles while I was in France—three in the trenches of the Vosges Mountains and the other two at Saint-Mihiel and Argonne-Meuse.

About two weeks after we arrived in France, I and three other boys went to a restaurant in a not too small town, and as we seated ourselves a French waitress came to take our orders. I took out my little pocket French dictionary and tried to speak the French language so that she would understand what we wanted to order, but she just could not understand me, so the other three boys took a hand in it, and it also was the same. In the meantime we would pass smutty remarks about her shape and legs, and that we would like to take her out, as she was a very good looking girl. After this had been going on for about fifteen or twenty minutes, she said in the good old American language "If you boys would speak the English language I could understand you better." Well, after that I just did not care to eat.

It seems to me that everything I saw in France, Belgium, or Luxembourg was about three hundred years behind our time, as everything was crude and old-fashion, and I was beginning to understand their language more and more, and also their ways and mode of living. As I read the daily papers of the accounts of the present war, quite a number of the towns I had stayed in are blown off the map by Hitler's armies.

After the armistice I was recommended for admission as a cadet to the West Point Military Academy, and on February 12, 1919, I left my organization for Beaune, France, to enter a prep school to prepare for my entrance to West Point. All the instructors were American Army officers, and the discipline was as rigid as West Point Military Academy. This preparatory school was like an extension from the University of France. However, it was plenty tough any way you look at it.

Up to this time I was in very good health—at least that is what I thought—but the first few days in March I began to feel the effects of the war, and on March 5, 1918, I entered the hospital with a high fever. I was very nervous and had a complete breakdown in health a day after I was admitted to the hospital. After being in the hospital for a month, I resigned my commission as a cadet to West Point, as I was not getting better very fast. I came back on a hospital ship and entered the hospital at Camp Merritt, New Jersey. There I stayed for a week before I was transferred to Fort Sheridan, Illinois, for further hospitalization, and on June 26, 1919, I received an honorable discharge from the U.S. Army.

After I was home a week at the old homestead with my parents I did not like civilian life and wanted to go back into the army, but I could not make the grade due to the condition of my health.

It was in the last battle I was in that I was helping a wounded comrade back to the first-aid dressing station when a gas shell fell across the road from us. It threw a piece of rock against my shoulder, near the shoulder blade, breaking one of the small bones, but I was so scared at that time I did not know I was hit until I was in the hospital for some time. I noticed I was losing my strength in my left arm, and to top it off I went totally blind in both eyes. Today I have my eyesight back but wear glasses, and my left arm is two inches shorter than my right.

With this physical handicap, I had to adjust myself to civilian life. I had to get a job—any kind of a job would do for the present—and so I finally got a job working for the Town of Oneida as a laborer repairing roads. I worked there about two months before the job ended, and shortly after I entered St. Mary's Hospital at Green Bay. There I stayed until spring.

I felt pretty good during the summer, so much so that I landed a job with a construction company, wheeling concrete for about three months. Then I operated a jackhammer about a month, before I received an appointment in the Indian Service as boys' adviser at Leach Lake, Minnesota.

I resigned from my position after being on the job two months, due to the fact the wages I received did not conform to the amount of work I had to do. In the meantime my parents had moved to De Pere, and later we moved to Green Bay, as we were renters instead of homeowners, and this was all due to bad mortgages and taxes.

It was in 1921 that I took advantage of the rehabilitation program for disabled world war veterans as set up by the Veterans Bureau. I entered the Larson Conservatory of Music as a music student in Green Bay, and I took a complete course in clarinet, history of music, theory, harmony, orchestra, band, and choral conducting, and September 22, 1922, I married the girl I threatened to strike for no reason at all at the little red schoolhouse fourteen years before. I continued my musical studies even after I was married, and received my diploma on June 16, 1924.

My musical career did not turn out as good as I had expected, and I had to join up with a small dance orchestra. In 1925 I moved my family to Milwaukee, where I was employed by the Nash Motor Company and played with a dance orchestra in a nightclub. At the end of sixteen months I received a medical discharge from the Nash Motor Company's doctor, as my physical examination conducted by the company showed traces of tuberculosis. Now that I was married with a wife and two children—boy and girl—on my hands, I got busy and looked for another job and in three weeks I landed a job as a truck driver. The work was awfully heavy at times, and I stuck to my job for a year before I had an offer to go on the road with a traveling orchestra. I accepted this offer, as I was just about ready to give up my work as a truck driver, and as soon as I was able to find suitable living quarters I moved my family to New London, Wisconsin, where the orchestra I was traveling with had their headquarters.

In the fall my family and I moved to Green Bay, where I jobbed around with various dance orchestras and made fairly good living. We finally moved out to Oneida and rented my father-in-law's house near the village, and I bought a used car and drove back and forth to Green Bay, which is ten miles from Oneida. As soon as my wife and I got settled in Oneida, my parents came from Milwaukee to make their home with us, as my brothers and sisters did not want to be bothered with them in their old age. I had quite a lot of band and orchestra work, and was kept pretty busy, and managed to stay off the relief rolls, and in 1929 we did feel the pinch of hard times. The bottom fell out of the music game, and the wages for musicians went with it. I do not know just how we lived through the winter of 1929–30, and in the spring of 1930 I was appointed enumerator for the Department of Commerce, Bureau of Census, Ninth District, and I covered the Town of Hobart, Brown County area. It took me about seven or eight weeks to complete the census roll in the area I was assigned.

During that year and part of the next I just picked up work—whatever I could find in the line of music—and managed to keep a-going, and as my parents made their home with me I had to feed and give them clothing as well as support my own family. In this way my living expenses became higher as time went on, and no help of any kind from my brothers, sisters, town, or relief department.

It became a problem that my wife and I had to figure out very seriously, and to make matters worse my parents both took sick at the same time. We had to have three doctors to take care of them for thirteen weeks; they both recovered, but it left them in very poor health, and a few years later my mother died; but Dad still makes his home with me to this day.

In the meantime I decided to run for the office of justice of the peace for the Town of Hobart, so in the spring I had some friends circulate my nomination papers for the spring town election. I was elected by the voters to the office I was seeking, and held the office for two years. In this space of time I only sent one man to jail for a period of ten days, and the rest of the cases that came before me were always settled in a manner that was satisfactory to both parties involved. I never knew that so many people had so much trouble until I became a justice of the peace and was glad when my term of office expired.

About this time in 1934 there was some talk about organizing the Oneida Indian Tribe to take advantage of some law that was coming up before Congress and the U.S. Senate, so a tribal council was called and at this meeting, there was a lot of discussion about organization. It was finally decided to apply for a non-profit-sharing corporation form from the secretary of state (Wisconsin). In this, the corporation would be the legal representative of the Oneida Tribe in dealing with the federal, state, and local government. This was done in order to quell two or three other factions who claimed to be the legal representative and had the tribe pretty well split up. I was elected secretary of this corporation.[13]

Then began some real work with no pay. Correspondence, travel, and speeches; we had to give socials and take donations in order to raise funds for expenses that we were running into every week. In June 1934 the Wheeler-Howard Act became law. It was called the Indian Reorganization Act (so-called New Deal among the Oneidas). The officers of the corporation worked that much harder to secure a federal charter and take advantage of the rehabilitation program that this act had to offer. While all this was going on I had found employment with the help of white friends in the relief department as an interviewer. In this work I interviewed relief clients and classified them for employment through the State Employment Bureau. With so much work on my hands, I resigned my office as secretary for the Oneida Tribe. While employed in the relief department I had occasions to meet officials that were connected with WPA, and it was through them that I got on a WPA project as timekeeper after I had completed my work with the relief department.

My Indian friends wanted me to run for the chairmanship of the tribe, and finally I decided I would, and after the votes were counted I was the winner, the new chairman of the Oneida Tribal Council. The next year I ran for reelection and again I won, but by the end of my second term I was getting pretty tired of this job and declined the nomination for a third term. However, my friends entered my name on the election ballots, but I was defeated.

The first year of being chairman, we the officers had to set up various programs, such as land buying, assignments, building houses, well drilling, WPA projects, CCC-ID, arts and crafts, canning, gardening, education, and establish credit funds for the Indians to borrow money to buy horses, cattle, poultry, and farm equipment. The second year was the continuation of what was started, or to be started. In all this work we were aided and advised by the various officials of the Office of Indian Affairs, who would spend a few days on the reservation at different times (about once a month or sometimes more).

In the last three or four years I have been employed off and on as foreman-timekeeper, foreman, superintendent of labor, and general foreman on a WPA project as a non-relief worker. Last spring (1941) I toured the East with an Indian band on a rodeo with Gene Autry and had a very pleasant trip. When I returned home I could not find any work. I went all over Green Bay and finally I went to Milwaukee seeking employment, but it was the same all over: no work, or I had to undergo a stiff physical examination, and due to the condition of my health I was never able to pass the exams. It was not until December 1, 1941, that I was certified for employment on WPA through the local relief department. But I still do not receive any grocery orders or surplus commodities from the relief department. Through all these hard times and knocks I managed to buy a home (house and lot), and if everything goes the way I hope, we will own our home in a year.

My son and daughter are attending the Nicolet High School, at West De Pere, this being their third year in high school.

All in all life has not dealt me harshly. Of course there were times when I did not know what to do after I could not find a job, but there was always a way, and my family always had plenty to eat and never had to miss a meal for lack of food in the house.

What will 1942 bring me? Only time will tell.

AMELIA WHEELOCK JORDAN

Amelia Jordan, then age fifty-four, gave this brief story of her life to Ida Blackhawk on August 6, 1941. The interviewer's questions about her experiences and views on childbearing, birth control, child rearing, and the soul brought forth some compelling thoughts.

Thoughts about Life

My mother died when I was about six or seven years old, and I had two sisters and a brother. My father gave all of us away for adoption to different families. I was adopted by quite elderly people who had no children. I was sent to the mission day school, and I attended the school all winter. The following winter I was sent to the government boarding school, and I went there two terms. Then I was sent to Tomah Indian School, and I was there three years; then I returned home. My foster mother had died during the winter. I was very fond of her because she was good to me, and although my foster father was very good to me, it was not the place for me to stay, so I next signed up to go to Carlisle Indian School in Pennsylvania. I stayed there five years. I was sent to work for some Pennsylvania people and I stayed one year. I could not learn for some reason. I learned to talk English fluently, but I was slow to learn anything. I guess I did not know how to study; anyway I made slow progress. I stayed at Carlisle as long as I could. I had no incentive to come home because I had no home as it were, and I was having a good time there with all my friends and schoolmates.

I was at Carlisle during the time Major Mercer was superintendent of Carlisle and the rules of the school were lax, and the students were more interested in social activities than in their studies.[14] We had social gatherings every Saturday night and we were allowed to dance and the boys and girls were allowed to sit down together and visit. In the wintertime they flooded the pond and we had nice ice for skating and they used to allow the girls to go skating after study hour for one hour. Of course the boys were there too. In previous years the girls were never allowed to go out at night, excepting when they went from their quarters to the school building, auditorium, or gymnasium, and they had to line up like soldiers in the army. Do you wonder that I had no inclination of leaving Carlisle? But when some of my girlfriends started to get ready to come home to see their parents or relatives I tried to think of someone whom I could come back to. I could not make up my mind. At last I thought of my father. He was married again. I came home with the rest of the Oneidas in 1909.

How well I remember that year. I was really coming away from school, and I could really do as I please. I was seventeen years old and I felt so grown up. My father let me stay there, but he was like a stranger to me. I helped with the housework, and whenever I wanted to go anywhere I got ready and went. I was actually doing as I pleased, and it was a grand and glorious feeling. During the summer my friend and I worked in Green Bay for some rich folks. We used to come to Oneida and attend all the dances and festivities. We had some Oneida boyfriends. In the fall my girlfriend went back to Carlisle and I felt lonesome for a while because I knew I could not go back. My friend was a senior and expected to graduate the following spring. I worked all winter, and early in the spring I got off the train at Oneida with another girl. As we stepped off the train I noticed a young fellow standing nearby. I had never seen him before, but I knew he was an Oneida. He kept looking at me, so I gave him a smile as I went by him. A little while after he started to talk to us, and as we walked down the road he walked along with us. He was going the same way. He came to his home before we did and he said good-bye and we went on. The following Sunday he came to my place and invited me to go out for a ride in a top-buggy.[15] He had a nice driving team and he was jolly and I am the same, so I guess we suited each other in that respect.

In the meantime I had found out who he was and no doubt he knew who I was. Anyway, I knew I was not related to him. [16] It was a quick romance, and that summer we were married. I had a little money at the agency, left to me from my foster father who had died while I was still at Carlisle. We built a small house on seven acres of land that my husband bought. We had not planned how we were going to make our living. The other married people were getting along some way so we thought we ought to be able to get along too. My husband used to work for his father and other farmers around us. White people had started to settle on the reservation. My father-in-law had his ninety-acre farm and he was beginning to get old, so my husband worked for his dad a great deal. We managed to buy two cows, and the cows brought a little income for us, and although I was having children about every two years, yet I used to make lace. We used to get a good price for our lace. I made about twelve to fifteen dollars a week. Every Saturday we went to town and bought our weekly supplies of groceries and what clothing we needed. We lived in that small house while the children were small. We have nine children. Of course as soon as the children were old enough to go away to school we sent them to Tomah Boarding School. We really had them only in the summertime. When his father got too old to farm he asked us to live with him, so we sold our little place and lived with the old man. After his death the farm was sold and the money divided among the heirs. My husband got his share and bought seventeen acres of land with a house on it.

We had quite a few cows by this time and we were getting along fine when my husband got a shock from lightning. I really think that he was almost struck. After that he was not himself and one of his eyes got infected, and that had to be removed. He had to use so much money that we were forced to sell our place. We next rented a seven-acre farm. We lived there two years then we bought the place, and we still have the place. We have three cows and we sell cream. Our monthly income from the cows is about twenty-five dollars per month. My husband always works for the big farmers, and since there has been the WPA he has been working on the government project, and that is how we make our livelihood. I always can some vegetables and as much fruit as I can possibly put up. In the summertime my children pick beans and earn a little money that way. Three of my girls are now married, and my son just got married recently. One of my daughters lives in Milwaukee, one in Chicago, and one lives in Oneida. We have only five left to support.

I really love children, and I never really dreaded to have children. I enjoyed taking care of them; of course after my oldest girls were five or six years old they were my nursemaids. I showed them how to hold the baby and how to take care of it. I only held the baby when I nursed it and when I bathed it. The girls would rock the baby to sleep. I did not have to buy dolls for the girls. They had a live doll to play with.

I always had a doctor engaged when I am expecting to be sick, and my sister-in-law usually worked for me at least ten days. My husband is very handy in doing housework, and after I get up he usually just hires someone to do the washing. I have been troubled with milk leg.[17] I suppose I was not careful of myself.

When a woman does something to cause abortion then I think she is committing a crime. I happened to know of a woman who had a miscarriage. I don't know what caused it, but she sent for me and my sister-in-law. It must have been just over a month but all we could see was a tiny head about a quarter-inch in diameter, but it showed the eyes, and the limbs were like white thread, but we did not see the hands or feet. We buried it and for a long time I remembered that.

I think that while the baby is a part of the mother that the child would not need a soul, but just as soon as it is separated from its mother, and starts to breathe, then it receives its soul. I think the breath and soul come together, because when a person takes his or her last breath then the soul leaves the body. It seems to me that the breath of life is a part of the soul. Of course it is just a supposition. Nobody ever told me anything in that line. The doctors and minister should know if anyone knows. I never think too long on that because it is so mysterious, and the more I think of that the more puzzled I get. I always remember what I was taught in the Sunday school, that God created everything in the beginning. But there have been times when I had my doubts and then I would stop and think that if God did not start [it all] then who did?

And I would not be any nearer solving it, so then I just renew my faith in God.[18]

I am beginning to feel old as I see my grandchildren, although they are small yet. I suppose it is time for me to try to learn some of the Indian remedies and be a medicine woman, but I don't know of any remedy. I am sort of alone, because I never had a grandma. My people all died early in life—my sisters and one brother all died while they were young. My father was the only one left when I grew up, but he and I had lived away from each other so that I was not attached to him. There was no one to show me this or that, to tell me about anything. For that reason I don't know any Indian stories or Indian medicine. I think it is nice to know some of the old Indian remedies, because they were really good remedies. They say that Peter Powless has the best remedy for any kind of rheumatism.

SARAH CORNELIUS

This autobiographical account of Sarah Cornelius, who was sixty-nine in 1941, ranges over a number of topics, including children and childbirth. She must have been in one of the earliest cohorts to go to Carlisle Indian Industrial and Military School. Colonel Pratt, for whom she worked, was the founder of the school. She was interviewed by Ida Blackhawk on August 19, 1941.

School, Marriage, and Work

I am the oldest daughter, and when I was quite small I stayed with my grandparents because my father and mother were poor and had other children younger than I. My grandfather was making money at that time. He used to make sleighs from hardwood timber, and he sold them as fast as he finished one. When I was big enough to walk to school, I attended the mission day school. They used to have a large frame building with desks for about a hundred pupils. There was folding doors in the middle of the room, and most of the time the doors were closed, making two schoolrooms. Reverend Goodnough was the teacher. He used to be very strict. I guess he had to be because there were boys and girls eighteen years old attending school. Father Goodnough used to issue clothing to the day school students. I don't know if it came from the government or if some missionaries gave it to the Oneida Mission. Anyway, they were new clothes, dresses, aprons, coats, and shoes. I remember the first time I went home with a big bundle—how glad my grandma was to get them. I went to school there until I was twelve years old, then I went to Martinsburg, Pennsylvania.

Martinsburg was a mission school set up by some wealthy friends of the Indians. There were about three hundred Indians there, but there were other tribes of Indians represented. I was in Martinsburg only a short time. Then the school was abolished, and we were all transferred to Carlisle Indian School. The Oneidas had just started to send their children to Carlisle or Hampton.

While at Carlisle, I was sent out to work for some Pennsylvania Dutch or German people. They were very rich farmers. They had their own cured meat of all kinds. They did not buy their meat from the butcher shop. There was another girl working there besides me, and Electa Skenandore (Mrs. Joe Powless) was working a little ways from us. We three girls used to have fun. There was a little lake there where we used to go canoeing quite often. We did not work hard, and I don't remember what wages I got.

Another place I worked was a farm too, and just the lady and her young son stayed there, but they had several men working for them. The husband worked in some city near there—I don't remember the name of the city but it was in the state of Maryland. One day the man came back there all beaten up. He said someone attacked him on the way coming home. Then one night some burglars came there and took some things from the hired boys' room. They entered the lady's bedroom and either they killed her or the shock killed her, but anyway the lady was found dead the next day. That man was married again in a little while after his wife died, and everybody suspected him but nothing was done while I was there. I was sent back to the school soon afterwards. That's the kind of white people I was supposed to learn nice things from.

While I was at Carlisle I used to work for Colonel Pratt in his home. There were about four of us worked there. Two of us worked in the morning until noon and the other two girls worked in the afternoon. Then in the evening we were all there. It was not hard because there were so many of us working for Colonel Pratt. I liked to work for him, but when the matron changed the detail, I was put in the employees' club. I liked that too, because we had good things to eat. I used to wait on the table and wiped the dishes. Government gravy is alright if it is eaten once in a while, but it gets tiresome if one gets that every day.

I did not learn in school, but I learned to speak the English language, so after staying at the Carlisle Indian School five years I returned home. I was seventeen years old. As soon as I got home my folks made a bargain with certain old people, who were well-to-do, for their son and I to get married. The young man made friends with me, and used to come to the house to visit, but I never hardly talked to him. I never had a boyfriend before, and I liked the boy. He would come there with his father's lively team and a new buggy, and I went out riding with him. He had been to school too, but to a different school, so he and I just got acquainted. All the girls of my age had their boyfriends, and it did not seem out of the way for me to have a boyfriend, but in a short time both of our parents told us we had to get married or we would have to stop going places together. They really had everything arranged for our wedding reception, and so we both agreed with our folks and we were married in the fall.

His folks had a farm containing about ninety acres, all under cultivation, and they had plenty of work. We stayed with his folks and I was expected to do most of the housework, and it seemed as though we were just staying there. My husband wasn't getting any definite wages and he was not satisfied, but instead of having an understanding with his father, he just got to drinking and he left me there to stay with his folks. I had three children, but my oldest boy died before he was a year old. I got tired of him drinking, and of us staying with his family, so I went home, but my father and mother made me go back and we kept on staying with his folks.

The next time he went on a spree I went away and worked for some people. I earned some money for myself, and when I got through there I went to another home. He finally went after me and begged me to go back, and he promised me he would quit drinking. I went back, and pretty soon it was the same old story. He went on a spree again. Again I left him. For a year or so we were separated for a month or so at a time, then one day I got the news of his accidental death. He was killed by a train on his way home while still intoxicated. That left me a widow with two little girls to support. At that time a widow with dependents did not get mothers' pension, and I had no income so I was left destitute.

I worked at the boarding school, and later at Wittenberg, Wisconsin. My salary was only about twenty-five to thirty dollars a month. When Mr. Pierce was transferred to Flandreau, South Dakota, he offered me a job to work for him. [19] I went and worked for ten dollars per week. Mrs. Pierce was the matron, and the next year then was a vacancy in the laundry. Mr. Pierce recommended me, and I became the assistant laundress. In the summer I came home for my vacation and saw my children, who were staying with their grandparents. I took the oldest girl back with me, and she stayed in my room and went to school all day. I didn't find it very hard to have my little girl there, so the next summer I came home again and I took my other little girl back to school with me. I used to hire two schoolgirls to look after my girls. One worked in the morning, and the other girl came in the afternoon. Both of my little girls attended school. I was getting along fine, supporting myself and my two little girls.

One summer I was home on my vacation when I met a young man at my cousin's place. We got acquainted and our romance began. It was a short romance, and before I went back to work we were married. I kept on working, and my husband went there and was employed as a school carpenter. We both worked and earned money the first year, and then I had to take a sick leave for two months. During that time I had a little baby. I went back to work and I had one of the big girls stay with my baby. I worked until I had another baby; then I stayed home and just my husband worked in the Indian Service. We finally got transferred to Lac du Flambeau, Wisconsin.

My second husband was an ideal man. He had no bad habits and was always pleasant and agreeable. In the summertime when he had his vacation we always came home to his father's place. His father was also a well-to-do farmer. We did not like Lac du Flambeau as well as we did Flandreau, so my husband resigned and we went to Green Bay. He did carpenter work, and we got along fine. Then my husband began to fail in health. We did not know what was ailing him—the doctor could not tell—but he lost weight fast and felt weak. I went back to work, and he stayed with some of my relatives. In the spring I was called home to his bedside. I stayed a few days and visited him; then I had to go back in order to keep my job. Not long afterwards he died, and I was again left a widow with two little girls. (My two older daughters both got married quite young.)

After paying my husband's funeral expenses I was again without funds to support my two little girls. The superintendent at Lac du Flambeau did not want my children there unless they were put with the other children, and I thought they were too small, so I left them with some relatives while I worked. The children stayed here and there with relatives until they were old enough to go to school; then I sent them to Tomah, Wisconsin. I resigned from the Indian Service and stayed with my son-in-law in Green Bay. I worked for different families by the day and was paid by the hour. The women were getting forty to fifty cents per hour for day work.

Then one say I met a white woman who told me about a summer resort where she worked one summer, and I wrote to the lady and I asked her if she needed a laundress. She answered my letter and told me to come, but I had to work in the kitchen. It was at Brown's Lake, near Burlington, Wisconsin. I worked there two months and got sixty dollars per month. That winter I got a letter from the Lakeside Resort to come and work about the first part of May. I helped clean the hotel and cottages and employees' quarters. I got twenty-five cents an hour and my board.

When the season opened for business, I started to work in the laundry, and I had my oldest girl work with me. She got twelve dollars per week and I got eighteen dollars per week. I used to wash for some of the guests, and I made extra money that way. We stayed about a week after the season closed and helped clean up. I left the resort with about three hundred dollars. I put some of that in the bank, and I used some of it through the winter months.

The next year I went again with some other Oneida women. When the school closed at Tomah the girls came to Burlington, and they both worked at twelve dollars per week. One of the girls used to wait on the table, and she got tips, and the other girl learned how to finger wave at the school.[20] She had a regular beauty parlor in our room every Saturday afternoon. The young girls that were employed there used to get her to fix their hair, and when some of the guests found out she could finger wave they came to her too. She made quite a lot of extra money that way. When my girls and I left that fall we had almost five hundred dollars. I bought some clothes for the girls, and one went back to Tomah and the other went to Haskell Institute, an Indian school in Kansas.

The third summer I worked there then I bought a home with ten acres of land. I paid eight hundred dollars down and was to pay on installments for the balance. In three years I had almost paid for the property, when I traded for a city property in Green Bay. I took the city property because I thought it would be handier for me to work in the city, but work was scarce then and I could not find any work. I worked short hours. I had to pay for paving the streets in front of my house, and I had a full basement made to the house, and it cost me some money. I found out my taxes was much higher in the city, so at the end of two years I was ready to trade for another place in Oneida. I traded my city property for a small farm containing thirty-five acres with a large house on it.

I had to repair the house and had a well dug, and it amounted to three hundred dollars. I rented the place, but I was not able to get much rent because the land was too sandy. I also had the house wired for electricity. Just as I got that done then I had a paralytic stroke and was laid up at Tomah hospital for five months. I am still partly paralyzed, but I am able to walk with the help of a crutch. I had to sell my property because I still owed about five hundred dollars and I had to let it go for much less than I would like to have sold it for, but I needed the money.

It is hard for me to sit still and see so many things that should be done. When I use up my money then I will be eligible for old-age pension. It seemed to me as I look back on the years I worked so hard that it was all useless. It is no use to try to accumulate so much property or money because you can't take it with you when you die. I should not have worked so hard, and maybe I would be well today. It seems to me that my father and mother did not work so hard to make their living. They used to go to Wausaukee in the wintertime, and my father used to take a contract for woodcutting for the winter. He used to have his crew to cut the wood and they camped there together, some of his friend and relatives. They really had nice times there in the northern woods. They killed all kinds of game for their meat while there. The women would make baskets in their spare time.

When spring came they would have some money saved up to be used for buying groceries in the summertime while they are taking care of their crops. They seemed to be taking their time, and yet they accomplished just as much as we do now. They had lots of time visiting each other and it was the custom to always give a visitor something to eat to show them hospitality, and they even offered it to strangers. They always had plenty to eat. I would not state that everybody was the same. There are always some who seem to be hard up no matter how much they earn. Those old people I am speaking of did not dress as we do now. They did not use their good clothes as often as we do, so they kept their clothes a long time; nor did they follow the style. They hardly ever bought ready-made clothes. They made their own clothes, and most of it was sewed by hand.

When I began to have children, we never called for a doctor. Most all the old women were midwives. I know I had a woman that took care of all sorts of sick people and knew a great deal about Indian remedies. She really was a doctor or medicine woman, as the people called her. She used to diagnose a case and went to the woods and gathered her medicine and proceeded to doctor the sick person, and maybe she did not always cure the sick, but she helped many sick people. If they had money they paid her; if not it was alright. A medicine woman was more like a missionary nurse.

My own grandmother was one of those that went about doctoring. Most of these old women were friends, and they taught each other how to treat for certain diseases and would show each other all sort of herbs, roots, or leaves to use for curing such a disease. In that way it was handed down to the next generation. But after the Oneida people began to use white doctors' medicine the old people ceased to tell about their medicine and the younger generation did not take any interest in learning the Indian medicine because they could get a doctor, and they relied on him more than an Indian doctor. I know a few Indian remedies, but I would be afraid to treat anyone because now it requires a license to practice doctoring. But fifty years ago the Indians were free to use their remedies.

There must be some reason why there are so many of us Oneidas getting the paralytic stroke. It seems to me it is more prevalent now than years ago. Many of the old people lived to be over ninety years old, and they would gradually grow weak and died without being sick very long. The Oneidas took care of their old people. There was always someone to take in an old couple and let them live in their home, or they would build a little log cabin for them by their place. Most of the old people were able to help themselves and so they were not altogether dependents. The old men were able to cut wood, or cut brush, and the old women made baskets or made quilt blocks. They were really useful to the very last.

With my two children by my first marriage I was taken care of by a midwife, but for my two other children a doctor and a nurse took care of me. I did not see much difference. I seemed to get along just as well with a midwife. I think any woman that is in good health will naturally not have a difficult delivery because nature made things that way and so nature takes care of it.

I never paid any attention to the old women's superstitions, and I had normal children. I never did anything to prevent myself from having children or to cause abortion. I just let them come; but I only had five. I guess that was all I was supposed to have. I have a daughter that has nine children, and I never tell her to do something to stop having children. I tell her that it is her fate. I used to try to help her all I could while I was able to, but now all I can do is advise. I am staying with my daughter who has no children and we always try to keep one of my grandchildren, but they get lonesome for their home. I like children, but they tire me now if I am with them very long.

Most of what I know about pregnancy is what I have been told or from my own experience. I know that about four months in pregnancy one feels the movements of the child, and anyone that would try to do something to get rid of it would be very heartless. Even though many of the old women knew some medicine that would cause abortion, yet they would not treat anyone or reveal to them what to do. It used to be considered a criminal act with the old Indians to cause abortion. It was also considered a terrible disgrace for a young maiden to have a child. A girl was ostracized by the church people and by the whole community. It is not that way anymore, and most of the girls that are unwedded mothers go about as though nothing matters.

Most all the women know that they must exercise during pregnancy in order to keep the baby from developing too much, and it is for the mother's safety. I know one woman that would not do any work for fear that she would hurt herself. She had someone working for her all the time, and when it was time for her to deliver she had such a difficult time, a doctor was called and he had to use instruments to deliver her baby; but the baby lived. The next time she was pregnant again she worked all the time and she had easier delivery although she had twins that time.

I think it is hard to say what period of its development that the soul becomes a part of the child. It would seem that as soon as it starts to live—and at the same time it is a part of the mother until it is born and no person has two souls—so I would infer that the child gets its soul at the time of its birth. The Indians say that a caul birth is a sign that the infant is talented or has supernatural power.[21] The change of life in a woman is like the period of puberty, only it's the ending of generative powers and the period lasts several years. Some women feel the effects more than others. I had no trouble at all, and I was working all the time. My menstruals gradually stopped and that was all there was to that.

Not very long ago there was a girl that had a baby outside on the ice. She claimed it was an accident and of course everybody believed her, and it's possible, but she could have done it intentionally too. That is how easy the girls get by these days. I think it is too bad that we have so many taverns around here, and most of the outsiders that come to the Saturday- or Sunday-night dances are the lower class of white people. The young girls are often enticed away from the dance hall for a ride, and if they drink beer they are sometimes doped by the fellows. The parents of these young girls are more or less to blame for allowing their young girls to go to those dance halls connected with taverns. The young girls are innocent and they really go there merely to dance, but they are treated to drinks, and one drink leads to another. If the parents would put in their protest, some of these taverns would close.

I have another incident I have heard of regarding how natural the Indian women had their offspring. One time a woman was home with all her children when she started to feel the labor pains of childbirth. There was no one living near them, and her husband was away. She took a quilt and went in the cornfield and delivered her baby. When she came out of the cornfield she was carrying her baby. She was an exceptionally strong and healthy woman. There was another woman that had a baby on the way to Green Bay, when the women used to go to Green Bay on foot. Her companions took care of her and then walked home. She must have been a strong woman too.

Lucy Elm, fifty-nine years old at the time she gave this account, spent years in boarding schools, receiving an education largely in domestic skills, as was generally the case with girls. On August 21, 1941, she responded to questions about issues surrounding childbirth and birth control that were put to her by Ida Blackhawk. Robert Ritzenthaler described Lucy Elm as "pleasant, hard working, and a swell friend to have."[22]

School, Marriage, and Childbirth

I was two years old when my mother died of childbirth. I was the youngest child of the family. I don't hardly remember my mother, but I do remember that I used to miss her, although my older sister was very kind to me. We were both sent to Wittenberg Boarding School, Wisconsin, and when we came home for the summer the following fall we were sent to Keshena, Wisconsin, another boarding school. After being there three years we again came home. I don't even remember where we stayed, but it was with some relatives.

That fall we signed up to go to Carlisle. I must have been about nine years old. I did not learn fast, but I learned to speak English and forgot my Oneida tongue. We were at Carlisle several years and I worked in different departments. I was detailed in the dining room, waited on the students' tables, and I worked in the laundry hanging out the clothes and ironing dresses and aprons. I also worked in the sewing room. First I learned how to darn stockings; then I learned how to patch underwear, then overalls, shirts, and dresses. Every month we changed detail. The last year I was there I worked in the sewing room and made dresses. I learned everything about dressmaking except to draft a pattern. That was before the stores sold dress patterns, etc. In the summer months I worked with my older sister, and I learned all about housework. We stayed in the country with some Quaker people and they were very nice to us. We went to school, but I was too shy and did not learn much.

Every summer we were sent to work for some white people. I always had a good, easy place and the people always liked me and my work. I never had any trouble. I don't think any of the people took advantage of me. Of course I had to work, but not too hard. I guess I always worked for well-to-do people. And everything was convenient; I never worked for country people. I have no complaints of any of them. I have nothing but pleasant memories when I think of my school days and the time spent working away from Carlisle. I presume that I enjoyed my school life because that was the only home I had. All my childhood was spent in school, and when I was leaving Carlisle I could not help but regret that my time was up.

My sister and I both came home. My father had a little place and we went there. We were grown up now and could do the work. My sister was eighteen and I was sixteen. We stayed home all summer and had a good time. My father just let us do as we pleased. We had all the boyfriends we wanted. My sister met the young man that she married, and later I met his cousin and I fell in love with him, and I was married the following fall. Then my sister, who was like a mother to me, lived away from me.

My husband was just a poor young man, and we had no idea how we were going to make our living, but he worked for different farmers and we managed to eat all winter. We moved to Green Bay and my husband worked in a coal yard. About a year after we were married we had our first child, a boy. My husband never tried to farm. We sold our allotments as soon as the Oneidas were permitted to sell their land. We always lived in the nearby towns, and Ed worked for different concerns as a laborer. He managed to take care of us, but it was a case of hand to mouth. I had a child about every two years, excepting the last one. He was three years younger than his older sister. I had five children.

I experienced lots of hardships while my children were small. We always had rent to pay besides our food, fuel, and clothing. My husband drank liquor now and then, and sometimes he spent more money for liquor than he intended; then that meant that I would have to skimp on our eats until the next payday. We moved to Manitowoc, Wisconsin, during the world war, and my husband worked in the shipbuilding factory. He made a lot of money, and he was able to rent a better place and clothe the children well. They were all attending school. My children all finished the grade school and my two daughters both attended the high school, but they both failed to finish.

Both of my daughters married outside of the tribe. One of my sons is not married yet, and the one that was married had an accidental death a few weeks ago when a car struck the car he was riding and he was killed instantly. My other boy died several years ago. He fell off the bridge and was drowned. My husband was sickly several years before he died, and he died about twelve years ago. My husband was a good man and a good provider, but he drank very heavily towards the end of his time. After my daughters and one of my sons got married I came back to Oneida and I am keeping house for Kay Hill. I am not very strong, so that is one reason I don't try to find some other work. I was badly injured when I was in a car accident.

I had a midwife take care of me when I had my first child, but it was because we could not get a doctor quick enough, but with the other children I always had a doctor. In each case I suffered alike so I can't say which I prefer. I never thought of preventing myself from having children. I just took for granted that I was supposed to have children while I was married. I would consider a person who does something to cause abortion to oneself, or to another, a very wicked person, but I think if a person knows what to do to keep from getting pregnant it is alright, as long as they are not hurting anyone.

A child must derive it soul from its mother, so when a child is born the soul becomes active just like the child. The child starts to use its own senses and gradually uses its power of motion. The child does not cry while it is in the womb, but it does have the power to cry right after birth. The old people used to tell me that it is very easy to mark a child at any time during pregnancy. I used to believe all they told me, and I used to be always cautious, but one time I was going to the neighbors and I came across a crippled man. He was very badly crippled up, and one just hated to see him because his feet seemed to be twisted around his body, and he moved around on his hands and knees. This fellow was sitting by the roadside in the grass. I was surprised and I went around him, but I did not stop to look at him, and he spoke to me and laughed. I went right on, but I made up my mind I was not going to be frightened by him. I thought of what the old folks had told me, but kept myself from thinking about it, and when my baby came I was a little anxious to see if I did not mark it, and I was glad to find out that nothing happened to it. From that I would infer that if a person can control oneself from getting excited about anything that they can prevent the impression on the child. All my children were normal and healthy, and yet I never was under a doctor's care during pregnancy, but really never had any trouble. When I began to have the change of life I never got sick, but my menstruation gradually stopped so then I knew I was passing that period of my life.

MILDRED SUMMERS

Mildred Summers, age thirty-four, also had serious troubles, above all with poverty. She shared this account with Ida Blackhawk on August 8, 1941. An account by her husband, Milton Summers, follows.

Poverty and Illness

My mother died when I was only six years old, and my father had died before my mother. I was just left here and there amongst the Oneidas. I had two half sisters. Their father kept them, but my stepfather just let me stay with one old lady. In the wintertime I went to the government school, but when I was out of school I stayed with the old lady. She did not adopt me, but I stayed with her and worked for her in the summer months. I attended the boarding school five years, then I stayed home and took care of the old woman until I got married. I was only seventeen years old, but I was glad to get away from the old woman, and I never thought of what I was getting into.

I married a poor boy, and of course I was worse off than him. I had no close relatives; I had a lot of distant relatives, but I did not know them. My husband had his parents, but they were very poor people. My husband was a good worker. He worked for some farmers in the summertime and went to the northern woods in the winter months and became a lumberjack. We went to Milwaukee one time and he worked in the factory, and when we came back he bought eleven acres of land, and he built this little log cabin, and we have lived here since. We lived here all through the depression. When the Oneidas were put to work on the WPA my husband was one of them. We have one cow, and that helps us out a lot. I even make butter once in a while, and the children get all the milk they want. Last fall my husband got sick, and as he is an ex-serviceman, he was eligible to go to the Milwaukee Soldiers' Hospital. He stayed there all winter, and my children and I stayed home alone. While my husband was working for the WPA he got about forty-five dollars per month, but since we have been on direct relief our budget is twenty-four dollars a month with the surplus commodities. Just once I got a separate order of eight dollars for clothing.

We have nine children. There are eight girls and one boy. My oldest girl is seventeen years old but is very slow to learn in school. Since our budget is not enough to pay their expenses to go to De Pere High School we tried to get them in a government school, but the agent did not approve of that because my husband is living, and besides we live too close to the highway where the government school bus goes by. But he don't understand that we can't even afford to pay for their lunches. The girls are beginning to realize that we are poorer than most of the other families, and they were anxious to go away to school. They would like to dress like other girls and have a room of their own, and they know we can't do anything for them as long as their father is sick. He is trying to get compensation from the government, but that is hard to get as long as he has been healthy for so many years after he was released from the army. But the doctors claim that his trouble now is from being gassed during the world war. His chest hurts him, and during the winter he had arthritis. As soon as he was well enough to be up and around he came home, but he has not been able to work. The girls were at the cherry orchard, and they made a little money for themselves. Of course as I said before we were always poor, and I had no home when I married Milton, so I did not miss the luxuries that other people enjoy. I was satisfied just so we had plenty to eat and a place to call our home, although we only had two small rooms and a place to sleep upstairs.

When the children were small it did not cost so very much to clothe them, and our groceries did not amount to very much. Little girls do not eat so very much. Of course now they are all getting big, and they are good eaters and their clothing amounts to more than it used to. Their shoes alone comes to over forty dollars a year, and I am not including the rubbers I buy in the wintertime. At the present time everything is so high that I don't know how we are going to get along this winter. We have an old car, and a radio that he got while he was working. Of course he used to always plant some contract beans, and potatoes, and other garden stuff for our own use, but since he got sick our land has been idle, and we pay twelve dollars a year taxes. We have never had to spend very much on doctor bills. The children are all well, just now and then have a cold.

I have had a doctor three times when I am sick with confinement. We always get a midwife because it does not cost so much, and I always get along alright. The midwife always stayed with one for at least ten days, and she would cook and wash for us too during that time. But we called for a doctor three times now since we had a government doctor. I have never been to Tomah Hospital. I always stay home; then I can be with my children. My girls do a lot of the work, but my oldest girl is not a very good worker. I have to tell her what to do each day.

I have never had a very difficult delivery. I have heard of some women being so afraid to go anywhere, or to do some things for fear of marking the unborn child. I never bother about it, and now and then we go to shows or fairs. I always go, but I never go in to see the freaks. I don't get frightened easily, so I guess that is why I never had a child that I would say was marked. One time I saw a show that I could not forget for a long time: the inhabitants of some lone island were very hideous-looking people. That was before my last baby was born, and I thought maybe I would mark my baby, but I didn't. I never make fun of people or make any remarks about anyone. I know a woman about my age who was a great one to make a remark of anyone she saw. As a young girl she was haughty and would make remarks about the way someone is dressed and also about their looks, and she would make fun of anyone if they were quiet and didn't say much. Her folks always dressed her real nice, and she was very proud of herself. When she had her first baby it was not a normal child. It died after it was a few years old. Later she went lame. She had tuberculosis of the bone. Now one of her legs is shorter than the other. I often think of how she used to be and wonder if she is still the same.

I have never given much thought of the soul. If the soul is part of the human being, then the child must get its soul as soon as it starts to live. It always seems to me so much of a mystery that I don't try to solve things myself, but take for granted that what someone tells me must be the truth. We are taught in church that every human being has a soul, and I never have asked anyone when we got it. I have heard that the soul never dies—that it leaves the body when one dies. But where the soul goes is also a mystery to me. They say it goes to heaven, but where is heaven?

I am a member of the Methodist church, but I don't attend the services very often. I suppose I should go to church more frequently, then I would be posted on religious things, but I am too busy bringing up children that I don't have time to go to church. I have been told that if you are married and shirk from having children that you are not doing right, so no matter how poor we are I would never think of doing anything to cause abortion. Of course now my problem is how to keep these little children from suffering on account of poverty, and I am sure that we are going to get help some way soon. I would like to see my children get as much education as they can possibly have, even if they never help us, but just so they will be able to take care of themselves. And I hope that none of my girls get married as young as I did—then possibly they will be spared from having as many children as I have.

MILTON SUMMERS

> Here is Mr. Summers's view of his own life and of his marriage with
> Mildred, as told in an interview with Guy Elm on February 12, 1942.

School, France, and Family

I was born January 1, 1897, in Oneida Reservation. I am a member of a large family of six children, five boys and one girl. My father left us when we were quite small; my mother raised us children. You might as well write down their names: the oldest Phillip Summers, Bangar Summers, Elmer Summers, Austin Summers, and one sister, Mamie Summers Cornelius. They all are living on the reservation. Phillip is a tavern keeper and runs a farm in the summer. Austin is a farmer and works in town in the summer at the docks. Elmer works on the WPA project. Bangar is disabled like me. Four of us boys were in World War I: Phillip, Bangar, Elmer, and myself.

I went to school when I was six years of age. I went to Methodist Mission School for one year. The next school was the Oneida Government Boarding School. I went to this school for six years. My mother used to go after us every month to come home and visit her over the weekend. If we didn't go back right away the Indian police used to come to our place and we all had to go back with him to school. Sometimes my younger brother and I would run away from there; this police would be there when we get home waiting for us. We ran away from that school so many times that he must have made lots of money from the government. We fixed him though, one time.

We had been home about two days, and it was in the spring of the year. My mother seen him driving towards our home and it was near noon. She said to us, "Now you boys stay right here and I'll do the talking. Anyway, you'll all have your dinner before he takes you back to school. Besides, I'm going to give him something to eat that will make him sick on your way back to school. That will give you a chance to get away from him." We were sawing wood by the house when he drove up. He came right over to where we were working and said, "Well, boys, get your coats and come along with me." My mother stepped up to him and said, "Now John, you see I'm out of wood and you come to take my boys away. You can take them, but first you must stay for dinner. I'm cooking a nice dinner for the boys, and I'm asking you to have a dinner with us." The Indian police finally decided he would stay for dinner.

When the meal was ready she called us all to dinner. The police I suppose was glad to stay for dinner because we had killed a woodchuck and we had that for dinner. He sure enjoyed his meal and didn't notice what she put in his dish to make him sick. After dinner, us boys got ready. My mother told us, she said, "Now you boys better be good. I'll be coming to see you in about two weeks," and she kind of had a smile for the policeman. The police was nice to her too. He said, "I want to thank you for the dinner; it's no wonder your sons are always running away from school and coming home to their mother."

We started for the school; the police had a rig with a nice horse for driving. He took a road to another man's home to get another runaway boy. Everything went alright until we were about halfway to the school, then his troubles started. He said, "You boys watch and tell me if you see anybody coming from both directions. I sure am a sick man. I wonder what the heck I ate to make me so sick." Just then he stopped his horse and got off his buggy. Well, we were in a clearing, and this Indian police was a big man; besides he was fat, so that he look like a woodchuck. "Well, boys, it's got to be done," [he said,] and walked back behind the buggy. Well he done it alright—I could hear all kinds of noise back there; but we were afraid to run from there because he had his wicked-looking gun with him, so we decided to wait and gamble on another stop. He finally got back in the buggy with us and we started on our way again, but we could tell that he was not feeling very well; he kept grunting and complaining about his stomach hurting him.

We went another mile or so, then once more we had to stop. He said, "Boys, boys, get out of my way I got to go again." This time there was a woods right alongside the road; he went running in there pulling his pants down as he ran. Just as soon as he got out of our sight we all jumped off and ran down the road as fast as we could run. By the time he came back to the road his horse had gone on; she was out of sight too. Well, we came back home and finished our work cutting wood for our mother. The next day then she took us back herself. Whatever he ate it sure fixed him alright, and I never asked my mother what she fed him. I know one thing: he never ate there again.

In 1910 I went to Tomah Indian School, and some of my brothers went there too. I was there three years. After I found out that I couldn't learn very fast I decided to quit going to school; besides I wanted to help my mother. I worked on the farms around near Oneida Reservation. I used to come home every week and visit my mother and gave her some of my money. I worked for the farmers until wartime.

I enlisted in the army April 6, 1917. I went to Camp Douglas, Wisconsin. I join up with the Thirty-second Division, Battery E, and later I transferred to D, heavy artillery. There were five Indians of all kinds of tribes from Wisconsin and Michigan. The Thirty-second Division received their training at Waco, Texas, Camp McArthur. We were there for almost six months training. We went from there to Camp Merritt in New Jersey, and from there to Liverpool, England, and to a camp called Winchester for about three or four days' stop. Then we got on the boats again for Le Havre, France. We stayed here for three days, then we went to a camp called Corkeltown in France for two months' training. From there we went into small-scale fights.

The real battles were at Château-Thierry, Soissons, and Argonne Forest. These were the major offensives where I saw plenty action. The infantry went into Germany; it was the first division to step on the German soil. The heavy artillery couldn't go any further due to loss of horses, and the men were pretty well crippled up. They turned us back, but the rest of the outfit marched to the Rhine. We were sent back to a station— the soldiers call it a delousing station. We stayed here to get rid of those pets. We were here for some time in the southern part of France, a town called Baladuke [Bar-le-Duc], recuperating. We were only supposed to be here seven days, but we were here for twenty-eight days. They couldn't spare the trains to bring us back to a deportation camp. It was in May 1, 1919, that we finally got on a transport, a troopship, and we sailed for the U.S.A. We landed at Boston, Massachusetts, and from there to Camp Grant, Illinois. We received our discharge May 19, 1919. I came home to Oneida.

I was married to my wife, Mildred Elm, March 26, 1922. I worked on the farms around here and done some work on the county road and town roads. When the depression came I was working on a farm. I was laid off from my job, and I had to depend on short jobs and the town for relief. This went on until I finally got on WPA projects. I have worked in a stone quarry, at road work, and in Kaukauna putting up a dam. I was forced to quit my job due to my health in 1940.

I have been to the veterans hospital in Milwaukee several times already for treatments. I like it there alright; they treat me just fine each time I have been there. But I always get lonesome for my family. I come back home to see them. Just now I am staying home, but I can't do any hard work, and so I just keep the stove supplied with coal and wood, and besides I go to stores for supplies.

We have four children at the district school; one at the high school, first year, and the oldest girl is working at Kaukauna and attending vocational school part-time. The children are pretty healthy, and they are plenty playful. We don't have much trouble with them; of course now and then they quarrel with one another over who should do this and that. When it goes too far and their mother can't restore order, then I usually step in and let them know who is the boss. They just have to mind me or there is sure trouble to settle afterwards.

Take my oldest daughter, Amanda. She helps her mother with the work in the house, and she can cook almost as good as her mother. She takes care of children when they go to bed and when they get up in the morning; that is, she helps them to get ready for bed and helps them to dress when they get up. She also helps at the table by dishing out the food and serving it to the smaller children. She makes the beds before she does other housework. In summertime she helped me with my planting, picking, and gathering crops in the fall. In fact, she is about the best worker in the whole family. All I can say is that she is good girl.

The rest of the family is all good as far as I know. We have never received any complaint from the teacher or from other people. All the bad things they do and the fighting is done right at home. When there is a big family like this there is bound to be some quarreling between different ones in the family. The only quarreling I and my wife have is that sometimes I get away from her when we are at a tavern. In the summertime when the weather gets too warm to work, we usually stroll to my brother's tavern and drink some beer, watch the people do their stuff, and relax after hard labor at weeding the garden or picking beans. And on Saturday nights we go there again. Sometimes we meet some live wire that is anxious to spend his money. Of course, we always accept the drinks—never refuse anything like that. We don't overdo it. I personally think it's lots of fun, don't you?

WILLIAM WEBSTER

> William Webster grew up mostly in Milwaukee, but his ties to the
> Oneida Reservation and community were very strong. Formerly a pro-
> fessional boxer, on July 18, 1941, he spoke to Guy Elm in Milwaukee
> about his career, his marriage, and his hopes for the future.[23]

A Boxer's Career and Marriage

I was born in Oneida, Wisconsin, on February 2, 1911, so that makes me about thirty years old. I was married once, but I got my divorce after I was married a few years. I have two children from this marriage. I am a professional boxer; that is, I used to be until I met an accident. My brother-in-law lost his life in this car accident; I guess my time wasn't up yet. Anyway, I came through alright, but I was in the hospital for a few weeks.

I am going to tell you first the education I have. You know that is the most important thing in one's life; I have found that out. The first school I attended was the old government boarding school here in Oneida. I went to this school for two years. The next school I went to was Tomah Indian School. I went there in the fall and I stayed there for two years. I finally ran away from there and came home to Green Bay. During the time I was away my folks had moved to that city. That fall I went to a public school called Tank School. I finished the eighth grade.

About this time my folks took a notion to move to another city, and this time it was Milwaukee.

In Milwaukee I went to Bay View High School. I attended this school for two years. I took up boxing the first year I was there, but I didn't do much fighting until the second year. I lick everything that was my weight in Milwaukee. I was fighting in the amateur ranks. I won many watches and medals as first-prize winner. I started in the flyweight; as I grew heavier and acquired experience I kept going up in weight. By the time I retired from the ring I was fighting in the lightweight division. I went one year to a vocational school and I kept on fighting on amateur cards during the time I was going there. I had over forty fights while I was amateur, and about that many after I turn pro.

I really think that if I hadn't got into an accident, I would be still fighting in the ring today. Because I know I was just getting to be a real fighter. I have fought in cities like Chicago; Detroit; Benton Harbor, Michigan; Racine; Kenosha; Cleveland, Ohio; Buffalo, New York; Elgin, Illinois; and St. Paul, Minnesota. Most of my fights were preliminary bouts. I was just starting to get on the main bouts when the accident took place. As a matter of fact I had just won a fight in Detroit, Michigan, and so I had quite a fat wallet when I got back to Milwaukee. I looked for my brother-in-law. We celebrated together that night. It was very hot weather in Milwaukee during the month of August, and so early the next morning we got up and took his car to go swimming. The accident happened on our way. We were traveling at a high rate of speed—we were cutting across away from the traffic and we came to a dead-end road. It was too late to stop. He put the brakes on, but we went over the embankment. About one hundred feet below was the lakeshore. We never knew what happened when we landed. My brother-in-law was killed instantly. When I came to I was in the hospital. I almost cash in too. I was crack up pretty bad myself. It took several weeks for me to recuperate from the injuries I received in the accident. I have never been myself since that time on. To continue professional boxing was out of the question for me, but I did try to fight a few more times afterwards.

When I first got married, I had a good job besides being a boxer. I was employed by the Milwaukee Cars Company. I was getting sixty-five cents per hour. We were working forty-eight hours per week. I also lost this job because I was off the job too long at the time of the accident. I looked for work all over the city, but on account of the depression jobs were hard to find and I was sort of crippled so I didn't have much of a chance for securing work.

I finally did get a job as a driver for a bootlegger and prizefighter promoter. I worked for him and he acted as my manager in securing fights for me. I had about six fights under his management. I lost all my fights and I decided I was all washed up as a prizefighter. I retired from the ring. I have fought on several occasions since that time, but I just can't get back in shape. My legs just can't hold up under me; a few good cracks and I start warppling all over the ring. The last fight I had was at Detroit, Michigan. A six-rounder. I don't know to this day how I managed to stay in there with the man I was fighting. Although I had a good manager and trainer, after the third round I just pounded away at the other fighter, hit or miss, and I guess most of the punches were missing their mark. After the fight my manager informed me that it was a good, close battle all the way through, but I lost the bout on points. I was encouraged to continue in my career as a prizefighter, but I knew better—that I couldn't possibly win my fights in the condition I was in at that time. I could give plenty hard blows, but I couldn't take it myself. And so that's how I quit the fight game.

Since I quit fighting, the manager also fired me from the other job I was working. I was out of a job for a few months, and then I got on another job, but not a steady one.

It was at this time that my beautiful wife had to go look for work herself. She found employment at once. She worked in a beauty parlor. Her wages were good, because that was her profession. We had the two children and we were living with her mother. When I wasn't working, I used to mind the children for my wife. Well, my mother-in-law also had few days a week job too. I got to be the housekeeper altogether for them. I knew then that I wasn't going to work very long like that. My wife had a chance to step out on me at nights. She would tell me that she was going to work at night at her job. I can't recall just how long this went on. After a while some of my relations told me that they saw my wife with another man at so-and-so's place, a tavern. At first I didn't care, because she was supporting me and the family.

I finally made up my mind to check up on her. And so on several occasions I would hire a maid to care for the kids. I went to make a call at the place where she was supposed to be working—but no wife there. The next day I asked her if she had to work that night. She told me she had to work late that night. I didn't say anything anymore. The first chance I got I stepped out too, and I was out all night. Boy did I ever catch hell. We got into a big quarrel and that was that; we decided to separate, which we did. In a few months she started to sue me for nonsupport. I didn't contest the case, so that she could get a divorce from me on that grounds on her own expenses. She got her divorce, and she is married again to a worse man than I am. He didn't last as long as I did. She is separated again. She has been good to our children, and I am friends with her, but I keep my distance as much as possible from them all.

I am permitted to see my children at all times, and so I make my visits every now and then, but not too often because I can't trust myself with my ex-wife. I don't figure on marrying again to another woman unless I am pretty sure she hasn't another sweetheart besides myself. I am going to stay single as long as I can because life is much easier for me to be single.

I have no steady job; I work at whatever I can find to do. Sometimes I work on the farm around near Milwaukee. I like to work on the farm the best because I get all I want to eat and I don't have to work too hard. Of course I don't earn big wages, but what I do earn is clear profit. I receive for my wages anywhere from thirty to forty-five dollars per month, beside my board and lodging. When I am not working I make my home with my sister, who lives in Milwaukee.

[Later in the interview, William Webster had more to say about the breakup of his marriage and his prospects for the future.]

You asked me about how did I get along with my wife earning the wages. Well, it was alright as long as I didn't ask her for some spending money for myself. I made my own spending money by going to the pool hall every chance I got, and I did a little gambling on the side.

I think perhaps I would still be married to her if I could have found a steady job. I don't think that she would have looked for a job herself. I got along good with her as long as I had a job myself. She stayed home to care for the children. She is a good housekeeper and a good cook, and she enjoys being a wife. But I noticed the change that came over her the minute that she started working outside of her home. I was like a little boy. She ordered me around, but she wasn't mean about it. And of course I did whatever she told me to do.

The first payday came around and she invited me out. We first went to pay our bills at the grocery store and bought some more groceries. We took this home. She got her mother to take care of the children. She took me to a swell show, and after that was over then we went to a dance hall and tavern. We had a swell time together. It went like that on her paydays for some time. I suppose about this time she met the man that finally broke up our home. I really don't blame her for falling in love with this man, because he was making good money then and I suppose he was nice to her. But then when they did get married it was a different story. He complained about caring for another man's children, and other things. She told me afterwards that she had made a big mistake in divorcing me. She said, "Why, he is so jealous that whenever I mention your name, he gets angry right away." He started to abuse her, and of course she separated from him at once. I guess now she has found out who is the better man between us, but I have had enough womenfolks to last me a lifetime. I will say that everything would have been alright if I hadn't got into that accident. It sure ruined my whole life.

I couldn't say how it would have turned out if both of us would have earned wages at the same time. No doubt it would have been alright. But then I was making plenty of money with my job and boxing and sparring with the other boxers in Milwaukee. About two hundred dollars per month average income—that wasn't anything to sneeze at, I'm sure. At least we made good living on that income. When I wasn't able to earn that, we all felt it terribly. They certainly can't say I didn't try to get a job. I must have worn out three pairs of shoes looking for work around town.

That's why I haven't much use for the present-day economic life. Do you blame me? I might say that times are changing to my favor, and I hope to take full advantage of it and get back on my feet again where I belong.

I am still a young man; I have nothing to lose but everything to gain. I am just waiting for my chance to get back in some factory and do my stuff. I really don't have a trade of any kind, so I suppose I could take up something to help the defense program. Whenever my chance comes I am going to take it, if I don't get drafted in the army by that time. If I get in the army it will be a pleasure and perhaps I will be able to stage a comeback at boxing.

I know quite a number of boys that went to the army. They seem to like the army life, and they are getting along fine. The training they will receive will do them good. That is one reason I would like to get in there myself and get all the training I can get. It might help to make a man out of me. At least that would be my ambition when I am drafted in the United States Army. I know I wouldn't be able to pass if I enlisted voluntarily; otherwise I would have enlisted already. So I think my only chance will be to get drafted. It wouldn't make any difference to me what branch of the army I would serve in, just so I got in there. I can swim like a fish, run when I get scared, fight like a wildcat, wrestle like a bear. I am a good walker, because I am a bum anyway, so I ought to make a good soldier.

I might tell you that training for my fights was really hard work for me. I usually get up at 5 a.m. I start off by doing the setting-up exercises; then I jump in a car. They usually take us out in the country. The road work consists of running about five miles at dogtrot; then punching the bag comes next. All good boxers practice shadowboxing. The best part of the training is going in the ring with your sparring mates for three rounds by each man. Some of the boxers have two or three sparring partners. I have trained in some of the best athletic clubs in Chicago, Detroit, and Milwaukee. I used to be in training most of the time. It was easy for me to be in condition in that way. I have sparred in the ring with some real good boxers. They tell me I could hit just as hard with either hand. There is plenty money to be earned, if a boxer knows his stuff and has a good manager.

The boxer's life isn't all roses by any means. He has to take good care of himself so that he doesn't get over the weight in his division. Some of the rules for good boxers are early to bed, plenty of wholesome food to eat, lots of exercise, and no smoking or alcoholic drinks. It is very hard sometimes to follow these rules, especially if you like to go out to a party and your friends are the drinking kind.

I used to be able to resist all the temptation that are liable to be injurious to my body. Women are chief causes for some boxers to break their training. Many a good boxing man has been ruined by the so-called weaker female sex. The women are so easy to get that sometimes it is better to run away from them. I know from my personal experience that it doesn't pay to play with the womenfolks when a fellow is in training and is ready to fight. I have seen some of the best boxers lose their fights because they had been out with some wild women. It's no use to argue about it because it is so that the womenfolks can and will ruin a man overnight. And so the boxers if they want to win their fights train with strict orders not to fool around with the women during the training period.

RUTH BAIRD

> On June 26, 1941, Ruth Baird told Guy Elm about her life, and espe-
> cially about her active participation in church hymn-singing groups.
> Indeed, she was a very strong leader of her group. She and her hus-
> band, Cornelius, worked at the Oneida Golf Club.

A Self-Portrait

I was born thirty-five years ago, here in Oneida Reservation. I can't tell you much about just how we lived when I was a child. I presume we lived just like the rest of the Oneida Indians. I know that when I was old enough to remember the way we were living my father and mother were on the farm. We had a few cows, chickens, and some pigs. My mother used to help by making bobbin lace. A woman from New York City came here and got the Oneida women to make this lace and do other needlework. Miss Hemingway was the woman's name. She held classes for the Oneida women. She was here for about six months. After she left here, Mrs. J. H. Webster took charge of the work.[24] She handed out the materials and took the lace and paid the women for their work. Some of them got to be very fast and good lace makers, and they made good money on this kind of work.

I was sent to Oneida Boarding School at the age of seven. I attended there for two years. From there I went to Keshena, to St. Joseph, a Catholic school. I was there one year. The next school I attended was also called St. Joseph, at Oneida, also a Catholic school. I attended this school one year.

About this time my folks moved to Green Bay, so I attended a public school. I think I was going to this school about three years. Then my parents sent me to the Flandreau school for the Indians in South Dakota. I was there three and a half years. I finished up to tenth grade; I came home and I didn't go to school anymore.

I worked in Green Bay during the summer. I met a young man who was divorced from his wife. We fell in love and we were married in 1924.

I have four daughters. The first child, the oldest girl, was born in 1925 and is sixteen years old, and the youngest is twelve years old. The twins are fourteen.

My first husband used to work at the Northwest Engineering Works at Green Bay. He was a machinist and used to make good wages. We got along good with his wages; I never had to go to work until the depression started and he was laid off. I think it was in 1932 that I got a job at the Prange Store in Green Bay. I had a few more other jobs, but not steady all-year employment. I had to work to help out in some way because my husband wasn't working steady.

He died about five years ago. I received a mother's pension, until I got married again to a bachelor about my age—but a bigger fool than I was. I found that out too late. Soon after we were married we started to quarrel over my children, and of course I'll stick up for my children anytime somebody tries to mistreat them, regardless what happens. Well, it did happen; we got into some fights, and finally I decided I couldn't stand it any longer. So we separated for a few months. I went back to live with my parents, and he went back to live with his dear mother. During last summer he took sick and almost died. So I took him back and he has been a swell fellow ever since. He has changed his habits considerably, so that we get along pretty good nowadays. He works on a WPA project.

Ever since I married this man I have been working at the Oneida Golf Club during the summer, until late in the fall. I make pretty good wages. I started off with forty dollars per month. For the next two years I received fifty dollars per month, and this season I am getting sixty dollars per month as a second cook. The work is hard, and sometimes I have to work at night too. But then where can I go to find a job that they'll pay that much.

I must tell you what my work is like. Sometimes we start at 8 a.m. and we are through at 5:30 p.m.—that's when we don't have the twilight golf games. And sometimes I start my work at 10 a.m. and work until late at night. The most busy days for us are the holidays and Saturdays.

There are lots of expenses connected with my work, because I have to have a car and drive it back and forth to my work every day. With the wages I receive I am able to dress my girls. One girl is attending the high school, and the other three are attending the public school.

My mother gets mother's pension because my father is not well and therefore is not able to do any kind of work. We are living together with my parents and my youngest sister, and sometimes my brother comes back there to stay too, and so it's a big family when we are all at home.

The New Deal came just in time to help us out. The land was assigned to my parents a few years ago, and a house was built on it. My brother helped the folks in clearing the land—about two acres—so that they could plant vegetables.

Last summer my mother also took sick, and it was one of the reasons that I moved in with them, to try to help them in some way. I have been with them ever since. The land assignment has been transferred to me and my husband. We are paying so much per month, like rent. These payments are to pay back the cost of building the house and drilling a well. The land is free of charge. I think we can get along on ten acres, with me working out. This spring we planted all kinds of vegetables, corn, and contract beans. We have enough planted to last us all winter.

My hobby is singing. I have been a singer since I was seven years old. I sang at Blessed Sacrament Church in Green Bay for twenty-two years. During that time there were many priests changed around. Some of them didn't stay very long.

I took lessons in singing from Miss Merril in Green Bay, and that is how I got my start. I have been very successful with the music. I have sung in many different churches throughout the state of Wisconsin. When Father Christian first came here in 1937 the church didn't have a choir. That was one of the first things he did, to organize a church choir. We didn't have books, vestments, and so we gave card parties to raise funds to buy the material. I think it was something like thirty-five members, men, women, and young girls, that joined when the choir was first organized. The first time we sang Indian songs in church it was like the olden times. The people took more interest in their church, and the attendance has been increasing ever since. The church choir, if it is well organized, is a good drawing card for any church. I have learned that from my personal observation.

Father Christian, when he heard the choir sing in English and in Oneida, was very much surprised and was very interested in the choir. He got a good musician to lead the choir and also to teach them music.

It was kind of hard to organize this choir because some of the older people can't read the notes, but they really are good singers in Oneida.

Us younger people can read music with the best of them, but most of us couldn't sing the Oneida hymns. Well, it took lots of practice and patience so that we really had to memorize the songs both in English and Oneida. For instance myself; I had never before sung much in the Oneida language, so I had to work hard to learn to read the Mohawk alphabet. Most all the Oneida songs are written in Mohawk dialect.

It is much easier for me to sing in English than Oneida because the notes are right before me. Of course, in solos I usually memorize it. The Oneida songs, you don't have a note to go by. The Indian words are written in the books, but no notes. The leader or the melody singer has to hit just the right pitch, or the rest will have a hard time to sing their parts. And I happened to be the leader in Indian songs and also the English songs; that is, I sing soprano. There is another lady that is a good soprano singer, and we alternate in leading the choir.

When the choir got to be pretty good, Father Christian scheduled a singing tour for the choir. We went to Wausau, Antigo, Appleton, Stevens Point, Fond du Lac, Sturgeon Bay, Green Bay, and Shawano. The choir surprised me; they made quite a hit wherever we went. The people were very nice to us, and we all enjoyed our trips very much. Father Christian chartered a bus on these trips, which was on Sundays.

I really don't know why some of the members, one by one, dropped out. The choir just went so far, then they started to disagree, and finally about half of the members quit the choir. I was the chairman of the organization, and so it was up to me to try to keep the choir together; besides I got some new members to join. In 1940 I didn't hold any office, but this year I was elected again as the president of the choir.

We have about thirty members right now in our choir. Some of these members are on sick list, so that we have about twenty-four active members. We have four bass singers and six tenors, male voices. And with the women, we have six alto singers and eight soprano singers. We have a soloist in each section. We have a choir that doesn't have to take a backseat to any other choir. It is the only choir that can sing in two languages as far as I know. The choir members have organized, within the group, a mixed-voice quartet, two women and two men. They specialize in Oneida songs. This is the quartet that went on an eastern tour last fall. I am a member of this quartet. We have been all over the state and have broadcast over the radio on several occasions. We have used the choir and the quartet to contact the other churches for aid to raise funds for our church. We have been very successful in this respect. I think that we, the Oneida people, should get help from our white friends from time to time, because we are trying to improve our church property as well as ourselves, so that we can be good Christians like the old Oneidas that first came here. I am very interested in the choir and other church work. I am always willing to help in whatever they ask me to do.

The choir puts on a play every year. They have been successful each time, both in their performance and financially. The choir has helped the people of the church in many ways. We sing at the wakes, funerals, and for the sick people that can't come to church. I am very happy and feel honored to be its president. The vice-president and the other officers and Father Christian have been kind and willing workers with this organization. Without their keen judgment and cooperation with me and the rest of the choir members I doubt very much if we could have been so successful with the achievements we have made this past year.

Father Christian is planning another tour this fall for our quartet. Last year we were gone for six weeks, and this year it's going to be a longer trip, about two months. I really haven't made up my mind yet whether I will go or not, but if I don't go I know that I will miss lots of sights and education. I firmly believe traveling to be the best education that a person can receive. Last fall when I went with the quartet I really enjoyed myself very much. I met lots of good people and saw many things that I never seen before in my life. We visited many place of interest.

I hope someday that the whole choir can go on a tour throughout the country. I believe that in another year the choir will be so good at singing that they can go anywhere and put on a concert of music that will be good enough for any public to hear. There is no question that this choir is good; they know how to sing both in English and Oneida languages.

My recreations are dancing, motoring, and to play softball. I have always liked to dance both the round dance and square dance; I still enjoy it.

Motoring is one of my favorite pastimes. My family and I do lots of traveling in and around Oneida. Sometimes we go up north to visit my sister and other relations. We always enjoy these trips. It's wonderful to see the woods at any time of the year. Good fishing is also to be had in many places in that part of the country.

When I was a young girl I used to play baseball with the boys, and so I learned how to play. I could run and hit just as hard as they could. When indoor baseball or the softball was introduced, I switched over to that game. I can really play that game even today, and I am not a spring chicken anymore. Last summer I still played a whole game, but believe me the next day I felt like I was an eighty-year-old lady. But it gave me lots of exercise and I felt good afterwards, when the aching pains went away from my legs and arms.

My social life is all taken up by my church work. In winter months when I am not working steady, I spend lots of my time for the church. The choir members are always in demand to appear on the programs given by the organizations connected with the church, and we also give plays and shows during the winter. The people of the congregation are very good in attending these plays and shows given by different organizations. We don't charge very much so that everybody can afford to pay the admission at the door. Our parish hall has been replastered, the kitchen has been fixed up, waterworks and sewer installed, and also new furniture.

The choir bought a new curtain for the stage this year; the cost is $125. We are paying that now on the installment plan. The choir has something like forty-five dollars yet to pay on it. Another thing that the church choir paid the bill for was to reshingle the roof of the parish hall, and that was also over one hundred dollars. They have contributed towards paying the coal bill and other expenses. So I think they are a handy people to have around. They are good Christians, well educated; they know how to work and scheme to make money for the church. I believe that in time we will be able to catch up with the repairs and other improvements to our church properties. And I hope that the younger generation will profit by our mistakes in the past. That is, we have been backward in trying to do all we can to help the church as much as possible, and we spent too much time elsewhere when we should be in church praying—besides letting the property go to ruin when it should be repaired.

I think I have told you enough about myself and my family, although there is plenty to tell yet. But I am afraid you wouldn't like to write it yourself, because it's about my love affairs with your younger brother, when we were at Flandreau going to school together. You remember when I came home and I met you at a dance, and you took me home to Green Bay? I fell for you and I changed my flag, switched over to you.

Well, you always have been a swell friend to me. I can always depend on you for help when I need it. So I guess I better stop teasing you before you write something in your book that I wouldn't want anybody else to read. You were lucky that today is my day off at the Oneida Golf Club. In case you want further information about my family, you can call again at any time, either here at my home or at the Oneida Golf Club.

CURTIS DENNY

> Curtis Denny was a young man who had had virtually no formal ed-
> ucation and could not speak English. In 1941 he lived just outside
> Green Bay and made his living as a farm laborer, but after World War
> II he moved to Milwaukee and evidently became a foreman for K and
> M Construction. He gave this interview with its genial self-portrait to
> Stadler King on November 4, 1941. "Associates" was the original title.

Associates

I am now thirty years, old but I sometimes feel like I am a hundred years old. I live in the Town of Oneida, about a half mile from the Village of Oneida. I have half the house my mother lives in so that my rent is not so high. I am married and have four children. I belong to the Episcopal church, but of course I am sorry to say that I hardly ever go to church, but that's because I have the stock to look after where I am working. I have no schooling to speak of; I went to school for two years, but all that I learned I have forgotten. I could not talk English to amount to anything. I am not able to say much more than "yes" or "no." I could understand fairly well when my boss tells me what to do, but he never talks to me about anything else. I suppose he knows I could not talk much, but I could swear pretty good when I get mad at the cows or horses.

I work for Mr. Percy Silverwood. I worked for him now about ten years, but of course not steady because I did work on the WPA part of this time. My boss puts me at driving a tractor so I ride all day, but that is a tiresome job. I get so tired that my bones ache when I straighten up, but after I walk around some that goes away when I start to milk the cows. He has forty cows and there are five of us that milk them, but we use the milking machine so some of us only strip the cows that the machine does not get. In this way it does not take us any more than one good hour. I like to milk the cows in the wintertime because it is not so warm and there are not so many flies. I tell you that flies were bad in the late summer about the end of August. There is no way of keeping them out of the barn. The cows would be switching their tails in our faces and some would kick and it was so warm that we would sweat and our clothes would be all soaking wet. I sometimes thought I would quit this job, but if I did no one else would hire me and I could not get right back on the WPA. It was only at milking time that it was bad, but during the day I always have a good job driving the tractor. I could work there all winter, but there is not so much to do then—only to look after the stock and get up a little wood. He keeps the same number of milkers all winter, but all the other workers are laid off.

I have two friends who are my real friends; that is, we are together more than anyone else. When we get our checks on Saturday nights us three would go together, we buy what we need and then we would go into a tavern and have some beer. We always feel that after working a whole week and earning a check of twelve dollars we should treat ourselves to a few beers. But sometimes we get too much. Our friend William could not stay with us so much on this because his wife always takes him away. My wife does not drink so much and she hardly ever goes along with us, but my friend Alphius's wife, she is right in it with all the drinks. Sometimes Alphius would have a hard time to take her home. She would want to dance with others after she gets a few drinks. He would have to hire a car to take them home.

Alphius and I are about the best friends of all. Sometimes we made believe we were quarreling and just about to fight, but we both know we would not do that. One time we fooled our boss. We were in the barn cleaning off horses when we started to argue like we were quarreling. I saw the boss coming toward the barn, but he must have heard us before he got real close so he stood outside where we could not see him. I knew he must be by the door, so I only talked louder and he did the same. I told Alphius that I will come over and clean him with the currycomb, and he said come on and see if you can do it. At this time I could see the boss through a window. He was walking away from the barn, and then I told Alphius that he heard us as he was right by the door—then we laughed at what we did. After he got his team out and I was starting out with my tractor the boss said, I heard you were quarreling with Alphius, what's wrong. I said ask him what's wrong, so he never found out. But there was no more fight in Alphius or I than in a baby.

Alphius and his wife come to our place often at nights because we live right on the way to the village. They always stopped in, either when they are going or when they are going back. I go to their place too once in while, but my wife has the baby so she does not like to be on the road.

William is a friend in another way: he likes to sing and he is a good bass singer, and I can sing soprano in Indian, so he comes and we would sing some songs. We got so we could sing good together, so once we started to make up a song like the Indian tom-tom. We made up our own words and a tone as near like the tom-tom as we could. We practiced this and soon we were able to sing it good, and someone heard us so they asked us to sing that at a program they were having at the hall. We told them that we would not be able to sing in a big crowd unless we had a few drinks because we are both so bashful, so when time came we got a small bottle of whiskey and we took a couple drinks each so when we were called on we were not afraid. We sang that and the people clapped their hands so much that we had to sing again. Everybody thought that was good and we had made it up ourselves.

My friend William is forty-seven years old; he is seventeen years older than I am. And my friend Alphius is fifty years old, so he is twenty years older than I. But the age does not make a difference. We could be friends to anyone who may be twice or three times older than we are or one much younger than we are. All we need is to have the same ideas or disposition and we could be real good and true friends. It must be the same with a man and his wife. They are good friends, in fact the best friends, when they are of the same disposition. They think alike, they have the same ways, and they work together more easily than those who do not have the same disposition. Some married couples are always arguing about something, and that's when they have ways and ideas that's different from each other.

I sometimes wish I was able to get up and make a speech at some of these wakes, but I never could. I would not know how to act if I would be called on to speak. But when I am alone working I have plenty to think of which I would say. I have been going to wakes since I was able to go, and all through these years I have heard men speak at these wakes, and they all say about the same thing as long as I can remember. But I never was called on to say anything, so I have a chance to listen to them. Most of these are talks on how we should prepare ourselves so that we also may go where that person is gone. They say that if we do not prepare ourselves we might be late and the door will be closed when we come along. They talk of little children as pure and spotlessly clean in their heart, but the grown-up people must work and prepare to be as the little children are. No one has ever come back to tell how or what the conditions are where all those who have died are, but it is only a few years after one dies that they are forgotten. Even our own parents are forgotten by us a few years after they are dead.

Some men speak at these wakes and tell us that only a few people will pass the judgment, and those are people who always had been really true in their belief. There must be a big place provided where all the souls go because people have been dying ever since the world started, and the world has been going on for such a long time. So how many people would there be if they all arose and mix in with us who are living?

I like to sing at these wakes, and as I have learned so many different songs and because I sing the most important part, which is soprano, they often come and invite me come to a wake. I and my friend William went to a wake one time and there were no other singers there, so he and I sang alone and we stayed way toward daybreak, but the people were good to us because we sang so much for them. They gave us breakfast and brought us home. It is rather funny that I am able to sing in a crowd at wakes but I would not be able to speak at the same place. Some people are given the ability to speak in a crowd or anywhere, and some people are given ability to sing, and there are people who are given both, but I am given only one. It is the same way with my partner William; he is a good bass singer and it makes no difference what hymn they sing, he is able to sing bass to it. That is the reason he and I get along so good together, because we sing good together. He also would not be able to say anything if he was called on to speak. But he could sing all night, but this is only in Indian too; he would not be much good at English hymns.

These two men with their families are the only real true associates we have, but they are true associates. I have a brother whose name is Sunrise, but he never as much as comes to visit us and we have grown to be that way too. My mother also comes in every day, but this would be no wonder because she lives just in the next room.

5.

Marriages and Families

Many people speak of their marriages and families, and quite a few are very frank indeed. They speak of good, warm, and loving relations among husbands and wives, siblings, parents and children, but also of troubled relationships, difficult and abusive husbands, wayward wives, and rebellious children. Most are quick to say that family relationships had deteriorated throughout the preceding half century, that morals used to be better, and that children used to obey their parents. They speak approvingly of the old days when Sundays were kept sacred, when people went to church instead of driving around and going to dances and shows. They lament that the presence of taverns and dance halls on and near the reservation has contributed to the deterioration of morals and family life.

Whatever the validity of these perceptions, these accounts do not remain at the level of general discussion but take us into their immediate families, giving us an intimate view of the sorts of partnerships and devotion, passions and troubles, anger, misunderstandings, and conflicts that occur everywhere, in all societies.

Minnie Decota Danforth shared these ideas about family, marriage, religion, and behavior with Ida Blackhawk on October 17, 1941. She was fifty-five years old and was also known as Mrs. Julius Danforth. Her husband later served as tribal chairman from 1947 to 1951 and from 1954 to 1963.

Family, Two Marriages, and Religion

My father and mother both belonged to the Methodist church, and that was where I was baptized and used to attend regularly when I was a child. I am sorry to say that I am not the religious type, and after leaving school I hardly ever went to church here. One reason is I went away to work in the Indian Service, and I met a Chippewa Indian in one of the schools I was working at, and he was a Catholic. I would not turn Catholic, so we were not married by his church but by mine, but he did not have to become Methodist. I did not get along very well with him, but it was not on account of our religion, but on account of something more private. We had five children when he and I separated, and I came away with all my children.

My father was working in Neopit, Wisconsin, and I came to his shanty. He was alone there working for some lumberman, and he had some lumberjacks boarding there. My mother died when I was small, and so my father was the only one I could turn to for help. Neopit is a little Menominee Indian village with a government sawmill. The town was in boom at the time I came there, and I am glad that they made us take domestic science at Hampton. Do you remember how we used to hate to go to the cooking classes? Well, I made use of my cooking lessons. I found employment as a cook in a hotel there mostly for sawmill employees. I worked there almost a year, and my children went to a day school. My father began to get tired of the children, and I knew I had to do something about it. I sent all of my children to a government school, except the youngest one.

I got another job that winter, with better pay, to cook in a lumber camp, and I could keep my little boy with me. I had a room next to the kitchen. The men had their quarters someplace else, and the only time I saw them was at mealtimes. At the same time I felt uneasy, because I was the only woman in the camp in the woods. One day I happen to look in the dining room when all were seated and I thought I saw someone I knew, and I guess he saw me too. Anyway, after work hours the boss and Julius came over to see me. Julius's wife had died, and he was in the woods to forget his sorrow; his children were in a government school too. Well, we got acquainted, and I came back to Oneida with him and we got married. His children and my children are all grown up, but they come home to see us now and then.

Julius belongs to the Episcopal church, but we neither of us are very active in religious matters. We help both churches whenever we are asked, but we stay home on Sundays because we have stock to look after. We have a good preacher and I have nothing to find fault with, but I just don't feel like going to church very often. I guess I committed a great sin when I left my husband, but it seemed the only thing to do in a case like that. At that time I thought I would never get married again, but I found Julius a different sort of a man than my first husband.

I used to send my children to Sunday school while they were with me, and I always told them to lead a decent life and urged them to get good educations. My oldest daughter got married quite young, and one worked a number of years and helped me, but she too got married lately. Now I just have one daughter left. She just graduated from a teachers college in Sioux Falls, South Dakota, and she is teaching in a government school in South Dakota. My youngest son is still in school at Flandreau, South Dakota, but my other son finished last year and he also studied to be a mechanic and he finished that too. He was here last winter, but finally found employment in Detroit, Michigan, in the Ford factory, but he was drafted, and in the meantime he volunteered in the army corps. He passed the physical and also the intellectual test and was sent to Tennessee, until recently he was transferred again. I suppose he will be a mechanic in an airplane. He is now near Chicago, Illinois, getting further instructions. I am rather proud of him, but I was wishing he would fail in something so he would not have to go. He used to send me ten dollars every payday while he was working in the factory, but I don't know how much he will be getting from the government or whether he will be able to continue to spare me some of his earnings. But I never tell my children that they have to send me their earnings. I am satisfied if they take care of themselves.

I think it is alright for some to be active in church work, but I think I lost my religion when I had trouble with my husband and prayer did not do me any good. I had to exert myself before I could help myself and my children, and I firmly believe that God had a hand in that—even though I never go to church. But he knows I am not against any church. In our church everyone has to testify once in a while in the prayer meetings and give their ideas of a Christian life. Well, I don't feel as though I am equal to give any advice to anyone. I would not advise anyone to take me as an example of how a Christian should live.

JONAS SMITH

> Jonas Smith, age forty-five, owned a farm and seems to have been doing quite well for himself. This is his account of his economic and personal life, with particular regard to women, as told to John Skenandore on August 29, 1941.

The Tale of an Oneida Bachelor Farmer

I am living all alone on this estate. I had four full sisters and one half sister, but the half sister doesn't come in on the will my father had made because she was legally given to a well-to-do couple when her mother died. My four full sisters and I are from my father's second wife, and it was mother's property.

My sisters are all married and left the place, and father and mother are both dead so I am left all alone because I can't find myself a wife. When my father died he had a mortgage on this place for thirteen hundred dollars, and half the property is suppose to go to my youngest sister and I get the other half and we are supposed to give the other three sisters one hundred dollars apiece. I am the only one left on the place, so it is up to me to make the payments. My youngest sister is not paying, but I am keeping up the payments and I do think I will pay up in time.

But I have had some tough luck. In the year of 1937 the cow testers condemned five of my milk cows and two heifers, which set me back a few years. But I was allowed on average $40 apiece for six of them and only $13.50 for one, as they said she was too far gone and it can't be used for meat. So until last fall I was able to milk seven cows again. I bought five more cows from the cattle dealer, and I borrowed the money from the bank to pay for the cows, which averaged $75 apiece, and I still owed $258 when the other day I got a chance to get another horse kind of reasonably so I took another jump in the hole for $95. So I still owe $353 at the bank, which I am paying $20 every two weeks, and $37 every six months on the mortgage, and $21 every three years for insurance on property. All these keep me very busy thinking what to do next.

I seldom work out, as I have cows to milk mornings and evenings. I only work out to farmers around when they need help badly, and I don't work for them to make money on them but only to get on the best side of them because I do need help too. Once in awhile, then, I could always fall back on them like for harvesting and threshing where one man can't do the job alone. I do not fool with small crops, only like potatoes and cucumbers. I plant about an acre of potatoes every year. It is more than I need myself, but potatoes are always in good demand and I do make a little money on that, but cucumbers I only plant a few hills of it each year only because I like it green so well and I pickle some for winter. All these small crops have too much work connected with them, so I won't have the time to work on them.

I make most of my living on my cows, so I spend most of my time in comforting the cows and seeing that they got plenty of water and feed at all times, and I keep their place clean and see that I put up enough feed for them during the summer months to last them a year around. I mostly grow field corn, barley, and oats for feed, and these three varieties grown together makes a splendid feed for milk cows in the winter months. My crops this year are not so hot, and the reason on that was one of my horses got old on me and can't work much anymore. But this one horse he made the difference on everything on my farm.

I am holding fifty-eight acres of land here; thirty-two acres of this is cleared, and I'm using it for cropland and the rest for pasture. I often wonder what would be my best bet to do on this estate because my sisters just won't do anything and I alone am keeping it up as it is. I often wonder if it wouldn't be best if we sold the whole works and I buy myself another small place elsewhere because this way it is going too slow and what money I make on the place is going right back on it and it is hard for me to buy my youngest sister out and she is holding half of the property.

I do like the idea of being alone because I can do as I please and [there's] no one to hurt and bawl me out and it don't cost me much on living expenses. I've had couple of samples of married life, and if it is like these with everyone then I would rather be alone and leave well enough alone. I am home most of the time as I have no car to travel with, and I don't want to have one either because I know well I would be neglecting my cows more. As it is now I am often invited to go out for a ride, and this kind of time takes my mind off my cattle and sometimes I don't get to milk them until midnight—more so when I get a few drinks with it, and that's nearly every time we come to a tavern stop. So a car gives me enough trouble without owning one.

My cows at the present time are bringing me around forty-six dollars per month on which I make my payments and living on. The milk truck comes every morning to pick up the milk, and if there is anything I need in the line of groceries all I would have to do is to make a slip for the things I do need and send it along with the driver and he brings the stuff along with his next trip, so I really have no need to get a car while the stuff I need is delivered right up to my door. I live so simple that it doesn't take much money to keep me alive.

I found it so much different when I got myself a housekeeper at one time. The way she worked to make a change in my house and my clothing had to be just so. And she had me going right and left getting things for her while she change things around about the house and can different kinds of fruit and pickles for winter's supply. I just left her have her own way and I just watched her and thought she was doing me too much work for what little I was able to pay her. But later I found out what that was all about. She didn't want no pay, but she wanted to get married. And she made me buy myself a new suit of clothes, white shirts, dress shoes, and new hat so that I can dress up when we went someplace. Which I never bothered before her. Wherever I went before I always went in my work clothes and never went to any public gatherings.

In a way I did like her ways and was rather stuck on her, and as we live together like man and wife I began to realize the expenses she was loading on me but I just didn't have the nerve to tell her my troubles. Where I could have paid my bills, I bought new things and clothes with my money. For two years she stayed with me, and we had troubles at times. But small ones as I always figured that she was not healthy as she was so often complaining of having pains so I did give in on her because when she did the bossing she felt better. In the mornings she got up early enough without me calling her, but one thing I didn't like so well that she didn't cook enough for breakfast. But at noon she piles it on plenty and she knew how to cook too, and prompt at twelve and supper at five, just as regular as a clock. She is good in many ways, but what made me stall around from marrying her was that I had noticed after being with me for a few days she got too bossy to suit me. She even wanted to have her say with what goes out of my place. Like close neighbors comes and borrow my tools, farm implements, but she didn't want me to loan anything out like that. Of course I had to step on that and I told her that my neighbors and I believe in helping one another and I am not going to make a devil of myself now when I always got along so nicely. She was good on other things but she was too quick in temper and wanted to boss, [and that] was why I couldn't make up my mind to marry her.

And one day during the winter months she saw me going outside with a gallon pail of salt and she asked me what I was going to do with the salt I was carrying out, and I told her that I was taking it out to the cows as I closed the door behind me. And just as I came back in she asked me if I gave all that salt to the cows, and I said, "Yes, I didn't just take it outside and spill it." These few words I said as a joke turned her right over and she started bawling me out for giving her a smart answer. So anyone can see it was only a joke but she took it bad. Well, we had quite a fight over this little thing and I was glad afterwards that she did spell [overreact] as she did; then I knew what to expect if I married her. And she told me at that time that she was going away the next morning, and she also said, "I hope you can get along alright." And I said, "You had been away fifteen years from our settlement and I got along just the same, and I am quite sure it won't be any different than before."

I was getting tired of the high cost of living anyway, so that very evening I fixed myself a different bedroom and as I laid there thinking about my troubles, the first thing I knew she came into my room and crawled in with me. Of course I was only too willing to help her with the covers, and she hugged me as if she had been away for years. So I just had no control of myself and right away I felt like climbing her and she took me like nobody's business. Twice in just a short time. So we were alright again and got along nicely for a few days until she got another spell. But we lived together like this for two years until she gave up on me marrying her and she started to go with another man and it wasn't long before he took her away from my place. And that was one of my experiences of married life with one of my own kind. So now I might tell you my experience with a white girl.

As I was always full of fun, and being an ex-serviceman from the army and belonging to the [American] Legion in Green Bay, I got acquainted with white girls at the Legion's Ball. So one winter evening after I had all my chores done and was reading the newspaper I heard a car drive up to my house and toot the horn and I went to see who it was and as I got outside I saw a taxi parking out there. A girl which I got acquainted with at the Legion dances got out with her suitcase and came to me and said that she had come to make me a visit, so I asked her inside. And it was after we got inside when she told me her troubles and asked me if she could park on me for about two weeks until she got another job. I said she was welcome to stay as long as she pleases, so she went and told the taxi driver not to wait as she has found a place. So she came back in and we both set down while we talked matters over. She told me that she was laid off from work at the five and ten cents store where she had been working for some time. Her parents are both dead and she has a few relations in Iowa but she has not saved enough money to go back to them so she said she thought of me as I had told her before that I was farming all by myself and she thought that she might be of some help if she came to stay with me. And she was right; she certainly was good company during the whole three weeks she was with me.

That night after we had a long visit together in my sitting room I fixed a bed for her in one of the bedrooms and put on all clean bedclothes and then told her that this will be her bedroom and she was well pleased. And I told her "good night" while I went into the next bedroom to sleep. I laid in my bed thinking what this was all about and wondering if I would dare go into her room and sleep with her. And believe me I never felt so darn cheap when she came into my room herself and asked me if she could sleep with me. I just didn't have the nerve, but at the same time I wanted to so I didn't hesitate a bit when she came in herself but I felt dagone slow. But I certainly made up for that in one night as I worked on her just about all night and that was my first chance to sleep with a girl stripped naked and I never knew the girls did work for it like this one did and I could tell that she went off nearly every time I did and took all of what I was able to give. I didn't keep track of how many times we did it, but we certainly didn't sleep much that night. And the next day whenever we felt like it—as we were alone and all the work I had was milking the cows and chores—and I even neglected some of that because I wanted to be with her all the time.

She didn't know anything about cooking so I had to teach her how, but she was very anxious to learn and it didn't take her long before she was able to cook a whole meal without asking me what to do. She was a nice girl and a good worker, but she didn't care about outside work and I don't blame her especially during the winter months. But she did wash my windows one nice day, both in and outside, and she did washing every week and was real good at it; she got the clothes real white.

And all the time she stayed with me there was never a dull moment. We were both real happy and got along very nice. There were times when white boys from town came and tried to take her out for rides, but she just wouldn't go and stuck right with me. I was going to ask her to marry me but didn't get around to it until her job opened up again and she went back to work again. This was real hard for me, to see her leave, because we got along so well and I certainly liked her in every way. I wondered a lot while she was with me just what she was, but I couldn't make out and asked her if she wasn't married many times. I thought she was only fooling with me. After she went back to work I expected that she would come back like weekends to see me, and I had the house all cleaned up ready for her Saturday evening as she said when she left she would be back Saturday. But she didn't come and I didn't bother looking for her until after the second week went by. I went to the place where she worked before and inquired and I was told that she was called back home on account of death in the family. So I gave her up and I have never heard from her since.

And the last girl I had here for housekeeper only lasted two weeks. She was also an Oneida and she was a good housekeeper, good cook, and has a nice disposition. All the time she was with me she never showed to be put out on anything but took everything with a smile. I liked that girl too, but she spoiled the whole works for herself after she saw the way I ordered my groceries. Then she went to work and did the ordering without asking me if it was alright, and her parents were having a hard time just then, and as they came to visit her often she must have been loading them up each time they came because I certainly noticed the drop on my milk check in just that short time she was with me. And even after I left her go, the slips I got back from the creamery showed that there was groceries taken on my name which I had never ordered and didn't get. But I didn't complain until it got so that I didn't have a check left. Then I asked how come my grocery bill was so high and they told me that the woman I had was getting groceries there in my name. Well, I had to put a stop to that before she would run me in too big a bill. She is alright otherwise; she was only supporting her parents and two of her children, as she was married before. I liked this girl, and if it wasn't for the tricks she played on me I believe I would have asked her to marry me. But I was afraid I would have to marry the whole family if I did and support them all.

Now, if I had my choice among all the women I had with me I won't have to do much thinking. I like that little white girl the best of all for the reason that she showed much more affection and more movements or get to her than the Indian girl when in sexual intercourse. Of course I don't know very many white women, but what few I know they are all good at working with the man, while the Indian girls are more bashful and have to be coaxed along, and if you do get them then they would just lay there like a log and let you do all the work and even hate to talk about it, whereas the white women doesn't seem to think anything of it and works right with you.

But there are a few nowadays that are more like the white women— unless it is because we are somewhat mixed. And when these kind of women are found it is likely among the drinking kind, so they must have learned that from the white men. I am still single because I cannot trust the womenfolks.

It will be obvious that many autobiographies are marked by loss, illness, and sadness, but few people indulge in self-pity. Elijah Thomas, age fifty, had his share of miseries, as he told John Skenandore on June 16, 1941.

Troubles

For the last seven years I have been living with my mother and stepfather; that is, I haven't been away much more than three days at a time as I never was well enough to do hard work since I had pleurisy in my lungs.

Before that I worked out most of the time and only came home for visits. I used to work up north mostly, cutting wood and logs and sometimes on the farm. But since then I didn't feel like myself anymore and just can't do hard work. This is about all I am good for—helping around the house and gardens where I can take my time and rest when I want to. My mother and stepfather are both very good to me and let me do as I please at home. Of course I always manage to do something to help along on living expenses. My stepfather is still holding twenty acres of his father's allotment and also the old homestead which his father put up in his young days: an old log house made out of number one pine, which used to grow all around here, hewed with a broad ax by steady hand. There are only four of us living in it right now. Just a grandson and I living with the parents. My mother is seventy years old and drawing the old-age pension, and my stepfather is sixty-two years old and has been on WPA since it has been in progress. With this and the garden we make a very fair living.

We raise our own vegetables each year, and mother cans lots of fruit each year for stormy days in the winter months. Last year we got eighty bushels of potatoes and he sold half of that at fifty cents per bushel. We always manage to raise enough white Indian corn so we can have all the corn soup and bread we want during the winter months. The bread is an awful lot of work, of course, so we don't have that so often anymore—only like when we have special meals. We have the best part of the twenty acres cleared for planting, but we don't use all of it ourselves as he rents some of the land on the further end to people living next to it. We clear the brushland as we get the chance and are kind of saving as much of the woodland as we can for fuel. We burn mostly wood and very little coal during the winter.

I am now about fifty years old and I was never married. I had chances to get married a few times. First when I was nineteen I went with a girl; I found my mistake too late—that I was wrong for not marrying her instead of going away. I used to like to travel when I was young, and this is what happened to me. I was going with this girl pretty steady when I made up my mind to go and look for work and left. I was gone for about one year, and when I came back I found my girl married to another boy. They got along very nice and made headway. I do blame myself for missing the good chance. I drink, for one thing; that she especially didn't like. And I was too blame slow is another thing. I often thought I should have proposed to her, as she is sure a nice girl and it is very hard to find them kind of girls nowadays. The more guys they can keep going nowadays the better they like it, and if you marry one of them, just as soon as you are out of sight there is another man in your place already. I've always said it is bad enough to lose a girl, so what would it be if it was a wife. But I do still think I would get married if I could find a good wife, and I certainly would try my best to quit drinking and lead a straight life. Of course I can't say I could, but it won't hurt to try.

I am also a great one to chew tobacco, which I learned to use when I was only six years old. My grandfather used to give it to me, but we used to hide ourselves from my dad so that he won't see me chewing tobacco. I often wonder what kick my grandpa got out of this, starting me off on a bad habit so young. And I still like my chewing, and as long as it don't hurt me for using it I don't think I could quit.

Staying single so long does not mean that I didn't have anything to do with the women, as every chance I got I steal one and got my scratching this way.

My own dad died when four of us children were quite young, and my dad had a farm near the west boundary line. He was quite a farmer and had horses, cattle, pigs, and chickens. He was a good worker and always had money, but he also drank about every chance he got, and since the whiskey was hard to get in those days he was able to have money on him at all times. He had quite a clearing on the place before he died, and mother sold the place and bought a small property in place of it. This was only eighteen acres, and that was where we lived until my mother got married again, and that was when she married the man we are living with today. We got along very nicely and lived with him at his place, and he took us stepchildren just the same as if we were his children. And his and mother's children, we all got along very nice. Of course, like all other brothers and sisters we did got into fights—more so when my half sister seem to be spunkier or quicker tempered than us. But as I say, like children we got over it in just a little while.

As I grew older I got into dances and sometimes a dance right at home, and in most dances the men would have beer or whiskey to drink and that's where I got my start. And look what I am today. I haven't got a thing that I could call my own and I am just living and that is all. Only looking forward for my next meal, where some people look for meals years ahead. I have nothing to look forward to as I am alone, and more so now in my condition.

There was four of us brothers and sisters from mother's first husband and four half sisters from her second husband. My full sisters are both dead, and all my half sisters are grown up and married and gone on their own. I have only one brother, a couple of years younger than I am, and he is up north most of the time cutting wood and logs for a living and he is only another one just like myself, working only for what fun he can get out of this world. He is single, and what he makes outside of living expenses he spends it for pleasure, drinking and dancing, and comes home here once in a great while. I do work on small jobs around here such as two or three days, but that is all I am good for; my lungs can't seem to take it anymore.

In this interview, which took place on February 10, 1942, Mrs. R. Hill told John Skenandore about the complexities of family life and bringing up teenage children. She also spoke of her satisfaction at being able to build a home for her family.

Raising Teenage Children

As far back as I could remember my husband and I got along quite well, but there are times when we disagreed and fought over little things when we should have passed things by without words. We also had serious troubles in our family which are hard to pass up without full understanding between us. But as much as I have seen some husbands and wives fight, I think our troubles are nothing compared with others. We had tough scratching right from the time we were married because our parents, as we call them, lost their properties soon after we were married. But we did the best way we know how and stuck together all these years. I won't say we never got into trouble, because we did. My husband gets cranky spells at times and hollers around at everything, and I would do the same thing and holler right back at him. I have found out that this was the quickest way to get it over with than to try and baby him along. And in no time everything blows over and things would go well again.

We have five children, three girls and two boys, and they get along very well; they didn't fight like some children do. My husband doesn't talk to his children; if there is anything that he doesn't like he gets me to talk to them and I often talk to them with my own idea. From little kids on I have talked to them and told them what I thought was wrong: never to take anything that didn't belong to them and not to be mean to others, not to tell lies, and to help people if you see they need help, and be good to everybody. But all my preaching didn't do much good to our oldest boy unless that he took after his ancestors. As soon as he was able to work out he started drinking, and he would spend all his money for foolishness and didn't help with our living expenses. So one day his father asked him to help next time he got his pay and give his mother some money—after all, she is always ready to feed you when you come back home. The boy didn't say anything and went back to work. He got his pay every weekend, and the following Saturday came but the boy didn't come home as usual, not until the next morning. So his father asked him if he had saved some money for his mother, and the boy told his dad that he didn't have to pay his mother any money. His father said that he didn't have to pay but he can give and have some respect for his mother. But the boy got just angry and quarreled with his own father, and finally his father got enough of it and told his son to pack up and go on his own if all he was going to expect from him is dirt.

The boy pack up and left us as he was ordered, and as soon as he had left the house I talked to my husband and told him that I thought he was wrong by ordering him out too soon and that he should have gave him another chance. But my husband was spunky too and just can't bear to hear his own son quarrel with him. And afterwards they met each other at the dance when they were both drinking and the same thing started again, and this time it turned out into a fight. And the old man was so drunk that he didn't remember anything and came to with a black eye, and the people got to talking as usual when anything happens, saying that his own son gave him a black eye. But we have found out that it was another boy that helped; the boy was the one that hit him and it wasn't his son. His father had his son arrested when he heard about this, and he went to see his son about it and they both made up to one another and he brought his son back home again. But the boy wasn't home much after that and every time he came home drunk that's the first thing he would bring up to me, that we didn't love him, and I always had to talk to him and begged him to forget about that. He certainly worried us enough while he was around here and it certainly is a relief since he volunteered in the army, and now we hear from him way down in Texas and [he] writes us real nice letters. And for a while he hated his father so much that he used to tell me that if father ever laid his hands on me that something was going to happen. And I've told him time and again that he would never do such a thing because after all I know him well enough.

Our oldest girl is very nice and behaves well and is as nice to both of us as we can expect. We had an awful time putting her through high school, and there were times that we thought she was getting out too much so I have talked to her a lot too and each time mentioned how we skimped many times on groceries just to keep her well dressed while she was going to high school. And she was always ready to do whatever we asked her to do. She is very kindhearted and tries hard to please us. Now she is working in Milwaukee and going on her own hook and she often invited us over and she even paid our fare up there and back again. We know everything that she does over there, and we are very proud parents with her.

And our next boy is about grown up and he also has started to work out, but he certainly is different than his brother. He is always ready to help me with a smile and never gets angry at us even when he had done something wrong and I would scold him, and many times he would only laugh at me and say, "You know me, Ma. I won't do it again." He is now in the CCC camp and we are getting fifteen dollars per month from his wages and I asked him when he first left what he wishes me to do with the fifteen dollars that is going to be sent to me. He said, "That's yours, Ma; you can do as you please with that money."

He has been back home twice since he has been working there. His father talked to him the second time he was back home. He left here going back to the camp, and about three days afterwards he came back home where he was only stalled in Oneida and couldn't get back to the camp so he lost some time. That was during the cold spell first part of January, and since then he hasn't been back home. He is not angry at us because he writes to us and tells us how he is getting along. The reason we would rather that he stayed away from Oneida is that a married woman is after him and we certainly don't like her. She was bad before she married her husband and married life didn't help any and now she is chasing young boys around. That shows that she will never settle down, and she is too old for any young boy of his age.

One evening during the time my husband and I were visiting our daughter in Milwaukee for a couple of days this younger son of ours had been roaming around taverns with some other youngsters, and as he tells us, just as they were getting ready to leave the tavern this woman came running to the car and crawled in with them, and the driver, or whose ever car it was, started right off and drove back here to our place to bring my son home. And as he knew that we were not home he invited them into the house for a little while, and he told us that they had been in the house just a little while before they heard a car drive into the yard and this woman must have recognized the sound of the car and ran upstairs to hide herself. And her husband stepped in with his brother and other men looking for her. And they convinced the youngsters to tell where she was and her husband found her in bed upstairs and brought her back downstairs and started pounding her just as they got back into the kitchen. He said if his brother wasn't along and stopped him he might have killed his wife right there. Someone must have seen her get into their car as they pulled out and told her husband about it. She also chased the oldest son for awhile, but I suppose he was too mean for her to stick.

In a way I am glad that they are both away from here. It gives me a lot of rest from worrying about them when they are out at nights. And the other two girls we have are still going to school without any trouble and seem to be learning right along. They help me a lot at home, and I can't complain much about them yet because they still mind me good. My husband works on WPA and I work one day of each week for our white neighbors, for which they pay me two dollars a day.

I was never so happy at any place as I am now living out here amongst the white farmers. They are all nice people around here and only too willing to help, and since I am not used to being treated like this I always wanted to pay for everything they did for me. And it makes me feel cheap when they bring us things and won't accept any pay. I tell you we had some mighty hard times on some places we rented, children going to school and father only working on WPA. Just as soon as we buy a little clothing for the schoolchildren then we would fall behind on our groceries and many times we had to borrow meat, salt, sugar, and different things between paydays from neighbors—which I am sure they didn't quite like the idea. But I was never in any neighborhood where I was treated as good as here.

Just as soon as the farmers around here saw that we moved out here in this brush, they keep coming over to see how we were getting along and if we need any help to just holler. We certainly have landed into a good neighborhood. Every time they butchered anything on their farms they would never forget us. They brought us fresh meat, sausage, liver, and pig heads, and between three white farmers around here they keep us pretty well supplied with meats. And all the things they gave me in the line of furniture that if I brought them all here it would fill my house right up and we won't have no place to get around. One of the farmers has been offering to cut wood for us if my husband got enough pole wood piled up at any time. And as I told him that we won't be able to pay for his work all at one time he cut me off short by saying, "I don't want your money; I want to help you." It seems rather funny to see a bunch of white people like these when we are so used to having white people taking everything we had away from us.

We moved out here and cleared just enough brush to set up our little shack we use for shelter and a bedroom; otherwise during the day when it was nice weather we sat around outside under our many shade trees and kept our dining table outside and ate outdoors, every meal, and when we went to bed at nights we just laid our mattresses on the floor in that little shack and laid ourselves down in every direction. We certainly started here right from the rocks, but I didn't mind it because now we won't have to pay rent and whatever improvements we make on the place it is ours. I think it is just fun, and when we get old we can say we started this place right from scratch. And now we already have a new house to live in and we practically built the house ourselves. Since my husband is working on WPA he didn't have much time to do the work himself, and the boys were working out for themselves so it was I and my two oldest girls that did most of the carpenter work.

My husband hired a carpenter for just about two days and got all the rafters up; then we nailed on the rest of the boards and just as soon as we got the roof covered we moved in already and that was inside of one month. My husband fixed me a frame for sawing boards at different angles, and since I wasn't any good on high climbing so I did mostly that and my two girls nailed the boards on. This way the work goes on even when my husband is away to work. And as soon as the roof was covered we put the shingles on next—just I and the two girls. Their ages were thirteen and fifteen. I helped them with the first three or four layers, and when we moved the scaffold up higher I was done because it was too high for me and it was bad enough where it was at first. I had the creepy feeling all the while we were on that, but the young girls liked it and kept on shingling right up to the peak of the roof and it took us just five days to shingle the whole roof and we moved from the shack into the new part. This was before the windows and the door were in but we had shelter then over our heads. We certainly enjoyed doing this kind of work, which was so different from housework. My daughter sure enjoyed it—especially shingling way up on the roof.

Every evening our boss was surprised to see how much we had accomplished, and he would help the girls then while I got the supper, and early before breakfast he would work on the house before it was time for him to go to work on the project. And by fall we had it nicely covered in and out, and since we have lots of wood we save on fuel by burning mostly wood and the house is plenty warm with wood alone. We are getting along very nicely this winter when some of the children are out working and the old man is working on the project and getting all kinds of meat from our good neighbors. So just by looking at our place here you might be able to see that most of us in the family are pulling together or we would have never got this far in just the short time that we have been living here.

But my husband and I get into trouble only when we are drinking. We both drink whenever we went to dances, and nearly every time we got drunk we quarreled; just what starts it I don't know. Whether he gets too cranky or I do, I just can't say; but one thing, he does scold around a lot, and I might be just as bad because I always gave it to him right back and plenty of it. I have always told my children not to drink because I did, as I don't mean to be a drunkard and am only doing it to spite father so that he may realize someday that we was never getting anyplace by it. And it only brought us plenty of trouble. I always told them to only use us for a lesson and not to try it themselves because they all see what it turns out to be and it never brought us anything that would be good for us.

ANONYMOUS NO. 2

> This forty-year-old man spoke frankly to John Skenandore on July 31, 1941, about his life, family, and his two marriages. He used his own name. We do not have his second wife's perspective.

Two Marriages

I am forty years old and have six children by two wives. My first wife was a white woman, and to tell the truth I may have to go a very long ways before I could find another woman as good and faithful as she was. I have three children by the white woman before she took sick and died. She had a little boy when I married her, and the way we got acquainted was that she worked for a neighbor farmer from where my dad was renting and this farmer hired me too once in a while and worked with the hired girl on that farm. As soon as she is through with her inside work she would come out into the field and work with me. And in the evenings after her work was done she would come to see me at our place, which was only a few steps between us, and each time she would ask me to take her back home when she got ready to go home.

And as I liked her ways I was always willing to do anything to help her, more so when she told me that she was poor and had no place where she could call her home. She had a brother and sister in Michigan, but they were spread out and had forgotten each other. This girl must have went through a tough life in her days because she certainly coax me to marry her so she can settle down and tend to her own business. She said she was tired of working for somebody else. At first I was a little bit afraid because I didn't think I could make her a living good enough to suit her, as being a white girl I thought she might be too particular. And I told her what I had in mind and she said that I didn't have to be afraid of that because she is only too willing to help me along where I needed. But I just couldn't make up my mind and at the same time I liked her company. This went along until in the early winter I took sick and had a very bad cold in my chest, and as she was so close to us she offered her service to mother and helped her with the work I have piled on mother. And she was only too glad to have her, as I was so sick that she was staying up a lot at nights. Well, she doctored me like I was a little kid, and I felt rather out of place to get such good care. Why, I felt like a big shot, sick with special nurse by my side at all time ready to wait on me. I was kind of sorry after I got better because she started to work with my mother more in her kitchen. She was the one that pulled me through and I certainly felt as though I owed her my life, so just as soon as I was well enough we got married and she didn't go back to work at all and stayed right with us. And just as soon as we got a chance we rented a place and went on our own hook. We had very good luck, and everything came our way and made a go much easier than I expected. She was more of help than me supporting her, and she was not a bit particular.

We got along very nice, and there was never a cross word said between us all the time we lived together. The boy she had before I married her lived with us for about two years until he took sick and started to break out on one leg. We had a doctor treated him and told us that he had tuberculosis inside of his bones and the only place for him was at the state hospital in Madison, so she sent him there but they couldn't help him and he died. Well, we got three more children before she got sick next, and that was seven years since we were married. I took her to the hospital in Green Bay as our children were quite small yet and they would only bother her, and I went to see her as often as I could. She had been there just about two weeks when I happen to come to see her again, and I was so very glad to see her looking better and she even said she felt better. But one thing: I didn't understand why she asked me to bring all of her clothes back home. She told me that she won't need them anymore and if she came out that she would have different clothes on. This made me think a lot because the way I saw her that day she was much better. But I told her that I would leave it until I came next time. And that same night I was told that she died and had a very peaceful death, no suffering.

She left me with three little children, and the day before she died she asked me to be good to the children and take good care of them. So my mother took the girl over, and one I had to send to the sanatorium for treatments. The doctors claim that he had tuberculosis too, but the other two are quite well and look healthy. My wife was strong and healthy looking and neat in every way. She kept our house just as clean as it could be at all times. And she was a very good cook and good at saving. Nothing goes to waste, and if there was anything left over after meals she always knew how to fix it up so it could be used for the next meal. And each meal was always different so that a person can't get tired of her cooking. And she also kept the children clean so there isn't one thing that I could say against her, but she was a real woman and I only wish I had her yet.

When I was a kid of two years old I was taken sick with infantile paralysis, and ever since then I had been crippled on one leg. But that had happened when I was so young that I didn't notice anything and never have any pains—only that I can't use my right leg as good as the left one and it didn't develop right and I always had to limp in getting about. For this reason it was hard for me to get work just anyplace but where I am already known. I get the job there before anybody else because it takes a good man to put out as much work as I can. So for that purpose I only worked about the neighborhood and only at farmwork. I can run any kind of farm machinery, and farmers often call on me if they have trouble with some machine that they can't fix themselves.

My first wife was drawing ten dollars a month of mother's pension on the boy she had before I married her. With that and what I made working out and on my garden we made a very good living. It has lots to do with the woman you have; I can prove that. You can live good on a small scale if you have the right woman—one that is saving and careful with everything. Now that I am married again and have the same number of children as with the first one—and I am drawing fifty dollars a month compensation and have nice crops of vegetables and even work out on odd jobs—I am still seventy dollars in the hole at the grocery store. What is wrong with that? It is the woman I have today that is driving me into that.

We have four children to support: three we got since we had been married and one from my first wife. That boy is neglected, but he has to do all of the work that the kids could do and hasn't much time to himself. I don't know just what it would be if I wasn't home so much as I am. Since I was hurt on WPA the doctors ordered me not to do heavy work anymore. I had been drawing compensation of thirty dollars a month, and later I was placed back to the county and they decided that my wife should get what they call mother's pension of thirty dollars a month. Later we were raised up to fifty dollars a month, and that is just what my wife is drawing now. This, and what money I do make outside, and the crops I have, can't keep up with our grocery bill.

The woman I married for my second wife is Oneida, from my own race, and she happen to be one that has all kinds of faults. She drinks, is unclean, a poor cook, and is very wasteful. Lots of the foodstuff spoils on her and is only thrown out. And since the check is in her name she pays only part of the grocery bill and drinks the rest of the money up, and many times she didn't come home for a few days. And I am rather afraid to say much about this because we might lose the pension again, and I am so very grateful to be getting this amount. I have tried everything to get her to stop drinking, but I just can't seem to succeed.

I do drink too, but I am always careful of my money and know what I am doing at all times. I have even tried like quitting on drinking, but that didn't do a bit of good. Where I thought she would quit with me, instead she would only call me names when she is drinking and make me so mad that I just couldn't help but drink also—just to forget my troubles for a while. She has even tried to put me in jail by making up lies that I was mean to her and beat her up, when I never thought of laying a hand on her. But she couldn't prove her complaints, and I had lots of responsible witnesses that proved that all she had against me were lies. And she was told that if she succeeded in putting me in jail that they have a place for her too. I often thought that she couldn't be right in her mind by the way she acts at times, and the funniest thing was that I never noticed it when I was only going with her. I went with her for two months and she was rushing me already to marry her and she was just as nice as any man would want then. But why did she change like this I can't understand.

I am renting this place for five dollars a month and I am holding two acres of garden where I have all kinds of vegetables planted and not a weed in it. The doctors told me that I could plant and weed all I want to, but no heavy lifting. I am in my garden so much that people or neighbors call me "field man." When I first came here the garden was full of quack grass, and now you can't see one. Just as I would finish one end of the field, then the other end was getting weedy again and I would start that end again and just keep right after them, and now I get all of my vegetables out of my garden. I am going to sell some of the vegetables, as I have more than we need ourselves. I expect to clear the grocery bill in a short time when I get started to sell them.

I have three different kinds of corn in my garden: sweet corn, and flint corn for my chickens, and the white corn which they call Indian corn. This is also good to eat green, but we use it mostly for soups and bread. Since my second wife won't learn how to make the soup and bread, I can make that just as well and she certainly likes to eat it too but you can't teach her nothing. She is just that stubborn that she doesn't want to be told anything. My first wife was a white woman, but her soups and corn bread were hard to beat, and I taught her how to make it myself and she wanted to learn. A person would think I would tell this story just the other way because my second wife is from my own nationality, but I am telling the truth—only that I might have got a woman of the worst kind from my nationality and the very best of the white race.

Of course my first wife was homeless and had worked through life roughly, which might have made her realize the difference when she was able to say "my home." She never wanted to go anyplace, only to my dad's, and both my father and mother were very good to her and they certainly felt for her and missed her a lot when she left us. She certainly spoiled me while we were together; now I expect all women should be like her. My second wife has both parents living yet and she has a home and is much younger than the first one and was badly spoiled by her parents. Unless she is just too young for me.

I hurt myself over lifting rocks in a WPA rock quarry, and the doctors ordered me never to do any heavy work again. So I consider myself lucky, as all records are on file and the doctors are backing me up hundred percent.

"CONFIDENTIAL"

> As Ida Blackhawk noted at the end of this piece, the narrator desired to remain anonymous. Again, it is remarkable for its frankness and for the portrayal of a young woman's life, attitudes, and motivations and her concern for infants and children. She was thirty-three years old, and the interview took place on September 10, 1941.

Children

My mother died at the time I was born, and my father gave me away for adoption. I was raised by a woman who had never had a child. She had two older children that she was raising. She was very good to me and treated me like I was her own. I really thought she was my mother until I went to school; then some of the children told me and I remember how I cried and cried. I went home and told my mother and she said I should not care, because she was like a mother to me, and she was always going to keep me. She used to comb my hair and dress me, and when I started to go to the government school I found out that I could not do as I please. I used to be just as anxious to go back to my foster mother as the other children were that had their own mothers.

My mother taught me how to make hull-corn soup and how to make Indian corn bread, and I am glad she made me learn how because now I sometimes make money making corn bread, and whenever I get hungry for corn soup I make it. Very few Oneida women of my age can make it good as they used to make it years ago. I was sent to Tomah Indian School for three years, and when I came home I stayed and helped the old folks, as they were getting old, and my mother was having heart trouble. My foster sister got married, and only my foster brother and I stayed with the folks.

I worked in Green Bay and gave my mother most of my wages. I met a fellow that later asked me to marry him, and we were quite intimate. I liked him, and he seemed in earnest, and so he took advantage of me and then changed his attitude towards me. After I had my baby I had him arrested and he made a settlement with me out of court. My mother stood by me through my trouble, and she took care of my son, and I worked for a while. Then when the state gave pensions to unmarried mothers, I put in my application and I got a mother's pension. For nine years I kept straight. I stayed home and took care of my sick mother, and after she died then I kept house for my foster father. He took sick and died; then I was left alone.

I got to drinking and I met a fellow that I went out with steady for over a year. Then I got drunk and I left him and went home with another guy, and he took advantage of me while I was intoxicated. I found out I was pregnant and I really could not say when it happened, but I knew the date when I got drunk. I went out with both fellows for some time, but not at the same time. I never got drunk again. When my baby came I knew who to blame it on, so I had him arrested, and the state backed me up. He too made a settlement, and the state increased my pension.

Since then I have had another baby. This time I hate to bother the man because he is a married man, and he got me drunk when it happened. I don't do this intentionally, and if I did not drink I guess I would be alright. I have not reported the birth of my last child, but I guess they will have to increase my pension or else they will have take the baby away from me. I love my children, although I hate to admit the circumstances of their origin.

I always have a doctor, and I have very difficult deliveries. The doctor put me to sleep and he took the baby out with instruments. My first baby was a boy, and that may have been the reason, but I always have a hard time. The second time I was confined at the Tomah Hospital, Tomah, Wisconsin, and I had a hard time too, but everything was handy there with all the doctor's equipment, and so I was given all the aid I could possibly have. I had to take the twilight sleep at the end. [1] With my last baby I stayed home and had a doctor come, and this time he was able to deliver my baby without the use of instruments, but I can't say that I had an easy delivery.

My foster mother told me everything that I should be careful of during my pregnancy when she found out I was in that condition. I stayed home most of the time and helped the old folks. I always work and walk every day, but yet I have a difficult delivery. The first two times I really was jilted, so I can't help that the children are fatherless. I admit that I have been more or less indiscreet since my misfortune, but I would like to take care of my children myself.

My oldest boy is going to the Episcopal mission school, and I am sending him there so that he will see the good things of life, and he can take his choice which he wants to follow when he grows up. They say environment has a good deal to do with the child's development, so if he is brought up by the mission and sees how good people behave, maybe he will grow up to be a good Christian man.

When I had my first baby I fed my baby whenever it seemed hungry, and he got along fine, but my mother took care of him more than I did excepting in feeding him. I nursed him until he was over two years old. When I went to the hospital the nurses would not let me have my baby but only to feed it. They had the babies in a different room. When I left they told me to feed my baby just so many hours apart during the first week, and so on as the weeks go by. I went by their schedule for a while; then I could not endure to hear my baby cry, so I fed my baby whenever it seemed hungry. And after I nursed it, the baby would sleep sometimes three hours, and when she awakened she would be ready to nurse again. My babies were never subject to colic, and I always eat everything excepting cabbage, turnips, and onions. My mother told me not to eat those vegetables because they are hard to digest. I always have enough milk for my children.

I would consider a child an infant while it is perfectly helpless and dependent on its mother or someone to do things for it. When a baby starts to walk and to talk, then I think they are in early childhood. There are children's diseases that one has to be careful of, such as colic, croup, whooping cough, chicken pox, measles, teething. Indian children are not as subject to croup as white babies. When a baby starts teething a mother can tell because the baby's saliva flows freely from the mouth, and they are usually fussy and irritable. Some children cut teeth easily; others get sick and feverish. Oneidas I guess have remedies for these ailments, but I always call a doctor when my children get sick. My little girl was troubled with adenoids and bad tonsils, and after she was two years old she was operated on for tonsillectomy and removal of adenoids. Since then she has been fairly well.

I never heard of infants being treated by the False Face doctors, but they treated them after they are four or five years old. [2] Usually if a child is nervous or has St. Vitus' dance, then they resort to the False Face doctors. The old people claim that a child is marked by some animal, such as a bear or some other animal, or by other things. The child is bothered by whatever it is marked by, and if it is a bear, then False Face doctors will mask to represent a bear and act like a bear and will eat on the floor from a big kettle of corn soup. They do other things to attract the patient. The child will not be bothered for a long time, and sometimes it cures them altogether. The False Face doctors are supposed to be a secret society of healers, and very few people know who they are.

G. O.

G. O. was another man who ranged widely in his employment and travel experiences. He gave this account to Guy Elm on February 16, 1942, shortly before the project ended. The narrator's identity was disguised, although he readily gave information about all of his relatives that could easily have identified him. We have edited out those names.

Travels and Travails

I was born February 15, 1893, here in Oneida. I don't know whether my parents were well-to-do or not, but one thing I do know—they sent me away to school when I was quite young. I went to Wittenberg Mission School. I stayed there about five years. At this school I wasn't allowed to speak Oneida. If I did I was punished for it, and I guess sometimes I got a good licking on top of it. Well, the thing to do was to learn how to talk English, and I had a dickens of a time to learn it for some reason I cannot explain. But once I got to talking English, I forgot all about the Oneida language. When I came home to Oneida I couldn't speak the Oneida language to save my neck. I stayed home during the summer and that fall I went to Carlisle Indian School in Pennsylvania. I stayed there another five and a half years.

I had a brother going there who was an athlete, a baseball and lacrosse player; beside he was a musician. Another brother, an ex-Carlisle man, lives in St. Louis, Missouri. He is a railroad man.

When I left Carlisle I worked around at common labor, clearing land and blasting stumps for the farmers. In winter months I used to go to lumber camps in Michigan, up to the time of World War I. I enlisted on March 29, 1918. After getting my examination I informed the army officers that I had previous military training at Carlisle, and they sent me to Camp Logan, Houston, Texas. I stayed at a detention camp about ten days, then went to training about one month. After that I was transferred to Fifteenth Division regulars. I put in fourteen months at that camp. After the war I enlisted one more year, and this time I was stationed at Camp Holabird, Maryland, near Baltimore. When I enlisted again it was in 1920. The outfit that I joined was motor transport.

I was with this outfit, as I said before, one year. When I left this outfit I went to Baltimore, worked there a while, then I went on the road traveling—you know what I mean—and landed back to Oneida. [3]

I got married to a Menominee girl. I worked at the Indian reservation and finally I moved to Green Bay. I was employed by a construction company each summer for about four years. In the winter we used to move back to Menominee reservation. We had our troubles shortly after we were married. She wanted to live in the reservation, and I was used to living in the city, where people are more civilized and have better living conditions. I suppose she had her reasons too. I know for one thing that she knew that I couldn't drink as long as I was on the reservation. And there were other things that I didn't like there in the reservation, so we decided to separate and later got a divorce. When this happened I left and went to Canada, not to run away from the law but because I wanted to forget everything about married life and I thought perhaps I could better myself by going there.

I met another Indian. We traveled together and landed a job at Toledo, Ohio. We worked in the shipyards for about eight months. We finally decided to go back into New York State to the Onondaga reservation; we stayed around there visiting our old friends from Carlisle. They certainly treated us like we were somebody, when we were nothing but couple of bums or hobos. Of course, I'll say, we were educated hobos. As soon as we get to where we were going, we always change our clothing and clean up before we go and hit the main drag. We always had money because there was all kinds of work. The only reason why we didn't ride the cushion was so that we could save some money for other purposes—other than a railroad fare. And it was lots of fun to bum our way from one city to the other. I did most of my traveling in that fashion. Sometimes it took me less time, and again sometimes longer, to get to my destination.

I worked in saltwater pipelines and salt-drying yards near Syracuse, New York, for two summers. I visited the salt mines, but I didn't work in any of the mines. This saltwater pipeline was a nice place to work. I had some instructions at Carlisle in plumbing so that I didn't have much difficulty getting the job and doing the work. My job was replacing worn-out pipes. I liked the work very much because it was easy, and besides I gained more experience in pipe fitting.

When I wasn't working, I used to go to the Onondaga reservation to visit some of the boys that I knew that attended Carlisle. I played lacrosse with the Onondaga lacrosse team one season. Every year they schedule games with Syracuse University, Cornell College, Hamilton College, Tonawanda Athletic Club, and some other athletic club in New York City. The season lasted about two months, April and May. In Canada they have regular professional teams and they have a league; they play about three months. Some other Indians that are still living in New York State had lacrosse teams yet at that time. I remember we played a Mohawk team at Hogansburg, New York. Some of the ex-Carlisle lacrosse players used to play with us, and some of them used to go to Canada and play professional. They really could play lacrosse. When we played against the college teams we used to hire these players so that we could beat the pants off the college boys.[4]

We had a goalkeeper that was a tough baby to handle. He sure could stop those balls and come out of his goal and shoot that ball back—sometimes clear across the field. It was a sight worth seeing. These players all could handle their sticks with skill, and when they did move it was like a flash, either to block or intercept the ball. I played with the team in 1927 in the spring. After the season, then some of the boys went to play baseball. The Onondaga also had a baseball club that was hard to beat. I didn't play on this team because I wasn't quite good enough. Instead I worked in the city of Syracuse the rest of that summer. I like

New York State and Canada very much. I certainly wish I didn't come back in this neck of the woods.

The three boys from the first marriage stayed with their mother, and of course she raised them. I really don't know just what kind of people they are other than what I hear about them, because I never did live with them. I have visited them at times but that's all. Since they have grown up, they have come to see me. They don't seem to like their stepmother, and so they don't stay very long. About one week is all that they can stand her home cooking and housekeeping. I know it's not very sanitary myself, but it's a home for me and my family. All the boys are taller than I am. Oh, they seem to think lots of me, and I do too with them. If I could have got along with their mother I think everything would have been alright. The boys treat me well when they come to visit me. They buy the groceries enough to last the duration of their visit with us. They don't all come at one time, but one by one, and not very often.

The youngest boy stayed with me part of the summer. You see those guns up there? Well, they belong to him. I certainly can't blame them that they don't like their stepmother, because I know that very few step-mothers like their stepchildren. They just can't get along, that's all, and my boys are like that. They don't come right out and say so, because I suppose they don't want to hurt my feelings, but they don't fool me; I can tell and know it to be so.

I have one boy from my second marriage, age five, and boy oh boy is he ever a bad actor. Well you can see for yourself the way he acts up right now. He is sure a spoiled child. His mother is the fault of that, because I usually give him a good thrashing but it doesn't seem to do him any good. The other day he almost punctured my eye while I was trying to sleep it off after I had been to a tavern. I said his mother was the fault of that because she babies him too much. It's just like talking to a cat; he'll do it every time.

Sometimes in the morning when I want to go to work I have a hell of a time trying to get my working clothes together. My pants would be where it should be, my coat would be under the bed, and my cap somewhere else. The car driver would be blowing his horn for me to come out for my ride to work. Well, I would have to go out and tell him to wait for me, then fly back in the house and chase around some more for my clothes. This kid plays tricks with me all the time, either by hiding my clothes or putting something in my pockets. His mother doesn't think he is bad, though. She spoils him by petting him too much and lets him have his way, and she doesn't correct his bad habits. And if I try to lick him then she is right there to take his part. To keep peace in the family, I always cool down and let it go at that. I suppose too it makes him bad because he is all alone, nobody to play with but his mother.

6.

Religious Life and Beliefs

The Oneidas were mostly Episcopalians and Methodists when they came to Wisconsin in the 1820s, and these two churches have had the greatest and longest-lasting impact on Oneida religious and social life. In addition to the influence of church doctrines on Oneida belief, the churches played—and still play—important roles in social life through their choirs, women's clubs, church mutual aid associations, and charitable activities.

Many people remained loyal to the churches of their parents and grandparents, but some individuals moved from one church to another, perhaps as a result of marriage. Still others were attracted to churches that came to the reservation later: Roman Catholic, Baptist, Seventh Day Adventist, Church of Christ, and others. Loyalty to the church of one's parents and the reasons for leaving are frequent topics in these accounts.

The narratives in this section discuss churchgoing, church activities, decisions to change churches, "conversions," beliefs, morality, and more. Abbie Schuyler explains why she is a "spiritualist," and Eddie Metoxen introduces us to the major remaining "traditional" Iroquois religious institution, the False Face Society.

In this narrative, Jerusha Powless Cornelius tells Ida Blackhawk how her views on religion have changed over the years. The interview took place on November 17, 1941.

My Changing Attitude toward Religion

I am going to tell you something that may surprise you, but it is the truth. I never believed in God until just lately. I also had the idea that the white people had a God of their own, and I always figured their God was strong and powerful and mean, because they are afraid of doing anything to displease him, and they try their best to live a good life so that he would give them a reward in the next world. They go to church every Sunday and pray to him and ask him things and implore him to forgive them. I always had the idea that it must be terrible to imagine that they have sinned and maybe they will be punished by being thrown in the fire. I said I am not going to be so foolish to believe in such a thing, and I did not think we Oneidas had the same God as the white people. I made up my mind that I was not going to be a Christian.

One reason I got in that mood was because my first husband was a drunkard, and he made my life as miserable as he could. We were poor, but he made it worse by drinking up what money he made by selling wood or logs from our land. Later we went to some woods, and I stayed home over a week there alone. He left to get some groceries and he never came home. I had no shoes to wear to go anywhere, so I made a pair of homemade shoes out of grain sacks, but there was so much snow that my feet were soon soaking wet. The neighbors gave me an old pair of shoes much too large for me, but I wore them. That was the time I made up my mind to leave that man for good, and I did. I worked for some people and earned my clothes. Then I went out to have a good time.

I started to use intoxicating liquor just to see how it was to get drunk. I soon found a friend to drink with me. I thought that if my husband could lead that kind of life, why couldn't I? I soon got the liquor habit, but the man that I was with drank moderately. I lived with this man for a number of years, and we got along fine. He used liquor, but he was a good provider and he worked all the time. He was good to me. He was a good man, but he was not a good Christian. I mean he was not an active church member, but he was a Methodist. The only fault he had was that he used intoxicating liquor, and I presume we got along because I used liquor too. We never bothered with the church, but we did not make fun of it. We knew we were not living according to the church regulations, but as long as I got along with him I did not care what the church people thought of me. And I really doubted the existence of God, so I never stopped to think of what God thought about me. I was always good and healthy until I was about seventy-five; then I noticed that I was beginning to fail in health. My husband died about this time, and I was free to get married again. I married the man I had been living with for many years. About two years ago my second husband died, and I was left alone.

While I sit in my home alone I ponder a lot. I try my best to make myself believe in God as a powerful person, but a good person, but I can't believe that he would make people suffer if he is a good person, and I have asked him to let me die too, but he does not seem to answer my request. I told my neighbor who always comes over to see me that I could not believe that God was good, but she believes that he is good and great. Not long ago there were some singers came from the Methodist church and sang and prayed for me. I heard some of them testify for Jesus Christ. Somehow while they were here I could not help but change my view about God. These people that came to see me made me happy, and I enjoyed their songs, so I invited them to come again, and the next time they came I repented before them all the things that I had done in the past, and I accepted Jesus Christ as my savior, and I felt better since I decided to become a Christian.

There are some things that are hard to believe about God, but as long as so many people believe in God I can't help but think that it must be true. I always consider everything very closely, and I can't help but think that if a person has children without being married that it can't be wrong, because it is nature and God is the creator of every living thing. The mice have their young ones, and all the little insects have to reproduce. We really are here for that reason. Every little bug is created for some reason, and that bug is created in such a way as to be able to reproduce. But human beings are made with a soul and a mind. They can think and realize that God put them here for some reason. We are supposed to have faith in God and believe in all the mysteries of his being. Three persons in one, but he is a spirit, and invisible. He is everywhere, so he must watch over a person who is in a tavern and guide them home whenever they get drunk. I realize now that he must have protected me many a time, because I never got hurt when I used to get drunk.

I have contacted some people that profess to be Christians, but I found out that some of them are pretty hateful and can say some evil things about another person. Since I became a Christian I made up my mind that I will love everybody, no matter if they hate me or say things about me that would hurt me. Sometimes I almost forget that I should not get impatient because I am suffering. God has given me just so much time to prepare myself to go to the next world. I am a little anxious to see what the other world is like. The good people that come here have told me that over there everything is going to be pleasant, no pain, sorrow, hardship, cold, hunger, or hatred. They say that we are going to meet those that have gone before us. I hope that is true, but how could they tell—no one has come back here to tell us just how it is in the next world. I think they are just guessing, but everyone will find out for themselves because we are all going to die sooner or later.

One thing surprises me, and that is I am not a bit afraid to die. I don't think God ever blamed me for deserting my first husband. I think I already had my punishment for my sins. Somehow I always imagine that God is merciful and would not want to see anyone tormented or suffering, but maybe I am wrong. But if I have anything to make up, I am ready, and if I am condemned I won't flinch. I have left everything to God and he can decide my fate. I never did any good deeds for the church. I guess I used to go to church when I was a child, but I did not attend church after I got married, about the age of fifteen. I did not believe in God; then later I was convinced that the Oneidas had a god, but different from the white people. What always puzzled me is that some people consider themselves good Christians, but they don't do any kind deeds. There is a man partly paralyzed that goes around in our neighborhood, and he always goes in people's houses to visit because he has nothing else to do. Some people won't let him in, and others don't treat him very nice. I always ask him to come in and sit down, and if it is mealtime I invite him to eat with us. That man can't help it if he is in that condition, and people should not treat him mean on account of that. I always try to treat everybody as well as I know how. I even adopted an orphan girl one time, and they took her away from me.

Religion and religious life are major themes for both men and women. Here, Ida Baird, an active member of the Episcopal church, discusses her beliefs and some of the changes she has experienced in her seventy-four years. She was interviewed by Ida Blackhawk on December 22, 1941.

Changes in Values and Behavior

I am an Episcopalian, and my husband was also a member of the same denomination. His parents and grandparents were all Episcopalians. My grandfather used to be the leader in the church choir. He had a very good voice, and he used to sing the church Te Deum in the Mohawk language. After he died then one of my uncles, Thomas Skenandore, always sang the Te Deum on occasions like Christmas and Easter. Since Thomas Skenandore's death different ones have tried to sing it. Lately Guy Elm sang it on several occasions, and he does very well. It is a hard Indian piece to sing because you have to put so many words to a measure. A person has to crowd his words and some can't do that, and it does not sound so well.

I was in the choir, but I am getting too old, so I had to give it up. I can sing any Oneida hymn or song. I have always been an active member, and although I had eighteen children I always tried to reserve Thursday for church work. I joined the women's auxiliary many years ago and they meet every Thursday to sew, and I have missed very few Thursdays. Since my children grew up there has been nothing to hinder me, only real severe cold weather. I always plan my work so I can take a day off on that day.

My children are all over the United States. Some married into other tribes of Indians, and some married white people. At the present time there are two living in Oneida. One of my sons came from Lisbon, South Dakota, to spend the holidays with us. I guess my children will miss my home that burned down the other day. Whenever any of them felt like coming home they knew that all they had to do was to pack up and come and they would always find me home. Now I don't know where to put my son.

I always tell my children to stick to the Episcopal church no matter where they are. My husband always went to church with me, but he never was a vestryman, because he drank intoxicating liquor heavily, but he was always ready to help when they had church "bees." When Father Goodnough was the minister they used to be very strict about communicants; if a person breaks the church regulations they had to wait until all the communicants have taken communion. Then they have to kneel in front and the priest gave them a special prayer of contrition, and then the person is permitted to partake of the Holy Communion. If a person does not repent they are excommunicated for some time. They still belong to the church, but they cannot take communion. But at that time the Holy Eucharist was celebrated only once a month. We used to go to confession on Friday but we just prayed for forgiveness; we did not have to tell the priest what sins we committed.

I believe that a person that has the power to bewitch people really can accomplish something. I'll tell you one case I know of. One time [a powerful man] took a yoke of oxen away from a woman that inherited them after her father's death. The woman vowed she would get even with him some future time. When his little girl was about eight years old she began to have fits, and she just kept getting worse until she finally died. The woman who claimed that she was going to bewitch his family remarked that she was going to do that again. Some years later his wife died, and in a few years he was married again, and their fourth child was paralyzed when she was about eight years old, and her left arm was helpless for some time. She had electric treatments, but she never fully got the strength of the arm and it did not grow to normal size. I had a daughter that used to go to a neighbor's place all the time. The neighbor had a daughter too about the same age, and the mother of the girl did not like the idea of my daughter having so many boyfriends, and her daughter did not have any, so she said she was going fix my girl, and she did. My daughter went insane and she was just in her youth. She is still at Oshkosh, but she seems to be alright now. She works for the superintendent and does not want to be released.

The old people were very careful of a person's hair because a witch can take a strand of hair and do something to it—either cause you to go blind or insane. Or if a man wants to make a woman chase after him, he will do something to her hair, and she will be in his power. So that was why they were very particular about leaving combings around. They take the hair off the comb as soon as they are through combing their hair, and they burn it. I used to know some Oneida women that could wish a person the worse luck, and they would invariably get their wish. A person that has a gift like that was considered almost as dangerous as a witch in the old days. A person will not wish anyone bad luck unless one did some harm, or made the person angry who possesses power of wishing and getting their wish.

An old woman went to her neighbor's and asked if she could borrow the team to go to town. The man said that he was going to use his team and could not let her take them. The old woman did not like that, and when she got home she remarked about the man, and she said, "We'll see if he will always have horses." The next day one of the man's horses died. When the old woman heard that the man's horse died, she got frightened, and she told the members of her household not to mention to anyone the remark she had made about the man. She was afraid he would accuse her of killing his horse. Sometimes too when a person is stingy with anything they have, and would not lend to anyone, something happens to the article they treasure too much. Then they say it is because they would not share their belonging with anyone. In other words, they get a lesson not to be too selfish.

I will tell about myself. I had a sifter that I always used to sift the flour when I am grinding corn to make Indian corn bread. I never would lend it to anyone, because it is hard to find sifters like that nowadays. I also had four quilt poles that I use in stretching out my quilt before I start to sew on it. I never would lend that to anyone for fear I would not get them back. Well, when my house burned down all those things I valued highly burned. Now I would like to borrow those things, and if I know a person has the things I want, I will not like it if they would not lend it to me. So that is the lesson I got: that one should always be willing to share what one has because one cannot tell when one may want to borrow those same articles for a short length of time.

The women's auxiliary was very particular who should become members of their organization. If a woman is just living with a man, and not legally married, the women would not welcome her in their sewing circle; and if a woman is known to drink beer, and gets slightly intoxicated, they would not tolerate her in their club. Nowadays some of the women in the auxiliary and some of those that are in the altar guild are the biggest beer drinkers. Of course some are total abstainers from intoxicating liquors. Most of the women drink moderately, and no one seems to think it is terrible, excepting the older women. Even the priest excuses the ones who drink. He tells them that it is alright just so it does not interfere with their church work.

My grandfather was a heavy drinker, and I mentioned that he used to sing in the choir and lead the singing. One time the vestrymen decided to take my grandfather away from the choir because he had been seen laid out on the street in Green Bay. My grandfather continued to attend the church services, but he sat in the rear seat of the church. One Sunday the choir started to sing an Indian hymn but they could not reach the high notes, so they had to start over again. The second attempt was just as bad. Then my grandfather started to lead the singing from the rear of the church. Everyone in church could sing when he pitched the tune. After that he was admitted back in the choir and there was no more complaint about him.

When he died, Father Goodnough gave a good eulogy of my grandfather. One of the things he said was that although he drank intoxicating liquor excessively, yet he never hardly missed a service to praise God with his voice, and as long as he dedicated his talent to the church he would be counted with the saints. He had his weakness, but that never interfered with his singing on Sundays. So when I think about these women that drink and still want to be connected with church work, I guess it is alright.

At one time drinking intoxicating liquor was considered one of the worst sins, and the worst fault a person could have. Cornelius Hill used to drink heavily, but when he became interpreter he still drank, but he drank alone.[1] He did not drink in saloons with other men, and so everyone considered him a temperate man, and no one could say anything [bad] about him. I think they used to criticize one another more at that time than they do now, and reported each other to their priest. The people used to observe Sundays more strictly than now. Nobody worked on Sundays. The men would not think of harvesting their crops on Sunday, or even to do any work outside besides feed their livestock, and the women would only cook the meals that is most essential for their Sunday meal. They never thought of having a church dinner on Sunday. If they have a church dinner or picnic it was always during the week. What made the change is on account of the men working on the different WPA projects. They have only Sundays at home because Saturday they usually do their trading in the neighboring towns.

We used to have two services on Sunday, one at eleven o'clock and another one at four o'clock, and choir rehearsal after the evening service. That kept us all busy on Sunday. We ate our dinner and we went to church again. The young people used to enjoy the evening service more than the old folks. When Mr. Pierce was superintendent at the boarding school there used to be a song service there at seven o'clock, and many of the young people never missed that. You see we had our time pretty well occupied all day Sunday, and we never thought of going to a tavern or to a dance hall. Of course there weren't any taverns on the reservation then, and that is why I blame the changes to the taverns and the opening of the reservation to the white people. We have to be like the white people, so I presume we are like the white people now.

I never thought I would like to see such changes. My husband has been dead now for seventeen years, and when he was dying he told me that I was going to live a long time and I would see lots of changes in our community, and I certainly have seen many things that just baffles me. My oldest daughter is about fifty-eight years old, and she was married quite young, and two years ago she was back here to visit. Her husband has been in the government service in Arizona, and she had not been home for several years. She certainly was surprised the way the young people have their pleasures nowadays compared to the way it was when she was a young girl, about forty years ago. My youngest daughter went out while she was here and never came home until about four o'clock a.m. She said to me, "Aren't you worried about her? Where could she be that time of the night? Only the worse kind of girl would be out at such a time." I said, "I am used to it now; there must be a tavern open at that time of the night. All the young folks are out all hours of the night nowadays, and they seem to be taking care of themselves. We old people just sit back and trust our young people."

Now take my two daughters, the oldest and the youngest. There are thirty-two years difference in their ages, and their ideas are quite different. My oldest daughter would not think of doing the things my youngest daughter does, and yet my youngest don't realize that the things she does seems outrageous to some people. She goes to church occasionally and considers herself a Christian. She drinks beer and goes to beer parties and thinks nothing of it. Her older sister was shocked. So that is the way with a lot of people, but there is nothing to do but look on. All the young folks are doing as they please regardless of consequence. Everything is changing: the way we travel, the way we farm, and the way we raise our children, and after awhile the whole world will be changed.

IDA BLACKHAWK

> On October 27, 1941, Ida Blackhawk wrote this brief essay about her feelings regarding religion.

My Beliefs: Religion and Values

My grandparents were members of the Episcopal church, and so were my father and mother. My mother was a Methodist but changed when she married Jacob Hill, who was a strong Episcopalian. I was baptized in the Episcopal church and attended the mission school until I was old enough to go away to school. I attended an Episcopal school in Philadelphia for two years, and I would have stayed there longer but the school was abolished while I was there and through Colonel Pratt's influence we were all transferred to his school, Carlisle Indian School. From Carlisle I was sent out to the country, and I lived in a German community, a little town about three miles from Germantown, Pennsylvania, not far from Philadelphia. The people I worked for were members of the Presbyterian church. They asked me to go to church with them so I did, and I was impressed by the way they held their services. It was so different from the way I was used to doing in the Episcopal church, but they had a good preacher and the choir sang some anthems. I enjoyed the music, so every chance I got I went to church.

At Carlisle, the Roman Catholics and Episcopalians were allowed to go to their own churches, and so I went to the Episcopal church, but it was the low church. When I came back here Father Merrill was here, and he used the gaudy vestments and officiated like the high church. Father Merrill was a good preacher, but at that time I was not so interested in the sermons. I went away to school again, and the next time I came home Father Thorn was here. He was a good preacher and a very good easygoing priest.

While at Hampton, Virginia, I used to spend the summers in the New England states, and one summer I was in Newport, Rhode Island. There

were four of us there from Hampton. Every Sunday evening we attended
a different church. One time we attended a Roman Catholic church, and
the priest said the mass in Latin. There was no sermon, and the choir
sang in Latin. We did not understand a word said during the service. I
told the lady about that where I worked, and she was much surprised at
us attending different denominations. I said, "We want to understand
the white man's religion, and in order to do that we have to visit all
the different churches." She said we were sinning and should go to
confession.

In my observation I concluded that the different churches are all
working for the same cause, and are all doing some good to humanity.
I might say that the Roman Catholic church has the most hospitals
and schools and institutions for the orphans and unfortunate girls.
But I don't believe in taking money way from the poor the way the Roman Catholic priests do. And the priests tell the people that the Roman
church is the only church, and the priests have the power to forgive the
people of their sins if you pay them, etc. There are some things in the
Episcopal church doctrine that I do not fully believe, but I never tell anyone. I may be wrong, and I may be right, and if I really went according
to my conviction I would not belong to any church. I was baptized in the
Episcopal church, so I try to support the church, while I don't take an
active part in the church activities. I pay my pledge and donate money
towards dinners, etc.

My father and mother were active members. My father was a vestryman for many years and was also in the choir from the time they started
to have choir until he was about seventy-five years old. My mother was
at the head of the church women's auxiliary for many years. It seems as
though I cannot find time to be at the auxiliary meetings, so I am not
an active member, but I pay my dues and help them in raising funds for
their society. I think it is a good thing to belong to some church, for
the church never influences anyone to do wrong. But I think a person
can be good and do good even if they are not Christians. Some of our
great men like Abraham Lincoln were not Christians, but he was a very
religious man and did great things in his lifetime.

Most of the missionaries to the Oneidas were very devout men, and
were good preachers, but some were not used to managing a farm or
running a mission. The priests left the whole thing to the vestrymen and
only attended to the church services, etc. Father Grant rented the farm

to some Oneida family, and they were doing alright, but some members of the congregation objected to that and found fault with the way the mission farm was being managed. Father Grant did not know how to beg for money to use for upkeep, and the result was that everything was neglected and the parish hall was soon in a dilapidated condition. The schoolchildren broke windows and no one said anything about it. Father Grant soon showed that he was addicted to strong intoxicating liquor, but he was a very intelligent man and I used to enjoy his sermons because he knew the ancient history very well, and he told us in his sermons how the Episcopal church branched out from the Roman Catholic church, and how the Christians were persecuted. St. Paul, before his conversion, persecuted the Christians, but after he changed he became a very strong Christian, and a great preacher. I had nothing against Father Grant; of course he officiated at the services more like the Roman Catholic church, but I never stay away from the church on account of any priest. I don't go to church to please the priest, but I go to learn something, and to worship God. I notice so many of our people change from one church to another on account of some priest, or if they get angry at some member of the church.

I think the reason the old Oneidas were so faithful to their church was, first, because they had no other social center; second, because they were in a strange land, surrounded by other tribes of Indians who were more or less hostile; third, they were led out here by a Christian man and they wanted to stand by him in his undertaking. They first built a little log cabin for their church and later built the stone church. Most of the work in masonry was done by the Oneidas. After the dedication of the church the Oneidas were very proud of their handiwork, and this gave them zeal to continue to support the church. The young Oneida people that returned from various government schools had no other place to go to but to the church they belong to, and later when the parish hall was built then they held dances there.

The white people started to settle on the reservation, and the opening of taverns and dance halls at Oneida changed the form of the recreation of the young people. The young people started to frequent the taverns and dance halls every Saturday night. During the week they attend the movies. The young people of the Methodist church are the same. The old Methodist people did not believe in dancing, but their young people attend the dances, and the white people are the same. If everybody stayed home there would not be anyone at the taverns on Saturday night and they would feel like going to church on Sunday. Some of the priests have told us that it is not a sin to use liquor, just so you don't do anyone any harm while you are drinking. They have also told us that it is alright to work or do anything on Sunday, providing you go to church first.

I think it is a good thing to belong to a Christian organization and to be willing to share in the church's expenses. I consider a person narrow-minded when they say the only way to be saved is to join the church, whichever denomination they belong to. Each denomination has a little different system in officiating the church services and their creed may be a little different, but I hope all the churches worship the same God.

I once read a poem written by James Russell Lowell called "The Vision of Sir Launfal." It was about a young knight that left his castle to search the Holy Communion cup lost during the Crusade. He fitted himself out with provisions and set out to search for the cup that Jesus used at the Last Supper. As he left his castle he saw a leper begging and he tossed a coin to him in scorn, but he thought it was his duty to give something to the beggar. He traveled far in the strange country, and he was an old man when he returned to his country. He came by the roadside, and there was the old leper still begging. He only had a crust of moldy brown bread left, but he sat down and shared his bread with the leper, and he took a tin cup and gave him some water. In his vision he saw the leper stand up, and a voice said, "Be not afraid. What you did to this beggar you did it unto me. The bread you gave him is my body, and the cup of water is my blood. It is not what you give but what you share, for the gift without the giver is bare." Then Sir Launfal realized that he had found the Holy Grail. After that he opened up his castle for the poor and the aged, and they were welcomed in his castle. This is what I believe in—a Christian should love his fellow men.

By 1940 a number of individuals had become members of other churches or at least had tried them out. Mrs. Abbie Schuyler, age sixty, was the sole adherent of spiritualism represented in this collection. Ida Blackhawk recorded her account on November 4, 1941.

The Comfort of Spiritualism

All of my people were Episcopalians, and my deceased husband and I were, too. In Milwaukee we attended All Saints Episcopal Cathedral. For some time I have been somewhat confused about religion. One thing, I don't believe that ministers should talk about another church or run any preachers down. The people as a rule don't like to hear that; so many preachers are apt to do that.

Lately I have been attending spiritualist meetings, and I am inclined to belief in spiritualism. I believe that our spirit lives forever and that people do not die—only their bodies die, but the soul and the spirit remain—and I believe that spirits of the departed are around us, and they can see us, but we can't see them. I also believe that we can converse with the spirits. They will hear us, but they cannot speak to us; but in some way they will manifest it to us that they answer. There are some people that are born spiritualist. They are not like those that study astrology and are supposed to know your destiny. The spiritualists deal only with the spirits.

I went to a spiritualist in Green Bay and she had never seen me before, so I was surprised when she told me that I was a widow and that she had a message for me from my husband. She said, "Your husband wants you to set a place for him at the table in front of you for ten successive days, for his spirit will be there to eat with you." So I did, and every mealtime I felt as if someone was there, although I could not see anyone. I said a prayer every mealtime and I prayed for my husband, but I did not notice any manifestation from his spirit, but I presume he was satisfied because I was not bothered with any strange noises and felt perfectly safe in my home alone. We should not be afraid of the dead, for they will not harm us.

The woman whose husband had an accidental death a week or so ago came here to stay overnight with me because she was afraid to stay home alone. I talked to her about spiritualism, and for her not to be afraid of her husband's spirit, for if he comes to her in her quiet hours it is because he wants her to remember him in her prayers.

I knew a young man who had a accidental death in Milwaukee. He was killed instantly by a car. I knew a lady who was a spiritualist, and she went with me to the funeral parlor to view the corpse. She stood there and said, "Oh, it is beautiful." So after we went home I asked her what she meant by saying "It is beautiful" when she was viewing the corpse. She said, "I wish you could have seen what I saw. The spirit of the dead boy was standing by his casket, looking at his own corpse, smiling. That was a beautiful sight to behold."

Some old Oneidas always said that the Indians are nearer the spiritual world than any other race, because from way back they believed in spiritualism. They called God the Great Spirit, and many of those old Indians knew when they were about to leave this world. The fellow that was struck by a car and died a few hours later seemed to have expected to leave. He and his wife went to Seymour the day before he died. He bought 100 pounds of flour, 100 pounds of sugar, 25 pounds of coffee, and 10 pounds of tea, and he piled up some wood by the house and said, "Now I can leave." His wife thought he meant to go to the woods in the northern part of the state.

When my mother-in-law was dying I asked her if she wanted to have the minister come to see her. She said, "No, don't call him." Later she asked me to give her the Holy Communion, so I just gave her a small piece of bread moistened with water, and she was satisfied. She asked us to sing for her, so we did; for two hours we sang some hymns. Then at the last minute she asked for the priest, but it was too late; we could not get him there in time. Father Christian seems to believe that the spirits or souls of the departed should have our prayers and that it will do them some good.

There used to be a big tree back of our house. When we were making a settlement here it was a small tree, and my husband was just about to jerk it out when I saw him and I stopped him. I told him to let it grow, so it grew there and got to be a large tree. Last winter I was short of fuel, so I hired some men to chop down the tree. In the meantime I asked my husband in prayer if he was willing to have the tree chopped down. For two days I did not notice any manifestation that he received my message. Well, they went ahead and chopped the tree, and that night

I heard some one chopping out there. I even looked to see if I could see anyone, but I could not see a thing—but I heard the chopping all night long. That was the way he answered me and manifested his approval—by making that sound.

The spiritualists that see into the spiritual world say that the spirits have a good time in paradise, or wherever they are. They have parties and they see each other and meet acquaintances, friends, and relatives, but sometimes it is a long time before they meet because there are so many spirits. Of course they have different parties than what we have. They don't eat or drink, but they have gay old times in the spiritual world, so there is no reason why we should be sorrowful when we lose any loved one. Of course we are bound to miss them here, but if their spirit lives and is around us we should not feel that they are dead. I feel just as happy here, seemingly alone, but in reality I am not alone. The spirit of my deceased husband is always here. My children all live in Milwaukee, and they always ask me to live with them, and I go and visit them and stay a while, but I feel as though I must stay home in order to be with the spirit of my departed husband, although the spirit can go anywhere.

I can't help in thinking that the Oneidas were believers in spiritualism at some time. It was customary years ago to have a tenth-day feast after the death of one in a family. I believe some do that now.[2] On the tenth day after a death in a family they held a feast. Only those specially invited go to the feast. Years ago they used to eat in silence, and a vacant place was supposed to be for the spirit of the departed. The food consisted of different dishes that the departed one liked, and the invited guests were supposed to eat a little of everything on the table. After they have feasted then the hostess gives away some of the departed one's possession, namely clothes, dishes, quilts, and other household goods, and if the departed one is a man then they give away his tools, implements, etc. I think at one time they even gave horses away. At the present time, if they hold a feast the invited guests talk and laugh like any other time, and sometimes they give things away and sometimes they don't. Usually the people invited are friends and relatives of the departed.

Melissa Cornelius, age fifty-nine, had thought a good deal about religion and the different organized religions that were available. She gave this account to Ida Blackhawk on October 22, 1941.

Christian and Indian Religion

My father and mother were Methodist, and so were my grandparents. For some reason my parents left the Methodist church and joined the Episcopal church, and my brother and I were baptized in the Episcopal church. Later my parents went back to the Methodist church. Then a Seventh Day Adventist came here and preached to the Methodist people in their homes, and he converted quite a few, and they started public meeting, and finally made enough money to build a church and the building still stands near our place. My father and mother left the Methodist church again and joined the Seventh Day Adventist church. They don't believe in Christ, and their Sunday is Saturday, same as the Jewish people. Their doctrines are all in the Old Testament of the Bible.

When I came back from the East I had my ideas of religion. I attended the Episcopal church services several times, and I was impressed by the form of worship. After visiting my people for a month I returned to Philadelphia, Pennsylvania, and found employment as a housemaid in a very wealthy home. One day a lady came to visit there, and I was surprise when she started to talk about religion to me. I told her I was baptized in the Episcopal church but that I was a little perplexed at the way the priest officiated at the services I attended. I did not believe in form and show that was used during the service. She told me to send for a booklet called Practical Christianity from St. Louis, Missouri, and to study that. I read the booklet and I believed a lot of what I read. I kept sending for the booklet, which is published monthly, and I noticed that it was written by the Christian Science church. I got a lot of information in those booklets. I began to go to the Christian Science church, and if there was a Christian Science church handy I would still be going there. I never say anything to anyone about what I believe in, but when I came back here I joined the Methodist church because the services were plainer and suited me.

It always seem to me that a person should worship God in a very quiet way. The Indians before the white man came had worshiped the Great Spirit, and the white people called that paganism, and I believe that the white people were mistaken. I think their form of worship in some churches, such as the Roman Catholic churches, seems to me more like idolatry. They have the images of Christ and Mary in front of them, and they bow and kneel before such an image and make a sign of the cross, etc.

My mother heard a story of how some great learned Christian came to the Six Nations in New York and tried to convert the Indians. At that time they had a leader called Za-go-yeh-wa't ᴬ. He officiated at these ceremonies to the Great Spirit. He answered the white man and said, we worship the Great Spirit in the open space. We don't have to build a church. The spacious sky is the temple of the Great Spirit, and we fast and pray in order to develop strong characters. The white men went away, and later, after the Revolutionary War, the white men said we have to ruin the Indians morally before we can ruin him physically, so they brought whiskey and practically gave it to the Indian. An Oneida gave a speech here one time during a centennial celebration. There were some prominent white men who spoke, including Bishop Weller. The speakers said nice things about the Oneidas, of their achievements, and that their drawback was intoxicating liquor. If they would only leave that alone, they would make a better advancement. The Oneida man said, "Before the white man stepped on the American soil, the Indians did not have any bad habits; they did not know how to steal or to say bad words, so if there is a devil, the white people brought him here and it is up to them to take him away." It is a fact that the old Indians were morally and physically stronger than this generation. Those Indians had developed very strong character up to the time they started to use intoxicating liquor, and if anything has ruined the Indian it is liquor.

Before the Oneidas came here they were already converted to Christianity, and the Methodists settled in the south side and the Episcopalians in the north side, and they were both very much against the Roman Catholic church. The Catholics had tried several times to come into the reservation to convert the Oneidas, but they were rejected each time. Then one time one very influential Oneida, a member of the church, got in trouble with the other members of the board and he offered the Roman Catholics to build a church on his land. He deeded the land to them, and that was how they got on the reservation. That man's name was Eli Skenandore (Ga-wihtha'g^). He used to be a good church worker and was a very well-to-do farmer. He often gave a feast at his home, and members of the Methodist church would go there and pay for their dinner, and at times he cleared one hundred dollars for the church. But in his anger he did something that was a detriment not only to the Methodist people but to all the Oneidas. There are very few Oneidas that are Roman Catholics, and because they have not been able to get membership the Catholics are really not friendly to the Oneidas. There are lot of Catholics on our reservation and most of the town officials are Catholics, and that is why the Oneidas had a hard time getting help during the depression, and they don't give them as much as the people of other localities get. Father Vissers, who was the Roman Catholic priest for the south-side Roman Catholic church, went around asking for donations for the Oneida Indian Mission, and people donated thinking that they are helping the Oneidas. He built a big day school and residence, and white people are getting the benefit of that. Very few Oneida children go there, if any. When I see or hear of a priest or a missionary doing anything like that it makes me wonder whether the white man's religion is really the best.

It seems to me that most of the present Oneida people have taken the same attitude as the white people. I think there are very few Oneidas that are really true Christians. They go to church, but they don't apply their religion in their everyday lives. While I was out East among the wealthy class of people, I could always tell when I met a good Christian and when I met one of the veneered ones.

I can't believe that a Christian can have any hatred in their heart, because Christianity teaches one to love everyone, but people are more interested in the material side. Even the priests are inclined to be more concerned about the financial part of the church than the spiritual part. What we need here on the reservation is spiritual help, and only spiritual people are going to be able to help us.

In the old country, they got so corrupt that they started fighting among themselves, and they are sending the poor people to fight, and maybe the poor people don't know just what they are fighting for. There is a motion picture called the *Sons of God* that showed the way things are in Europe. It seems that the Nazis think that they have conquered the French nation, but the French government hired some prostitutes to kill the German officers who frequented the French resort, called

"Mademoiselle Guillotine." A German officer of high rank was sent there to investigate the resort, and he discovered what had happened to the German officers. So that is the way with all the little nations that Germans have conquered. They have hatred in their hearts and are ready to strike back if they get an opportunity. If all those European countries were really Christian nations they would not be at war today. We all need more spirituality in our religion.

CORA ELM SINNARD

Cora Elm Sinnard, age fifty, served as an army nurse overseas during World War I. While in nursing school, she participated in demonstrations for women's suffrage. On January 8, 1942, she shared with Ida Blackhawk some of her feelings and beliefs about education, religion, and related topics.

Life, Belief, and the War

My parents and also my grandparents on both sides were Episcopalians, and so they had me baptized in the Episcopal church when I was an infant. I was taught all the doctrines of the Episcopal church. I became a very firm Episcopalian. Although I went to school when I was quite young, yet when I was with my father and mother I spoke the Oneida language, and I presume that was the reason I never forgot the Oneida language. My father had some education. He may have gone as high as the seventh grade, but anyway he was very good in arithmetic. He could work any problem mentally and always got the correct answer. My mother was not very far advanced in school, but she was very handy in sewing and working, and very thrifty, but she could hardly speak English.

My parents sent us all to school, and although my father had a one-hundred-acre farm, yet he did not want the boys to miss school on account of working on his farm, so he sent them away to school and most all of us have pretty fair education. We all went beyond the seventh grade. My brother and sister are postgraduates of Hampton Normal School, and one sister finished the Commercial course at Haskell, and I was graduated at Carlisle. I then went to Philadelphia, Pennsylvania, and trained in the Episcopal hospital, and I was asked to stay and be a supervisor nurse after my graduation. When the U.S. got in the last world war I joined the Red Cross U.S. Army Corps and was sent overseas for two years.

My father used to tell us a lot of the old beliefs and customs, but he did not believe in them. He used to tell us that witchcraft was all the Devil's work, if there was such a thing as the Devil. He said that it was prohibited to practice witchcraft when his grandmother was a girl. He used to tell us a story about what his grandmother told him. She used to tell him that she remembered when a group of old men and women were killed by order of the chiefs because people accused them of being witches. She used to speak especially of one old woman who was making corn bread when someone came and told her that she was wanted too. They did not even give her time to wash her hands, so she went with her hands covered with corn meal dough and she was killed with the others. It seemed that the Oneidas learned witchcraft from the Dutch people, and they were already prohibited to practice it before they moved to Wisconsin, yet even now and then some old woman or old man gets accused of being a witch, in whispers. But no one dares to accuse anyone openly because in Wisconsin the laws are different from the laws of the state of New York. They would have to prove their accusation before they could punish them.

In regards to religion I would say that the Christians believe that Jesus Christ is the most important, because they believe that he is their salvation. But if a person is not a Christian, then they must believe that God is the most important in religion. It seems that humanity forget God; only in time of disaster—then they get closer to God. A true Christian should lead a Christian life every day, and if everyone practiced that the world would be altogether different. There would be no hatred between individuals, marriage vows would not be broken, and a nation would not go against another nation, if people practice their religion. No nation would think of killing off people just to get possession of land or to dominate the world, if people did not forget God or their religion. An individual who is following his or her religious belief respects other people and is not so apt to break the civil laws. In other words, they have a sense of right and wrong.

I think religion is a good thing for the masses, because when they turn against religion then humanity is at stake. Religion soothes those that have faith. This world would be worse if there were not religious people. I have read about the corruption in some religion circles, but not all religious people are connected with that and that's why every so often then there is a revival, or maybe a new religious organization will start what we call a church. I believe that all the different churches are working for the same cause, and no matter what denomination they belong to they are all doing good work.

Magic deals with supernatural power, and religion deals with spiritual or divine power. The soul and the spirit of a person is about the same if not identical, and sometimes I have been inclined to believe that the conscience of a person is a part of the soul of a person. The soul of a person is the real self, and the body is the shell or the place where the soul lives. When the person dies, then the soul leaves the body and the soul lives on. But I have heard it said that a person can be so bad that his or her conscience will not be able to distinguish between right or wrong, but they continue to live, so then the conscience is not the soul according to that.

When a person has supernatural power they are born with it, and they are not aware of their extraordinary power until they are old enough to realize things around them. Some do not develop their supernatural power, and others do. I am not so sure that anyone can possess supernatural power, but I have heard that Indian people are more apt to have supernatural power than any other race, because they are closer to nature and it is more of an instinct. When a person dies his supernatural powers end. I don't know why the old Indians always said that after baptism children lose their supernatural power, so they infer that the supernatural power comes from an evil spirit, and when a person becomes a Christian one loses the power because one becomes a child of God.

I never heard anyone speak of an animal having supernatural power or to be sacred. The Oneidas had a "red stone" that they considered supernatural. That was the stone they were named after. [3] They claim that this red stone followed them wherever they went. But they did not consider it sacred and never worshiped it. I am just assuming that they thought Dehaluhyawá·gu sent the red stone to them. I used to hear my father relate about Dehaluhyawá·gu as the Great Spirit that the Six Nations worshiped as their god many years ago, before the white man came to America. [4] The Indians spoke of him as having a great power, and he looked over them. At times they said he came to them as a human being, and again that he was a spirit. They prayed to him for protection and thanked him whenever he answered their prayer. They have a story about his origin, but I don't remember all of it. This Dehaluhyawá·gu had a brother, and his name was Dawìsgala, and Dawìsgala was the bad spirit.[5]

Because the Oneida already believed in a spirit, it was easy to convert them to the white people's religion with comparatively few exceptions. If the Oneidas thought Dehaluhyawá·gu and God were the same Great Spirit, they were anxious to learn more about the powerful spirit that the white missionaries told them about. After the conversion of the majority of the Oneidas, I think they had to believe in God only and deserted Dehaluhyawá·gu altogether. After the white people ruled over, then they must have been forced to accept their God as having more power than Dehaluhyawá·gu. My father spoke of Dehaluhyawá·gu more as a myth, and although I often heard him talk about Dehaluhyawá·gu and Dawìsgala, I have forgotten those stories.

I have heard very little of False Face doctors, but I would imagine from what I have heard of these False Face doctors that it is a case of mind over matter. The old Indians then knew something of psychology, and where they learned it nobody knows. It seems to be a gift, like the knowledge of medicine. My grandmother was a medicine woman, and she was known as a very good midwife. She took care of my mother in time of childbirth with all of us, with the exception of the youngest one. She was too old then and was sickly. She was a member of the False Face doctors, but they used to keep that secret, so even my mother did not know of it until after her death. Although she was a member of the Episcopal church, she was not an active member.

I believe in dreams, and I have dreamt some things that have come to pass. For instance, I dreamt that I was going to cross the Atlantic Ocean, and it was before I signed up to join the nurses' U.S. corps in my hospital. And before the war ended I had another dream that I could not help but remember, and that was that I was going to sail for America, and I got in the boat when I woke up. I remember that at the time I was so disappointed that it was only a dream, but a few days after that the armistice was signed. I usually dream of a person I am going to get a letter from.

It is altogether different the way the present church members behave than even in my father's time. The vestrymen were chosen by the people, and they were men who were active church workers and good, strong Christians. When my father was a vestryman he was often chosen to go and lecture a married couple if they were known to be having domestic troubles, or if two church members have a dispute, it was the duty of the vestrymen to straighten things out for them. The vestrymen had to be very careful of their own behavior. The moral standard of the Oneidas has become much lower. Nowadays people not legally married have a good standing in church if they attend the church and pay their pledge. The vestrymen and the priest overlook the conduct of the members of the church. Even the Sisters of the Holy Nativity are very earthly. They are just gossip collectors. They are supposed to be missionaries, but I have never known them to really do any missionary work.

The first two sisters that were here when I was a child used to teach us Sunday school lessons every Sunday afternoon, and also taught the church catechism to the confirmation class. In our church a child is baptized in infancy, but the child is not confirmed until it can understand the doctrine of the church and what the Holy Eucharist stands for. After confirmation the person becomes a member of the church and can take part in the church election for vestrymen. But if they neglect to take communion on Christmas and Easter then they are not considered eligible to vote. I think the general ideal most valued years ago was righteousness, but nowadays I think it is different. I think a person with money, no matter how they have acquired it, is looked up too, such as a tavern keeper, etc.

It seems to me there is such a thing as being too religious, and as being too self-righteous. I would say that there are a great many people better than the religious people, and many of them do more good in the world. I would say the most good an individual gets is education, because through education a person may get high position and money, which is the most essential in getting along in this world. Of course, having religious interests may give a person the prestige in a small community such as Oneida, but in my profession I have to give my credentials in order to get a position. People can try to ruin my reputation, but they can't take my profession away from me.

My experience with this Oneida community is that everybody looks down on the other. There is more jealousy here than one could imagine. I think if they got out more to some other community they would get a different outlook on everything. I have been asked so many times by some of these Oneidas how I happen to join the Red Cross Army Corps. I try to tell them that I could not have been admitted if I was not a graduate nurse, and then they would give me a surprised look and ask me when and where I trained. After my graduation at Carlisle I went to Philadelphia, Pennsylvania, and started to train. Some wealthy people I worked for helped me, and my father paid my tuition. I came home to visit only once while I was in the hospital. I never ran around here on the reservation like some do. I had a strenuous youth. My life overseas was not very easy. Although I was in a base hospital, I saw a lot of the horrors of war. I nursed many a soldier with a leg cut off, or an arm.

EDDIE METOXEN

In 1941, Eddie Metoxen, age fifty-two, was one of Oneida's leaders of False Face, a practice that had roots in the traditional religion and culture of the Iroquois and was shared with their relatives in New York and Canada. Stadler King took down this account on June 30, 1941.[6] The title given here is the original one.

A Sacred Ceremony

I have a great feeling because my garden is coming so good. I have almost one acre of canning beans. The best thing a person could do is to plant all they can because everything is going to be high next winter. If the war keeps on for some time they will run out of some things, and that will make everything cost so much. So we will have to plant all we can so that we may be able to avoid buying everything. I know that if I have enough potatoes it would save a lot.

I am buying this land. I will have to pay one hundred dollars for about three acres, and the CCC have told me that they would help me fix up this land. That is, they will level off all those holes where gravel was taken out. I will have a good gravel pit if I get that fixed up. I will start building a house next spring.

I think the best story I can tell is about the way we cure this sickness, when people are being bewitched, by this masked face. This sickness is known only to Indians. I have had a chance to perform these ceremonies to this young son of Mr. and Mrs. X. When a neighbor's boy was sick and we went there to cure him, this boy was there and he made fun of the way we did. He laughed so much and joked about it. In a few days he came down with the same kind of sickness. He was just about to die when I got a note asking me to come and see what could be done to cure him. I went over to see him, and I could see that it was the masked face that was bothering him. I got my bunch of Indian dancers, and we all went at night. When we were all inside, and all of us were ready for the ceremony, I started to burn tobacco at the opening of the stove. Then we all could smell the smoke and the boy began to move. I could tell by the smoke that there was a chance of helping him. Then I said the word *waz•z*ᴵ. And we started the dance. This word means "dance spirits" in English. We did these dances three nights, and the boy got up and took part in the dance. The boy was so happy because we were able to help him. He had faith in what we were doing because he was so much better and he seemed very happy. If people had good faith in this they are more likely to be helped, but if they don't have much faith or if they were in doubt, this would not help them.

I could not charge anyone for doing this kind of cure; it must be done free. I have now helped over one hundred people, so I could have had lot of money if I was getting paid. There are three of these sicknesses, and it would be rather hard to explain in English just what these are, but it's the spirit of either one of these three classes of sickness. When I perform these dances I get some form of extra spirit. This spirit is a super being and I could see small men in a vision and they would all dance with us, but no one sees them—but I have seen them. They are all small Indian men. These are the spirits of Indians, and it is them that could cause the sickness. Sometimes the person who is wished this sickness by the spirits would get deformed in some way. I have doctored a lady whose face was getting deformed, one of her eyes was turning gray and she could not laugh like people do, so I took some of my helpers and went to doctor her. She seems to be getting better now. A doctor would not know what this is; he would say that it was paralysis or nerve wreck. When I am doing this curing I am always aware that some greater spirit is with me, and that is God the supreme spirit. If I was not a believer in God I would not be able to do this.

The three of these spirits are the *wazá•z*ᴱ, which means the dance spirits, and *ohgwá•l*ᴵ, which means the spirits that makes the scare or the Bear. That's when people seem to be scared of something or like they were expecting to see some sort of an animal like a bear. And then there is the otguhzó•l ᵁ. This would mean a masked face. These are all supernatural spirits, and no one should make fun or joke about them because they have power to wish one of these sickness on anyone.

We have a real Indian tune which we sing when we are curing a person. I have heard that long ago, maybe as far back as the days of our great-grandparents, that Oneidas used to worship the Great Spirit in this way. That is, they would dance when they pray and worship God. Some tribes of Indians do that yet when they pray. I have seen Winnebagos dance what they call corn dance. This is held in the fall when corn is ripe and they get together and dance, which is to thank God for the corn they got. Some tribes dance when they ask for rain. These are all sacred dances, which is the belief and customs of Indians. So this curing people is sacred belief, and when people believe in what they do it is most always granted if they ask for one special thing.

I also believe in singing Indian songs for people when someone has died and they have wakes. It is the belief of Oneidas that they help the dead when they sing some hymns because the spirit is still among us. The Oneidas always did believe that the soul of a dead person does not go until ten days after death. I believe in the traditions of the old Indian people and in this curing of people by dancing for them in a sacred way.

Some people would not believe this, but it is true. I could tell when I see a person which one of these three spirits is ailing a person. When I burn the tobacco in the fire of the stove I could tell which spirits they are, and I could tell if they could be helped. The smoke of this tobacco seem to go round and round and then all at once it would be swept up the chimney. When the smoke does this I know that the person is curable, but if the smoke spreads and goes downward then I know the person could not be cured. If a person is bewitched by the Bear spirits they will act and move like a bear. This is when they are sick in bed, they will jump up and try to climb a wall, and they will stand like a bear with their arms stretched out but at their wrists the hand will bend down. If they get so bad they will make noise in their mouth like a bear. They have a feeling like they expect to see some animal; they will look out through the windows and act like there was something outside that they are afraid of.

When I am asked to cure these persons, I get my dancers together and we would all come to the house and not knock on the door but we rush right in and stand by the sick person. The dancers make motions like a bear before the sick person. When I have put the tobacco in the fire I say "*ohgwá•l¹*" (bear), then the dancers would start to dance as a bear would. Someone would spread acorns and other nuts on the floor, and some blackberries in small pails. When I stop the dance we would all grab for the blackberries and nuts and eat them. I mention each one of these spirits starting from the one this person is bewitched by. If the person is bewitched by the bear I would say "*ohgwá•l¹*" and "*wazá•z*ᴱ" and "*otguhzó•l*ᵁ" and the dance would start. Then the dancers would do all they can to scare the sick person. We do this three nights, and the second night the sick would make moves to get up. The third night they usually get up and dance with the dancers and we know that the sick will be well.

Then there is the *waza•zé*, which means dancing spirits. They are small people which could not be seen by other people, but I could see them when I am performing this ceremony, and also by the sick person. If these are the spirits I burn the tobacco and say "*wazá•z*ᴱ" and also mention the other two, but for this we eat ground corn siftings in soup fashion. We do this for three nights too when the sick would be dancing along with the dancers. The other spirits are the *otguhzó•l*ᵁ. This is the masked face, so I start off with saying the word and the other two. The dance then starts, but this time we have candy and peanuts on the floor and each dancer tries to get some of these peanuts or candy and I take the coals of fire with my hands and shower this over the sick person. I do not get burned and when I pour these coals of fire over the sick person, they do not get burned either. The only time we do not do this three nights is when the sick is not so far gone or not so sick. But if they are very sick we do it three times. But most always they are up the third night and join in the dancing.

Some people have been known to have their face twisted one way or the other and they get stiff in the joints. But when they are cured their faces turn straight again and they are once more limber as anyone else. When I do this performance I ask the spirit of God to help me, and this is what makes it sacred. I am aware all through that God is with me, and if someone was sick across the ocean I could perform the ceremony here at home and they would be cured wherever they are. So sacred is this

Indian ceremony that if I was a mean man and someone made me mad, I could wish this spirits on them and they would get sick with one of these sickness. But I know that it would be wrong because it is a great sin if a person wishes any bad luck on another person.

When we are performing this for some sick person we do not talk— only make noises like the spirits which are ailing this person. Each man knows just what to do, and no one is told what to do. When I stop the dance I hit the floor with my Indian club. When I start to pour fire coals on the sick person they start to dance. All this ceremony is carried on without a word, but we all do make motions to scare the sick all we could. When the scare comes off of the sick he begins to feel better and he wishes to join in the ceremony. The nuts and blackberries are supposed to be the best foods for a bear, and this ground corn is best food for these little Indians who dance with us but could not be seen by anyone else but the sick person and the performer of the ceremony. One time we were performing this ceremony for a sick person when there was an old lady there who thought she knew better than I did and kept talking to me as to what I should do. This ceremony did not help the sick because no one is to talk but to keep their minds on what we are doing. They must have faith and believe in this, but if they don't they will not be helped. There are a few other men who could perform this ceremony, but they are old men who really believe in the old customs and traditions of the Indian. It is the same with singing in Indian: we must believe in it, otherwise we would not be able to sing at all.

I had taken a notion to sing when I was a boy, but I was not sure I can do it. But at the age of twelve I was not afraid anymore because I had been with other men who always did sing at wakes. After I had sang once then the rest was easy, and I have kept on singing all through these years. I could now sing over one hundred different songs without a book. If a person was so interested in singing and keeps their mind on that one thing, they could not help but become able to sing hymns. When I was still a small boy I used to try to sing and I got to be pretty good, so I did try it out at a wake. I did not go to school, so I could not talk English and I could not understand if someone was talking in English. I am a poor scholar in English, but it was not so hard for me to learn how to sing in Indian.

I rather think that someday I will be able to get my bunch of singers to sing on radio, because this country is becoming more for singing every year and the time will come when there will be nothing else but singing. If my bunch would sing once a day they will have made a day's wages because the singers all make big money. I may be more able to earn and save more money than I am doing now. There is not so much cost to what my wife and I live on because she is a saving kind of a woman. She makes use of everything there is—like if some bread would be left over she makes bread pudding out of it, and this is what I like. And she makes what she calls hash from meat that we would not eat at one meal. And there is plenty of times when we have potato soup, and this is the best kind of dish; and it's saving too because this is half water. Also we don't have any tea or coffee for supper because that would keep me awake very much during the night. And there are only two of us so we could go without butter and milk, but if we had children we could not do this. That is the reason we are able to save money easily when I am working, and my canning beans will bring me sixty or seventy dollars, so I am almost certain that I can buy this land and get a house started next spring. I have only a small debt which I can pay a little at a time.

When I get this place up I can start to raise chickens which could always be sold if cash is needed. I also may be able to keep one or two pigs for my meat. This is the way I want to do so that I may be a little more independent. I would not be without a home now if I did not get sick about three years ago. I came near dying that time in the hospital, and the doctor who took care of me had over $150 coming from me when I got better, so I had to sell my place. But I was satisfied because it would have been worse if I died. I have now joined an insurance so things would not be so bad for my wife if I was to die now. I think it very important that men should belong to some sort of insurance because if I had been insured when I got sick I would not have had to sell my place. The company would have paid all the hospital bill and doctor bills and possibly some would have been paid to me while I was laid up because they usually pay so much a month. I would not be without a policy now because I learned a good lesson.

Just now I am out of a job because we are all laid off for a while on account of running out of funds, but they told us that we may be going back to work in about ten days. This is on the CCC project. We have a good job which surely will be of benefit to people and to their lands. We make ditches on the government lands so that it would dry off quick in the spring, and we also make fences or lines between allotments. This would save the people who are allotted on these lands the trouble of paying for these fences. Also there are good fences along the roads of these lands. It was through this system that I was promised help if I get this land all paid for.

7·

Boarding Schools and "Outing"

The first selection in this chapter presents a succinct picture of the worst life at a government boarding school, this one at Oneida. (This is the same school at which Anonymous no. 1 lost a leg; see chapter 4.) The remaining selections are about life in the big non-reservation schools. Andrew Beechtree and Stadler King speak of their experiences at the Carlisle and Chilocco schools, respectively. The last two selections, by Guy Elm and Cora Charles, give accounts of the "outing" system, originally conceived by Colonel Pratt for students at Carlisle.

Students at boarding schools were encouraged to live with Euro-American families during the summer months, working for their keep and a small salary. Or students could stay with a family for a year or more and attend a local school, as Guy Elm did. According to the Carlisle catalogue, "No branch of the educational work is of so much benefit as the 'Outing.' The school itself is too large to allow of home training on a small scale, as the Indian should learn it in order to become Americanized. In a majority of country homes to which pupils go, they are made members of the family and are carefully trained as sons and daughters of the family are trained" (1902).

Another reason for outing was that the school authorities did not want students to return home to their families in the summer, fearing that they would "backslide" and return to their Indian culture (this was referred to as going "back to the blanket") or even refuse to return the following school year.

John A. Skenandore was one of the most prolific writers and skilled interviewers on the ethnological project. He had also worked on the earlier project, writing in the Oneida language. This is the only piece in the book that has been taken from the first collection. Mr. Skenandore was also a noted joker, and Robert Ritzenthaler called him "the happiest fellow in the world." This was in spite of his experience at the Oneida Reservation boarding school!

Oneida Boarding School

I must have went to our old mission school a very short time, as when my parents took me to government school I still didn't understand a word of English. And that was the place where I had many hardships. We were not allowed to talk in our own language, so we had to hide ourselves before we could have any fun and talk as we liked.

And then our disciplinarian caught us at it many times and gave us a whipping each time, and sometimes we were punished by carrying in wood to the boiler house which heats all the buildings. We were made to haul twenty-five sticks apiece on our shoulders, and there were times when we had to haul from quite a distance.

We were made to work half a day and went to school the other half; the children that went to school in the morning had to work in the afternoon.

As I said, I didn't understand a word of English so I just guessed when I went to school. The teacher made lots of funny noises in her mouth which didn't mean a thing to me, but finally the boy next to me told me in our language that she said that I was supposed to come to school in the mornings and that I could go back to "the building."

So I went out, and it happened I met Ben Green as I got out; he too was sent out. He said the teacher told him that we were to go home and come back the next morning. We were just glad and started out straight across through the woods and went home.

The teacher must have meant that we go back to the boys' building and come back to school the next morning. Ben was further advanced in English then I was, so he partway understood what the teacher said, but she did not tell us to go all the way home. Our parents brought us back to school early the next morning, and they must have explained for us as we were not punished.

I still got another mishap the very same day. That time I was walking back towards the boys' quarters when I met the disciplinarian. He stopped me and rattled off a lot of his stuff, which I didn't understand a word and just could not answer. To my surprise he slapped me with both hands both sides of my face, and I stooped down to hide my face; then he pounded my head with his fist, but that didn't knock the English into my head. At that time I only wished he was still alive after I grew up.

We were hungry a lot there, but the reason was that they only put on just so much food to one table and some of the boys were as greedy as pigs. So if a boy was not a fast eater he would never get enough to eat. I was going to that school when I was twelve years old, the time I met an accident. The way this happened: as I have said before, we were made to work half a day and the other half did schoolwork. We were detailed to work different places, and at a certain time we were changed about. At that time I was detailed to work in the laundry and all the machinery was run by steam.

I must have worked in this laundry about two weeks with a very mean boss who was always scolding, and she was so very big, weighed about three hundred pounds, so it was not very pleasant to get a scolding from her. A boy was sent to this laundry when I was at work, with his bedclothes to do his own washing, as he was troubled with his kidneys and gets his bed wet at nights. This made her very angry, and one day she took all his clothes off and put him into a washer, closed it up, and even turned on the steam a little and turned the washer by hand.

When she opened and took the boy out, the boy was so scared that I thought sure he went crazy. From that time on I was so scared of her and she made me very nervous. There was two of us boys running these machines, but one day when my friend had gone after some coal from the boiler house I was setting by the window watching the machinery when I saw that the wringer was at a standstill. This made me very nervous, and I rushed a tubful of bedclothes over to the wringer. First I took a sheet and doubled it nicely and put it into the wringer. Just as I got this inside the wringer, the sheet was snatched off my hands and my left hand had to go along with the sheet.

It all went so quick that it seems like just a wink of my eye, and there I was with my left hand off. It didn't bleed until after I had some clean towels wrapped over it; then the boss came and took more towels and wrapped more on my arm before she led me out through the door. By the time we got to the door I could only see a little light ahead of me, but as soon as we got through the door and got the fresh air, everything cleared up—seems to feel so good, no pain of any kind—and she led me and walked about seven hundred feet to the school hospital. It wasn't until we got to the hospital then they tied my arm to keep from bleeding. And then I was taken in bed until they got a woman, a government doctor. She then put me under ether, as she had to saw off about two inches of the bone so as to stitch the flesh over the bone. I didn't feel any pain for three days; only from my shoulder down it was numb. After the third day the pain came on, and that's what made me cry a little. She had to saw my arm off twice. The first time she forgot to tie one of the cords and infection set in, so she had to do it all over again. I must have been just about still alive after all the suffering this woman gave me.

And she still did a very poor job after it was all knitted. I lost a good many days of school, and my classmates left me behind in class. I was so weak from lack of blood that my bed was placed near lots of windows so as to get plenty of sunlight and fresh air. It took some time before I was able to get up from bed, and I had to start way back and practice how to walk and I had to be very careful not to hurt my arm. Time came when I was able to go outside and play with the boys by the hospital.

I have never forgotten the funny feeling I got when I thought I was strong enough to run around with the boys. The ground I started to run on raised up and was about to hit me in my face when I reached out with both hands. But instead of the ground raising, it must have been my head as I found myself on the ground instead of the ground on top of me.

And as I was not used to this left hand off so naturally I reached out with both hands to protect my face. And I often hurt myself, and there were times when the whole scab peeled off again.

I hurt this arm many times before I got used to it. I finally got back to school, and I was very discouraged to learn that my class had left me so far behind. I had been in school long enough, but my parents did not tell me to work hard in school and never told me what I could do with a good education, so I just had my own way and every chance I got I stayed out of school and much rather work. I was nineteen years old when I quit school altogether, and my father was getting quite old so I did the farmwork then.[1]

While I was out west I have tried a day of school, but my eyes failed me as I went one week in school and was sent two weeks in the hospital. And I had no one to buy me eyeglasses, which would have helped me a lot in day school.

I often wonder why the government never offered any kind of reward for all the damages it has done to me. They didn't even as much as give me a good job, and I have asked many times for some kind of a settlement. If I was only playing when this happened I would not expect a thing, but I was put to work among the machinery at the age of twelve.

ANDREW BEECHTREE

> This selection is a compilation of material about Andrew Beechtree's life at Carlisle Indian Industrial and Military School, taken in bits and pieces from a long autobiographical account. Born in 1895, Andrew had attended several schools in Wisconsin before going to Carlisle. He has critical things to say about Carlisle, but he is also clear about his appreciation of this school.

Education and Life at Carlisle

At that time it was the practice of the large government schools to have representatives solicit for students from the different reservations. I suppose my sister wanted to go, so my parents thought they might as well send me too. I can't recall now whether I knew about going beforehand.

At last in the fall of 1905 we were shipped to the famous Carlisle Indian Industrial School. This school was located in south-central Pennsylvania about twenty miles from the famous battlefield of Gettysburg. It is in the beautiful Cumberland Valley. It was originally a military post. One of the buildings, the one that was used for a jail or guardhouse, was built by the Hessian soldier prisoners of Revolutionary War days. The school is the fruit of the imagination of one Major R. H. Pratt, U.S.A., Retired, and it was also because of this military training that he, as the first director, was able to make it a successful undertaking. It is said that stern measures were used to subdue the students from the more independent western tribes.

(It is my contention that the words *uncivilized* and *savage* as a distinction between a white human and a red human does not apply. I need only to call attention to the turmoil in Europe in this present year of 1940, and to European history, to make my point clear. I believe it is only a cultural difference.)

To show how much I learned in the four-odd years I went to local schools, allow me to present the following story. It is said that at my first interview with the matron I was asked what my name was and I gave the name of the place where I came from, and when asked my home address I gave my personal first name. If that is true or not, I know it was a possibility. And my crying at school only brought rebuke, so I had to make the most of it.

Naturally, at a place like that, with something like six hundred students, there had to be a regular routine of duties. It didn't take me long to get used to it, and I enjoyed the life. We went to school half a day and worked the other half. Our routine was patterned along military duties. The regulation bugle calls announced the different duties. We formed into lines and moved only on command. At different times we had regular army drills.

But we had plenty of time to ourselves, too. Like after school let out at four o'clock until five thirty when we went to supper, and again after supper until nine o'clock, our bedtime. We, the smaller children, went to school to what was called the normal department. This included grades from kindergarten to about third grade. But only small children were allowed in this class, although at that time many a young man of present high school or even college age was only in the first grade. This, however, was no reflection on the student. He just never went to school before due to ever so many reasons. As a matter of fact, some of these men were the material for athletic sports, for which the school's name became famous.

The small children were taught by the advanced girl students as training for a later teaching career. This course and nursing were two courses open to coeds who wished for a career.

Contrary to general belief, this school did not have courses in what is known as higher education. In fact, it was only an eighth-grade school as far as academics were concerned. But on the vocational side it was different. Being a community of some seven hundred persons, with limited financial outlay, life was carried on much after the everyday life of a small country village. As the population of the place was stationary, the enrollment being set by the Department of Interior Office of Indian Affairs, only a few new buildings were constructed. Yet we maintained the operation and appearance of the place, made repairs and alterations, and produced local produce on two farms.

The first farm, or the closest farm, contained a grape vineyard where once I got caught stealing grapes and had to spend a whole day in a dark lockup. We were instructed on and we did actual work in masonry, carpentry, blacksmithing, cabinetmaking, printing, etc. My first lessons were to sweep and scrub the halls and assembly room of our barracks. This school, like all the rest I have attended, was divided into three living quarters, and like at all the schools I was relegated into the small boys' quarters.

Whenever there was an athletic contest, which usually took place on Saturday afternoons, we were marched in a body to the arena, and there we would sit watching Jim Thorpe go through holes in the opposing lines made by [Alex] Arcasa, Peter Calac, Joe Guyon, Elmer Busch, William Garlow, George Vetterneck, Roy Large, Samson Bird, Gus Welch, "Possum" Powell, Joel and Hughie Wheelock, and many other stars. That was football under the tutelage of the world-renown Glenn (Pop) Warner.[2] In the track contest, I live again in the scene, with Frank Mount Pleasant flashing by in his dashes, Skenandore flying over the hurdles, Sundown pole-vaulting close to twelve feet, Jim Thorpe defying the laws of gravity in the high jumps, Louis Tewanima showing his heels to many a worthy opponent—and I sitting in the stands watching. I once ran in one of those races and managed to come in third. I don't know what would have happened if there had been more than three of us running.

[Andrew came home from Carlisle after several years, and he gave this description of his linguistic situation upon his arrival at his parents' home.]

On my way back, I was bloated with self-esteem and expecting to be welcome back with open arms. As I sat there entertaining myself I had a chance to meditate, and as a result much of my egotism oozed out with each succeeding hour. Finally the rig and ensemble appeared out of the brush. So I welcome my folks home. So they said "More?" to me in the native language and I said "How do you do," in English. The Oneida word denoting the word "more" is from a contracted clause which would say "You live some more?" or "You are still alive!" But it seems to imply that it is a pleasant surprise for them to see you again.

After this greeting we all went into the house, and shortly thereafter my mother started to cook dinner. The sitting room and the kitchen were combined into one room so that we were all together, and we went on talking. I didn't notice at first, but soon it flashed on me that they were talking broken English. But imagine our surprise when they started using their native tongue and I couldn't understand but a few words of it. In fact, it sounded so strange to me that it was comical. And if it was comical to me to hear them talk native, it was a scream to hear me try to talk it. The meaning of the Oneida words I learned back gradually, but to converse or talk in Oneida—that was beyond my poor power to master.

A peculiarity of this Oneida language is that if you do not pronounce the words just right, you are likely to say words whose meaning would not be nice to say in public. After a few embarrassing experiences I decided that I could get along better if I left the making of speeches in Oneida to someone else. Again I wish to state that my case is in the majority of a large number of those coming under similar circumstances. Those who were sent to a faraway school like Carlisle or Haskell or the many other so-called large schools, when they were far advanced in years, are a pitiful people. Their second- or third-grade education prevents them from having free and intelligent conversation, and their self-respect prevents them from chancing a bad remark in speaking in the Oneida language.

[After several years at a boarding school in Tomah, Wisconsin, and working during summers and at other times, Andrew went back to Carlisle.]

When the snow started to fly my work stopped so I looked for another job, but to save my life I couldn't find any. It then dawned on me that I might be able to enroll back at Carlisle. Although it was way past entering time, I used up most of my remaining money and bought a railway ticket for Carlisle. They took pity on me and took me in. After a grade examination it was decided to place me in the junior class because this was such a big school. Again this was a misfortune, as I had all these lessons the previous year and I was forced to loaf throughout the school term. I found to my sorrow that loafing dulls the senses and power to proceed again.

The following year the course of studies was changed again. But instead of raising the grades, the stress was made more on the vocational side. Before this they had a commercial course, teaching typing and shorthand. But as I came late there was no vacancy for me in the class, so I took carpentry vocation until such time as I could find a place in the commercial course. When they changed the courses they knocked out the commercial course also. My pet subject being abolished, I then decided to specialize in carpentry.

In the schoolrooms we had rudiments of chemistry, algebra, bugology, geometry, animal husbandry, and like subjects. We were required to read books like *Julius Caesar*, *Evangeline*, etc., as time went on. It wasn't so difficult to pass the grades. And to utilize my spare time I took to tooting a horn. I have forgotten to state that. All of these larger schools train men or boys in band music. The girl has a chance to play in an orchestra, such instruments as piano, guitars, mandolin. I chose for my instrument an alto, sometimes called a French horn. When I first tried to play on it, it sounded like an alley full of cats and dogs. About a week of this noise which seemed to get worse and I took the darn thing back to the music instructor and told him something was wrong with it. "Well" he said, "let's see what's wrong with it." He took the instrument and started playing the tune of "Yankee Doodle" so melodiously that I could hardly stand still. He handed back the horn and said, "The horn seems to be alright; I wonder if it isn't you that's no good?" Well, I had formed that same conclusion already and I accepted the new challenge. From that time on my playing improved. I might have become a good player had my eyes been good. As it was, my eyes would be too slow to follow fast time. Although I took treatment for my eyes, still it did not help. At this place, there being so many students, a doctor was retained on a full-time basis. At the Tomah and Oneida schools, a doctor was called only when his services were needed.

As this school originated from things militaristic, it naturally retained much of its military character. All calls and signals were announced by a bugle call, and to perform the several functions we were first formed into military formation and given instructions. The boys' battalion was composed of about six companies. A company was composed of four squads; a squad was composed of seven men and a corporal. A company was commanded by a captain. The other officers, in order, were first and second lieutenants, first, second, third, and fourth sergeants. The third sergeants acted as right guide and the fourth sergeant as a left guide. The companies were identified as companies A-B-C-D-F-G and band.

Every spring, competitive drills were held. My company was company F, and we won three of the four competitions I was in. I had my ups and downs here too, but every spring I always came back to be the third sergeant or right guide. The main reason for that was that I was about the average-size man of the company. My natural stride was not too long for the small one nor too short for the long-legged fellows. I was also in the higher grade, which would, by the law of averages, give me advantage on intelligence. However, I am too modest to claim the point. . . .

One day in the spring of 1914, word went around by way of mouth—that is, one told another—that there would be a gathering of boys at the YMCA hall. The meeting was called to order, and we voted on something to which I didn't pay much attention. Well, several mornings after that while we were eating our breakfast, we noticed an elderly man walking around among the tables. Up to that time it had been the custom for the cook to put out a certain amount of bread at each meal, and when that was gone we were so told and we couldn't get any more. So this time, someone raised his hand near where this man was and the waiter told him that there was no more bread. This man took the plate and went into the kitchen. Soon we saw them coming out with another batch of bread. We heard later that a conversation took place in the kitchen that went something like this: "I am the kitchen matron, and I said that they shall not have any more bread at this meal." The stranger replied: "I am the Commissioner of Indian Affairs, and I'll say that they should have more bread yet." First person: "Alright, Sir." I found out that what we signed was a bill of complaint. The superintendent was accused of misappropriating the money of the school and using it in giving private parties. We knew that he was giving many parties, and wondered why we should be deprived of such pleasures.[3]

Shortly thereafter there was a complete shakeup in the personnel of the school. A good man was engaged to be the new superintendent. If ever a man had the welfare of the Indian at heart, he was one. His name was Oscar H. Lipps. A short time ago I read an article on the Indian and his treatment, and later I read where he was retired. I said to myself, that's one way to get rid of a man.

One time those of us that could afford it went on excursion to New York City. I think that was in the fall of 1915. We arrived at the New York [Grand] Central Station about ten o'clock in the morning. There were about fifty of us, and we went in our uniforms of light-blue trousers with gold stripes running along the outside seams, navy-blue blouses or coats with gold trimmings on the lower sleeves. Over this we wore navy-blue capes with gold linings. Dark-blue caps and black shoes completed our attire. With the corners of our capes thrown back over our shoulders exposing the gold linings, we presented a pleasing sight.

We stayed together in the morning while we viewed the Woolworth Building, the Flatiron Building, the Brooklyn Bridge, and several other places of interest. While we were looking at different places and things, the people were looking at us. We then separated and spread out in small groups to look for eating places. After lunch, a friend and I went to visit the famed Metropolitan Museum. We were a little early, for the doors did not open until 1:30 o'clock at that time. So we went window shopping for a while, and when we returned we were admitted into the building. We were so interested in the many new and strange sights that we could see, we forgot to keep track of the time and our location. When we did take note of the time, we found that it was nearly train-leaving time, so our first task was to find the exit. We found out that we were in the upper floors. After we got out it was some time before we got our bearing. The trip would have been a success but for one thing. I got myself a pair of new shoes to wear on this trip, and that was one of the worst things that I could have done. Was I ever glad when we got back on the train and I took off my shoes.

In the second inauguration of President Woodrow Wilson for the presidency of the United States on March 4, 1916, our boys' battalion was privileged to participate in passing in review before His Honor, the President. When my company got before the reviewing stand, their line took the form of snake tracks. We were suppose to be reviewed, but they exercised their Indian conception of democracy and did some reviewing too. Also at that time, some of the girls got up an Indian play called *The Feast of the Red Corn*. They rented a hall there and played to the people of

Washington for a week. They were assisted by our first band, that of the best musicians.

I believe that the officials of the school and commissioner's office had learned by experience that only a small percentage of the race would hold positions where they would sit at a desk and push a pencil. Therefore everything possible was done to make them strong physically so that in the chosen employment as transient workers they may be able to withstand hard work.

In this connection, then, permit me to present my humble opinion for the existence of such a situation. In the past the Indian's educational facilities were very lacking; therefore the average Indian started to school at the age of ten years. Then he went to a school where he was taught only half of the time, thereby still putting him in the rear of his white friend. If he finishes this school and continues on to high school, then his age relation to the white children is that of a grandpa. Such condition would strain anybody's pride. So it should not be a surprise nor a reflection on the Indian for forgoing education under these conditions. Furthermore, in the ten years prior to his entering school, he will have spent much of this time in running, playing, and other physical activities. When he goes to school and has to sit still for long periods of time, those muscles of his crave for action, and he is unable to concentrate on his lesson. But put a lot of children—including Indians—to doing something that requires action and observation, and the Indian will be above the average.

[He follows this with a rich description of some of the sports and athletes at Carlisle, including football, lacrosse, and ice skating, and the activities of the teams' supporters.]

When our team goes away to play at some other place, we always give them a rousing send-off. And if they bring home the bacon, we gave what is known as a nightshirt parade, especially when they win from a tough opposition. This nightshirt parade is held after dark. We would put on our nightshirts over our clothing, and by turning one corner of our pillowcases inside the other corner, we would use them as hoods. Then, with the band in the lead, we would parade through the main streets of the town. The main part of the town was about two miles from the school. We also had many football songs which we sang at the games. The one that strikes my fancy went like this:

> Harvard, Yale, and William Penn and half a score or more,
>   Of the other colleges are looking for a war,
> Wouldn't they be surprised to see, among the red and gold,
>   A big chief like Kennedy who was a warrior bold,
>   And that's what we've been told,

Chorus
> Captain [name of present captain], Captain [ditto], He big chief, he make a rush, The whole line goes down like mush.
> Captain ———, Captain ———, Keep them humping by your bumping.
> Captain —————————

I must not omit to state that at times there were casualties.

[There was a lot more than sports, work, and classes, however.]

That winter we gave a play called *The First Continental Congress*. My part was to represent Richard Lee, and I had the difficult task of saying, "West Virginia votes aye." More difficult, however, was the making of the forms of deer and lambs from boards, which was to be used in a girls' play, the name of which I have now forgotten. This play was given by the members of the Susan Society.

Carlisle at that time had four debating societies, two for the girls and two for the boys. The name of the girls' societies were Susans and Mercers, the boys', Standard and Invincible. Once in a while the boys' societies would debate before the whole school; that is, that's where the debate would start, but sometimes it ran on for several weeks and several socks. I belonged to the Invincible Society, and the only office I ever held in it was vice-president, and that's all I did was hold that office. Never once was I called on to preside in three months—that was the term of office.

Before the end of school, each society would give a social—the Carlisle etiquette for a party. At these parties, each member was privileged to invite a friend of the opposite sex. For some reason I didn't go to many of the other parties. But I got even with them; I wouldn't invite them either.

Well, I was too busy that spring anyway. I was a member of the band; I was again third sergeant in a competitive troop; I was a member of a chorus; I wrote three articles for our class edition of our weekly paper; I was trying out for a half miler on the track team; at the same time, I couldn't take a chance to neglect my studies.

At last, I started cashing in on my efforts. For winning the competitive drill with a rating of 100 percent, we were given a chicken dinner. Our captain won the right to use the gold sword the next year, but as he was my classmate he was graduating that year too. However, the previous year he had won an expensive good watch. It takes a real good man to inspire his men to cooperate 100 percent. His quality was demonstrated when, after the competition, he marched us to a secluded place, he called us to attention and said, "My friends, I thank you." Then the tears in his eyes expressed better than words the thoughts that were in his mind. For being in the band, we were given a picnic with their—not mine—lady friends.

For being an officer of a company we were given a picnic, and thereby hangs a tale. It happened this way. I had a group of three pals, all of whom possessed an ability to sing. So we had formed a quartet and used to sing together. Two of us were officers and two were not. One of my buck private friends had a girl and a rival. This girlfriend was a company officer, as was also the rival. As I was unattached, my friend came to me and asked me to entertain his girlfriend. Always wishing to oblige a friend, I consented.

In due time we arrived at the picnic ground of a place called Cave Hill. Sometime before this, the class's attention was called to this saying: "Seest thou a man diligent in his work, he shall be . . . ," etc. [Proverbs 22:29]. So I set about diligently to entertain my friend's girlfriend. I bought candy for her, I took her for a canoe ride, I took her hands and made it my business to tell her how soft and ladylike were her hands. I looked into her eyes and compared them to the serene blue sky, her laughter I compared to the ripple of a laughing brook. I looked at her lips—well, I just did everything I could think of to make my friend's friend forget about my friend's rival all that day, and never once did they talk to or about each other. I reported that evening to my friend that my mission was well executed.

Imagine my dismay when, a few days later, I realized that I had overdone my mission, that my acting had been too realistic. Now I was in a pickle. I did not want to hurt my friend's feeling, and my explanation and efforts to discourage the girl's attention to me fell on deaf ears. And I was too much of a gentleman to tell her right out to go to blazes. Luckily for me that in a few days it became time for me to go to a summer resort near Farmington, in the state of Maine. Of course I went there to work and not for pleasure. But that's ahead of my story.

In due time I received two diplomas, one for academic or class work and the other for shop work. Then the juniors gave us a farewell banquet and party. Next came the track meet. I went out to run the half-mile race, which meant that we had to run twice around the quarter-mile track. I ran around the track once and then decided that that was too much hard work for nothing. So I ran right back into the dressing room and sat puffing for a long time. Well, it is said that experience is the best teacher.

When we held the graduation service, we of the chorus sang a cantata called "Oh Italia." An afternoon and an evening were also devoted to gym drills and exercise exhibitions. I was in a wand drill and setting up exercises.

At last came the parting of friends and classmates. Each handshake of farewell and each farewell wave brought a pain to my heart until at last I could not make a verbal reply. What a contrast develops at this time. They gleefully bid me good-bye, leaving me to see their dear families and to enjoy freedom and excitement; I, sad and disconsolate, knowing that the excitement is now over and that I must now return to the monotony of daily routine. My sense of fairness prompts me to admit that I owed a debt to the young lady of the picnic episode. She alleviated a lot of the weight of sadness in the succeeding days.

Few of my twenty-seven classmates have I ever seen since. Some have died but most are just mediocre individuals, like myself, plugging along buying that proverbial "shoes for the baby." Of the girl, I heard later that she married and lived in a manner that her good graces entitled her.

In view of the fact that the school is no longer in existence and that the memory of it exists in so many real Native Americans, I wish here to revive in memory the words we used to say in the song of the institution:

Nestling 'neath the mountains blue,
O Carlisle, our fair Carlisle. We ne'er can pay our debt to you,

O Carlisle, our fair Carlisle. Remembering thee will never fail.
We'll weather every storm and gale, while o'er life's troubled sea we sail,
O Carlisle, our fair Carlisle, time passes, men must ever struggle ahead.

STADLER KING

Stadler King, age fifty-three, offers this account of his years at the
school in Chilocco and of his feelings over leaving it. [4] The title he
chose for this piece draws on the idea that, even after years of enforced
immersion in "white" ways, many students returned home to they
ways of their people; they put "the blanket" back on. [5]

Back to the Blanket

When I was at school I heard students say those words "back to the
blanket" so many times, but I did not have a blanket when I went so
I could not have come back to it when I did come home.

I went to a school where there were forty different Indian tribes, and
most of these were western tribes such as Cheyennes, Pawnees, Peo-
rias, Kaw, Arapahoes, Navajos, Pueblos, Pimas, Cherokees, Choctaws,
Creeks, Miamis, Sioux, Sac and Fox, Shawnees, Poncas, Winnebagos,
Chippewas, and many other tribes that I have forgotten. The big Chilocco school had about seven hundred students.

This school had one purpose and that was to teach Indians the three
R's, and also occupational trades such as the carpenter trade, mason,
painter, shoe and harness maker, blacksmith, steam and electric engineering, farmer, poultry farmer, dairying, horticulture, and maybe
some other trades. When the school was busy teaching all these things,
there was not time to think of the blanket. There was the daily routine
of events such as mealtimes, school time, study hour, drilling, and then
there was the ball games, socials, dances, inspections, parties, church
services, and maybe some other doings. All these kept each one of its
students busy all the time.

There were rules in the school which forced students to come within
the routine changing of events. I was eighteen years old when I went
there, so I was then old enough to realize that this may be my last chance
to learn something, so I got right down and did what I could to learn

as much as I can in the three years that I had signed up for. It did not take long before I knew some students by sight, but I had a hard time to remember the names of these students because there were so many of them and they all had different names. I was very much interested when I heard the sergeant call the roll. There were names like Big Eagle, Big Smoke, Blind Woman, Tall Bull, Fly Man, and many different names, and somebody answers to each of these names. I soon knew those who were in my classes and I knew those who worked in the same trade as I did, and those with whom I roomed. After a while I knew all the boys who were in the same "home" as I was.

These big buildings were numbered like Home 1, Home 2, Home 3, and two homes for girls which were 4 and 5. Each home had different sizes of boys or girls. I was put in Home 1.

I arrived at the school the first of September 1906, and the first of October I was made a second sergeant, and the first of December that year I was made the first sergeant. Then it was my chance to call the roll at each time we lined up. I was first sergeant all that winter, but in the summer when vacation started our captain went home and I was made captain of my company of sixty-six boys. It became my duty to give clothing and shoes to those in my company whenever any one of them needed it.

After I was there one year I was made an adjutant of Home 1, which gave me charge of the whole home, which had two companies. I held this office the balance of the time that I was there. It was rather funny but I felt proud, too, to have charge of boys, some of which are twice as old as I was. However, I did not have any trouble, and none of them ever were disobedient to the rules laid down.

I knew how to make indirect friends with these western tribes, and it worked out pretty good. As an officer I was at all socials, dances, and other doings, so the way I made friends with the boys was by associating with girls of their tribe. Like the Cheyennes: I made friends with a nice-looking Cheyenne girl, and I danced with her a few times and took her to a booth where they sold lunches. The Cheyenne boys saw this, and I could do anything with them. They seemed to be good to me, and they obeyed in all requirements which I had charge of. When I needed a haircut I could ask one of them who was a good barber to trim me up. He was willing to do it for me, and then when my lessons were new and I needed some assistance I would ask one of the higher grades to help me and he would show me how to do the problems. They were willing to give their time to help me in what I wanted, so I made use of having friends which I had made indirectly. This was the way I got along at school.

I was the busiest student while I was there. I worked in the mason trade for some time when I asked the disciplinarian to put me in the creamery. He was glad of it; he said the dairyman was having hard time to carry out the work in the creamery and at the barn. The dairyman put me in charge of the creamery, and he was at the barn. It was no trick for me to do the creamery work because I had younger boys to do it, and I only oversaw the work, but I made four hundred pounds of butter every week. I had lots of time to study my lessons because I had these boys to do the work. The girls who worked in domestic science would come to my creamery to get milk, cream, or some other kind of milk which they call "whipped cream." I did not know what whipped cream was, but she knew so she helped herself. I worked hard all the three years there and I surely liked the life in school because an officer had all the privileges, but time was going faster than I thought, for before I knew my three years were coming to an end.

Time came when I was to leave my school that morning. I had all my belongings packed in my big trunk, and I was ready to leave any minute. The team and wagonette drove up to my building and waited for me to come with my trunk and suitcase, but I was still working. I was in the storeroom giving a pair of shoes to one boy. I fitted him out and then ran and got two boys to help me with my trunk. I ran over and gave up my big bunch of keys that I carried. I gave them to the disciplinarian and told him good-bye. He got up and came with me to the wagonette. He said be sure to come back next fall—then I stepped off of the land that I never would step on again. It came to me at that moment, and it touched my very heart to think that I did not know if I will come back and to think of leaving my dear old school and all my friends.

We drove to the girls' home, where I told the driver to stop for a few minutes. I jumped off and went into the building. I knew the room and went straight for it. She was standing at the window, looking down at my wagonette. I went in and said, "Cora, I am leaving." She turned to me but was unable to say anything. Tears came to her eyes, so I gave a last farewell. I stepped out with a very heavy heart. As we drove away I gave a last look at all the beautiful buildings. The Oneidas who came home at the same time never knew of my feelings.

I felt comfortable after I got on the train, but when we got to Kansas City we changed cars so we waited for another train. While we waited another train going the other way came. There was a man somewhere who had a loudspeaker. He called the names of cities this train would pass, and after a few names he mentioned the place where I had just come from. This made my heart burn like and nearly choked me. I was unable to think. After this train pulled out our train came. We came to Chicago and finally to Green Bay.

Things seemed to change when I got off the train and saw Frank Cornelius and his wife standing there to meet me. I was glad to see them because they were good while I was gone. They sent me money every so often and told me that I was missed at home all these years. Frank said, "Let's go on the east side. I will get a new suit of clothes for you so you will be really new." He bought a good blue suit and paid thirty dollars for it. It was a good suit that cost that much in 1909. This made me happy, and we went home that evening. I was happy, much more happy than I had figured on. I was raised by these people from the time my father died, and I was only thirteen years old then; now I [was] a grown-up man of twenty-one.

This was in the days of land sales. Frank was in the business of selling land for different people. He was making money, and very often I would be with him in Green Bay, De Pere, Appleton, and sometimes Kaukauna. We went to these land buyers, and often he got a hold of three or four hundred dollars. It was nothing for him to hand me twenty-five dollars. Times were easy, and everybody seemed to have money. I met my own girl in Seymour, and at this time all things took a new light. I felt like she was really the only girl.

I carried on this carefree life for one year. I was twenty-two years old when I first took a drink of beer. Frank had been drinking more and more for some time, and he offered me drinks but I did not drink until I was that age. I began to drink more and more until I would sometimes be pretty drunk. This easy life with much money nearly did spoil me but in 1912 I married my real true girl. I did not think any more of my school and my friends—only when I [would] get a letter or card from them, and they also would be gone home. I heard from different ones and in many cases they sent me cards with pictures of them in Indian blankets. I had no Indian blanket but I had good clothes to wear. I was a good worker, I was the healthiest, I was the happiest man when I started a life of a married man with a good kind wife.

GUY ELM

> Before World War I, Guy Elm attended Carlisle, where he became
> a prominent athlete. For some years he lived outside Carlisle in the
> framework of the outing system, "to learn the ways and means of
> the white people." In this piece from June 11, 1941, to which he gave
> the title "Attitudes in the Oneida Families," Guy recounts his varied
> adventures living and working outside Carlisle.

Living and Working Outside ("Outing")

From observations and studies that I have made amongst the Oneida for some time, I have discovered many interesting facts concerning their habits, hobbies, social life, sports, occupations, and church activities. I am in position to know, because I have lived, worked, played with them, both socially and in athletic contests. I know the white people just as well as I know the Indians, for the simple reason that I have spent about half of my life with them at different times of my life. I spent my childhood days with the Oneidas from the time I was born until I was fourteen years of age. Then my parents sent me to Carlisle Indian Industrial and Military School for boys and girls, and also for women and men, in the fall of 1910. At this school they had what they called the outing system for the students. That is, the student could go out in the country, work for some white people during the vacation, and if they prefer to go to public school during the winter they could do so, and work before and after school hours for their board and lodging.

The wages they earned, the students could spend one-fourth of the total sum while they are out in the country, and the balance is sent back to school, the money placed in the bank. Whenever the students goes back to Carlisle and decides to stay there to continue his or her schooling, the money that they have on deposit they can withdraw— again, one-fourth of the total sum. When the student graduates or stays to complete his full term of enrollment, either three or five years, whatever the case may be, they can go home. The money is sent to them afterwards if they decided that they are to stay home for good. That is what they call Carlisle outing system.

Well, when I got there I was young and didn't know much, and I was advised to take this outing system to learn the ways and means of the white people. I stayed with one family for three years, and then I decided I want to visit my folks. The place where I worked was called Robbinsville, seven miles east of Trenton, New Jersey. The people I worked for were Germans. I have never found better people to work for since that time. They were hard workers, kind and very religious people. The man was middle age at that time; his wife was much younger than he was, and they had one daughter. They had a farm of about sixty-five acres. They specialized in truck farming, poultry, and besides they had some cows, pigs, and horses.

I'll never forget the different crops that we used to raise there and the acreage of each crop, because I took as much interest in helping raise the crops as the owner. This farmer had about five acre of peaches; five acre of asparagus; two acres of strawberries; one acre of blackberries; two acres of apple, pears, plums, and grapes, all in one orchard; ten acres of early potatoes; and about fifteen to twenty acres of late potatoes. Alongside of these trees and between the rows where there were young trees, he had his vegetables—anything you can think of. So you can see what a big job we had on our hands.

The first big job was cutting the asparagus, which usually are ready to be cut after the fifteenth of April. We keep on cutting it every day except on Sundays, until last part of May. My boss usually had about eight men to cut asparagus first thing in the morning, and two women to do the sorting and to tie them in small bundles. The asparagus were sorted into three grades. Number one were first grade; in this grade was the best quality. They had to be straight, tender, and so many inches long. The second grade is asparagus that are shorter in length, some crooked ones mixed in, but they have to be same length too. The last grade is those that the stalks are small in size and the heads are not so good. They have a machine that they used to bundle them together tied with a red cord, trim, and cut at one end. Then they are packed into crates, twenty-four bundles to each crate. Towards evening we take it to the village station and shipped it to New York City. The price for first grade was anywhere from three to four dollars per crate. The second grade was sold cheaper, and the third grade was sold cheaper yet. Every day we get the returns, the price received for the shipment.

We usually have about twenty-five to thirty crates per day; that's about one hundred dollars per day. After paying the workers, the crates, and other overhead expenses, my boss used to tell me that he makes a clear profit of sixty dollars per day—not bad wages for any man.

Just about the time we are getting through with the asparagus, then the strawberries are ready to be picked. He hires pickers—as many as he can get. He pays the pickers two cents per quart or box. These quart boxes are packed into crates and shipped to New York City or sometimes Philadelphia, and besides we used to take turns going to Trenton, New Jersey, to sell from house to house.

When we went to Trenton, we had to get up about three o'clock in the morning, take care of the team, and have our breakfast. We had regular market wagons, two of them, one wagon for a team and the other for a single horse. The wagons are covered so that the fruit, or any other foodstuff, doesn't get wet if it rains. At five o'clock we are parked at the city market. Then the fun starts. I usually hang around there just two hours; if I don't get rid of the load by that time, then I hook the team back on the wagon and start peddling from house to house. In that way I used to sell out my load and beat it back home sometimes for dinner.

Going around town like that I came into contact with people of different nationalities. I treated them all alike. I was fair, honest, I joke, and I sometimes told Indian stories to them. I had friends in every part of the city, and Trenton is not a small city. I think to this day that was the best time I had in my life and the best education I ever received.

On these trips, after I sold the farm produce and I knew I would be late for dinner at home, I used to put the team in a barn for the farmers to feed their horses. Then with my bag of money I would go uptown to a swell eating place, clean up, take my coveralls off, and order me a steak dinner. On one of these stops at the restaurant I met a cashier, a pretty girl, but I could tell that she was older then I was. I was seventeen years of age then. I noticed that she was all smiles and she looked me over. Anyway, she asked who I was, where I was from, and many other question about myself. And she told me about herself: that she was a Polish girl, she had worked in Chicago, New York City, Philadelphia, and that both of her parents had died. And finally she invited me to come back there again.

I like the girl right from the beginning. From that time on I saw to it that I always got late for dinner at home so that I could go and see the girl at the restaurant. Young whipple snapper as I was, she took me to town like nobody's business. Before I started going with this girl I used to go to Trenton about once a month; now I was going there every Saturday, and sometimes I didn't come back until Sunday night. I didn't have to worry about money because she had a good-paying job. I would get broke on Saturday night, and she stood the expenses on Sunday nights. My folks back on the farm begin to wonder what was going on in the city. I tried to keep secret about the girl in the city, but I couldn't fool my boss; he kept teasing me every Monday morning.

This went on until towards the end of the summer. So one Saturday night I invited the girl to a good show and we were enjoying ourselves. The lights went on and I happened to look back and there was my boss and his wife sitting right behind us. Well, after the show I introduced my girlfriend to them. She talked to them, and they liked her very much. My boss went so far and asked me if I was going to marry her. I told him no sir, I said, not me, I'm going back to school in about two weeks to continue my education. I said I'm only a kid and she is a woman of about twenty-five years of age. He said to me, but she is a swell girl. She has the looks, educated, good job, and has a wonderful personality. He said, I wish I were you—I would marry her on the spot. He said, if you get married and settle down, you can work for me on the farm during the summer months and work in town in the wintertime. I can find you a job in town at the rubber company plant. Or you could live with us on the farm; we have a swell home, and besides you have been with us so long that you are just like our own son. You better think this over in the next two weeks.

Well, I did. I asked the girl if she would marry a man if he asked her to. She told me it all depends on who the man was. She said of course if you was to ask me to marry you, I would say yes at once. That was enough for me, I got scared out. I said to her, no, I don't mean that; I was just fooling. The time came for me to go back to school. I told my boss that I would be back the following summer to work for him again.

I went back to Carlisle, and from there I came home for a short visit with my folks. I was home about two months, then I went back again to Carlisle. I corresponded with my girl for almost one year, but I didn't go back to New Jersey that summer. I went to New Hope, Pennsylvania, instead. But I started to go to Trenton to see her again. Everything went swell with us that summer; we had lots of good times together, dances, shows, and private parties. In the fall I went back to school, and that following spring she wrote me a letter telling me that she had married. And that was the end to our romance. Although I received many letters afterwards from her, I kept clear from her and sometimes I didn't answer her letters, and she finally stopped writing to me altogether.

In this family I never noticed any quarreling going on between husband and wife. Sometimes they argued about this and that, but it was always a fair argument; when it was over they were just as good friends again. The daughter was very obedient to her parents. When she was told to do this and that with the work, she went and done the work without any delay. The clothes she wore, her mother picked out for her. The company she associated with, her parents had their approval of it. She never went to parties unless one of her parents was along with her.

The family worked together, and they were getting richer every day. Besides the farm they had other properties in the city: a store building, auto garage, and about half a dozen houses in Camden, New Jersey, that they were renting out. I knew that they were making lots of money on the farm.

The wife raised each year about one thousand young chicks. That was one of my jobs, to feed them. She kept about two hundred hens over winter to lay eggs. They had a regular egg route in the city. Every Friday the eggs were delivered on this route. I don't remember just how many dozen were sold each week. I know this much: the Mrs. always had lots of money with her when she went to make a deposit at the bank.

I learned many things while I was there. I went to public school and I kept up with the white kids that were attending full-time, while I used to start going to school first of November and I quit first of April each year. When they had their examinations I would go and have my examinations too. My tests were always near the top of the list. All the education I received was part-time schoolwork. No doubt if I had attended full-time on my schoolwork I would have went through high school at least. When I went to school I used to study hard and did whatever the teacher told me to do in line with my studies.

I don't remember ever having any trouble with my teachers or the students at any of the schools that I attended, both Indian and white schools. The first teacher that I had used to tell the class that obedience, perseverance, honesty, and cleanliness were the stepping stones for building a person's character. I have followed the golden rule as much as possible, and I have no regrets or am I ashamed of my character even today. I make friends wherever I go, both men and women.

One summer I was placed on a dairy farm near Langhorn, Pennsylvania. These people were Quakers. We had about thirty cows to milk. This farm was a large one, something like 180 acres. The family was a large one: man and wife, six children, besides the grandparents and the wife's sister, and us two Indian boys, altogether thirteen people. There were four boys and two girls. The oldest was a girl sixteen years of age, and the youngest one a boy six years old. The grandparents were both over seventy-five years of age. The farmhouse was a stone building. It had about ten rooms altogether. The farm was located just outside of a small village called Humerville. It was the first time I ever worked on a modern dairy farm. At first I couldn't quite get used to it, that is, milking the cows. I had to milk from six to eight cows morning and night.

The boss used to wake us up pretty early—about 4:00 in the morning—because the milk had to be shipped to Philadelphia at 7:00 a.m. Sometimes we had to hustle like everything so as not to be late for the train. I really didn't have time to go out in the fields to work because I spent most of the time cleaning the barn, washing the milk cans and pails, and feeding the younger stock, besides other livestock. I sure was busy all the time.

It took me about one week to decide whether I should stay there or go back to school. I was glad that I stayed. After I learned and got used to the work, I began to like my work, and I stayed with these people one year.

I thought perhaps that the people would be quarreling, because there were so many of us together. But the boss and his wife knew how to manage a big family. Every member of the family had their own work to do. I had the job as I said before, in the barn. The other Indian boy had his job in the fields. One of the boys had to look after the water pump; another, chickens and ducks; another, the hogs and small pigs—about twenty of them. The womenfolks had a plan just like ours. One woman did the cooking, another was a helper, and one did the cleaning around. When one got through with her work she would help the others out.

There were jobs on the farm when the whole family would turn out to work together. Everything as far as I know worked like a clock; no arguments, quarrels, or fights. Well, anyway, these Quakers don't believe in fighting at any time. I suppose that's why we all got along so good together. I noticed that they are not so noisy like other class of people. But I used to make them laugh at the table, during mealtime. If I was late for a meal they would wait for me at least fifteen minutes. I asked the Mrs. one time, I said, "How is that you folks always wait for me? You shouldn't wait for me; whenever the meal is ready go ahead and eat." She said, "You don't know how much we enjoy your jokes, stories, and other talks we have at the table. My husband and the rest just won't eat until you come around." Sometimes I have to repeat my stories several times to them.

I went to church several times with them. They don't have a minister. They go in and sit down, everybody as quiet as they can be. Then all at once somebody gets up and offers a prayer to God. They claim the Holy Spirit moves them to do this—and anyway that's their belief. Sometimes they stay in church for a long time and again sometimes it's just a short service.

I was very interested in one thing about these Quaker people, and that is playing different games of sport like football, baseball, basketball, tennis, hockey. I found out that this people don't engage in sports where there is body contact, like football, that might cause a serious injury. The younger people might have a different idea in regards to this, but the old people sure don't like to hurt other people.

I am writing my experiences with the other race of people to show the contrast between whites and Indians, and furthermore to prove that I have been with them. And in this instance the Indians are just the opposite of the Quakers. When they play any kind of a game, they like to hurt the other player, so that they can be forced out of action. But they do it in a fair play. However, sometimes their fighting spirit gets the best of them, or if the other player tries to pull some underhand stuff, then they too get rough and pull their tricks and violate the rules of the game. In other words, they are ready to give and take.

I have been told time and again, that is one reason they make the best football players and also the best soldiers in the army. I think it's quite true, and I'm satisfied of the fact that they are great performers in all kinds of sport and in the army too. Every now and then I see in the newspapers or hear over the radio they are mentioned for their achievements in sports and in the army—which has been increased to over a million men on this new defense program.

I worked for the Jews at a summer camp at Camp Becket, Massachusetts, near the state line, in the summer of 1917.[6] We had as many as two hundred young, rich Jewish boys from New York City for the summer. We went there on the fifteenth of June and stayed until after Labor Day. These jobs were under the supervision of the Carlisle outing system. There were ten of us Indian boys that were sent there that summer as assistant physical directors.

The boys were divided into groups, so that we all had about fifteen to twenty boys to look after. The quarters or buildings where they stayed were arranged so that they were all in the groups. We were held fully responsible for these boys at all times. The head physical director gave us his orders every day. The program for the day was worked one week ahead of the schedule. Our job consisted of setting up exercise the first thing in the morning before breakfast. After breakfast they were required to make their own beds, clean up their quarters. They had about one hour to do it. At nine o'clock we call the roll to see if any boy is missing. The training was then in order for the day. Instruction in swimming, boxing, wrestling, baseball, basketball, and track work. About 11:30 a.m. the boys are told to get cleaned up for dinner. At 1:00 we call the roll again. We take them out to the athletic field again; then the different groups organize their best men to form a team—either basketball or baseball.

The athletic field had four baseball diamonds in it, tennis courts, basketball courts, and a big lake nearby. Besides, the camp was at the foot of a mountain. Woods—plenty of it. Well, these boys kept us busy from early in the morning until 9:30 at night. When they all go to bed, then we had one hour to ourselves, either to write letters or visit one another. These boys played different games under supervision of us Indian boys. We also had organized a team of our own. We went out and played the village teams around there on Sundays. That was our day off at this boys' camp.

Some days we took our lunch along with us and went hiking up the mountain about eight miles distance one way. These hikes gave the boys plenty of good exercise. We would also show the boys how the Indians used to blaze through the woods so that they wouldn't get lost. The leader usually did the blazing as they went along through the woods.

These hikes took place about once a week. Some of the boys stayed there all summer, others stayed two weeks, and some one month, but as soon as a group of boys left another group would come from the big city to take their place, so that we had about two hundred boys all the time.

Another job we had was to row boats for them. We also gave instructions how to handle the canoe with the paddles. Sometimes when we have visitors at the camp the Indian boys would put on exhibitions going down the fast swirling rapids. We had two small rivers that emptied into the lake a short distance from the camp. And also we usually put on a canoe race on the lake. We had an Indian quartet that could sing any kind of music, and also an Indian orchestra. There were other camps close by for girls and grownups, so that gave us a chance to go to dances. The Indian orchestra was very much in demand for music around there at these camps. They made extra money because all these people were rich; whatever they asked, the Jews were more than willing to pay for it. Besides, it was something different, and they sure enjoyed and danced to the music.

On our way back from Becket, Massachusetts, at Albany, New York, we took a riverboat, a small passenger boat that makes its run of the Hudson River between New York City and Albany. That evening somebody suggested to hold an entertainment. They asked for volunteers, and we responded with a few selections with the quartet, and the orchestra got their instruments out and started to play dance music: waltz and two-step. It wasn't long before everybody was dancing on the deck. The captain invited the orchestra and the quartet into the main ballroom and asked us if we would entertain the crowd with our songs and the orchestra with their dance music. We all consented and accepted the kind invitation.

The ballroom was so packed that some of the people couldn't get in. The dance went on until after midnight. The people certainly enjoyed the orchestra music. We worked together with the orchestra by putting on our quartet songs in between the dance numbers. This quartet later was recognized as the best quartet that Carlisle ever had. The quartet and the orchestra were invited to the captain's quarters. We had a swell dinner with him, and afterward we counted the donations from the people that were given to us for entertaining them. The total amount was almost two hundred dollars. We divided it up into ten shares. It came in very handy the next morning when we got to New York City.

We went on a sightseeing trip and visited Central Park and other places of interest. We were there all day and part of the evening so that we were able to see a good show. At midnight we boarded a limited for Philadelphia, and there we changed cars for Harrisburg, Pennsylvania. We got back to Carlisle next day at 9:00 a.m.

All during this time we never quarreled or had arguments; we got along good and made many friends with the people. We were congratulated on good behavior at the camp, and on our trip going there and back again. The first school assembly at the auditorium when all the students meet together to start their classes, the superintendent spoke to the student body. He mentioned our group of boys that were at the boys summer camp. He said, last spring when I received a letter from a wealthy Jewish man who owns and runs these summer camps in Massachusetts, [7] he asked me if we had some young men that could be depended on to fill these positions as guides and physical directors. At first I was inclined to write back to him and tell him that we couldn't possibly fill the bill. I thought it over and called in the staff of my officers. We discussed and argued the matter over and over again. The more we talked about it, the more I was convinced that perhaps I wouldn't make a mistake to send you boys there to do this work. I finally decided to look at your records. The teachers were interviewed about this and that boy in regards to his conduct in the classroom. The disciplinarians were consulted as to your characters and also the coaches and head physical director. It wasn't an easy task to select the twenty-five young men that we send out to different camps this summer as an experiment to find out whether you boys would make good or make a failure. We pick you boys out on the basis of your past records here at Carlisle. I was very glad to hear from your employers, each month, how you were getting along with the work you were sent out there to do. I'm proud of you, and the school can also be proud of the wonderful record you all have made there at those camps. I'm glad that I sent you boys out there and that you all looking so strong and healthy. Next summer we plan to send more boys to these summer resorts in Massachusetts and New York State, now that we know you young men can handle those jobs out there. I want to thank you all for what you have accomplished this past summer.

I always wondered why the Indians got along so good at this school at Carlisle, because it was a large school—more than one thousand students attending there. But I suppose it was the discipline that kept us from arguing and quarreling at one another. There were all kinds of ways in which to cause quarrels, but they usually just say a few words and let it go at that.

In the summer of 1918 I was sent to Hog Island shipyard, a government shipyard, the biggest in the world.[8] It had fifty shipways. About fifty Indian boys from Carlisle were sent there. I was given the chance to decide whether I want to go to summer camp or the shipyard. I went to the shipyard because I knew I could make more money there. We went there first part of June and I stayed there until first of September. We were put in the barracks with the United States Army men that were stationed there for guard duty. We didn't have to pay for sleeping and staying there, but we had to pay for our meals. They used to serve cafe[teria] style. It was a large building; they had several of them like it in the yard.

They used to tell me that about thirty thousand people were employed there at that time. They had three shifts of eight hours so that they kept going night and day without stopping. When we first got there, those of us that didn't have trades, we were asked to pick a trade like corking [caulking],[9] riveting, rimmer,[10] and crane man, signal man, rigger, and many other jobs that required skilled labor.[11] I chose riveting. We had instructors that gave us lessons just how it is done. I might say we went to school for a period of two weeks before we were placed on shipways and joined different crews of working men.

I worked with a crew of all new men—that is, we all started at about the same time. I started off with passing the rivets to the bucking-up man. The first day we went on the shipways to work, our riveter told us to take our time. He said, after we get organized with our crew then we'll speed up. Well, the first day wasn't so bad. It took one week on the shipways before I noticed we kept getting more rivets in. From that time on we went to town full speed. The crew stuck together all summer. Sometimes we would double over on the shifts; that is, instead of working only eight hours per day we would work sixteen hours. In that way we earned more money. I averaged about eight dollars per day; some got more, depending on what they were doing. We had a few arguments at times in that sometimes one of us didn't want to work on Sundays, but we usually settle the question by voting or pulling matches to see if we would work. We would always settle the argument one way or the other, and it was final. Our crew of men was made up of a Polish, Irish, Mexican, and Indian, all about the same size, and we all could speak good English and swear in four different languages.

It was a happy and crazy crew of men. When we want to celebrate in the city of Philadelphia, it was necessary to bail out somebody at the jail every time. And we were all pals so we had to help each other out. I never, since that time, have run into another gang of men that would work so good together. And I have worked with many different crews of men since I started working for my living. When I told them I was quitting my job at the shipyard back there at Philadelphia, they kept asking me to stay on. But I told them that I want to get in the army to see what kind of a life that was like. I finally quit and went back to Carlisle, and from there I came home. I was here in Oneida about two weeks, and from here I went to Camp Shelby, Mississippi. I got into the army just long enough so that I can say I was in the world war—about five months. During the time I was in the army, I was obedient to my superior officers and I worked hard trying to learn as much as I could about the soldier's life in the army. I really didn't get a chance to drill very much because I was put on the football squad and did my training on the football field.

I might say that is one place where you can't argue or quarrel; you either do it or get off the pot. I seen several arguments, and each time it was settled by a fistfight. After it was over the men would shake hands and make friends again.

The army life was OK with me, and I'm very glad that I had the chance to join it. I have received state bonus, government bonus, and other help from the United States government. In the army a soldier can't argue very much. You can't even talk back to the officers. You have to take it on the chin with a smile.

The most quarrelsome family that I have known was an Oneida family. They lived in Milwaukee, Wisconsin, years ago, when I was working in that city. I had to board at their home for one month. I never seen anything like it. They quarrel at one another from morning to night. And it wasn't just two of them, but the whole family. There were two boys and two girls. The boys were older than the girls. The parents were just as bad; I suppose that their children, hearing them quarreling all the time, decided to do the same thing.

The two boys would argue as to who was to take care of the furnace, or clean the basement, and to carry the ashes out from there. They quarreled over the family car. When the car had something the matter with it, they blamed one another about it. They were constantly quarreling at the table at mealtime, so that I sometimes would get up and go downtown to a restaurant to eat a good meal and enjoy myself. I had just started to get used to them when I found another place to board. It was a regular boarding place. After I got settled down it was like a heaven to me. I didn't hear any more quarreling or arguments—only on Saturday nights, when the men had a few drinks. Then they would argue about this and that until one of the parties would give in to the other.

I never in my life like to quarrel, but I do enjoy arguments when it comes in the right place, like for instance at card parties, lodge meetings, in a football or baseball game. The arguments sometimes have good results in deciding the score of the game. And sometimes in lodge meetings, to help the organization correct their past mistakes.

But quarreling is altogether different with me. When I quarrel over something that is a worthwhile affair, I just as soon fight and get it over with. But I have changed that attitude in late years; nowadays when I have to quarrel I usually try to laugh it off or make myself scarce. I have found it to be a good policy and worthwhile to remember at all times and places.

I have a pal—we have been almost constantly together from boyhood. We attended the same schools here in Oneida, and also at Carlisle, and we have worked at different jobs together. He has more education then I have, but I have traveled the country more than he has. We are always trying to outsmart one another, but it's no use. Sometimes he gets the best of me in discussions of the events of the day: politics, the kind of government we have today, the people's economic life, church affairs, and its prospects for the future, and past experience. And the different sports, horse racing, for example, and also baseball, football, boxing, wrestling, and many other games of sport enjoyed by the American public. And about our past experiences with the weaker female sex, our downfall and our weak spots, drinking habit, tobacco smoking, our social activities, work being done for different Indian tribes by this so-called New Deal, the present world war.

There isn't a day that goes by but we are arguing about one of these subjects. My pal usually gets the best of me when it comes to writing about these subjects, but I get the best of him when it comes to discussion in public. That makes him quite angry at me, so much at times that sometimes it looks like we are just about to come to blows. But then I usually spring a good joke on him—what has happened to him in the past. Anyway, I always succeed in getting him back in good humor. If we do get mad at each other, it doesn't last very long. We have been such good friends for a long time that either of us gets lonesome, and then before we know it we are talking to each other again, good friends as ever. If we don't see each other again for a few days, when we do get together again, look out for jokes and stories about him or myself. We help each other out in many different ways by exchanging our point of views in many questions and what is happening in general. He is an ex-veteran and so am I. In business we advise each other carefully. We belong to the same church. Sometimes we get to arguing about who is the best Christian. We both drink beer, smoke, chew tobacco, and sometimes step out and celebrate on Saturday night. I don't know who is the best looking between the two of us, but one thing I know: he is a better liar than I am.

CORA CHARLES

> Cora Charles, age fifty-nine, was educated at the Hampton Institute, an institution better known as a pioneer school for the education of African American children. Like Guy Elm, Andrew Beechtree, and many others, she had adventures while participating in the outing system during the summers. Cora was evidently the wife of Josiah Charles (see narratives in chapters 3 and 8). She was interviewed by Ida Blackhawk on June 25, 1941.

My Experiences Working for New England People

I went to Hampton, Virginia, when I was only twelve years old. The reason I was sent away to school when I was so young was because my mother was dead, and I had no one to take care of me. My older sister and three brothers were also at the same school. At that time Hampton Institute was like an elementary school so anyone that was in the third or fourth grade was admitted to the school. Later they raised the age limit to seventeen years of age, and above the eighth or ninth grade. At the present time it is more like a college.

Hampton Institute is a school for the Negroes, but at one time the American Indians, Puerto Ricans, and Cubans, and Indians from Jamaica were also admitted there. At the time I was at Hampton there were many Oneidas there, and also Indians of other western tribes. We Indian girls had our own quarters, and the Indian boys had their quarters. The Negroes had their quarters. We all ate in the same dining room, only there were separate tables for Indian students. We all attended the classrooms together.

The classes consisted of Indians, Cubans, Puerto Ricans, and Negroes. The wealthy New England people used to pay the Indians' scholarships at Hampton, but the government paid the Indian students' board, clothing, and transportation, while the colored students paid their own expenses while in school, excepting that their scholarships were paid by the rich New England people. I doubt if there are any Indians attending Hampton Institute today. There were still a few in 1918, but not any Oneidas. I did not mind going to school with the colored people at the time, but now I am always ashamed to tell that I had colored people as my classmates. It seems to me, at that time I did not realize how it would seem to other people.

After I was there a year I was told that I had to go to the New England states to do light work for the summer, because Hampton would be too warm during the summer months. So early part of June all the Indians were getting ready to "go up north," as they called the New England states. Every Indian girl was in hurry-scurry, including myself, although I really did not fully realize what it was all about. The girls stored some of their clothing and books in the storeroom upstairs and packed the rest of their belongings in a suitcase or two, or sometimes in a trunk, to take along.

We went in a boat from Old Point Comfort to New York City; then from there we all went to different places in the New England states. Everything was new to me and I was really enjoying the sights, etc. New York City really thrilled me. I just wished we would stay there a few days and go sightseeing every day. It seemed good to eat in a swell restaurant. I think we ate in a YWPA [YWCA]. The immense high buildings surely impressed me, but I did not have time to stop and look at them. The lady who had charge of us was trying hard to keep us together so no one would get left behind as we got in the elevated cars. Every time I stopped to gaze at anything, someone would poke me in the back and tell me to keep moving.

We finally all got to the depot, where two of us girls were met by a lady that took us to the Adirondack Mountains, to her summer home. She seemed like a good-natured lady and was very nice to us. The other girl was Lavinia Adams, now Mrs. Lavinia Skenandore. She was older than I, and she did the cooking and I was her helper, or second girl. We went on the train for three or four hours. It seemed like ages to me, as I was beginning to be anxious to see the place where we were going to work for the summer. I was wondering if the other girls had reached their destination. At last, the lady told us to get ready to get off, as the next station was where we were going to get off. Someone met us, and we rode in a fancy buggy, pulled by lively horses. When we arrived at the lady's place I noticed that there was another lady there, so there were two ladies occupying the summer home. We were shown to our room, which was right over the kitchen.

The next morning, I took a good look at the place. The house was situated beside a huge rock, and one side of the place was a wooded, rocky hillside. They had a golf course there, and the grounds were kept in good condition. It was a beautiful place. When the lady came down she assigned us our duties, so we both started to work. It was the first time I realized that I was sent there to work. I used to have to take warm water upstairs for the ladies to wash with in the morning, and then I had to wait on the table. Lavinia did the cooking, but one of the ladies directed her. I just carried the food in the dining room and placed it on the table. I also helped with the dishwashing and prepared vegetables. I really was kept pretty busy, but we always had an hour or two in the afternoon.

Our room used to be so hot that we could not go up there to rest in the afternoon. Finally I told the lady, and she fixed up another room for us. She had another window put in, and oh! what a difference it made. We were comfortable the rest of the season. Once in a while these ladies took us out riding to another country home. We stayed in the buggy while they visited their friends. I noticed that most of the owners of these country homes had residences in New York City or Brooklyn and only lived in the mountains during the summer. They hired someone to take care of their homes, or estates, in the wintertime. We stayed at this place during June, July, and August, and I got about a dollar per month, but Lavinia got more. I was not used to working and I felt as though I was working hard for such little wages, but I really was not doing any heavy work. There were no conveniences there in those mountains. When we washed we had to rub by hand, and iron the old way.

These people had lots of company—or else they were operating a summer resort. Anyway, there were people coming back and forth from the city. One of the ladies had a wealthy son who came there with his friend, another young man. They made so much work for us. They got up later than the other people there did, and we always had to serve breakfast for them later than the other people. They played golf every day. When they were getting ready to leave, Lavinia and I were both rejoicing, and when we thought they were about ready we went out and climbed behind a big rock back of the house, and we could see them down below us. The last minute they ran in the kitchen and called us, but neither one of us answered, so they left without seeing us. The lady told us afterwards that the young fellows were going to give us a "tip" or give us money, as a gift. We said, "We don't accept presents, but we wish they would pay us for the work we did for them." Since then I found out what a "tip" really means.

We stayed there all summer and worked hard for those wealthy ladies. By the time we left there we knew why they were rich. They were very saving—in fact, they were stingy. They worked us hard for the wages they gave us, but of course they were not mean to us. We told the lady that places the girls in the New England homes that we did not want to go back there again, so I was sent to another place the following summer. This time I was sent to Newport, Rhode Island. I worked for a young couple. They were well-to-do people. They had a nice home, but they were not society people. They treated me as though I was one of the family. Of course, I was a little more experienced to do maid work, so the lady liked my work. She made it as easy for me as she possibly could and let me have all the afternoon to rest or go see the other girls working in Newport.

There were several of the Indian girls there, but they were not all Oneida girls, but they were all from Hampton. We used to go to the beach and see the ocean waves come to the beach. We enjoyed watching the people in their bathing suits, but we used to just sit on the beach and take in the sea breeze. We went around the cliffs several times. On the cliffs are the mansions of the "400" society people, the Vanderbilts and others. [12] As Newport is a summer resort, everything was very high in the summer time; we could not afford to buy any clothing. We used to attend the band concerts, held every other evening at the different parks. Newport had more beautiful parks than any city I know of.

When I left Newport to go back to school I really hated to leave the people I worked for, or stayed with, as they were so good to me. Mrs. Barlow told me they had a child that died and she was born the same year I was, so I seemed to remind them of their little daughter. After I was back to Hampton I used to hear from Mrs. Barlow, and after I finally came home to Oneida I still corresponded with Mrs. Barlow. Now and then she would send me a present. She used to send me all her discarded clothes. She was a large woman, and so I had to always fix or alter them. Sometimes I gave some of the clothing to my relatives.

One day I was fixing a suit when I came across a little bag sewed onto the lining of the sleeve. I ripped the little bag and inside I found a little bundle, and after I unwrapped it I found a sparkling stone, and it was a diamond. I did not know what to do about it. It seemed to me that it was a funny place to hide a diamond, but I took for granted she wanted me to have the diamond, so in order not to lose it I had a ring made and had the diamond mounted. But I was always ashamed to wear the ring, for fear people would criticize me on account of my circumstances. I knew myself that there are a lot of other things I would buy before I would think of buying any kind of a ring.

About that time I received a letter asking me to visit the Barlows for a month or longer, so I made preparation to go. I went on the train all the way. I got there in the evening, but no one met me at the depot, so I looked around for a taxi. They were all driving away, but there was a big limousine and I hailed the driver, and he opened the door and I told him the address I wanted to go to, so he drove there, and I got out and went to the door. The house was all lit up and the folks were home. They were glad to see me, and were evidently expecting me. We got to visiting, and after a while someone said that my driver was out there waiting; then it occurred to me that I had forgotten to pay him, and it happen to be the boss of the taxi company.

While I was there she told me about losing a diamond. She had no idea how she lost it or where she lost it. She said she was going to give a diamond ring to her niece, and then she changed her mind and she had the diamond taken out and a ruby put in its place. She thought she put the diamond away but she could never find it. Then I told her that I found the diamond in the sleeve of a suit she had sent me, and that I had it put in a ring, and I took it out of my purse and gave it to her. She was very pleased and asked me what I paid for the ring, and I told her nineteen dollars so she handed me twenty dollars. I thought afterwards how foolish I was to return it, because she did not give me a reward. I stayed about a month. I helped her and worked as hard as when I used to work there.

I finally started home, and came back the same way, on the train. We used to go on a boat from New York City to Newport on the Fall River Line when I was sent from Hampton, Virginia, and I knew how rough it used to be. We always got seasick going in a boat. When I got to New York City I went to some of the big department stores and did some shopping, then I came home. I enjoyed the trip very much, and I often wished I could have another trip like that.

After I came home I felt like working, and I appreciated my home. A home sometimes gets monotonous, especially a home without a child, and I have not been fortunate enough to have children. Of course I have tried to occupy my time with something, so sometimes I plant potatoes or beans or corn and spend my time taking care of the garden. I also raise chickens and I make a little side money that way. I also go away to work at a summer resort some summers.

One summer I went to Burlington, Wisconsin. There was a lake about one and a half miles from town. I worked in the kitchen and had charge of the electric dishwasher and the girls that did the work. I enjoyed my work because it was not hard and we had plenty of time to rest between work hours. The busiest time was from Friday evening to Sunday evening, as most of the people came only for the weekend, and sometimes there would be about 500 people there during Saturday and Sunday. During the week we would have about 250 to 300 people and we were not rushed at all. We had lots of time to go in swimming in the lake, and in the evening we went to the dance hall and watch the people enjoy themselves. Sometimes they gave pretty good programs of home talent. I made about fifty dollars clear money and had a good vacation besides.

I was there during July and August, and after Labor Day my husband came there with another couple and we went on to the Chicago Fair and stayed three days; then we returned home. That was another treat that I enjoyed. My husband is now laid up and not expected to live very much longer, so I do not expect any more pleasure trips anywhere.

About the places I was in the New England states, I will say that at one place in the Adirondack Mountains I outgrew my clothes. I was still growing and I did not earn enough to buy new clothes, so the lady let me have her old dress to wear back to school. She paid me twenty-five cents per week, and when I left she gave me a sealed envelope and told me not to open it until I got back to Hampton. Do you suppose I could wait that long? No, I opened that envelope as soon as I got out of sight, and I found that there was five dollars in the envelope. She had actually given me two dollars more than what she told me I was going to get. They surely did not pay us very much for our work those days.

My brother was the first Oneida that attended school at Hampton, and he told me that when he was sent up north to work, the farmer he worked for wasn't going to pay him anything because he was going to teach him everything. But my brother learned at home—how to rake up hay, how to use the scythe, and how to cut grain with a cradle on a scythe, and most everything about farmwork. My brother told the New England farmer that he would not work unless he was paid, and that was the beginning of the students getting paid for their work in the summer months. But even then they paid as little as they could, and they made the Indians work hard for their money.

I stayed with the Barlows one winter and went to school with the white children. I learned more that year than all the years I was at Hampton. There were some good rich New England people, and these people were surely good to me. They dressed me like any white child, and I only worked after school and Saturdays. But I did not feel at home with white children, and although I made friends among them, yet I felt rather sensitive. When we studied history, and whenever there was something about the Indians in the lesson, they all looked at me, and that used to make me furious. The children did not dare say anything to me, but I could just guess what they had in mind. Although the people coaxed me to stay, I decided to go back to Hampton and finish my education there.

I was graduated in 1902 and returned home. My old grandmother, who had taken care of me after my mother died, was failing, so I decided to stay with her and take care of her, and she died about two years later. Then I was married soon after that. I never used my education in a way

I had planned to use it; I thought I would apply for work in the civil service. But of course I have used it in my work at home and in the way I conduct myself wherever I am.

My husband was also at Hampton, so we often talk about our experiences while going to school. Most of the teachers at Hampton were rich New England people who donated their time to the school. Later when the school increased in attendance the school had to hire teachers, and of course they got paid, but they hired college graduates, so they had very efficient [effective] teachers. Hampton taught college studies even when I was there, but now it has turned into a regular college. The Indian schools such as Carlisle, Haskell, and other large schools used to have very poor white teachers; many of them were not qualified to teach, but if they have pull with the superintendent they could hold the job. It has been only recently that the standard of the teachers has been raised. They now have to take a civil service examination and be under forty years of age.

Years ago we used to have old ladies for our teachers, and they did not follow any method and were not really interested in their work, but were there for one reason, and that was to make money. Some days they just let the class pass time away by drawing while the teacher wrote letters or did some fancywork. When an inspector came around, then they made a good showing. Most of the government employees were there because they were friends or relative of the superintendent. They used to abuse the Indian children too. Sometime they punished them severely when it was uncalled for. They would give little girls heavy work to do. That was finally reported, and the Indian Office put a stop to it. The Indian schools were more like the industrial schools for white children. Everything was strictly on a routine and not a bit homelike.

It was Commissioner Collier, the present commissioner of Indian Affairs, with the help of Mrs. Roosevelt, that put the Indian government schools on a different basis. Now everything is more like a home, and instead of having a mean matron they have a young woman who is sort of a companion for the young girls, and she is called "Girls' Guide." The boys and girls are allowed to mingle together on the school campus. The large institutions are more like the white colleges or universities, but I still don't think it is right. They should hire mostly Indian employees, because only an Indian can fully understand an Indian's ways. There are plenty of educated Indians that could qualify for these positions, but many times the white people get the preference. Look at the colored people. They have their own teachers, and see how well they are getting along in the educational line.

I think that the government is not doing right by trying to make farmers of all the Indians. They are not all interested in farming, and this giving land back to the Indians is not for the Indians' benefit. It only means that they have to work hard and make money for the government. If they stop grinding away, then the government will step in and take it away from that individual and give it to the next foolish Indian. My husband tried to farm, and we just could not make money on the farm. We finally sold the farm and we opened a grocery store, but we did not have enough money to keep up. It was during depression, so we finally sold the store and bought a small tract of land and built a small log house and a little addition to it, and then my husband worked on the WPA. He worked there until he took sick, but he has just reached the pension age, so he began to get a pension. That is how we live today, but after he is gone I don't know just what will happen to me.

I really don't know what would have happened to the Oneidas if they were not given relief at the time. There was no more wood to cut and sell and no work of any kind in sight. There were a lot of young people that had found employment in some large city who came back to the reservation thinking that they could find something to do here. They were given relief too. Now that the factories are hiring help again, many of them have gone back to the cities, and some are getting ready to go back and try city life again. I think eventually the young Oneida people will all go away from here, excepting the ones that like to farm.

It seems to me that the older generation of Oneidas were better farmers then this generation, or else the land was new and fertile so the crops yielded more. But most of the old fellows had pretty good farms and were getting along fine, but as soon as their sons or heirs got hold of the land it began to get run down, and white people got a hold of the farms and they seem to make improvements.

I often wonder how those New England farmers are getting along. No doubt the old-fashion farmers are all dead, and their old farms are under new management with all the modern farm machinery. But at the time I was in the New England states I thought those farmers were a little behind times. Some farms looked as though they might have been flourishing farms at one time, but at the time I saw them they were in a dilapidated condition. I really wondered how they made their living, as some of the land is rocky, but some of the farmers had boarders in the summertime. The business people of New York City and Boston and Brooklyn and other large cities all spent their vacation in the country. Some of them would go just for the weekend. I enjoyed that climate, especially in the mountains. I often wished I had enough money to go back there and stay all summer.

8.

Sports and Recreation

For many Oneida men, especially those who had gone to the major boarding schools, sports were of considerable importance. Carlisle and Haskell, as we have seen, were noted for their great teams and athletes, but there were many other Indian athletes who became famous, especially in football and baseball. And the Oneida Reservation fielded teams that were a source of pride. This section contains several accounts of exploits and experiences on playing fields as well as some accounts of hunting and fishing.

This narrative carried the title "My Economic Life," but Howard Elm
seems to have been even more interested in talking about his sporting
life. He may have reckoned that the interviewer, Guy Elm, would be
interested in that topic as well. The interview took place on September
18, 1941.

My Economic and Sporting Life

I was born in Oneida twenty-nine years ago. My father and mother are
both Oneida and still living. I went to school at the public school when
I was seven years old. There are four of us in the family, two brothers
and two sisters, and I am the youngest. One sister died last spring.

My father was a farmer when I was a young boy, and I am sure we
didn't have hard times like the families today because my dad and
mother were hard workers. When I was old enough to remember, my
father had a team of horses, eight cows, lots of chicken, and some hogs
on the farm. They raised about a hundred bushels of potatoes every
year; his land was suitable for this kind of crop, besides raising other
crops like tomatoes, corn, cucumbers, beans, pumpkin, melon, and
strawberries. Cash crops were peas, cucumbers, and navy beans. The
times were good for farmers as well as for workers in any trade you
could think of. Everybody was making a good living.

During the winter months my mother used to make lace—bobbin
lace, they called it. She used to be one of the best lace makers, and she
earned good wages. With the income from the cows, her wages, and the
food supplies on hand they were able to get along good.

We lived in a frame house—three rooms downstairs and two bedrooms upstairs. We had a barn big enough to take care of twelve cows
and three horses, a chicken coop for one hundred chickens, a hog pen
for half a dozen pigs, a small corncrib, garage, and granary to hold feed
for the stock. My father owned a car; the make was Overland. Evidently
it was the first car that he bought for the family. Since that time he has
bought a Cleveland, a Ford, a Nash, and a Chevy.

Sometime in 1924 my dad sold his farm and we moved to Milwaukee.
He was employed at the Federal Tire Company for about two years. I
continued to go to school in Milwaukee.

He and my mother got a job as first and second cook at the big dairy farm of Williams near Milwaukee. There were about fifteen people employed by this man. We stayed there over one year, then we moved back again to our home in Milwaukee. And this time he was employed by the city department. He worked there for about three years. The depression was at its height about this time and some of the men were laid off, and of course my father was one of them. So he sold out and came back to Oneida and he bought ten acres from my grandpa. The next year he started to build a small cottage and planted some contract beans, cucumbers, carrots, and beets.

About this time I went to school at Haskell at Lawrence, Kansas. I was there two years, and then I came home to visit the folks. I stayed home during the vacation months and helped with the work. That fall I went back to Haskell to finish my education. The last two years that I was there I played football, but I wasn't able to play very much because I was troubled with a leg injury. But I was able to make the varsity. We traveled around considerably. We played at Omaha, Nebraska; Grand Forks, North Dakota; Sioux Falls, South Dakota; Denver, Colorado; Pittsburgh, Pennsylvania; Philadelphia, Pennsylvania; New Orleans; St. Louis; Seattle, Washington; Jefferson City, Missouri; and two home games. These were the days when Haskell Indians were known as a traveling team. They went from coast to coast, and they had a great team at that time. Some of the greatest stars that Haskell ever turn out were on this team, namely the Levi brothers, John and Joe; Anderson; Weller; the Oneida boys Powless, King, Smith; and Wilson Charles Jr., who became a second Jim Thorpe. He was an all-around athlete; he had a perfect physique for an athlete: six feet tall and weighing about 180 pounds stripped. Well put up man all around.

I was 175 pounds, and I played end position on the team. Our line from end to end averaged over two hundred pounds per man. We had one man named Miles that weighed 270 pounds; they nicknamed him "Baby" Miles. He was six feet and four inches tall. When he was in the game, the other players looked like kids alongside of him. He played the guard position, either right guard or left guard. Every time when the coach would send him in to play, the crowd would yell, "What a man!" And the opposing team members would whistle, "Boy-oh-boy! What are they going to send in next?"

One year before I was on the squad, these Haskell Indians played against the Minnesota Thundering Herd, as they were nicknamed at that time, because they were turning out the best teams in the country. This game was played at Minneapolis, Minnesota. The game was one of the greatest since the days of the famous Carlisle Indian who also played Minnesota University. In 1907, that year Carlisle had a champion then and Minnesota was no match for this powerful Indian team. This game at Minneapolis, Haskell outplayed the Minnesota team for three periods. At the first half the Haskell Indians were ahead by the score of 7–0 in their favor. It was a tough game because the two teams were evenly matched, but the Haskell team had only twenty-four players along with them, and Minnesota had its full squad of thirty-five players to enter the game.

Towards the end of the third period the Haskell players were getting tired, and so Minnesota managed to tie the score on a forward pass play. The Haskell coach had ordered his man at the start of second half to play a defensive game; that is, whenever they got possession of the ball to run two plays then punt. It worked for a while, and besides he benched his star players about halfway in the third period for them to get rest for the final drive in the fourth period. Well, Minnesota scored again right after the fourth period got under way, after recovering a Haskell fumble at midfield. This time they scored by rushing through the Haskell line for short gains. The second-string linemen were in there for Haskell and they just couldn't hold the Minnesota backs from breaking through. The score stood 7–14 in favor of Minnesota, when Coach Hanley sent his entire group of regulars back into the game. The twenty thousand people that were watching the game got the thrills of their lives.

Minnesota had the ball on Haskell's ten-yard line when the regulars got back in the game. They held Minnesota down for no gain and drove them back to their thirty-five-yard line and blocked the ball for a field goal, which Minnesota tried to make on fourth down. The ball was recovered by Haskell, and on the first play John Levi, Haskell's star fullback, crashed through center and ran through the whole Minnesota team for a touchdown. But a Haskell player was charged with holding and the play was recalled; the score didn't count. Haskell was penalized fifteen yards for holding, so that the ball was put on Haskell's twenty-yard line. The Indians were quite angry for the penalty the officials had invoked against them; they protested [valiantly] but to no avail. And so they were fighting mad. They unleashed everything they had and tore the famous Minnesota's line to shreds. They went up the field with end runs, off-tackle plays, smashes through center, and some short forward passes until they got to the Minnesota ten-yard line. This Levi was all-American fullback. He proved it to the crowd that day because each time he took the ball he ran right through the line, over the goal line, and two times Haskell was penalized for offsides, but on the third try he circled the end this time and scored. Weller missed the try for an extra point after a touchdown and the score stood Minnesota 14 and Haskell 13. Haskell kicked off to Minnesota, and they failed to make first down and were force to punt. These Indians almost scored again; they were within Minnesota's twenty-yard line when the whistle blew ending this great game between these two teams. I saw the game because I was connected with the trainers; we took care of the boys on the rubbing tables after each game. I witnessed some big games played by the Haskell Indians that season, and it was the only game that they lost that season. After these boys got through playing college football, some of them played pro football and others went to coaching college and high school football teams.

I joined the national guard, which was composed of Haskell Indian students, a company of cavalry. I was a member of this outfit for two years. This outfit later made its name and became famous for being the world's finest at drilling, jumping stunts, and horsemanship. They were at the World's Fair in New York, and later took part in parades in Washington DC, Philadelphia, and Baltimore, Maryland, before coming back home to Lawrence, Kansas.

I left Haskell and went to Oklahoma and stayed with my aunt who lives there for one year; then I came home. After I was home all summer I went to CCC camp near Park Falls, Wisconsin. I worked in the CCC for two years, but I came home several times during that time to visit my folks. I learned lots of useful things during the time I was enrolled at this camp. I drove trucks and done other work, which I was called to do. I went to night school and took up some studies that I knew would help me later in life, so that I have about just as good an education as any you can see here on our reservation.

When I came home, I worked on the WPA for awhile to take my father's place on the job, and when I wasn't working on the project I helped him on the farm. We went into partnership raising contract crops such as carrots, beans, cucumbers, and beets for Larson Canning

Company and Seymour Canning Company. We double the crops all around and raised some chicken besides, so that last fall I managed to get married.

Early this spring I went to farming on my own. The girl that I married has a big farm—but heavily mortgaged. When her mother took sick they had to sell out everything that is personal property on the place. She paid some of the debts; in fact, she didn't have much money left when she died. So this spring my wife and I decided to go back to farming. We had to start with nothing, so we sold the car for four hundred dollars. We managed to buy a horse and few cows and some farm equipment, and also seed to plant. I had to rent my dad's horse so that I could plow. Well, everything was tough, but I managed to plant corn, some grain, and cash crops. Now I am crossing my fingers and just waiting to see how I will come out with my crops. We have made up our minds that we are going to rent out or sell out this fall and go working out ourselves and earn some of these high wages they are talking about. We are both young and hard workers, so all we care is to get jobs so we can go to town and make some money for ourselves.

The subject "recreation" covers lots to my mind; however, before I was a married man I enjoyed myself taking part in all the sports, namely football, baseball, basketball, track, tennis, swimming, boxing, and wrestling. I still play baseball, basketball, and softball, but not in a league competition. I like to watch all the games that are played by Oneidas here in Oneida and also by the white people as well. The Oneidas usually put up stiff competition in either baseball or basketball.

I always wished that I could become a good ballplayer when I was a young kid, but I was troubled with a rupture. I had my operation when I was over twenty years old. I never could quite get used to being careful not to get hurt; in so doing I wasn't able to perform like the players that were in pink condition, so to speak. And to play your best a player has to be in tip-top shape.

Other recreation for me and my wife are dancing, shows, movies, taverns, motoring, and fishing. My wife is just as good at fishing as I am. This summer we had lots of good times together fishing, at picnics, and hiking in the woods or parks.

We usually get up early, do our work, eat our breakfast, get our fishing equipment ready, and our lunch. Next we drive around to our friends and pick them up for the trip. The trips are usually sixty to seventy-five miles. With forty to fifty miles per hour, we get there in two hours and sometimes longer. We hire a boat and start fishing at once, and fish until lunchtime. Then we lunch and go fishing again and by three o'clock we have enough fish to eat. I always clean my fish as soon as I get home, and I let my wife fry them while I do my work around the farm. I can eat lots of fish sometimes, that is, certain kinds.

Social activities with us are dancing, parties, private parties, and church doings. I am not much of a churchgoer, but I do donate whenever they ask me to do so.

Since I have been married I have changed my ways and habits to suit my wife, and of course she has too. We try to get along with each other the best way we know how. Sometimes I think it's tough to be married; then again I am glad that I am.

ANDERSON CORNELIUS

As with Howard Elm's narrative, interviewer Guy Elm seems to have inspired Anderson Cornelius, age forty-five, another Carlisle alumnus, to turn his discussion of "Present Economic Life" into one of athletic pursuits and fishing stories, surely a more agreeable topic than depression-era economic life. The interview took place on June 29, 1940.

An Athlete's Life

My parents always told me that I was born in 1895 here in the reservation. I am forty-five years old. I got married in 1924 to a girl by the name of Lilly Powless. We have seven children; the oldest is a girl, sixteen years of age, and the youngest is a boy, five years old. We are struggling along like most of the big families here in Oneida. We are poor, but we have been able to eat three square meals a day. I am a world war veteran. I own my home and a few acres of land. I am an ex-football and lacrosse player at Carlisle Indian School. At the present time I am working on a WPA project. Now then, I will have to go back and tell you about my education. I will try to tell you just about everything I know about myself and my family.

When I was nine years of age, I started to go to school at the Oneida boarding school. I had older brothers attending at that school. I had a hard time at first because I couldn't speak a word in English. I was punished almost every day for almost a month until I was able to say yes or no, but then sometimes I make bad mistakes. I say yes when I should have said no and the other way around, no when it's yes. I finally was able to speak broken English. I used to scrub the floors in the hallway for talking in Oneida language. I guess I was pretty bad alright.

We had to go to school half a day and work half a day. Anyway, it seems to me I was always scrubbing every day. I don't know why they made us work—perhaps to pay our board bill. The grub they put on the table wasn't fit for pigs, but sometimes they fed us pretty good, I suppose when they knew the inspectors were coming around. My folks used to visit us every Sunday. My mother used to bring lots of good eats. And, Oh! Boy, the way we used to eat the food she brought. She would tell us to be good and not try to run away from school. We were allowed to go home every month from Friday until Sunday evening.

What I like the best to eat was butter, so whenever it was time for us to leave home I would take a baking powder can and fill it with butter to take back to school. Some of my playmates played a trick on me one time. I used to hide my can in a woodshed. The boys stole it and refilled the can with wagon grease. It was after supper in the wintertime that this thing happened. It was dark already when we came out. And so the boys asked me if I had any butter left. They said we got the crust part of the bread for everybody, let's go and put the butter on our bread. I said alright, follow me, I will show you where I hide my butter. So we all went to the woodshed. I got the can out. I couldn't see what was in the can; well, I thought it was butter—that's what I had in there. We all spread the stuff on our bread. I took a good big bite on my bread. I chewed it; I notice it had kind of a bad taste to it. And so I took another good bite; then I knew I was fooled. They all started to laugh at me; I said to them, you just wait you fellows, I'll get even with you someday, just watch your step.

I waited for my chance, and it took long time until I was able to get even with them. I got a quarter from Dad, a brand-new one; so I showed the boys what I had, and at that time twenty-five cents was lots of money for us boys at that age. They were all excited and asked me where I got it. I said, Superintendent Hart is giving every boy twenty-five cents to go to village store to buy whatever he likes to eat. They all went over and went in his office and asked him for the money. He was surprised and he got pretty angry at these boys. He said to them, what do you think I am, a banker? You boys beat it, before I call the disciplinarian, and he started to chase them out of his office. Well, sir, I got a good laugh on them, and I watched my step from that time on. I knew that they were great for playing tricks on one another. We were all good friends, and those that are living are my best friends today.

I went to Carlisle in 1909. I enrolled for five years. I stayed there at the school for one year and went out in the country for two years and I spent the last two years back at the school.

Out in the country I worked on a farm near Newtown, Pennsylvania. It was a big dairy farm. The people were kind to me. I made friends with the neighbors and many others around the village. I really like the farm, and my work and the people. I received ten dollars per month the first season; the next summer my boss raised my wages to fifteen dollars per month. I thought that was lots of money at that time.

When I got back to Carlisle that fall I went to try out for the football team. I was able to make second team. The next year I made the first team and also I was on the lacrosse team. I was a goalkeeper.

When the period of my enrollment expired, I came home to visit my folks. I stayed on the reservation all summer, worked around so that I had about one hundred dollars saved up. I took this money and went back to Carlisle. The football season was in full swing when I got back there, so I join the squad. It prove to be my best season, that is, I done my stuff on the football field. The following spring I played on the lacrosse team. The position I played is called goalkeeper. I guess I had about the toughest position to play on the team. I had to stop the balls that were shot at the goal. The goal is about six feet in height and about four feet wide. The goalkeeper stands just inside of this goal. Sometimes I have to run with the ball out of there and shoot the ball down the field again. And with half of the opposing team swinging their stick and trying to block you off, that's when the goalkeeper has to think fast and figure out how to get rid of that ball. I used to practice every time I had a chance by having the players shoot the ball at the goal. I got so I could stop about nine out of ten shots that were shot at the goal. Good shooters usually shoot the ball so that it will hit the ground before it goes in the goal.

The Carlisle Indians were one of the best lacrosse teams in the East at that time. I remember the first season that I played on the team, we played fifteen games and we won twelve games, lost one game, and tied two games. The teams we played were Pennsylvania, Penn State College, Lehigh, Swarthmore, Syracuse, Hobart College, Cornell College, Albright College, Lafayette, Crescent Athletic Club, Rutgers, Maryland, and the two service teams, Army and Navy. These two teams, Army and Navy, were the hardest teams to beat; we tied with the Army, but we lost to the Navy by one point. The score was 4–3.

Our coach was an Irishman named O'Neal. He was from Canada. He was a good coach, one of the best in country. He turned out some good teams at Carlisle. I think that lacrosse is a rougher game than football. It requires lots of running, blocking, and clipping, and also a player has to know how to handle his stick in catching the ball and passing it around to his teammates. Besides, the players use the sticks in scrimmaging for the ball. Some of the teams played a clean game—that is, no rough stuff—but there is always one or two players on the team that are dirty and rough players. When they are caught the penalty is ten or fifteen minutes in the penalty box; that is, they are removed from the game for that length of time, and no substitution can be made for them. The team has to play without them, and in a close game, if they are short one good man, it makes lots of difference in the outcome of the game.

I remember one game that got pretty rough. Both sides were playing a fast defensive game, and the score was tied 2–2. The players started to get rough; some of them went too far. Soon after that two players got in a fistfight. They were banished from the game, and that started the whole thing. Some more fights got under way, until it seemed to me there were more players in the penalty box than on the field of play. It was just about ten minutes left to play when they started coming back into the game again. The game was a close one. Each side scored one point apiece. We had one Indian player that we always depended on in close games. He was very light in weight so that he couldn't stand playing against the big fellows in a regulation one-hour game. The coach used him as his last card for a score, and he usually came through with the deciding point.

This little fellow weighed not more than 135 pounds, but he was the fastest runner on the team. He was like a flash; he could dodge, twist, do tricks with his stick while carrying the ball; believe me, he was a hard man to catch. Well, the coach took one player out and put this little fellow in his place. The two teams were scrimmaging around our end of the field near the goal. They had missed two shots at our goal. And still they came back for another shot. This time I caught the ball and passed it to another teammate, and he passed it to the little fellow before the opposing team knew what it was all about. The little fellow wormed his way through the whole team, almost ran into the goal for a score, and that was all we needed to win the game. The coach and the trainers used to take care of him just like a racehorse. He save the team from getting beat quite few times. His teammates were very friendly and kind to him. When he made his twisting runs the whole team would form interference for him just like football. It's a wonderful sight to see those boys block clip. Sometimes they used what is known as Indian block, that is, they leave their feet off the ground and fly through the air headfirst and block opposing players trying to catch up with the runner. Sometimes they block from the side, in front, and from behind. It's very dangerous for the blockers as well as the runners. From where I stand I can see everything that goes on the field.

All during the time that I played lacrosse I never really was hurt seriously. I got scratches and bumps now and then. I was goalkeeper for two seasons at Carlisle. I played several games here in Oneida. The last game was at the De Pere fairgrounds some twenty years ago, but I'll never forget some of the exciting games that I happened to be in.

After I got married I used to work around Appleton, Neenah, and Menasha for a contractor. I also work on road construction jobs around the southern part of the state. I always had a good garden, like potatoes, beans, cabbage, melons, cucumbers, and corn—both Indian and sweet corn. I manage sometimes to buy small pigs to butcher late in the fall and have meat for the winter.

We always had plenty to eat anyway. The house where we lived wasn't such a swell place to live in, but it was better than paying rent for a better home. The family kept getting larger every other year until we had seven in the family. They are all living and they are all in good health. It keeps me busy and thinking how to figure out the best way to make our living. It's a man's job alright, but I enjoy it. I am very interested in raising my family.

The kids are very good in helping with the work around the place, and when the school is closed the older children go out and work. They earn enough to buy their own clothes and some spending money for themselves. The children are easy to manage; they all mind their mother, and when I tell them anything they know that it's no two ways about it. They either do what they are told to do or there will be trouble and plenty of it.

I have found out that if you are too easy with the children, you'll have trouble with them later when they grow up. But if you let them know who is the boss when they are young, they will always obey your orders. I never lick them, unless they do some thing or disregard my orders, but as a rule one good thrashing is all they need. After that they usually mind what I tell them. I don't know whether I am right the way I discipline them. Anyway, it seems to work for me and my wife as well as the children.

As I said before, I work on WPA. I have done almost everything on the project from water boy to mason work. I have been transferred from one project to the other. The wages I receive is from $40.00 per month to $72.50 per month. We manage to live on this income, and we have to be satisfied with it. It won't do to kick, because it's a "take it or leave it" work program. I have tried to get private employment on several occasions, but I guess it's on account of my age; they always tell me that there are no jobs open.

My recreation in sports are football, baseball, basketball, and swimming. What I mean is that I am interested in these sports and like to see them played.

I do lots of fishing, and I like to eat fish. I like to fish the suckers with spear and with a dip net. Every spring I get my share of the fish. In the spring of the year, the first fish that come up the river are pickerel. Later on then the sucker, and in May the redhorse. For trout fishing we Oneida usually go up north.

There are lots of stories about the Oneidas—what happens sometimes when they are caught fishing with spears at night for suckers. The game wardens sometimes get angry at them and they take a notion to arrest them. I have several good stories about that, and it really happened.

This happened a few years ago. One Oneida was caught fishing with a spear and a lantern, and he had a half a bag full of suckers with him. The game wardens asked him what was he doing. The Indian answered them, he said, "Why, I'm fishing. What did you fellows think I was doing, swimming for my health?" He went on fishing. He said, "Now is the time to fish: the game wardens have all gone back to town, the fishermen have all gone home to sleep, the river is full of fish. Why don't you fellows join me and fish all you want?" The game wardens said to him, "Come up on the bank and show us your fish." The Oneida went up on the bank, and one of the wardens showed him his badge and said, "You are under arrest for fishing with spear and lantern at night." The warden said to him, "Don't you know it's against the fishing law to fish with a spear at night?" He told him, "You can fish all you want with a dip net. I'll have to take your fish, the spear, and your lantern; besides, I got to take you to town and lock you up in jail for the night, and tomorrow the judge will tell you what is your fine."

Well, the next day he went up for the hearing. The judge asked if he was guilty; the Oneida said, "Yes, Judge, I was fishing, but these two men bothered me. They took my fish and my fishing equipment." The Oneida had been before the judge before, so he knew him. The judge let him go but warned him not to fish again at night with his spear.

A year after, the Oneida kept waiting for a good fishing time. So one night he got ready. He didn't have the dip net, but instead he rented a dragnet from his neighbor. He went to his old fishing place and got his dragnet across the river. Some other fisherman came along and they fished with him. They all got lots of fish. They divided it up among them and went home to sleep. But this one Oneida—he went home with his fish, then decided that perhaps it would be best to go back and fish some more as long as it was good fishing and nobody would be around. He had make himself a jacket out of calf hide; he took that along with him, also the dragnet and a bag for the fish. He went to his fishing place and put up the net again. It wasn't long before a car drove up the road not very far where he was fishing. Two men got off and started to walk up the river where he was fishing. The wardens were the same men that caught the Oneida the last time. One of the wardens spoke to him; he said, "I thought I told you last spring not to fish at night." The Oneida said to the warden, "I know, but this is a net I am fishing with." "Yes," said the warden, "so I see, but it's not the kind that you suppose to use. The dip net is alright, but a dragnet is against the law. I'll have to arrest you again. This time it's going to cost you plenty money."

When they got to the car he threw the bag with the dragnet in it in the rumble seat. He asked the Indian if there was any more Oneida fishing in the river. The Indian said, "Sure, lots of them, just around the bend." The warden got the Indian's name; he said, "You stay here while we go look around for some more of your tribesman." And so the two wardens went up the river with their flashlight blinking.

As soon as they went around the bend, the Oneida got the bag out, took his dragnet out, and put the calf hide in its place; he put it back in the rumble seat. When the game wardens returned, they found him sitting on the running board of their car smoking his pipe. The wardens were quite angry at the Oneida. One of them said to him, "I thought you said there were lots of Oneidas fishing. If you ain't the biggest liar on the reservation; just for that we going to send you over the road this time."

The next day the Oneida went before the same judge in the court. He was questioned; the Oneida pleaded not guilty. The judge set the date for his trial. The Oneida got out on bail, and two weeks after he had his trial. When his case came up he took the stand, the district attorney fired questions after questions at him, but each time he got around him. And finally he asked him if he own the net that was set across the creek. The Oneida said, "No, I was just on my way home and I saw the net and there wasn't nobody around so I thought I would fish as long as there wasn't anyone around. I will get some of the fish for myself. I was in the creek when the two officers came along and caught me with about one dozen suckers." The district attorney told him that was all.

One of the game wardens took the stand next. He told the court how he caught the Oneida fishing with a dragnet. The judge then asked the warden if he had any evidence on the Oneida fisherman. The other warden spoke up and said, "Yessir, Judge, we have plenty. This time it's a dragnet he was fishing with." The judge looked at the Indian, then asked the warden to show it to him. The warden got the bag and dumped its contents on the floor near the judge. Out came the hide instead of the net. The whole courtroom was in uproar; they all had a good, healthy laugh, including the judge. But the two wardens just looked at each other with disgusted expressions in their faces. The judge looked at them, and then he winked at the Oneida. He scratched his head, then he said to the wardens, "Well, men, I guess the joke is on you two gentleman. The Indian pleaded not guilty, and I certainly can't find him guilty; besides, next time you take nets from the Oneida fishermen be sure it's a net. First thing I know you'll be showing me skunk hide. The case is dismissed"—and so the Oneida was free again to fish.

My social life doesn't take so much room. I go to house parties but not to public dance halls. Most of the members of the family go to church, but not every Sunday. I don't dance the white man's dances, but I like to dance the old war dance—what the Oneidas used to dance long ago.

I saw service overseas; I am glad that I was in the world war. I hope I will be pensioned off when I get too old to earn wages, so I can live in peace the rest of my old age.

JOSIAH CHARLES

> This story about lacrosse was taken from the account of the life of Josiah Charles, the rest of which appears in chapter 3.

Lacrosse

My recreations are basketball, baseball, football, swimming, boxing, wrestling, and a long time ago, lacrosse, an Indian game. The lacrosse game was a tougher and rougher game than football. They used to play lots years ago. They had different teams that were usually called after whatever locality they were from—for instance, Duck Creek, Methodist, Seymour, and Freedom, and so on. They played on Sundays and sometimes during the weekdays. The teams played for some articles of clothing, skins of animals, beaded belts, blankets, and also foodstuff. All of these things are donated by the supporters of the respective teams. They have their coach, as the white man calls it. The trainer was called the medicine man. The Indians used to believe that he had supernatural powers, which he alone could decide the score of the games played by his team. Besides the players were treated with some kind of liniment before each game. What I mean is that this medicine man would have a sort of dressing hut at the scene of the game, with all his medicine such as a liniment-smelling thing that would wake up a dead man, some salve that was flavored with catnip and evergreen, and medicines for bruises, sprains, cuts, and dislocating of the joints, and, too, some kind of a drink for exhausted players. The medicine man had all these things in readiness for his ballplayers. A big bearskin, woollen blankets, and already made handmade splints for broken legs or arms. These players when they played really went for blood. They played until they have to be carried off the field in case of serious injury. They blocked and checked with their bodies. Sometimes three or four players hit the runner with the ball if they want to stop him from scoring a point.

The goals were set at each end of the field. The distance between the two goals is about the same as in football, although there is no rule as to the length of the field. The width of the field applies the same rule, but I would be safe to say that it's about the size of a football field. These goals I am telling you about are two poles stuck in the ground about four feet apart and about eight feet long. In scoring a point, the ball has to go through between these two poles either along the ground or in the air. When it does go through it counts one point. The number of players on each side is twelve. The positions on the team are as follows: a goalkeeper, center, first attack, second and third attack, first defense, second and third defense. There are five men on the attack and five on defense. The sticks they use are about three and one-half feet long; at one end there is a net, and the shape of it is something like a broom. They use this to catch the ball and to scrimmage with. Sometimes they sock you on the head and on the legs with it. Well, to tell you the truth they are not careful where they hit you with these lacrosse sticks. It's a great game to watch, but it's rough and bloody sometimes.

My uncle used to play on the lacrosse team. You know, you could be a lacrosse player at forty-five years old at that time. Among the Oneidas and other Indians, at that age a man was just then at the prime of his life. Well, my uncle must have been over fifty then. The Civil War veterans were having their Fourth of July celebration at a grove on the old De Pere road. On one side of the grove was a field; the owner had cut the hay off and put the field in shape for lacrosse and baseball games and footraces. This uncle of mine (his name was old man Powless), he prove to be an all-around athlete. He ran the races, played baseball, and also was the star of the lacrosse game. He wasn't such a big fellow. He was about five feet, ten inches and couldn't have weighed more than 170 pounds. But he was a fast runner, quick as a cat, and could handle his stick with the best of them. I watched closely the way he played. Whenever he got the ball he would start off with just a dogtrot and dodge the players. When he got about thirty yards from the goal then he would put on all the speed he had and dart in there and shoot the ball at the goal. Sometimes the goalkeeper stops the ball and sometimes he will miss the goal altogether. Anyways, that's the way he scores. But sometimes he is blocked off before he can get within shooting range to the goal.

I saw another play that I thought was good. The play started at the other end of the field, and this same player got possession of the ball. He threw the ball to one of his teammates and started to tear down the field. His teammates just passed the ball around to one another until he was past midfield; then one of them threw the ball towards him. The ball sailed through the air just high enough so that the opposing players couldn't get it with their sticks. He caught the ball on the dead run and went on and took a good shot at the goal and scored with sticks swinging all around him. I saw him nail players with his famous flying blocks from behind and sideways. This player was all over the field. But to my opinion the best play of the game was when three opposing players tried to stop him. They formed a human wall in front of him. He came up to them very fast and took a jump—he went up in the air about five feet and jumped over all three men. The men didn't know where he went until they look back and saw him going downfield dodging through the rest of the team, and his teammates were blocking and clipping their opponents left and right. He finally scored, and as I found out later, it happen to be the winning point.

After each game the players are rubbed off with cloth and massaged with witch hazel, and salve is applied all over their bodies. The cuts and bruises are treated by their trainers; sprained ankles and other injuries are also taken care of so that the players don't look so bad after they are dressed up. They used to play right by our house at one time, when I was a young boy. The place is right east of the cemetery by the little creek.

In this game the players were all big fellows. During the game, one of these big fellows was blocked by two other players. He was hit so hard that he landed on the other side of the little creek, and got up and crossed the creek and then fell and went down. They had to throw water on his face, and he finally got to his feet and said, "Well, it took two men to do it."

On March 20, 1941, during a general discussion of the loss of Oneida land, Guy Elm gave this account of a memorable football game. The first paragraph sets up the story in the context of that narrative.

A Football Game to Remember

The scheme of the white man to beat these Oneidas was so worked out to perfection that there was no recourse from any angle for them in the courts. Besides, I doubt if they did get a case of lawsuits in the court, if they would get a fair trial, because the majority of the white people in our neighboring cities are prejudiced against us Oneida Indians for reasons that I must say I don't know. Perhaps they haven't forgot the Deerfield Massacre in New York State years ago, or it might be that in recent years we have met the white man's football teams on the field of battle. [1] It was our only chance to get revenge on them from all the cheating they have committed against the Indian throughout the United States. And usually the Indians gave them a good beating at football. Just look back at the records of Carlisle, Haskell, and some other Indian schools, and the proof is right there.

This reminds me what happened to me one time, when I was playing football at Carlisle Indian school back in 1917, during the world war. We were playing Albright College. It was our third game of the season, and the game developed pretty rough at the start of the second half. In fact, it got so rough that the players from each team were complaining about the unnecessary roughness to the referee constantly. Fistfights ensued after almost every play. The referee started to expel players from both teams out of the game. Injuries also forced some of the players from the game, so that the coaches were up in the air.

A player on the opposing team playing right tackle position was spotted out to be the one causing "heap big" trouble to the Indians on their line plays. The coach edged up to me on the bench and said to me, "Elm, go in there at halfback position and instruct the quarterback to shoot the player right smack into that right tackle, and you carry the ball in every play and see if you can crash through on that side of the line. We want to score another touchdown before they get going. The way they going now, I am afraid they are liable to overtake us. Hit 'em low and hard and be sure of your tackles. Now you have your orders—go in the game." Well, I went in. The Indians were holding their opponents on about the twenty-five-yard line. On the last down they elected to attempt a field goal, which was blocked.

Now was my chance to tell our quarterback the coach's instruction, and which I did. Our backfield was composed of players bigger and heavier than I was. The fullback was 195 pounds and the quarterback and the other halfback were 180, and I weighed about 170 pounds, but I was faster, and once in the open I was hard to catch because of my ability to dodge and straight-arm the opposing tacklers. Well, the quarterback looked at me and said, "Me call plays through there? Why! That bird will break you in two. He is tough; we been trying some of our best plays through there and he has stopped them cold; we haven't gained an inch in that slot. Well, orders is orders with me, Elm. You'll have your chance right from here on."

When we lined up he called my number for off-tackle smash. I fooled the tackle right from the start; instead of me going between the end and right tackle I cut back between the guard and him, shot through there with all the steam I had. It was a five-yard smash, but he made the tackle himself, and he tried to twist my leg at the same time. When we got back on our feet, he tap me on my shoulder and said, "Lucky break for you that you didn't come through that other opening. I would have nailed you so hard that now you would have been on the stretcher on your way to the sidelines. I don't like you Indians." "Well, just for that, Brother, I'm coming through there on the next play coming up. Watch my smoke," I said to him.

The captain called time-out and we rested up; we talked things over. The quarterback didn't want to send plays through there again after I told him what the big tackle said to me, but the rest of the players insisted that we carry out the coach's orders. It was finally decided that we try two more plays, mass on tackle where the guards would pull out of line, run interference for the ball carrier, and smack the tackle with the rest of the backfield.

The quarterback told the players that if we made a first down in two plays, the third play would be Carlisle's "pet" play, a double reverse, which has fooled many a team, and when used, and if every man carries out his assignment, usually resulted in a score. And so we smash that line, we pile up on the tackle, which took some of the wind from him.

That made him "spit fire"; he was so angry because it was another gain of three yards through his position. And a player when angered can't play at his best. The next play through there some Indian stepped on his hand, so that he has to take time-out to have it bandaged. And sure enough it was a first down and yards to spare. He kept shaking his fist as me, because each time I had carried the old pigskin through there he had failed to stop the plays. To complete his humiliation, the quarterback called the next play double reverse. Everything went like a clock. I came through there like a scared deer; he made a diving tackle at my legs, but our powerful fullback was running a few steps behind me, waiting for just that kind of a tackle. He came down on the tackle like a ton of bricks, and Mr. Tackle was done for the rest of the afternoon. I scored on that play, a run of sixty-five yards, and the team had easy going the remainder of the game.

After the game, we were in the dressing room. The big tackle came in there; he was quite lame. He said, "Where is that little halfback?" The players pointed to where I was dressing. He came over and extended his big hand. He said to me, "I want to apologize for what I said to you this afternoon. I have found out I had the wrong opinion of you Indians. I have been playing regular on the varsity for three years, and it was the toughest game I have ever been in. From now on the Indians are my friends." I accepted his apology and told him that we had never run across a better tackle then he was. We all shook hands with him and wished each other good luck. Now getting back to the subject of my story, I will continue.

Stadler King set down ten consecutive stories about his varied experiences fishing and hunting. Here are three of them with his own titles.

Fishing with White Men

One day in the spring of the year, shortly after I was married, I was getting some garden ready to plant. It was plowed so I was getting it dragged. A wagonload of men came along and stopped right in front of my place. They were all talking at the same time and I could not make out just what they were saying, so I went up to them on the road and they said come along with us, we are going fishing. We will be there just when it gets dark. They were all white men from Seymour, but I knew them all and they were all good friends so I went in and told my wife. She said what time will you come back. I said I will be home sometime toward morning and she made lunch for me and I took my spear and I put on some old clothes but I took along an old overcoat; in case I get cold I could put it on. So I got on the wagon with them and we went.

It was about six or seven miles to the fishing grounds, but they had a good team so we went right along. We had gone some ways when one of the men pulled out a bottle of whiskey and said take a drink so it would not seem long ways for you. I took one drink and gave it back to him, but he passed it to the other men and each one took a drink and I thought it was no wonder they were all talking at the same time; they all seemed to be happy. Well, we did get there just about getting dark so they put the team to the wagon and gave them some hay and some of us went around looking for wood. It did not take long and we had quite a pile of wood together; then they made a fire and we stood by the fire. We waited for the fish to start running, and every so often this man with a bottle would pass around his whiskey; each time I would take a little drink.

Then I thought of my lunch, so I went to the wagon and got it and I ate my lunch and one after another they got their lunch and after a while we were all eating lunch. By the time we got done eating we could hear the water in the creek like fish were running, so we lit our lanterns and went in the water and sure enough there were fish running and I caught one just as soon as I got into the water. Then all the men got into the water, but one man stayed on the banks so I threw my fish to him, as he was to take care of all our fish. We stayed in the water maybe two hours and I got ten fish, and when we went to our fire they counted the fish and we had sixty fish. We stayed by the fire a little while and we each had a couple drinks of the whiskey; then we went back in the water and now there were more fish. We stayed in the water another two hours, then we all went by the fire again and now we counted 215 fish.

The man who had the whiskey always passed the bottle while we were on the bank. He said you will not catch cold even if you go in the water if you take a little drink once in a while. That's why we all take a drink when he gives us one, and he must have more than one bottle because he still had some when we were going home. We stay there until three o'clock in the morning. Then we divided the fish and put them in separate bags and each man got eighty fish and each bag was so heavy that one man could not raise it, so we all helped to load the bags of fish on the wagon. So we were ready to start for home about half past three in the morning.

It was already daylight when we came to my place. One man got off and helped me to take my bag of fish to the house; then they went on back to Seymour. My wife was not up yet, so I woke her and told her that I had eighty fish and I said would you cook them all right away. She said, why we can't eat more than one apiece. So I did not sleep a wink that night and I just made a fire in the stove; then I started to clean the fish and we had some for breakfast. But we did not have salt to salt them down, so I went to Seymour and bought ten pounds of the coarse New York salt. (We had heard that the common table salt would not do because there is some mixture in it that the fish would not keep if you use that kind of salt.)

When I got back I cleaned all the fish and salted it down in a big lard tub, and a week after this I took all the fish out and washed it and salt it again. In this way the fish would keep all summer, but when we want fish for a meal my wife would always soak the fish in water for a couple hours so that it would not be too salty. I thought that it paid well to have some friends like those men to come and invite me to go with them and get so much fish. We didn't buy much meat that summer because we had so much fish, and it was good after it was salted for a while.

Fishing with Indians

This was another time and a different experience. While I lived toward Seymour, we had a neighbor whose name was Mitchell Denny. He used to come to visit us quite often, so one day he came and he told me that a bunch of men had made up a fishing crew and that they were going that afternoon, toward evening, and he came to ask me if I didn't want to go with them. Then I asked him who were all going; he mentioned a few men, then he said your brother John is going to take a team and he will take all the crew; only three can ride with me. So I agreed to go but I said I would ride with my brother. He said I'll be here and pick you up about three o'clock, then we will go to John's place and you can then go with them. I said alright.

In the meantime I got things ready; I got my lantern filled with kerosene and trimmed it and sharpened my spear with a file and put on old clothes. I ate lunch early so that I was all ready when he came with his horse and buggy; so I went with him to my brother John's place.

By this time all the other men were there waiting, so they hooked up the team and got everything ready. In those days the roads to the fishing grounds were bad—that is, it was not even graded—so they decided to go around on the Shawano road which is on the north side of the reservation. This is a better road, although it was farther around that way.

We got to the Elm Tree Saloon, and we stopped there until it got dark and some of the men began to drink. But we went down to the creek which was only a little ways from there and we began to fish for a while, and after we had about twenty fish some of the men said it was too early in the evening for the fish to run and they said we might as well go back to the Elm Tree Saloon and wait a while. So I told them that I would stay and fish until they get back because I could tell that they wanted to drink some more, so I stayed there and they went back to the saloon. Well, I stayed and I had twenty-two fish and it was now eleven o'clock and I was beginning to think uneasy about my bunch of men; these were all Indians and most of them do like to drink. I thought, I will wait until midnight, and if they are not there then I will go to the saloon and see what's keeping them so long. I met other men there and I fished with them. It was midnight and they were not back yet, so I took my fish along and went to the saloon.

My bag of fish was heavy already, and when I got there they were all drunk. I went into the saloon with my fish, and one of them said you better sell your fish so we could buy whiskey, but I would not do that because they sold the fish I had with them when they came up. So they must have got mad at me because when the proprietors of the saloon was closing up I was talking to another men who was not in our bunch and they went out and they must have sneaked away because when we came out my brother's team and Mitchell's horse and buggy were nowhere.

So I was left all alone there with half a bag of fish and about ten miles from home. I knew that my brother was drinking too so I suppose he didn't care about me or maybe he didn't know that I was not in the bunch. Well, there was nothing else to do—only go home on foot—so I fixed my load good and started to walk home. So I walked and walked, and the best and shortest way was the railroad track so I walked on that. It was almost daylight when I passed through Oneida Village, but no one was up yet. From there I still had four miles to go, but I kept right on. The sun was up when I got home, and my family was eating breakfast, but after I told them what happened with my bunch of fishermen my wife said, I was expecting something like that would happen because they are all soaks that you went with. But I got my fish home and I cleaned them all but by this time I was so sleepy and tired that I went and laid down and I must have went right to sleep. I slept until noon. When my wife woke me up she said come and eat some of your well-earned fish.

I had quite an experience that time. For going with a bunch of men that drink that's what is likely to happen.

Hunting Muskrats

My neighbor Mitchell Denny used to come to visit me so much when I lived not far from Seymour; he came to our place one evening. He used to always come just about suppertime, and we always invited him to eat supper with us.

So this evening he came—it was late in the fall, about the first part of December—anyway, it was during trapping season. He told us how he was trapping muskrats; he said he had quite a few furs now but he wanted to get more before he sold them. I suppose he wanted to make himself friendly so he said, if you could catch some muskrats I would buy them from you as long as you have no trapper's license. So I told him that I would see if I can catch some and I would let him know. I knew that there were some muskrats along the little creek behind our place.

I asked him how much they are worth. He said he would give me thirty-five cents apiece for them. I told him that I did not know how to take the fur off. He said you don't need to take the fur off, you just catch them and I will take off their fur myself.

The next day I went to this creek with my dog and an ax. I looked all over and there was ice over this creek about two inches thick, so I could walk on it. All at once my dog barked, and he seemed to be looking in the ice and he was moving forward so I wanted to see what he was looking at so I went where he was, and under the ice was two muskrats, so I said get away Bobby and I turned my ax and hit the ice above them. The ice must have hit them hard enough to kill them, so I just chopped a hole big enough and I got them out. Well, I thought, here was seventy cents. I let them lay on the ice and went down farther on the ice.

I came to a spring where my mother-in-law got their water. I looked around there and all at once my dog chased something in the tall dry grass. They made toward the creek, and I ran over and there was another muskrat and I hit the ice again over him. That killed him so I got him out too. While I was getting this one out another muskrat ran into the same hole at the edge of the ice. I could see him crawling under the ice coming toward the hole I made, so I hit the ice again with the ball side of my ax. Well, I got him out too. Then I went home. I had four muskrats, so I put them where they would not freeze so much.

That afternoon I went to a big marsh about a half mile from my house. I knew I had seen some muskrat houses over there. I took my old dog and my ax. We found the houses, then my dog began to smell around and these houses were just marsh hay piled up and they were about three feet high and maybe five feet round at the bottom. I began to chop into this pile of hay and I had quite a lot of hay apart when I noticed that there was something in there because my dog began to get excited. He would jump right into the pile and dig as fast as he could, so I just chopped the hay loose and he pulled them away. We soon got most of the long hay off and came to some fine hay, and all at once I noticed that something was moving under this fine hay. I ran over to a bush of willows and chopped a stick about six feet long, but it was light enough so I could handle it easily. Then I went back and I took my stick and scraped away the loose dry hay and there were a number of muskrats, so I began to pound right over them with the stick. Then after all was still I thought I must have killed them all so I took them out one at a time. I took six muskrats out and I could not find any more in that hole. I thought I had enough to carry home as they were quite heavy, but I already had ten muskrats and that would come to three dollars and a half. That was the first day at hunting muskrats.

Some schoolboys who had to go by Mitchell's place were coming along on the road, and I went out and asked them if they would tell Mitchell that I wanted to see him that night and to tell him to come over. They said alright; we'll tell him.

That evening he came just as he always does, in time for supper, but I told him that I had ten muskrats and to my surprise he had the money. He paid me just as he had agreed, thirty-five cents apiece, so that made three dollars and fifty cents. Well, I thought that was pretty good for one day, especially at that time of the year, and he still wanted more so he told me that he will come again the next evening to see if I got any more.

Then he just warmed the muskrats a little by the stove and he took one outside and in just about five minutes he come back in; he had only the fur. Then he took them out one at a time. It was not long before he had the fur off all of them, then he said, well, I'll see you the next night and he went home. The next morning I got up and went outside and there was a pile of muskrat meat outside. I had to throw all of it in the woods.

During that fall he came there every other night and I always had a few. Then after a while he took them home and skinned them at his place. One time I found couple of them dead. I picked them up and took them home, but he bought them and never said anything. Afterwards I heard that he was getting one dollar and a half apiece for them, so he was making one dollar and fifteen cents on each one I sold to him. Of course he had to take the fur to town to sell them and he had to have a license, so he had some expense while I did not. And I thought I was making pretty good money because at the end of that season I had made seventeen dollars and the hunting I did was only toward evenings and in those days there were not many jobs, so I was satisfied with what I made. Besides, I thought it was quite a sport and fun to look for them and find them.

9.

Four Memorable Days

Several of the writers composed essays regarding four days of their lives that stood out in their memories—each day representing one of the seasons. In this section there are two stories by Stadler King and two by John Skenandore.

Stadler King crammed twenty notebooks full of his own stories as well as interviews with many others, often writing on both sides of the page, which was unusual. "Winter" gives an account of his involvement with a depression-era political organization, the Workers' Alliance. Floyd Lounsbury evidently accepted a role, and Morris Swadesh would have been an enthusiastic supporter.

Fall

This story is of a time when I was young and still single. I remember it well because I wound up that day rather funny. I had worked all summer for people on a nice farm just four miles from the city of Seymour. I had worked for these people since the death of my parents. They were good people, and they used to call me their son because I had no parents. This was just home for me, and they paid me thirty dollars a month and board and washing.

It was in the fall of the year in the month of November, and as all of the important work on the farm had been done there wasn't so much to do. I had a girl who was working in Neenah who had written to me and said that I should go and see her whenever I can. She gave the address in her letter so that I could find her easily. So on this beautiful November morning my boss woke me up, he said "daybreak." I was awake already but I just laid there in bed, so when he came into my room I pretended I just woke and stretched myself full length and said "alright." When he went out I got up and I could see that it was going to be a swell day as this was during what was called Indian summer.

I dressed up and put on my shoes and went downstairs. When I got downstairs I found that there was fire in the dining room heater, and in the kitchen the fire was burning good with kettles on. I put on my jacket and went out to the barn with milk pails and milk cans. The boss was already feeding the horses some hay, so I started to milk; we each had certain cows to milk. I was almost done with one cow when he came to start on his cows. The cows used to stand in two rows and the cows in each row faced away from the other row, so it gave us a good chance to be talking to each other while we were milking.

So when he was settled down to milking I asked him if I could have two or three days' vacation at this time, and he said sure if you wish, I'll get the neighbor boy to help me milk while you are gone. I said I'll be back in three days. Then he said where are you going, and I didn't like to tell him right out so I said I want to visit some of my relatives, and he kinda smiled. I thought maybe he guessed where I want to go, so he said I will take the milk down myself and you can ride along. So when we were done milking we fed the cows and gave the horses their grain and fed all the calves and pigs. Then we loaded the milk cans and just then we were called in to eat breakfast, so we did, and after the mistress had said the grace we started to eat. The boss told the Mrs. that I was going away for a few days and he kinda hinted that I was going to see somebody whom I loved.

When I was done eating I went and cleaned up and put on my best clothes and shoes. Then I went down again so we were getting ready to go out when the Mrs. said I wish you good luck and a good time. Then she said have you enough money and I thought here was a good chance, so I said I could take a little more, so she said wait a minute. By this time the boss went out and she came back and she had a ten-dollar bill in her hand. She said you better take this so you will not be afraid of running short. I took the money and thanked her and said good-bye and she said be a good boy.

I went out and helped hitch up a team; then we went to take the milk to the Seymour Creamery. We got to Seymour and emptied the milk at the creamery, then we drove to a barn where we tied the horses and we went into what was called Hotel Seymour and waited until it was nearly train time. I thought the boss would go home before but he stayed until I went to the depot, which was only a block from the hotel. When I heard the train whistle for Seymour I said well I'll be going and he said I'll go home too. And he said when shall I come to meet you, so I said I'll come back on the evening train on the third day, so he said alright take good care of yourself, and I said Oh yes, and I started to run for the depot. I bought a ticket for Green Bay, and the train came to a stop so I went out and got on the train. It was then quarter to ten o'clock and the train started to move forward. There was no one on the train that I knew, so I sat alone in a seat. As I looked out of the window I saw that nearly all the plowing was done. The trains in those days, that is the Green Bay and Western, had small engines, especially the passenger train. We got into Green Bay at eleven o'clock.

There wasn't much time before dinner, so I just walk over to the east side and I had dinner in a restaurant; I ordered ham and eggs and coffee. When I was through eating I asked the cashier how much was my dinner and she said forty cents so I paid. Then I came back across the river, and at twenty minutes to twelve I got on a streetcar for Kaukauna and on this car I knew no one. We went through De Pere and got in Kaukauna before one o'clock, and there was another car there waiting for connections so I got on that car and went into Appleton and still I changed cars in Appleton for Neenah.

I got into Neenah at two o'clock and I started to inquire where Mr. J. R. Bloom lived and someone directed me to what street I should go on to find the home, and I knew the number so I walked and walked until I came to the street (which was given me in the letter) and I kept my eyes on the numbers on the doors.

After a while I knew I was getting closer and then I came to the number and I knew I was on the right street so I made myself bold and went to the door and rang the bell, and who should come to open the door but the very person for whom I came this long way to see.

I suppose that we were both so surprised that we must have lost our consciousness, and I came to again as we let each other go. Then we sat down and I began to look around the room and I saw that rich people must live in this house because everything was so nice and the furniture must be expensive.

She began to tell me that she likes this place; then she said the owners were good people and they both had good jobs and the children were all at school. She told me what time the children would be back and what time the owners would be back so I said I will be gone by that time, but I said I will come back tonight when they are all home—then we can go to some show. She said come here at seven o'clock; I will be done with everything then and I will be ready.

I only stayed about an hour because I was afraid that something might happen that would make them come back earlier and find me there with their hired maid and this might spoil her good reputation with them so we bid each other good-bye until seven o'clock. As I went back to town I took good notice of the way I went, so that I could find the place again easily even if it was at night. It was then nearly four o'clock, so I had three hours to bum around. As I did not know anyone in that city I did not know where to go, so I just walked in the streets and visited some stores and I found that Neenah was a beautiful little city. It was a clean city, and I could imagine that there were many rich people in this city as there were so many beautiful homes.

It was not quite suppertime when I went in to a restaurant and ordered a good supper. I ordered ham and eggs and french-fried potatoes and coffee and a nice piece of pie, and I still had lots of time so I took time in eating. But finally I was done; then I went to the railroad depot and inquired about trains going north to Green Bay, and I found that I could take a ten o'clock train which would get me in Green Bay before midnight. Then I went back to the home where my girl was working, and when I got there I rang the doorbell and the owner came to the door and the first thing I did was to inquire for Olive and he says yes she is here and he let me come in and he took me into the kitchen where she was. She pretended to be surprised, and she gave introductions to us and the mistress of the house. Then we were left alone and she went in her room only a little while and she came and said well I am ready, so we went into the streets toward the main street where the show house was.

We did not walk alone but two in one. She knew the city better than I did, so she took me to the show house where I paid thirty cents for the both of us and we stayed there until nine o'clock. When we came out we went into a drugstore and I treated her to some refreshments. Then we went back to her home, but this time we did not walk fast—we took our time. Finally I had to bid her good-bye at the door. Then I went back toward the town and up to the depot and I got me a ticket for Green Bay. It was not long before the train pulled in and came to a stop, so I got on it to a seat where I could be alone.

The conductor came by collecting the tickets, and I gave him mine. He took a look at it then he pulled out a small slip and wrote something on it then he stuck this in my hat and went on. As the train went through a number of cities, and it was nice and warm in the cars, and I must have got tired making this trip, and I was not used to staying up so late, the last city that I remember going through was Kaukauna. I must have went to sleep. I did not know when we went through De Pere, and the train must have stopped in Green Bay and I was asleep. I did not wake up until the conductor woke me. He says wake up and after I woke he said where are you going; I said Green Bay. He smiled at me and said, well we are way past Green Bay. He said you must have been sleeping when the train got to Green Bay and he said we changed crews in Green Bay and that's where I got on. Then he reached up and gave two jerks on a rope that runs above from one end of the car to the other and immediately the train slowed up and he said you will have to get off here and walk back. So he went ahead of me and I followed him. He took along a little stool, and when the train came to a stop he went down and he placed the stool down so I might step on it as I got off. Then he told me that the best way for me would be to walk in the middle of the track and follow it back to Green Bay, so I thought he was good to me and he went up and got on and the train pulled ahead. After it went by I stepped onto the tracks and walked toward Green Bay.

I walked and walked and finally I could see signs of getting closer to town and I could see lights, but it must have been a long way because it took so long to get back to the depot. Everything was closed up when I got back, and I had to look for a place where I could sleep. The hotels were all locked up so I tried other hotels, and as I walked from one hotel to another I thought that I was spending my vacation very well as I was looking for a place to sleep way after midnight. I went into the Blackstone Hotel. This was not locked but there was no one around, so I went right upstairs and I found a room that was opened so I just took off my clothes and laid down. I thought I will tell the proprietor how I got in, in the morning. I laid there and I was thinking that I would stay in Green Bay all the next day and go back to Seymour on the day after, so I must have went to sleep soon after I laid down.

This was the end of that day and part of the next.

Winter

One winter morning in 1938 I got up real early because all arrangements were made for a bunch of five men to go to Madison to a big conference that was to take place that day.

There were circulars distributed to all WPA projects and the Workers Alliance of America. At an earlier meeting, five men were elected or chosen to go to Madison on this day. The conference was called by the head officials of the Workers Alliance in the state to discuss certain problems concerning the Alliance. Delegates came from all parts of the state to talk about what could be demanded from the WPA. I happened to be one of the delegates elected to go; there was Mark Powless, George Peters,

Lawrence Kerstetter, and Floyd Lounsbury. Mr. Morris Swadesh, who was from Madison, was very much interested in the Workers Alliance because he knew that many people cooperating would have more power and influence than one single person, so he donated the car for this bunch to ride in going there.[1] So I was up early and made fires in both the heater stove and the kitchen stove.

It was not long before the rooms were warm and my wife and I got up. It was still dark, so I had lighted up all lamps. I helped her to get breakfast cooked and I got plenty of water for her for the day and I hauled in plenty of wood. Then she said breakfast is ready and we called the boys to get up so they got up and when every one of us was ready we sat down to eat.

After breakfast I went and got ready; I put on my best clothes and shoes and rubbers and dusted off my overcoat and winter cap.

It was just then getting daylight outside but it was nearly seven o'clock. We had made an agreement that we should start at seven-thirty, and as I never like to be late or behind time I started out at quarter of seven, I only had quarter of a mile to go to the Village of Oneida, where we were suppose to meet.

When I went out I could see that it had snowed some and there were places where it had drifted quite a bit, and when I got on the road it was all full of snow so I thought of our trip. When I got in the village George Peters was there, so he and I waited there for Mark and our car. We waited and waited and it was after eight o'clock when Kerstetter came walking up, so he told us that Lounsbury could not start the car so he wanted a mechanic to go down and start the car for him. But there was no one at the garage yet, so we three waited for him too.

While we waited there, Mark came and told us that he would not go, and just about this time Lounsbury drove up there. He had got someone to push his car and got it started in that way. Well, Mark was wearing his overalls and they all told him that he must go and they told him to get in the car with us and we would drive to his place so he can change clothes. Finally he agreed, so we drove down the road to his place. The snowplow had made one trip down so we went along pretty good; we were out about two miles when we met the snowplow coming back, and we had to drive into a farmer's yard so the snowplow could go by. After it went by we turned around to go on the road again but we got stuck in the snowdrift. We all got out and pushed until we managed to get on the road again. The snowplow had made the road wider and there was ice in the bottom, and as we speeded up again somehow our car zigzagged and Lounsbury could not keep it in the road and the car just turned right around and into the snowbank, where it stopped.

Well, we had to get out again and pushed the car out and turned it the other way; then we went on again and got to Mark's place. Then he went in to change clothes, so we waited there for him until he came out and that seemed like hours. After a while we were all set again, so we drove back to Oneida. We could tell that our car was not working just right, but we went right through Oneida and took Highway 54 until we got to Highway 55; then we went south. We passed Freedom about a mile when our car got worse so we stopped, and none of us knew much about cars so we waited until a farmer came along and they asked him to push us back to Freedom—so he did. He pushed us to a garage where they got the garage man to work on it, and this took some time so it was ten o'clock before we started out again. We got to Kaukauna and then we took Highway 41 to Appleton and continued on this road right into Oshkosh, and it was so close to dinnertime that they decided to stop there and eat dinner. We had a good dinner, and George Peters, who kept our expenses, paid for it.

Well, we were all set again and out of Oshkosh we took Highway 26 until we came to 155, and this road runs right into Madison. We got into Madison at four thirty, and Mr. Lounsbury knew just where we should go so we drove right up to the hotel where the conference was to be, but there were so many cars that we had to drive quite a ways before we found a place to park. Then we walk back to the hotel and registered as delegates, and then each one of us was assigned what department he was to represent. I was assigned to go to the relief department, and we were given the room number and the floor so I went on an elevator to the right floor and got off. I looked through the halls for the door number, and finally I found it way at one end of the hall. So without knocking I went right in.

Soon as I went in I saw that there were a great number of people there and it was a big room like a regular hall and I went right up and presented my card with my name on it, which told that I was a delegate from Oneida. I gave it to two men who sat at a table and appeared to be the chairman and secretary, and they said alright we shall tend to your questions after a little while, so I sat down on one of the chairs with the rest of the people and I just listened to what was going on. There were so many questions that they talked about. One man or woman would get up after another and present their question. Then it was suppertime so the chairman said we will now adjourn until seven thirty tonight, and I hope all of you will be back here again. So we all came out and went downstairs; some got on the elevators, but I preferred to walk down the stairs.

When I got down on the first floor I find my gang was waiting there for me already. Then we went out to have supper, and we got in our car and went to the home of Morris Swadesh. We went a long way before we got there and we parked the car in the street and then we went up to the house and Mr. Lounsbury knocked on the door. Then a man came and opened the door and we could see that this man knew Mr. Lounsbury and we all went in. Then Lounsbury introduced us all to this man. This man's name was Sam Swadesh, and he sure was a nice man, and he and his wife gave us a good supper. After supper we sat in the front room for a while and all they talked about was what problems we should present, and they asked me what they said about my question about Oneida, but I told them that my turn did not come yet. So they told me a few questions which I should ask.

It was not long before we went again to the hotel where we are having the conference, so we got back there and went to our rooms. A few people spoke, and then the secretary got up and said we also have with us tonight one real true American. He is from Oneida, and I know the conditions in Oneida, and we should help them because I know that they are deprived of many things from the relief and work to which they are entitled. So he said I will read what they want and what they need, and he read the requests that was written on the paper I had given him. Then he asked if I had any more to say, so I got up and said that the main purpose of me being here was to complain of the fact that so many men who are able to work could not get on the work projects, and those who can't work are getting relief which is not sufficient for them. That is, they are not getting enough.

About this time they started to ask Mr. Flanner, who was the head man in the state for the WPA, a lot of questions, and he answered them all, and he said that he was doing the best he can with what money he gets but he said that he would be willing to do still better if there were more money and the Alliance could ask for more money from the government and state and that he was with them.

This meeting lasted until ten o'clock, when we were told that the meeting will continue in the morning and that a general meeting of all the different departments will meet in the big assembly room in the afternoon the next day. That meeting adjourned till morning. Then we went down and I met my partners again, so we went to our car and then drove to the Swadesh home. When we got back it was getting late, so we did not stay up very long as we still had the next day in which to tend to the conference. They showed us our rooms and we were all glad to see a bed so we did not hesitate when they said do you want to rest now. We said yes, then we went into our rooms and I got ready to go to bed and it was not long before I was sound asleep and that finished that day.

JOHN A. SKENANDORE

> Mr. Skenandore began his off-farm work life as an unskilled laborer on the roads and eventually become an assistant to the Brown County highway commissioner, checking on the quantity and quality of road-building materials supplied by contractors. The depression ended this career, of course. His "Summer Day" tells how he began that job.

Winter

Early one winter morning about the year of 1914, as I awoke I got to thinking what I was going to do for spending money for church entertainment coming up within three days. I didn't have any money, and I certainly wanted to go and see it. So as I lay there thinking I thought I would try hunting first. So I got out of my bed and did my chores in a hurry: that is, feed the horses and water them and clean the stable; then I hurried back to wash up for breakfast.

Mother saw that I was in an extra rush that morning and asked me what I was going to do that I seem to be in such rush. Well, I said, there's an entertainment coming soon and I haven't any money so I am going to try and make some. Well, she said, I think I can help you out on that. No, I said, give me a chance to earn it first, then if I can't make it I will accept your help. I still have three days to earn a little money. Alright then, she said, but how are you going to make that? I said, that's very simple. I am going to make that money with pleasure. I said, I am going hunting and what game I get I am taking into De Pere tomorrow and sell it.

I ate my breakfast and hit for the woods. At that time there was lots of small game left, plenty of woods for them to hide in. Everything came just my way that day. It had snowed a little first part of the night, so I decided not to take my dog along and I tied him up so he won't follow me. I just got in the woods and there was rabbit tracks already. I tracked him a little ways and found where he was sitting, so I wasn't going to take any chances by letting him run and shot his head off in his nest, picked him up and dropped him in my hunting bag.

I went a little farther and saw another rabbit track and tracked him next, and while I was tracking this one a partridge flew up in front of me, but I was too ready for anything like that. I let him have it and down he came and I put him in the hunting bag too and continued tracking the rabbit, and this one didn't get very far and his head also came off and he jumped in my bag.

I only had twelve shells to hunt on, so I took special pains in shooting so there won't be any waste. These shells lasted me until about three o'clock in the afternoon and the load I was lugging around was getting very heavy so I was rather glad when I did ran out of shells so I made a beeline for home. And while I was walking by a small swamp I noticed a rabbit's tracks had gone into the little swamp, so I took the pack off my shoulder and laid it down on the ground and put my gun on it, then tracked the rabbit into the swamp. I only walked a few steps into the swamp and saw the rabbit sitting in the grass. I slowly backed up until I got out of his sight, then I looked around for something to hit him with, and the only thing I could find was a pine notch. So I took this notch and went back to where the rabbit was sitting, and as soon as I got close enough I threw the pine notch at him. But the rabbit jumped about the same time as I threw the notch and met the flying notch and it hit him right on the head and he keeled over. If this rabbit only set still I would have missed him by about two feet, but it looks like he knew that I was making the money for good purpose and helped me out. I then dropped him in the bag with the rest of the game and went home.

After I got home then I started to clean the game—took all the inwards out of them and hung them up. I got six partridges and seven rabbits out of the twelve shots. I would have got more partridges if I had more shells, as I had left a few go which I was not sure of getting.

Partridges at that time used to sell for forty cents apiece and rabbits at twenty-five cents apiece, so I made lots more than what I needed.

After I got these animals all ready it was time for my chores again, so even though I was very tired from walking in the jungles I got at my chores early, and before supper cleaned the stable again, gave the horses lots of bedding, and fed and watered them again, as that was all they had to do for that day. And by the time I got my chores all done it was time to eat supper, and I got cleaned up again, ate my supper, and soon after that I went to bed as I was very tired. I was figuring on a long trip the next day with horse and cutter to De Pere, which is about eight miles one way. At that time we used to think it was long ways as we traveled so slow with horse and rig.

Well, as I say I went to bed. I'll never forget the way my mother used to fix my bed. She had an old-fashion mattress on which she had shredded corn husk for stuffing—and the way she used to work these husks every day so that my mattress would look like a balloon. And when I lay in it, why I would almost go out of sight. And believe me it was comfortable. I appreciated this particular mattress more when I am tired and that night I must have went right to sleep as soon as I hit the bed.

Summer

On one summer after having all my garden weeded I thought of looking for a job, so I got up early enough and went to Green Bay. I rode in with my sisters as they were working in town and had to start by seven o'clock in the morning. So I got off of their car as we got in town and went straight for Brown County Highway Commissioner Office. I knew at that time that the commissioner is always in his office by seven in the morning, so I got there just before seven and walked into the office.

The highway commissioner and the engineer were both in the office as I walked in. They both looked to see who came in and then looked at one another and then laughed. The commissioner said, "Who told you that we need you?" he said. "We were just talking about you, and we were just getting ready to come over to your place to hire you on a damn good job." I said, "OK, that's just what I came for is a damn good job." He said, "You are on a road-paving job in Wrightstown, but can you be gone for a week at a time as this job is in Wrightstown and it will be hard for you to get back every night without a car." So after telling me that he wants me as a material inspector then I wondered if I would be able to handle it and didn't know if I should try. But I thought as long as I was looking for a job I might as well grasp the first chance. And he said, "Art the engineer here will take you back home to tell your family good-bye and take what you will need for the rest of the week, and he will take you on the job and start you off with what we want you to do." "Alright," I said, "if I can't handle the work I'll quit and you can put someone else on."

Then we pulled out of town and came back home. My wife didn't know what to say when I asked her if she can manage the rest of the week without me as I had hired out by the week. Of course after I told her what I was going to get and to meet me every Saturday afternoon in Green Bay, then she said she would manage. Then we pulled out all the way down; I didn't have much to say, as I was rather nervous to think of the responsible job I was going to do.

And being the only Indian on that job, I didn't know just how the Pollarks [Polacks, Poles] would take me, and the contractor has a full crew of them. We finally got to where they were working just outside of Wrightstown. The engineer took me around to a different part where these men were working, and the way they looked at me was enough to scare a lion. He introduced me to the foreman and I found him very nice and he invited us over for dinner as it was just about noon. So we came back to his camp and I noticed all of his men were boarding with him, but he gave us a special table to eat on and told us to come to this table every day and without charge. After dinner we went into town to look for a place for lodging, and after we found a place then we went back to the bins and checked on the scales and weights and he told me not to let anybody change the weights unless he said so. He said my place will only be by these bins and to see that the material is weighted right to the needle and with the right kind of material. He also said, "If you see anything wrong shut them down and send for me. I'll be out on the grade every day."

And the rest of the afternoon we spent our time on the grade cross-sectioning until quitting time when we went back to eat again. After supper I got a chance to talk to quite a few of the men and gain friends. The mixer was suppose to start the next day, so I had a chance to gain friends even out on the grade. About nine o'clock then I went to my room and went to bed.

The Oneida Ethnological Study under Attack

These three pieces chronicle an attack on the Oneida Ethnological Study by a white farmer, E. P. Boland. His letter to Congressman Joshua L. Johns (which was published in the *Congressional Record*) is followed by a speech by Oscar Archiquette, mostly in response to Boland's letter. This is supplemented by a letter from the chair of the Menominee tribal council in support of the Oneidas.[1]

Letter to Rep. Joshua L. Johns

WPA Projects
EXTENSION OF REMARKS of
HON. JOSHUA L. JOHNS of Wisconsin
IN THE HOUSE OF REPRESENTATIVES
Friday, August 1, 1941
Letter from E. P. Boland, Green Bay, Wisconsin

Mr. Johns, Mr. Speaker, under leave to extend my remarks in the RECORD I include the following letter:

Green Bay, Wis.
July 15, 1941
Congressmen Joshua L. Johns,
Eighth District of Wisconsin
Washington DC

Dear Mr. Johns:

I want you to know that I have enjoyed reading your weekly letters, They certainly contain a lot of information and it is too bad that everyone, not only in the eighth district but throughout the Nation, does not have an opportunity to read them.

I also want you to know that I enjoyed [your?] last talks over the radio, and as I listen to you talk and read your weekly letters, I often wonder what the American people are headed for.

There is one thing at this time that I would like to bring to your attention although I believe you are very familiar with conditions, and that is when farmers are begging for men to do their haying and harvesting, there still continues to be operating a lot of useless, worthless WPA projects. The one that I am going to describe should be one for the book.

Out in the town of Hobart—that used to be part of the Oneida Indian Reservation—there are still quite a number of Indians who, up to the time the relief took over, were all willing to work and able to make their own living. This took a period of about 25 years to bring them up to this point. Within 30 days after the relief set in, it put the Oneida Indians back about 25 years. One of the WPA projects which I have in mind is about 12 big fat lazy Indians

sitting up at the Episcopal Hall for about 2 years, supposed
to be writing the Oneida Indian language. After they had
it written, they didn't know what to do with it, so they continued
with the same project, or a new one, to write a dictionary
for the Indian language; each one of them getting $70 a month.

(Now can you tell me who wants to learn the Indian language,
and what are they going to do with the dictionary?)

The reason why I set this project out is because of the fact that
many of the farmers in this locality are unable to get help to put
in their hay. Four of these fellows used to belong to my crew, but
while they can get $70 a month writing the Indian language they
will never work for me or for anyone else owning a farm, and the
best part of it is that most of the money those fellows earn on
WPA goes for booze.

Now, in my opinion, that is one project that should be halted
immediately, as there is plenty of work right in their
neighborhood that they can do and get, and would be doing
something for the good of their country. (Of course, these
fellows are our New Dealers).

Then we have several projects over in our courthouse. A
bunch of loafers are sitting around tables blocking the hallways,
supposed to be working on old records or trying to clear up the
family tree of a lot of the old, early French frog catchers or
muskrat hunters who lived along the banks of the Fox River in
early days in little shanties.

I feel, Mr. Johns, that you will agree with me, and I know that
it is hard, single handed, to do anything to remedy matters and
break up the political machine, but I believe that if more
publicity were given to the useless, worthless projects of WPA,
that today there is absolutely no cause for it, and that some of
the "rubber stamp" Congressmen would wake up.

In closing, I will say that it is just too bad that 75 percent of
our Congressmen and Senators are not men of your caliber and
ideas, and the other 25 percent could be "rubber stamps." With
kind personal regards, I remain

Respectfully yours,
E. P. Boland

. . .

Report and Speech at General Tribal Council
by Oscar Hobart Archiquette, Vice Chairman of
Oneida Indians Incorporated of Wisconsin²
At Epworth Hall
August 20, Wednesday 8 p.m. 1941

Mr. Chairman, government officials, ladies and gentleman,

I do not know since when I became a white man. I have been
asked to make a report for the Executive Committee in English
and in my genuine American Indian language. I don't like to
speak the white man's language because I am an Indian, but I
can, when I have to. Disregard all mistakes I make.

We the Executive Committee approved of a community hall,
high school, and a CCC project for drainage ditches, building of
fences, improving of roads, and to build a recreation park with
fire places where a person can fry hotcakes, and ball ground
where the womenfolks can play basketball.

The executive and other committees met once a month with
government officials at Oneida and Hobart Relief Office for the
past 12 months; most of the committeemen were present at
these meetings. We have reclaimed the land adjoining the state
reformatory property; same can now be assigned to Oneidas.

We recommended the following to the government officials
for a business enterprise for Oneidas: first, beef cattle; second,
sheep; third, a canning factory. That is as far as we went with it.

Our future program is the following: first, high school;
second, community hall; third, more land; fourth, more
rehabilitation funds; fifth, defense program or ammunition
plant for Oneidas. The reason I mention this is because I
understand the wages paid to employees on defense work is
$1.00 an hour and they are everlastingly striking for higher
wages. We Oneidas only get $0.40 an hour, and if the
government would set up some kind of defense project and pay
us one dollar an hour, we would be very glad. We, the Oneida
tribe of Indians, are willing to set aside a tract of land for a
building site for defense work. We Oneidas have been in every

war this country has ever had. We have defended our country even before the white people had war between themselves in this country. We Oneidas are offering our language for defense. We Oneidas are still ready to defend our country by one hundred percent.[3]

Sixth, WPA building project; seventh, project to quarry limestone for foundation of houses and barns; eighth, cooperative store. I think I better not say anything anymore. The superintendent might change his mind about installing us. I will say a few more words after our installation.

Report of application for land by chairman of land committee, for which I interpreted. There are 92 applications for land, totaling 5000 acres. There are eight families assigned land during the past year. We wish to help everybody but what can we do when there is no land to assign.

I am going to read a letter written by E. P. Boland to Congressman Joshua L. Johns of Washington DC. The letter is attached herewith. I want you to know the contents of this letter; it is not a secret.

Mr. Boland claims he couldn't get anybody to put a few spears of his hay in the barn because there are 12 fat lazy Indians sitting in church writing Indian language getting $70.00 per month. There is nobody getting $70.00 per month on our project, and it is not a language project; it is Ethnological Study of the Oneidas. Most of what Boland said in his letter is a lie; if there is another English word which means "lie" it's that too. I will never work for Boland as long as I breathe on this earth. If anybody wants to tell Boland what I said, they are welcome to it. I don't care if I lose my WPA job tomorrow on account of it. I mean every word I said.

Boland claims up to the time relief was set up we were self-supporting, and it took the white people 25 years to get us to this point. Within 30 days after the relief was set up, it put us back 25 years.

I wish Boland could put us back 25 years. Twenty-five years ago most of us Oneidas had homes and were self-supporting. Friends, I think it is now time to wake up and cooperate. We should all hold our hands together and not let a hayseed like Boland keep us down in the mud with his low wages. What Boland wants is for us to everlastingly haul manure for him at the low wages he pays. He does not want us to elevate ourselves to better living conditions; he does not want us to work on a job where they pay more than he does. Boland acquired land from Oneidas for little or nothing, made a few dollars by hiring Indian labor, paying the lowest for labor in this community. Mr. Boland is biting the hand that feeds him.

The meaning of Boland's letter, about 25 percent rubber-stamps, means just this: according to his judgement there are 75 percent rubber-stamp congressmen today. The wording of his letter tells he is no businessman. I have very little education but I can write a better business letter than Boland, even if his skin is white. Let us not lay down doubled up and not say anything. Let us brace up and defend ourselves. And we will defend ourselves as long as I am a member of the executive committee!! If we don't, our whip will be this. Oh, the Oneidas are too ignorant to defend themselves; they depend on someone else to do the talking for them. Friends, let us forget our petty hard feelings against each other—just because maybe I passed you without looking at you and did not greet you.

It is now time to stick together, help each other, and we will! We are going to answer Boland's letter. We will show that the Oneidas have enough gumption to defend themselves at this time. Our neighbor the Menominee Indians are backing us one hundred percent. I will read you the answer given Boland's letter by Mr. James G. Frechette, chairman of the Menominee Indian Advisory Council.

According to this letter the Menominees knew about Boland's letter to Congressman Joshua L. Johns before we did. We, the Oneida Tribe of Indians realize our neighbors the Menominee Indians have come to our rescue. We therefore hold the Menominees in the highest of esteem.

· · ·

Letter to Rep. Joshua L. Johns

The response to E. P. Boland's letter from the chairman of the
Menominee Indian Advisory Council, James G. Frechette.

Keshena, Wisconsin
August 12, 1941

Honorable Joshua L. Johns
House of Representatives
Washington DC

Dear Congressman:

The relationship of your office and the Menominee Indian
people has been none other than pleasant and most helpful (on
your part) when it comes to aid for our Indians. The past years'
records show that with your assistance the Menominee Indian
people have gained much needed Congressional aid for their
future social and economic welfare; for this we are very
appreciative and thankful. The Menominee people are very
conscious of the fact that Congressman Johns is our friend.
However today it becomes our duty to come forward and defend
our neighboring Tribe and Friends of the Oneida Nation who
were so unjustly used as an example in a political brawl by a
certain Mr. E. P. Boland, of Green Bay, Wisconsin, and printed
in the Congressional Record-Appendix, August 1, 1941, Page
A3945 under title WPA Projects.

It is very unfortunate that Mr. Boland must use the Oneida
Indians as an example for his attack on the WPA Projects,
especially when he quotes so little of the facts. A short review of
the history of the Oneida Indians may be of interest to the
people who read the Congressional Record.

In 1821 the Oneida Indians were removed from their home in
the East by their government and transplanted in the wilds of
the Middle West and left to survive as best they knew how. They
left homes that were as progressive and modern as the times
permitted but the advance of what was then termed
"Civilization" had caused our government to pass a law to move

all Indians west of the Mississippi River. When the Oneidas
came west they were befriended by the Menominee Indians who
in the Treaty of 1821–1822 ceded to the Oneidas a strip of land
four miles wide at right angles to the Fox river, with what is now
Little Chute in the center. Later they were led into the unholy
allotment system, a system the government had devised where
Indians were allowed to cut up their reservations and dispose of
their holdings to the white men. The Oneidas fell victim to this
scheme and surrendered their holdings in this state for let's say
"Thirty pieces of Silver." But this is not the whole story; under
the allotment system these unfortunate Indians were bled white
by the very alert land sharks of the time. Many a choice piece of
land was bargained for after the Indian was thoroughly doped
with intoxicants.

Sure the depression that hit the whole country found its way
into the Oneida Community (what was left of it) the same as the
rest of the Good Old U.S.A., but fortunately for all the unfortunate people of this Great Nation we had a Government capable
of finding a way to battle starvation, famine and sickness,
a Government capable of stepping in and lending a helping
hand to its unfortunate wards (even including the Indians).

Can Mr. Boland qualify his statement that the WPA has put
the Oneida Indians back about 25 years simply because these
Indians no longer work for the Peon wage *some* of the farmers in
his locality paid during the great uplift trend toward teaching
the Oneida Indian to work (a period of 25 years according to Mr.
Boland's statement)? I'm wondering how many of these Indians
still have money coming for work done for such problem
solving masterminds as Mr. Boland and their big farms capable
of hiring a crew of men to do the work. What I'm wondering is
where were these depression wizards before the WPA.

Mr. Boland also states that 12 big fat lazy Indians at Oneida
were writing a dictionary and the Indian language and each
drawing a salary of $70.00. My, what a disgrace to find such
extravagance in this great country of ours. Can it be possible in
this day and age? Would it meet with Mr. Boland's approval if
they wrote a masterpiece on "Why don't all the people in this
country own and operate large farms sufficiently large enough

to hire a crew of men (such as Mr. Boland's)?" For Mr. Boland's
information I'd like to say: the only thing that the Oneida people
have left that the white man could not take from him is his
language, and if our Government is willing to pay them for
making their language history I say GOD BLESS OUR
GOVERNMENT, for it won't be long before men like Mr. Boland
will want to deprive them of their language also. (Only ten years
or so ago the past administration in the Indian Service forbid
Indian children to speak their own language in the schools.)
Further I'd like to answer Mr. Boland's query, ("Now can you tell
me who wants to learn the Indian Language, and what are they
going to do with the dictionary?"). Does Mr. Boland also wish to
know why our great institutions teach Greek, Spanish, French,
German or any other language or maybe you don't have to know
anything to be a big farm operator. Also maybe he wishes to
discredit the works of Noah Webster.

Mr. Boland also is an authority on quoting the fact that MOST
of the money those fellows *earn* on WPA (now he admits it), goes
for booze. It is common knowledge that plenty of others not on
WPA can qualify for this honor and since when does Mr. Boland
rate sufficient to challenge an American right to do as he
chooses with his daily wage.

Ah, and at last it comes out, he puts in parenthesis (of course,
those fellows are our New Dealers). Shame on you Mr. Boland,
your politics smells. Maybe you rather see them still in the bread
lines.

Might I say in closing that the Oneida Indians as a whole are
among the most industrious and hard working class of people
in the State. They have an established record as the best
woodsmen ever to work in our industry, The Menominee Indian
Mills Operations. Many have intermarried in our Tribe and are a
credit to any Community; industrious and hard working is
second nature to this hardy race of people.

I also know that many have established themselves in the
Government Service throughout this country and also in many
of our Industrious Cities and are a credit to our Nation as Good
American Citizens who mind their own business, respect their

fellow man, and are always willing to lend a helping hand to
their unfortunate neighbor.

It is also to be remembered that the Oneida Indian today has
no industry of his own, no natural resources that he may take
advantage of such as we, the more fortunate Indians here on the
Menominee Indian Reservation. All he has to depend on is the
GOOD EARTH and his GOVERNMENT. Yes Mr. Boland, we are
not all Rich Farmers who need a crew of men to do our work,
but we thank our God each day that we live in a Country where
our Government knows what to do in a Crisis. That we live in
the land of the Free and our country right or wrong will always
find the American Indians ready to defend Her Principles and
Her beliefs, but above all we are fully convinced that the system
of government devised by the American people is the greatest
system of government that God has ever permitted to exist. We
had long learned that the great leaders we have at the seat of our
government are chosen by the voice of the American People, and
once that choice is made, whether in the President's chair, the
Senate or the House of Representatives, whether he be
Democrat, Republican, or any other Party, is all forgotten the
minute he takes the oath of office. He then becomes the image
that we the common people look up to as our Leader, Him we
love, Honor and Respect. It is no small wonder that we sing to
our heart's content, so the whole world will hear us, "GOD
BLESS AMERICA".

Very Respectfully and sincerely,
James G. Frechette
Chairman, Menominee Indian Advisory Council
Keshena, Wisconsin

NOTES

Introduction

1. By the time of the second undertaking, the name of the WPA had been changed from Works Progress Administration to Works Projects Administration.

2. In the language of the Oneidas, their name is usually given as Oneyote-ʔa·kâ·, which means "People of the Standing Rock." The five original nations were, from west to east, the Seneca, Cayuga, Onondaga, Oneida, and Mohawk (Tuscarora, the sixth nation, was admitted to the league later, in 1722). The nomenclature of these peoples is complex. Each nation of the league had its own language and names for itself and for the others, and the intruding Europeans had their own ways of rendering the same names in French, Dutch, English, and German (see Fenton 1978:319–321 on the variety of Iroquois names). Today there is some tendency for young people to reject the term Iroquois (whether pronounced /kwoy/ or /kwa/) and to prefer the term Hodenoshaunee.

3. Population estimates are at least as difficult to deal with as nomenclature. Elizabeth Tooker's table for the estimates of the number of fighting men in the league between 1660 and 1779 suggests that there could not have been more than ten thousand people encompassed by the confederacy (1978:421). And these numbers were drastically reduced by losses in epidemics and war. Campisi doubts that the Oneidas numbered more than a thousand before the nineteenth century (1974:34).

4. That the league frequently failed to maintain internal peace or unite against outsiders has often been noted, but this organization certainly played an important historical role.

5. The eastern end of Lake Oneida was the center of their home territory, but they controlled a large hunting area that, in today's geographical terms, stretched south from the St. Lawrence River to the northern border of Pennsylvania, and from just west of Syracuse to beyond the city of Utica (see Campisi 1974:27–29; Hauptman and McLester 2002:2, map).

6. Aside from their importance in the wars that decided the destinies of Canada and the United States, it is often said that the confederacy may have been an inspiration for some of the founders of the American republic, and

their influence has been felt in numerous other ways. The earliest indigenous Anglo-American literature, the works of James Fenimore Cooper, filled with Cooper's version of the Iroquois, had an impact on the image of America and of Indians, both in America and in the rest of the world. Iroquois society and culture played a central role in the origins of American anthropology through their role in the writings of Lewis Henry Morgan. Iroquois claims to land and monetary compensation for the land that was taken from them two centuries ago continue to haunt New York State and the courts, even while the depressed economies of that region gain from the recent development of Indian gaming and other enterprises.

7. These events are well documented. See, e.g., Hauptman 1999; Campisi 1988b; chapters by Vecsey, Locklear, Campisi, and others in Vecsey and Starna 1988; and chapters by Hauptman, Horsman, Campisi, and Locklear in part 1, pp. 9–89, of Hauptman and McLester 1999. Iroquois nations, including the Wisconsin Oneidas, are still pursuing claims for land or monetary compensation for lost lands in New York State (Vecsey and Starna 1988). The writings of the Oneida Ethnological Study include numerous accounts of several political organizations that worked in vain for compensation in the 1920s and 1930s. See also Hauptman 1981:70–79.

8. This movement was inspired by a Mohawk prophet in Ontario who, in 1798, called for a return to the old rituals as well as for reformed behavior, including abstinence from alcohol. Handsome Lake, the Seneca prophet who created the important reform and revitalization movement known as the Longhouse religion (Wallace 1970), had little following among the Oneidas (Campisi 1974:104).

9. Much has been written about Eleazer Williams, a dynamic man who also created quite a stir when he claimed, in 1853, that he was the "Lost Dauphin," the son of King Louis XVI and Marie Antoinette of France (Ellis 1856; Bloomfield 1907:145ff., 193ff.; Martin n.d.:20–22; Cornelius 1999:129–133).

10. For documentation of the numerous treaties, sales, and litigation see Hauptman 1999. The Oneidas were not the only Indians from the East who were induced or forced to move to Wisconsin in those years. The Stockbridge, Brotherton, Potawatomi, and Munsee groups also found their way there (Lurie 2002:8–12).

11. Foremost among these were Jedediah Morse, a prominent minister, famous geographer, and sometime congressman and federal commissioner (and father of the inventor of the telegraph); Lewis Cass, the powerful governor of Michigan Territory; and David A. Ogden, land speculator and onetime congressman (see Hauptman and McLester 2002:9, 31).

12. This reservation of 65,400 acres was far less than they had been promised originally. They had been led to believe that they would be sharing six mil-

lion acres with the Menominees and Winnebagos (Ho-Chunk) (e.g., Horsman 1999; Hauptman 1999; maps in Campisi 1974:108, and Hauptman and McLester 2002:49).

13. Basehart 1952 documents these changes over the centuries.

14. These are the custom of going from house to house (*Hoyan*) on New Year's Day, the collection of "holy water" at dawn on Easter Sunday, the Tenth-day Feast, and perhaps certain practices at wakes.

15. Oneida singing groups and their activities are a frequent topic in the WPA interviews. Choral groups sometimes went on tours sponsored by the church missions, and with the advent of radio they were heard on local stations. Choral singing continues to be an important part of Oneida culture and identity—at least for the older generation. The same hymns are sung today, in church, at wakes, and on other occasions, and cassettes and CDs are available (see Campisi 1974:184–185; O'Grady 1991).

16. This region remains an important center for the lumber and paper industry today, with timber grown further north and paper mills located throughout central Wisconsin and the Fox River Valley.

17. The Civil War brought other blows to the Wisconsin Oneidas. Whether out of loyalty to the United States, from their own fighting tradition, or through the financial inducements that were offered in 1863 (a salary and a three-hundred-dollar signing bonus), between 110 and 142 Oneida men—out of a population of approximately eleven hundred—joined up to fight in the Union army. Estimates of those killed, dead from disease, or missing run from forty-six to sixty-five. During the same years the Oneidas suffered losses at home from three major smallpox epidemics between 1862 and 1866 (Hauptman 1993; Hauptman and McLester 2002:136.)

18. See, e.g., the brief account in Campisi 1974:148–149. Those who tell of these transactions usually claim that particular white officials of the Bureau of Indian Affairs and certain educated Oneidas participated in the deals that deprived them of their land.

19. Basehart (1952:217–218) gives the 3,590 figure, which includes about 733 acres of trust land and 2,857 acres of taxable fee-patent land. He notes that 60 percent of the holdings were ten acres or more, far below the eighty acres estimated by experts to be the minimum for an economically viable farm in that region. Only five of the holdings, or 2 percent, were over forty acres.

By 1941 the Oneidas had regained an additional 1,313 acres of trust land through purchases on behalf of the tribe by the New Deal program. Today, as a result of their recent economic success from gaming and other tribal enterprises, the Oneidas have been able to buy back another portion of this land. By 2001 the nation owned, either collectively or individually, about fifteen thousand acres (Webster n.d.).

The WPA papers contain a number of first- and secondhand accounts of how the land was lost. See Solomon Wheelock's story (in chapter 2 of this volume) or Chauncey Baird's story (Campisi and Hauptman 1988:136–37).

20. In 1941, Harry Basehart carried out a survey on part of the reservation and found 610 dwellings occupied by whites and only 306 occupied by Indians (Basehart 1952:219).

21. This topic has been discussed in detail in Hauptman 1981 (esp. 70–87). Robert Ritzenthaler's brief monograph (1950) gives a vividly illustrated introduction to Oneida during the summer of 1939, when he did research for his master's degree in anthropology.

22. The Civilian Conservation Corps (CCC) organized more than three million men, usually young and inexperienced ones, for public works projects. They were primarily engaged in conservation (in such activities as reforestation and erosion and flood control), building roads, creating public parks, and raising telephone poles. The men often lived in tent camps near their work sites and were fed and given clothing as well as salaries of about thirty dollars per month. There was a CCC camp on the Oneida reservation.

23. Hampton Institute was established in 1868 as Hampton Normal and Agricultural Institute for the education of newly emancipated Negroes (as African Americans were called then). From 1878 until 1923 it also had a program for Indian students. The institution exists today as a university, one of the Historically Black Colleges and Universities. Haskell Institute is now the Haskell Indian Nations University.

There is a large and growing literature about these schools. Any autobiography might include accounts of boarding school experiences, but here are some recent works dedicated to the subject: Coleman 1993 (includes a large bibliography of Indian autobiographies); Lomawaima 1987, 1994; Adams 1995; Child 1998; Archuleta, Lomawaima, and Child 2000. See La Flesche 1963 (orig. 1900) for testimony written a century ago. Fritz 1976 gives some of the theory and debate behind the planning of the schools.

24. Some recent works on Indian boarding schools draw upon student letters and diaries and the memoirs of former students. The authors note the complexity of the subject, the varied reactions of the students, and their ambivalence about their experiences, both while they were in school and in later years. See, e.g., Coleman 1993:192–198; Lomawaima 1994; and Child 1998. Several accounts of boarding school life are grouped into chapter 7 of this volume, but other discussions can be found elsewhere, especially in the autobiographical narratives.

25. Since the late 1960s there have been some attempts at "reclaiming a tradition" at Oneida (Cornelius and O'Grady 1987). There is now a Longhouse, and some young men and women have adopted the big drum and the style

of pan-Indian singing common at intertribal powwows. Many Oneidas now attend powwows and participate in various ways. The Soaring Eagle Drum was "known and respected widely . . . as a competitive performing group on the powwow circuit" (Cornelius and O'Grady 1987:270–271; see also Campisi 1974:193–197).

26. The Wisconsin Oneidas always had politically alert leaders and activists. After the era of the chiefs, and after they had lost political control of the local elected councils, several individuals arose in the 1920s and 1930s to lead separate movements for compensation and the return of land. These movements are often discussed in the project writings (see Hauptman 1981:11ff.). Hauptman (1986:65ff.) documents more Oneida political struggles in the 1950s, this time the successful fight against "termination." Termination would have meant the dissolution of the reservation and the end of the Oneidas' special status as Indians. They would have lost the badly needed services provided by the Bureau of Indian Affairs and would have become totally dependent on the mercies of the county and state governments, in competition with the non-Indians who outnumbered them so greatly.

All the early leaders were men, but women began to play larger roles beginning in the 1920s. Laura Miriam "Minnie" Cornelius Kellogg, an extraordinary political figure whose activities in the 1920s stretched far beyond Wisconsin, prosecuted various suits for compensation and attempted to revive elements of the old Iroquois matrilineal system and its "traditional" chiefs (Campisi 1974:153; Hauptman 1981:11–15, 74–77). Beginning in the 1930s, women served on the reconstituted Oneida tribal government, and Irene Moore served as vice-chair and chair of the tribe from 1953 to 1964 and then served on various committees (McLester 1988). Women are frequently tribal chairs these days, and they often comprise a majority of the members of the business council.

27. For information about Oneida life on the reservation and in Milwaukee after the WPA project and World War II see Hauptman 1986; Ritzenthaler and Sellers 1955; Richards 1974; and Lurie 1988.

28. The depression and his family's straitened circumstances forced Lounsbury to drop out of school several times. According to Conklin (2000:860), "Lounsbury turned the numerous economically forced delays in his academic program . . . into opportunities to harvest an abundant array of offerings (courses, audits, and informal tutorials) that could never have been fit into a normal sequence of four uninterrupted years." He went on to become a leading linguistic anthropologist and theoretician, an expert on the Iroquoian and other American Indian languages, and an inspiring mentor to many students in these fields. He was Sterling Professor of Anthropology at Yale University until his death in 1998.

29. He continued, "During this twenty-two months my family has lived hap-

pily. It has been about the best living as long as I have had a family even tho my earnings is not so much that any could be laid aside, but we eat what we want to eat; our clothes is not the best but it is really good enough for common people." Stadler King was appreciative of the New Deal. "These better conditions are all brought about to us by one great man with a true and honest heart, Mr. Franklin D. Roosevelt."

30. For example, see "Three WPA Stories," translated by Amos Christjohn, in Campisi and Hauptman 1988; Marie Hinton's *A Collection of Oneida Stories*; and the Oneida dictionary that Clifford Abbott, Amos Christjohn, and Marie Hinton produced (see Abbott, Christjohn, and Hinton 1996).

31. Although the initial plan may have been for a historical study, Harry Basehart saw it more as "an 'acculturation study'—a study of the process of culture change or simply, of the manner in which cultures change when exposed to the influence of other cultures" (Basehart letter, April 15, 1941, Maxwell Museum, University of New Mexico–Albuquerque).

32. Tillie Baird, Dennison Hill, Amelia Jordan, and Morris Wheelock each contributed one or more notebooks to the second project but apparently were not employed full-time for very long.

33. Harry Basehart's education, like Floyd Lounsbury's, was deeply affected by the depression. Basehart (1910–88) did not enter the university until he was almost thirty, in 1939, and he completed his undergraduate work at the University of Chicago by examination at the same time that he began his graduate study. Thus he was in the middle of his second year of university study when he began his first fieldwork and the supervision of the WPA project. Like Lounsbury, he did a remarkable job. He completed his dissertation at Harvard University and became professor of anthropology at the University of New Mexico, teaching there from 1954 until he retired in 1975 (for an appreciation see Newman 1980).

34. For the Oneida Language and Folklore Project everything was written down in the Oneida language and then translated into English. Although some of the material for the Oneida Ethnological Study was collected in the Oneida language, especially in the early months, they soon switched to English almost exclusively. Some of the accounts they got from interviews with informants were given in Oneida but were apparently translated as they were recorded.

35. The tale of the discovery of this collection consists of a string of fortuitous but prosaic events and coincidences—about seven of them—that led me to the box and gave me the necessary leads to identify its contents. There are no dramatic moments other than that of the actual discovery—and the reader may imagine my excitement and wonder when I found such a treasure in the vast and cluttered storeroom (details supplied on request).

36. We hope to publish a second volume that organizes more of the material

according to topics and draws upon historical recollections and sociological observations in order to present a detailed, synthetic account of Oneida history and society.

37. There are also a number of short pieces—jokes and funny stories, lists of useful plants, recipes—usually in Oneida and then translated into English. Most of these were collected for the first project. Many of the jokes are ribald and depend on mishearing or misunderstanding Oneida words. (It is said that some of the men were cutting up when they wrote these down, and not everyone was pleased.)

38. This is similar to the decision made by Peter Nabokov, to freely edit the transcription made by William Wildschut of the autobiographical account by Two Leggings (Two Leggings 1982).

39. In some third-person accounts that discuss particular Oneida individuals and families, letter and number codes are used to keep identities secret.

1. A Brief Economic and Social History

1. The Oneida Indian Reservation runs from southwest to northeast on both sides of Duck Creek. There is a ridge of raised land on each side of the creek, and a road ran along each—and still does. They are informally called First Ridge and Second Ridge, and presumably she is speaking of First Ridge here.

2. Hoops were strong, flexible wooden strips that were lashed around the staves of barrels in order to hold them together.

3. A bolt is timber that has been trimmed, cut to a certain length, and then split lengthwise into halves, third, or quarters. These are shipped to mills to be further split into shingles or barrel staves.

4. The Oneida Indian Boarding School was in operation from 1893 until 1918. It had been offered to the Oneidas by the government as an inducement to get Oneida agreement to allotment (Bloomfield 1907:335–336). For an account of some aspects of its history as an institution see J. Cornelius n.d.

5. A smudge is a smoky fire made for the purpose of keeping away mosquitoes.

6. The Treaty of Buffalo Creek in 1838, between the U.S. government and the Iroquois chiefs, was supposed to provide lands in Kansas for Oneidas who would give up their land in Wisconsin (Metoxen 1999:134; Campisi 1988b:61). Few went to Kansas to see the land, and fewer stayed (an amendment to the treaty a month later set up the boundaries of the Wisconsin reservation). After years of complex negotiations and litigation, the government gave small cash payments instead.

7. The fee-simple patent gives the owner unrestricted ownership of the land, including the right to bequeath it or sell it. "Fee patents would be issued to the

allottee if he or she were determined to be competent to handle their own affairs as decided by the Indian Agent" (Metoxen n.d.).

8. Josiah Powless was the first Oneida physician. He was killed in action during World War I.

9. Ida's sister, Cora Elm Sinnard, tells her story in chapter 6.

10. Cara Richards (1990) discusses the differences in typical work experiences of Onondaga men and women, based on a study she conducted in the 1950s and 1960s. She suggests that women who have worked as maids in the homes of middle- and upper-class white families acquire different sorts of cultural information than the men and learn things that can be useful as they deal with the wider society. This makes sense and may indeed be the case for these Oneida women, but it is not evident from the narratives.

11. Carlisle Indian Industrial School was established in 1879 and closed as an Indian boarding school in 1918. Much has been written about Carlisle, the prototype of the non-reservation boarding school and the most famous of them (see Witmer 1993 for a brief but profusely illustrated history of the school). Hampton Institute ended its program for Indian students in 1923.

12. Cf. Stadler King's account of town relief. The relief office was set up under the New Deal.

2. Recollections and Opinions of Elders

1. Mr. Elm's age was given in various places as eighty-seven, seventy-eight, and seventy-five.

2. Dr. Rosa Minoka-Hill (1875–1952) was the second American Indian woman to receive a medical degree in the United States. Born on the St. Regis Mohawk reservation in New York, she was adopted by a Quaker physician in Philadelphia after her mother died. She received her medical degree from the Women's Medical College in Philadelphia in 1899, and after marrying Charles Hill, a Wisconsin Oneida, in 1905 she moved to Oneida, where she served as a physician until her death. One of her six children was the late Norbert Hill Sr., an important educator and political figure.

3. The Iroquoian peoples had long been planters of corn (maize), and the crop was of central importance for ritual as well as in their diet.

4. A "spider" refers to a frying pan, perhaps with legs or feet, doubling as a trivet or tripod for supporting a vessel over a fire.

5. He is speaking of the Holy Apostles Episcopal Church, a striking stone building whose tower can be seen for miles around.

6. This refers to the game usually called "snow snake" in English. It was widely known among North American Indians. Morgan (1962:303–305) de-

scribes it, and comparative descriptions and illustrations can be seen in Culin (1992, vol. 2:399–420.)

7. A reader familiar with the literature on Iroquois kinship might be tempted to see this relationship as a survival of matrilineality with its emphasis on the mother's brothers. There is nothing in the WPA accounts or in the ethnographic literature (Basehart, Campisi) that supports this, however.

8. Linguists consider these to be distinct languages rather than dialects, even though Oneida and Mohawk, in particular, are very closely related (see Lounsbury 1978).

9. Followers of the Longhouse religion, mostly in New York, regularly perform dances as a part of their worship ceremonies. At the time Tom Elm was speaking, this did not exist at Oneida. See the introduction for discussion of the more recent adoption of drums and dancing at Oneida.

10. The U.S. government made all Indians in the United States citizens by decree in 1924. Some had become citizens earlier as a result of having obtained land in fee simple pursuant to the Dawes Act; others received citizenship through military service. Although there were individuals and factions among the Oneidas who wanted to resist being made citizens (as this passage suggests), in 1924 that option was taken from them.

11. Franklin K. Lane was secretary of the interior from 1913 to 1920. An account of this event, "Novel Ceremony at Oneida," appeared in the De Pere News on November 19, 1913. There was also a recording of a speech by President Wilson (Daniels 2003:130).

12. Ash-splint baskets were still made by a few women in 1940. See the photograph and brief comments in Ritzenthaler (1950:24–26). Lismer (1941) presents a well-illustrated account of splint basket making among the Seneca at the same period.

13. The Indian sport of lacrosse was widely played by peoples throughout the eastern half of what became North America, and it was particularly popular among the Iroquois. To some extent it still is. Although the game is played by thousands of non-Indians, especially in prep schools, colleges, and universities, Iroquois and other Indian men have their own teams and leagues and style of play. There are several accounts of lacrosse in this volume. See Vennum 1994 for an unrivaled portrayal of Indian lacrosse.

14. Dennison Wheelock and Chester Cornelius were both lawyers and prominent members of the Oneida community. They attended Carlisle, and Dennison and his brother James were both accomplished and widely admired musicians and bandmasters. Chester was the brother of Laura (Minnie) Cornelius Kellogg, one of the most prominent Wisconsin Oneidas in history. Mason Wheelock is not alone in accusing these men; similar comments appear quite a few times in the WPA papers. But it is also true that Dennison in particular had a notable

record as a champion of Indian treaty rights and other causes. The "truth" of what role certain Oneidas played in the loss of the land has yet to be discovered and written.

15. For a recent source on Iroquois pharmacopoeia see Herrick 1995.

16. The Oneidas adopted the practice of singing Christian hymns in their own language long before they moved to Wisconsin. Hymn singing has played a central role in their religious and aesthetic life, and the singing societies continue to be important today. O'Grady 1991 lists 179 Oneida hymns by their English titles and presents a short but useful account of the music and the societies.

17. Ellen Goodnough, the wife of Rev. Edward A. Goodnough, Episcopal missionary to the Oneidas for thirty-five years, wrote about such a marriage in her diary, November 22, 1866. "The bride but 15 and looked modest and child-like. As a rule the young people have not had a word to say in regard to their own marriages. The mother of the young man picks out a wife for him and makes a bargain with the girl's mother. Then the young man sends the girl a present of cloth, etc., through his mother, in value according to his circumstances. As soon as my husband understood the matter he refused to perform the service unless the parties gave their full consent" (Bloomfield 1907:272–273). He must have slipped up this time.

18. Captain John Archiquette (1847–1923), Oscar's father, was a prominent member of the Oneida community. He was a Civil War veteran, an interpreter, a vestry in the Episcopal church, a member of the Oneida National Brass Band, and a captain of the Oneida Indian police force.

19. "I had eleven children, but ten of them died before they grew up. Just one grew up, and he is now about forty years old. I did not experience what it is to have a grandchild" (Jerusha Cornelius to Ida Blackhawk, I-23, Oneida Language and Folklore Project, American Philosophical Society, Philadelphia).

20. It was not uncommon for Oneida farmers to contract to grow beans or other crops for large producers, especially the Larson Company. They would take the seeds from the factory, then plant and harvest them on their own (or rented) land, and take the harvested crop to the factory. They were paid by the pound.

3. Working, Earning, and Struggling Through

1. This work was part of a long-term survey, the Wisconsin Land Inventory, or Bordner Survey, which produced maps of land resources and land use. The survey recorded the land cover, the types of vegetation, wooded areas, cultivated land, pasture, cranberry marshes, as well as drainage features, roads, quarries, cemeteries, and such built features as schools, garages, factories, stores, hotels, farms, etc.

2. This and the next two paragraphs required a bit of editing, both because of the technical aspects of the machinery and the processes and because it was not a simple matter for Stadler King to describe these in words. I have consulted experts on papermaking, John Klungness and Edward L. Springer of the U.S. Forest Products Laboratory in Madison, and Doug Greisenz of Georgia-Pacific.

3. This would have been a debarking drum (cf. the "Green Bay barker," below), while the second set of machines, which Mr. King calls "beaters," appear to be what are called "chippers." When he first speaks of "pulp," before it is debarked (or barked), he is referring to the wood that is to be used to produce pulp for paper, which can be called either "pulp" or "pulpwood."

4. Apparently the pulp was in a "digester," from which it would then be "exploded" to become a high-consistency pulp slurry or paste.

5. The pulp at that point might be used for paper for bags or cardboard boxes, but it would have to undergo more processing to make higher-quality paper.

6. According to Dixon Skenandore, body wood is "the part without branches so the wood was free from knots."

7. When a new Oneida Language Program was begun in 1974, Melissa Cornelius, one of the remaining fluent speakers of the language, was a leading participant for several years. Professor Clifford Abbott, who was and still is directly involved with that project, reports that she was outspoken and vibrant even in her nineties (personal communication). Among her passions were Shakespeare and the books of Helen Hunt Jackson (1830–1885), especially A Century of Dishonor. For a brief account of her years at Carlisle see her "Reminiscences of an American Indian" (1982).

8. "Grained" refers to the practice of feeding grain to the animals directly rather than depending on feed from pastures alone.

9. A drag is used for leveling off the ground.

10. "Cribbing" refers to the supports underneath the house or other large object being moved. These consist of four-foot lengths of wood set across each other in layers.

11. William "Fat" Skenandore was a prominent figure in Oneida politics in the 1920s and 1930s. A "self-styled attorney" (Skenandore 1988:126), he was notable for his legal research and organizing activities related to Oneida land claims and treaty rights (see also Hauptman 1981:77–79).

12. A boiler was a large cast-iron tub in which the water used for washing clothes was heated and kept hot. In the photograph of the classroom at the Oneida Indian Boarding School, there is a drawing of a boiler on the blackboard on the far left.

13. Basehart writes: "Older Oneida views explaining intense emotional involvements of men and women as due to love magic have persisted, particularly among those with little education" (1952:262). The only other account of love

magic in the Oneida Ethnological Study comes from a man who believed that his second wife, a Chippewa, had him under her power by using magic. For a famous case in the Iroquois literature see Haring 1992.

14. Dust tea is the lowest grade of tea—what remains when tiny pieces break off the broken leaves of higher grades of tea during processing. It is often used in teabags.

15. Sister Amy was one of the Sisters of the Holy Nativity serving the Episcopalian mission. The "Sisters' House" was next to the priest's house.

4. The Lives They Led

1. See the introduction to this volume.

2. All the games on this list are typical Euro-American games of the period, and none can be considered survivals of any of the Iroquois games written of by Culin (1992). The only exception is snow snake, spoken of by Tom Elm in chapter 2 of this volume.

3. Elsewhere Oscar Archiquette tells a different story about his last days at Flandreau. A teacher accused him of writing his name in a dictionary that she thought was school property. He told her that the dictionary had been given to him by his sister, but she sent him to the "head teacher," who slapped him; he fought back and was "sent home" (see Campisi and Hauptman 1988:137–138).

4. Iroquois have long celebrated what is known in English as Midwinter, or Indian New Year, with elaborate rituals and dances that take place over several days (see, e.g., Speck 1949 and Tooker 1970). Hoyan seems to be derived from the earlier "thieving parties" that collected food and other material for the Midwinter ceremonials. See Morgan's description of this activity, with its treats or tricks (1962:213; cf. Ritzenthaler 1950:34).

5. The roads were laid out along the lines that the surveyors drew, dividing the landscape into large square sections.

6. Societies or clubs were a prominent feature of Indian boarding schools, as they were in American high schools generally. One of the writers, Alma Thomas, listed the organizations she knew from Flandreau in the 1930s: sixteen for boys, nineteen for girls, and seven for both girls and boys. These included, for both sexes, Glee, Drama, and Pep clubs as well as the student council. For girls there were Big Sister, YWCA, Girl Scouts, St. Theresa Sodality (for Catholic girls), Hiking, Home Economics, Travel, and Florence Nightingale clubs as well as ones called Pocahontas, Minnehaha, Naquaah, Busy Bees, Merry Madcaps, Sacajawea, Katzenjammer (after the popular comic strip), and Sunshine Strivers. The Girl's Athletic Association had the motto "There is a sport for every girl and there should be a girl for every sport." For boys there were Hi-Y, 4-H, Big Brother, Bachelors Club, and clubs with such names as Lions, Wildcats,

Vikings, Racketeers, Aces, Gentlemen of Riggs, and Royal Knights. The "F" Club "aimed to promote athletics, school loyalty, and sportsmanship."

7. "When not in school, pupils receive regular wages, a fixed portion going toward their personal expenses, the remainder being deposited for them in the school bank. As sufficient amounts accumulate, interest bearing certificates of deposit are issued, and so held until the holders leave school for their homes or go to higher institutions of learning" (*Catalogue of the Carlisle Indian Industrial School*: n.p.). Evidently Haskell had a similar practice.

8. A runway is a route or pathway that the deer take in their regular movements from place to place.

9. "Dropsy" is an old term for unhealthy swelling (edema) caused by excessive collection of fluid in the body.

10. Hauptman (1981:79–87) presents an interesting discussion of Morris Wheelock's political activities in the 1930s.

11. It was popular in the 1930s to compare little boys who were all dressed up to "Little Lord Fauntleroy." This story has been filmed on a number of occasions, but the 1936 version with Freddie Bartholomew all dressed up as a little English lord particularly captivated the public at that time.

12. The Wittenberg School at Wittenberg, Wisconsin, was established in 1887 as a Lutheran mission school. It served as a government non-reservation boarding school for Indians from 1895 to 1917.

13. See Hauptman 1981:74ff. for more on these significant events. The outcome has shaped Oneida development and tribal government to this day.

14. Colonel Richard H. Pratt, the founder and director of the Carlisle Indian Industrial School from 1879 until he was removed in 1904, was succeeded by Major W. A. Mercer, who led the school for just three years. According to Witmer, "Two major consequences resulted from the Mercer administration: the deterioration of the industrial and academic programs, and an increased emphasis on athletics, especially football. The strict discipline was relaxed" (1993:59)—just as Amelia Jordan suggests.

Moses Friedman, an educator rather than a military officer, took over as superintendent in 1908. He tried to strengthen Carlisle's academic curriculum and the industrial training program, but he was unpopular and was accused of mismanagement. He lasted in office only until 1914 (Witmer 1993:73ff.). The school declined after that and was closed down in 1918.

15. A horse-drawn "top buggy" was a small, two-seat "runabout" with a soft, folding canopy top.

16. Perhaps this means that she knew there was no barrier to sexual relations and marriage. Although by this time there was no longer clan exogamy, marriage between first cousins was prohibited (Basehart 1952:265).

17. "Milk leg" is a painful swelling of the leg soon after childbirth, due to thrombosis of the large veins.

18. For a discussion of breath, soul, and person among Iroquois in earlier times see Druke 1980.

19. Charles F. Pierce was the first superintendent of the Oneida Government Boarding School. He was sent to Oneida in 1892 by the commissioner of Indian Affairs to oversee the construction of the buildings. It opened in 1893 (Bloomfield 1907:336).

20. "Finger wave" refers to a technique for styling women's hair that was popular in the 1920s and 1930s.

21. When a part of the amnion covers the head of a child at birth it is called a "caul birth" and thought to bring good luck.

22. Robert Ritzenthaler, later professor of anthropology at the University of Wisconsin–Milwaukee and curator at the Milwaukee Public Museum, spent a summer doing fieldwork in Oneida in 1939, when he was a graduate student. He took the pictures that we have of the project participants and of many other people at that time.

23. Mr. Webster went on at some length about his athletic activities and economic ideas. Some of this has been edited out.

24. Mrs. Josephine Hill Webster gave a similar account of the origin and organization of lace making in Oneida to Tillie Baird (T-53, Oneida Language and Folklore Project, American Philosophical Society, Philadelphia). She coordinated the production of lace by sixty to one hundred women until 1926, when the New York organization gave up the enterprise. "I always sent the finished work every two weeks, sometimes one to three hundred dollars' worth of finished work in one sending." They made bedspreads, pillowcases, handkerchiefs, and altar lace, in particular (see Bloomfield 1907:345ff. for more on lace; also McLester 1988:116–118 about Josephine Hill Webster, a daughter of Chief Cornelius Hill). Bobbin lace (some versions are called "pillow lace") is made by placing a series of pins on a board to make the template for the design and then running threads around and through the pins. Each line of thread is wound on a bobbin or spool, and the thread is played out from it.

5. Marriages and Families

1. The "twilight sleep" was an anaesthetic intended to put women to sleep and to cause an amnesia so that they would not remember the birth process. It consisted of a combination of scopolamine and morphine.

2. See the explanation of False Face in note 6 for chapter 6.

3. He means that he was "riding the rails," hopping trains, and bumming his

way, as he says explicitly later in the account. Even before the depression there were many men who traveled as hobos.

4. See Seabrook 1998 for evidence that a similar relationship prevails today between Onandaga lacrosse teams and those from prep schools and colleges.

6. Religious Life and Beliefs

1. Chief (or Reverend) Cornelius Hill (1834–1906) was one of the most prominent figures in Oneida history. He was both a pinetree chief from the Bear clan, noted for his oratory, and a pillar of the Episcopal church. Called the "last chief" of the Oneidas, Hill was educated at the Nashotah Episcopal Seminary and served prominently for many years as an interpreter for church services. In 1895 he was ordained as a deacon in the Episcopal church and in 1903 was installed as a priest. He married the granddaughter of the leading chief, Daniel Bread, but later became Bread's main rival (Bloomfield 1907:326–334 [date of 1905 on p. 328 should be 1895]; Hauptman and McLester 2002:153–159).

2. This ceremonial practice was reported by the earliest ethnographers of the Iroquois, J. F. Lafitau in 1724 and Lewis Henry Morgan in 1851. The feast is given to start the journey to heaven of the spirit of the deceased. Campisi and Ritzenthaler add some contemporary observations about Oneida practice, and Tooker gives a more general overview (Campisi 1974:214–215; Ritzenthaler 1950; Tooker 1978:462).

3. This refers to the standing (or "erected") stone, one•yóte?, from which the Oneidas get their name, Oneyote?a•kâ•, "People of the Standing Stone" (Campisi 1978:489).

4. This is just one of many different transcriptions of this name, which is often rendered as "Sky-holder" or "Upholder of the Heavens" (Elm and Antone 2000:17).

5. A number of versions of the Iroquois creation account have been published, and Andrew Beechtree gives his own distinctive telling of it in the WPA notebooks. See Beechtree 2004 and Elm and Antone 2000.

6. False Face refers to a healing society whose purpose is to drive out illness by scaring away disease. There are many published accounts of False Face beliefs, rituals, masks, and the effects of healing rituals. The most comprehensive source is William N. Fenton's *The False Faces of the Iroquois* (1987), which contains many illustrations of masks and artists at work on them and gives descriptions of rituals and accompanying prayers and songs, with diagrams and photographs. Ritzenthaler found that False Face masks and costumes were not in use in Oneida in 1939 but that "the basic idea of curing a patient by pouring hot ashes over his head has been used in at least a dozen cases within the last two years" (1950:32). Campisi believes that curing ceremonies were no longer

performed after about 1950 (1974:208). Although some people today contend that False Face should be kept secret, the people who practiced it in earlier days do not seem to have felt that way.

7. Boarding Schools and "Outing"

1. John Skenandore spent at least a few years at Flandreau, too. He completed seven grades in these two schools.

2. Jim Thorpe, who excelled at football and track and field and played professional baseball as well, is generally considered America's finest all-around athlete. In 1912 this football team had a record of twelve victories, one defeat, and one tie. They played such teams as Syracuse University, University of Pittsburgh, University of Pennsylvania (their only loss), Brown University, and Army, and outscored their opponents by 504 points to 114!

3. The superintendent, Moses Friedman, clashed with the commissioner of Indian Affairs, Francis E. Leupp. "Friedman was exonerated on the charge of mishandling funds but not on his failure as a Superintendent" (Witmer 1993:82). He was dismissed and replaced by the last superintendent, Oscar Lipps. The legendary football coach Glenn ("Pop") Warner was also fired, in 1914.

4. For more about the Chilocco Indian Agricultural School see Lomawaima 1987, 1994.

5. "In the past, when our Grandmothers and Grandfathers returned to their traditions after trying other ways, it was said (as an insult) that they had gone 'back to the blanket' " (*Back to the Blanket Journal Homepage*, www.angelfire.com/biz/BackToTheBlanket/)

After his days at Carlisle, Luther Standing Bear (1933:189–191) wrote, "To clothe a man falsely is only to distress his spirit and to make him incongruous and ridiculous, and my entreaty to the American Indian is to retain his tribal dress."

6. This was Camp Greylock in Becket, Massachusetts, which is still in existence. While the founder and owners were Jewish, it would no longer be considered a "camp for rich Jewish boys," if it ever was.

7. It is interesting that it was assumed that he was a "wealthy Jewish man" who owned more than one camp. In fact, Camp Greylock was founded the previous year by three idealistic young brothers, immigrants from Russia, whose father was "only a moderately successful businessman" with a paper and twine store on the Lower East Side of New York City. Gabriel R. Mason, the brother who was Guy's official sponsor, was a teacher who later served for many years as the principal of Abraham Lincoln High School in Brooklyn, New York. He was

also a founder of the Teachers Union, now the United Federation of Teachers (Mason 1972:6–9, 50–54).

8. Hog Island was the site of a number of shipyards that were constructed rapidly during World War I for the mass production of vessels for the war effort. The massive effort began in early 1918, but none of the ships were produced in time to serve in the war before it ended on November 11, 1918.

9. Caulking involves driving material into the spaces between planks or plates in order to seal the joints.

10. The riveter, the rimmer, and the bucking-up man are members of the team that does the riveting. The rivets must be heated, passed on to the riveter, hammered into the holes, and flattened on the other side.

11. The crane man, signal man, and rigger form the team that hoists materials aloft and into and out of the holds.

12. "The 400" was Mrs. Caroline Astor's reckoning of the elite of the elite, the richest and "best" families in America, according to her *Social Register*, first published in 1887. And Newport, Rhode Island, was their summer playground.

8. Sports and Recreation

1. Deerfield, a colonial village in Massachusetts (not New York), was attacked in February 1704 by a French and Indian war party. Some inhabitants were killed and others abducted. There is an interesting and not irrelevant connection between the Deerfield Massacre and the Wisconsin Oneidas. Eunice Williams, the daughter of the most famous Deerfield prisoner, Rev. John Williams, chose to remain with her Indian captors when the rest of her family was released, and she eventually married a Mohawk man (Demos 1994). Her great-grandchild was Eleazer Williams (see the introduction to this volume and Tom Elm's narrative in chapter 2).

9. Four Memorable Days

1. Unfortunately, Morris Swadesh's enthusiasm for workers' rights and other causes got him fired from City College of New York in 1949, during the McCarthy era.

Appendix

1. Congressman Johns, who was an opponent of the WPA in general, also had Oscar Archiquette's response read into the *Congressional Record*. Farmer Boland was neither the first nor the only citizen of Wisconsin to object to this project. The prominent Republican senator Alexander Wiley complained that it was "a

financial boondoggle wasting the taxpayer's money" (Campisi and Hauptman 1981:447).

2. Oscar Archiquette was the vice-chair of the executive committee of the General Tribal Council that had been established as a result of the Indian Reorganization Act in 1934 (see the introduction to this volume).

3. This speech was made about four months before the entry of the United States into World War II as a result of the Japanese attack on Pearl Harbor on December 7, 1941. A number of accounts recorded in mid-1941 suggest that people expected that there would be a war and that war would mean more industry, more work, and rising prices for agricultural produce. Alma Thomas drew up a list of eighteen young Oneida men who were already in the army as of March 1941. Oscar suggests here that there were already Oneida code talkers serving in the armed forces.

WORKS CITED

Abbott, Clifford, Amos Christjohn, and Maria Hinton. 1996. *An Oneida Dictionary*. Clifford Abbott, ed. Oneida WI: The Oneida Tribe.

Adams, David Wallace. 1995. *Education for Extinction: American Indians and the Boarding School Experience, 1875–1928*. Lawrence: University of Kansas Press.

Archuleta, Margaret L., K. Tsianina Lomawaima, and Brenda J. Child, eds. 2000. *Away from Home: American Indian Boarding School Experiences, 1879–2000*. Phoenix: Heard Museum.

Basehart, Harry W. 1952. "Historical Changes in the Kinship System of the Oneida Indians." Ph.D. diss., Harvard University.

Beechtree, Andrew. 2004. "The Origins of Man." Brian Swann, ed. In *Voices from the Four Directions*. Herbert S. Lewis, ed. Pp. 532–545. Lincoln: University of Nebraska Press.

Bloomfield, J. K. 1907. *The Oneidas*. New York: Alden Brothers.

Campisi, Jack. 1974. "Ethnic Identity and Boundary Maintenance in Three Oneida Communities." Ph.D. diss., State University of New York at Albany.

———. 1978. "Oneida." In *Handbook of North American Indians*, vol. 15: *Northeast*. Bruce G. Trigger, ed. Pp. 481–490. Washington DC: Smithsonian Institution.

———. 1988a. "From Stanwix to Canandaigua: National Policy, States' Rights, and Indian Land." In *Iroquois Land Claims*. By Christopher Vecsey and William A. Starna. Pp. 49–65. Syracuse: Syracuse University Press.

———. 1988b. "The Oneida Treaty Period, 1783–1838." In *The Oneida Indian Experience: Two Perspectives*. J. Campisi and Laurence M. Hauptman, eds. Pp. 48–64. Syracuse: Syracuse University Press.

———. 1999. "The Wisconsin Oneidas between Disasters." In *The Oneida Indian Journey: From New York to Wisconsin, 1784–1860*. Laurence M. Hauptman and L. Gordon McLester III, eds. Pp. 70–84. Madison: University of Wisconsin Press.

Campisi, Jack, and Laurence M. Hauptman. 1981. "Talking Back: The Oneida Language and Folklore Project, 1938–1941." *Proceedings of the American Philosophical Society* 125(6):441–448.

————, eds. 1988. *The Oneida Indian Experience: Two Perspectives.* Syracuse: Syracuse University Press.

Catalogue of the Indian Industrial School, Carlisle PA. 23rd Year, 1902. Jamestown NY: The Journal.

Child, Brenda J. 1998. *Boarding School Seasons: American Indian Families, 1900–1940.* Lincoln: University of Nebraska Press.

Coleman, Michael C. 1993. *American Indian Children at School, 1850–1930.* Jackson: University Press of Mississippi.

Conklin, Harold C. 2000. "Floyd Glenn Lounsbury (1914–1998)." *American Anthropologist* 102(4):860–865.

Cornelius, Judy. 1999. "Additional Notes on Eleazer Williams (1787–1858) and the Origins of the Episcopal Tradition among the Oneidas." In *The Oneida Indian Journey: From New York to Wisconsin 1784–1860.* Laurence M. Hauptman and L. Gordon McLester III, eds. Pp. 129–133. Madison: University of Wisconsin Press.

————. N.d. "Oneida Indian Boarding School, Oneida WI, 1893–1918." Unpublished paper prepared for 2003 Oneida History Conference.

Cornelius, Melissa E. 1982. "Reminiscences of an American Indian." In *We Were Children Then.* Vol. 2. Clarice Dunn and Gen Lewis, eds. Pp. 64–66. Madison: Stanton, Lee.

Cornelius, Richard, and Terence J. O'Grady. 1987. "Reclaiming a Tradition: The Soaring Eagles of Oneida." *Ethnomusicology* 31(2):261–272.

Culin, Stewart. 1992. *Games of the North American Indians.* 2 vols. Lincoln: University of Nebraska Press.

Daniels, Susan G. 2003. *Chronology of Events: Research on Oneidas in Wisconsin, 1634–2000.* Privately printed.

Demos, John. 1994. *The Unredeemed Captive: A Family Story from Early America.* New York: Knopf.

Druke, Mary A. 1980. "The Concept of Personhood in Seventeenth and Eighteenth Century Iroquois Ethnopersonality." In *Studies on Iroquois Culture.* Nancy Bonvillain, ed. Pp. 59–70. Occasional Papers in Northeastern Anthropology, 6. Rindge NH: Franklin Pierce College.

Ellis, Albert G. 1856. "Some Accounts of the Advent of the New York Indians into Wisconsin." *Wisconsin Historical Collections* 2:415–449.

Elm, Demus, and Harvey Antone. 2000. *The Oneida Creation Story.* Floyd G. Lounsbury and Bryan Gick, trans. and eds. Lincoln: University of Nebraska Press.

Fenton, William N. 1978. "Northern Iroquoian Culture Patterns." In *Handbook of North American Indians, vol. 15: Northeast.* Bruce G. Trigger, ed. Pp. 296–321. Washington DC: Smithsonian Institution.

————. 1987. *The False Faces of the Iroquois*. Norman: University of Oklahoma Press.

Fritz, Henry E. 1976. "The Board of Indian Commissioners and Ethnocentric Reform, 1878–1893." In *Indian-White Relations: A Persistent Paradox*. Jane F. Smith and Robert M. Kvasnicka, eds. Pp. 57–78. Washington DC: Howard University Press.

Haring, Sidney L. 1992. "Red Lilac of the Cayugas: Traditional Indian Law and Culture Conflict in a Witchcraft Trial in Buffalo, New York in 1930." *New York History* 73:65–132.

Hauptman, Laurence M. 1981. *The Iroquois and the New Deal*. Syracuse: Syracuse University Press.

————. 1986. *The Iroquois Struggle for Survival: World War II to Red Power*. Syracuse: Syracuse University Press.

————. 1993. *The Iroquois in the Civil War: From Battlefield to Reservation*. Syracuse: Syracuse University Press.

————. 1999. *Conspiracy of Interests: Iroquois Dispossession and the Rise of New York State*. Syracuse: Syracuse University Press.

Hauptman, Laurence M., and L. Gordon McLester III, eds. 1999. *The Oneida Indian Journey: From New York to Wisconsin 1784–1860*. Madison: University of Wisconsin Press.

————. 2002. *Chief Daniel Bread and the Oneida Nation of Indians of Wisconsin*. Norman: University of Oklahoma Press.

Herrick, James W., ed. 1995. *Iroquois Medical Botany*. Syracuse: Syracuse University Press.

Hinton, Maria. N.d. *A Collection of Oneida Stories*. Oneida WI: The Oneida Tribe.

Horsman, Reginald. 1999. "The Origins of Oneida Removal to Wisconsin." In *The Oneida Indian Journey: From New York to Wisconsin 1784–1860*. Laurence M. Hauptman and L. Gordon McLester III, eds. Pp. 53–69. Madison: University of Wisconsin Press.

Hymes, Dell. 1972. "Morris Swadesh: From the First Yale School to World Prehistory." In *The Origin and Diversification of Language*. By Morris Swadesh. Joel Sherzer, ed. Pp. 228–317. Chicago: Aldine, Atherton.

La Flesche, Francis. 1963. *The Middle Five: Indian Schoolboys of the Omaha Tribe*. 1900. Madison: University of Wisconsin Press.

Lismer, Marjorie. 1941. *Seneca Splint Basketry*. Indian Handicrafts 4. Office of Indian Affairs. Chilocco OK: Chilocco Agricultural School.

Locklear, Arlinda. 1988a. "The Allotment of the Oneida Reservation and Its Legal Ramifications." In *The Oneida Indian Experience: Two Perspectives*. Jack Campisi and Laurence M. Hauptman, eds. Pp. 83–96. Syracuse: Syracuse University Press.

————. 1988b. "The Oneida Land Claims: A Legal Overview." In *Iroquois Land Claims*. By Christopher Vecsey and William A. Starna. Pp. 141–153. Syracuse: Syracuse University Press.

————. 1999. "The Buffalo Creek Treaty of 1838 and Its Legal Implications for Oneida Indian Land Claims." In *The Oneida Indian Journey: From New York to Wisconsin 1784–1860*. Laurence M. Hauptman and L. Gordon McLester III, eds. Pp. 85–89. Madison: University of Wisconsin Press.

Lomawaima, K. Tsianina. 1987. "Oral Histories from Chilocco Indian Agricultural School 1920–1940." *American Indian Quarterly* 11:241–254.

————. 1994. *They Called It Prairie Light: The Story of Chilocco Indian School.* Lincoln: University of Nebraska Press.

Lounsbury, Floyd G. 1978. "Iroquoian Languages." In *Handbook of North American Indians: vol. 15, Northeast.* Bruce G. Trigger, ed. Pp. 334–343. Washington DC: Smithsonian Institution.

————. 1988. "Recollections of the Works Progress Administration's Oneida Language and Folklore Project, 1938–41." In *The Oneida Indian Experience: Two Perspectives*. Jack Campisi and Laurence M. Hauptman, eds. Pp. 131–134. Syracuse: Syracuse University Press.

Lurie, Nancy O. 1962. "Comments on Bernard J. James's Analysis of Ojibwa Acculturation." *American Anthropologist* 64:826–33.

————. 1988. "Recollections of an Urban Indian Community: The Oneidas of Milwaukee." In *The Oneida Indian Experience: Two Perspectives*. Jack Campisi and Laurence M. Hauptman, eds. Pp. 101–107. Syracuse: Syracuse University Press.

————. 2002. *Wisconsin Indians.* Rev. and expanded ed. Madison: Wisconsin Historical Society Press.

Luther Standing Bear. 1933. *Land of the Spotted Eagle.* Boston and New York: Houghton Mifflin.

Martin, Deborah B. N.d. "Eleazer Williams, 1821–1921." Pamphlet [29 pp.]

Mason, Gabriel R. 1972. *Gabriel Blows His Horn: The Evolution of a Rebel.* Philadelphia: Dorrance and Co.

McLester, Thelma Cornelius. 1988. "Oneida Women Leaders." In *The Oneida Indian Experience: Two Perspectives*. Jack Campisi and Laurence M. Hauptman, eds. Pp. 108–125. Syracuse: Syracuse University Press.

Metoxen, Loretta. 1999. "The Oneidas in Wisconsin: The Early Years, 1822–1848." In *The Oneida Indian Journey: From New York to Wisconsin 1784–1860.* Laurence M. Hauptman and L. Gordon McLester III, eds. Pp. 133–135. Madison: University of Wisconsin Press.

————. N.d. *Subdivide and Conquer: The Dawes Allotment Act.* Oneida Cultural Heritage Department. No. 6.

Morgan, Lewis Henry. 1962. *League of the Iroquois*. 1851. New York: Corinth Books.

Newman, Stanley. 1980. "Harry W. Basehart: An Appreciation." In *The Versatility of Kinship*. Linda S. Cordell and Stephen Beckerman, eds. Pp. xii–xvii. New York: Academic Press.

O'Grady, Terence J. 1991. "The Singing Societies of Oneida." *American Music* spring:67–91.

Richards, Cara E. 1974. *The Oneida People*. Phoenix: Indian Tribal Series.

————. 1990. "Women Use the Law, Men Suffer from It: Differential Acculturation among the Onondaga Indians in the 1950's and 60's." In *Iroquois Women: An Anthology*. W. G. Spittal, ed. Pp. 164–167. Ohsweken, Ontario: Iroqrafts.

Ritzenthaler, Robert E. 1950. "The Oneida Indians of Wisconsin." *Bulletin of the Public Museum of the City of Milwaukee* 19(1):1–52.

Ritzenthaler, Robert E., and Mary Sellers. 1955. "Indians in an Urban Setting." *Wisconsin Archaeologist* 36:147–161.

Seabrook, John. 1998. "The Gathering of the Tribes: Preppies vs. Indians on an Old American Playing Field." *New Yorker*, September 7: 30–36.

Skenandore, Francis. 1988. "William Skenandore." In *The Oneida Indian Experience: Two Perspectives*. Jack Campisi and Laurence M. Hauptman, eds. Pp. 126–130. Syracuse: Syracuse University Press.

Speck, Frank G. 1949. *Midwinter Rites of the Cayuga Long House*. Philadelphia: University of Pennsylvania Press.

Tooker, Elizabeth. 1970. *The Iroquois Ceremonial of Midwinter*. Syracuse: Syracuse University Press.

————. 1978. "The League of the Iroquois: Its History, Politics, and Ritual." In *Handbook of North American Indians*: vol. 15, *Northeast*. Bruce G. Trigger, ed. Pp. 418–441. Washington DC: Smithsonian Institution.

Two Leggings. 1982. *Two Leggings: The Making of a Crow Warrior*. Peter Nabokov, ed. Lincoln: Nebraska University Press.

Vecsey, Christopher. 1988. Introduction. In *Iroquois Land Claims*. By Christopher Vecsey and William A. Starna. Pp. 1–16. Syracuse: Syracuse University Press.

Vecsey, Christopher, and William A. Starna. 1988. *Iroquois Land Claims*. Syracuse: Syracuse University Press.

Vennum, Thomas. 1994. *American Indian Lacrosse: Little Brother of War*. Washington DC: Smithsonian Institution Press.

Wallace, Anthony F. C. 1970. *The Death and Rebirth of the Seneca*. New York: Knopf.

Webster, Loretta. N.d. "Land Acquisition History." Unpublished paper prepared for 2003 Oneida History Conference.

Witmer, Linda F. 1993. *The Indian Industrial School: Carlisle, Pennsylvania, 1879–1918*. Carlisle PA: Cumberland County Historical Society.

INDEX